bad girls go everywhere

bad girls go everywhere

THE LIFE OF HELEN GURLEY BROWN

Jennifer Scanlon

OXFORD
UNIVERSITY PRESS
2009

OXFORD
UNIVERSITY PRESS

Oxford University Press, Inc., publishes works that further
Oxford University's objective of excellence
in research, scholarship, and education.

Oxford   New York
Auckland   Cape Town   Dar es Salaam   Hong Kong   Karachi
Kuala Lumpur   Madrid   Melbourne   Mexico City   Nairobi
New Delhi   Shanghai   Taipei   Toronto

With offices in
Argentina   Austria   Brazil   Chile   Czech Republic   France   Greece
Guatemala   Hungary   Italy   Japan   Poland   Portugal   Singapore
South Korea   Switzerland   Thailand   Turkey   Ukraine   Vietnam

Copyright © 2009 by Jennifer Scanlon

Published by Oxford University Press, Inc.
198 Madison Avenue, New York, New York 10016

www.oup.com

Oxford is a registered trademark of Oxford University Press

Library of Congress Cataloging-in-Publication Data
Scanlon, Jennifer, 1958–
Bad girls go everywhere : the life of Helen Gurley Brown / Jennifer Scanlon.
        p.   cm.
Includes index.
Summary: "The first biography of Helen Gurley Brown, author of the 1962 international
best-seller Sex and the Single Girl and 32-year editor of Cosmopolitan magazine. Scanlon
had unprecedented access to Brown's papers, and she presents Brown in the context of the
feminist movement, highlighting her role as an advocate of professional accomplishment
and sexual freedom for women"—Provided by publisher.
ISBN 978-0-19-534205-5
1. Brown, Helen Gurley.   2. Periodical editors—United States—Biography.   I. Title.
PN4874.B768S27 2009
070.5'1092—dc22   2008030466

1 3 5 7 9 8 6 4 2

Printed in the United States of America
on acid-free paper

Frontispiece: Helen Gurley Brown in her *Cosmopolitan* office in the 1980s.
Sophia Smith Collection, Smith College

To Michael, Fynn, and Maeve

contents

Preface   ix

1   GROWING UP GURLEY, AND A GIRL   1

2   WORK LIFE, ROMANTIC ENTANGLEMENTS   23

3   DAVID BROWN   40

4   *SEX AND THE SINGLE GIRL*   57

5   SENSATIONALIST LITERATURE AND EXPERT ADVICE:
Selling *Sex and the Single Girl*   79

6   SEXY FROM THE START: The Early Years of Second-Wave Feminism   94

7   PACKAGING A MESSAGE–AND A MESSENGER   112

8   NORMAL LIKE ME: The Single Girl on Television   132

9   GOOD GIRLS GO TO HEAVEN–BAD GIRLS GO EVERYWHERE:
Helen Gurley Brown's *Cosmopolitan*   143

10   SEXUAL LIBERATION ON WHOSE TERMS?: Defining the Second Wave   168

11   AGING, RESISTING, REDEFINING   192

12   AN EDITOR STEPS DOWN, RELUCTANTLY   212

Acknowledgments   226
Notes   229
Index   263

preface

Helen Gurley Brown, celebrated author of the 1962 international best-seller *Sex and the Single Girl,* diva of the New York magazine world, Living Landmark of New York City, and more than thirty-year editor of *Cosmopolitan* magazine, offered her *Cosmo* readers several pieces of advice in her farewell column in February 1997.[1] Among them: every woman has something that makes her unique and gifted; pursuing beauty can be a delightful endeavor, not just a preoccupation; sex is among the best things in life; and men are not the enemy.[2] With these brief directives Brown summarized the philosophy that made her such an important and contested figure throughout the second half of the twentieth century. To conservatives, Brown's books and magazine released the single woman from all social constraints, making her an autonomous, sexually liberated threat to the institutions of marriage and family. To many feminists in the nascent and then evolving women's liberation movement, Brown's views enhanced men's rather than women's lives by turning women into sexually available playmates.

For her legion of fans, however, Helen Gurley Brown represented another arena, one in which female independence and sexuality, heterosexual

■

xi

relationships, and the celebration of beauty coexisted amicably, if not always altogether peacefully, with feminism. Her message, that "men are wonderful and children are wonderful and you may need both to fulfill your life," paired with "you should not, you must not live through those people," resonated with American women who wanted to claim sexual and personal satisfaction in addition to economic independence. When Brown repeatedly claimed, "I am a feminist," she spoke not only for herself but also for her "girls," first for her Single Girls, then for her Cosmo Girls, and always for millions of mainstream American women.[3]

Nearly four decades after *Sex and the Single Girl* hit the bookstores, *Sex and the City,* an overnight television sensation, introduced a set of "lipstick feminist" characters and social mores, and few among its fans or critics made the link between the contemporary feminism of Carrie Bradshaw and that earlier philosophy espoused by Helen Gurley Brown. The feminism of Brown's day, known now as the "second wave," seems in many ways contradictory to the contemporary "third wave," *Sex and the City* approach to women's lives.[4] The second wave's studied lack of attention to if not antipathy toward fashion, suspicion first of lesbianism and then of heterosexuality, and disdain for women's various pursuits of beauty seem incapable of spawning a movement whose practitioners obsess not only about women's professional opportunities but also about their dating prospects and their Manolo Blahnik stilettos.

But the life and work of Helen Gurley Brown, always irreverent and daring, always celebratory of femininity and of any and all sexual practices enjoyed by women, provide the necessary corrective to this understanding of the second wave and a vantage point from which to view the third. Arguably, in the "long decade" of the 1950s, and now again in the twenty-first century, lipstick feminism, like that practiced and promoted widely by Helen Gurley Brown, is one significant way in which feminist ideas and practices survive and thrive.[5]

This book, the first biography of Helen Gurley Brown, considers her not simply as a wayward practitioner of the second wave, an aberrant lipstick-toting girlie girl, but instead as a pioneer, a founder of the second wave, whose 1962 best-seller, *Sex and the Single Girl,* preceded Betty Friedan's formative work, *The Feminine Mystique,* by a year.[6] Brown's particular version of feminism, more likely practiced by single women than by housewives, and by working-class secretaries rather than middle-class college students, has largely been left out of established histories of postwar feminism's emergence and ascendance. Yet Helen Gurley Brown was there from the start, documenting and promoting the beliefs and practices of the sexy single girl, who challenged the status quo with her unrelenting presence, her sexual and economic desires, and her refusal to give in to the dictates of postwar domesticity. Claiming Brown's rightful place as a feminist trailblazer, this biography pursues three central themes: the life experiences and contributions of a woman who was both present in and pivotal to crucial moments in postwar American history; the nature of her "Gurley Girl feminism," which appealed to so many American women outside the organized women's movement; and the ways in which Brown's particular philosophy and example help fill in this chronological and ideological gap between the second and third waves of American feminism.

Several elements of Brown's life and work have contributed to her omission from feminist history.[7] Among those, her focus on individuality rather than on the group identity of women stands out. As a child of the Depression, a hard worker who achieved professional success after many years of steely discipline and without the benefit of education or traditional beauty, Helen Gurley Brown wanted no less for her readers. In her Horatio Alger version of feminism, it was difficult if not impossible to accept the notion that structural barriers would effectively prevent her or other women from achieving a fair amount of success. As someone who worked her way up from secretary to copywriter to popular writer to magazine editor, Brown believed not in overthrowing the system but, rather, in working it. She did just that throughout her career and most decidedly at *Cosmopolitan,* where she exercised impressive editorial and entrepreneurial skills, made an unparalleled mark on the women's magazine world, and, arguably, developed her mass movement of women, a loyal cadre of readers who embraced Brown's philosophy.

Interviewed by the feminist Gloria Steinem during her *Cosmo* years, Brown nearly exploded with frustration at what she perceived as Steinem's repeated attempts to make her into a victim.[8] When a group of feminists staged a takeover of Brown's offices at *Cosmopolitan,* she shot back at them, declaring her magazine already feminist rather than in need of liberation. Steinem and others defined Brown as naive or antifeminist, yet her writings and her relationships with readers reveal a practice easily as complicated as theirs. Brown's particular approach linked her not only to other members of her generation but also to successive generations of women, through a philosophy of feminism compatible with both capitalism and popular culture.

Brown's version of the actual and potential equality of women and men also differed from that promoted in other feminist circles. She believed women were equal to men in sexual desire and in their right to be sexual inside and outside of marriage. She promoted equality both of economic access and of sexual freedom, avidly supporting the Equal Rights Amendment and featuring the ERA, along with abortion rights, in the pages of *Cosmopolitan*. Unlike some feminists, however, she refused to view men as the enemy, as she considered women equal in almost every way to men, including in their potential to abuse power. In addition, she saw no reason for women to refrain from playing the system by exploiting the inequities in the dating game. In *Sex and the Single Girl* and then in *Cosmopolitan*, Brown argued that since men made more money, they ought to be expected not only to pay for all dating adventures but also to keep women in jewels, alcohol, even cash. This particular version of equity troubled many feminists but spoke to longstanding realities of life for working-class women, many of whom faced the as-yet-unnamed glass ceiling in employment. When others called Brown on her allegedly having "sold out" to the system that oppressed women, she argued simply that she lived in the real world. If men made the rules, women could at least manipulate them.

Much to the horror of conservatives and feminists alike, Brown considered sex a "powerful weapon" for single women, one they had to draw on as necessary to claim their right either to pleasure or to survival.[9] This never meant, however, that Brown envisioned her readers as doing anything less than everything in their power to provide for themselves. She believed above all in work—hard work. She urged all women, whether they worked as secretaries, flight attendants, Playboy bunnies, or corporate executives, to consider themselves professionals and to set professional goals. After all, as she stated repeatedly in one way or another, "Nothing is as much fun as achieving."[10]

Helen Gurley Brown's ideas about female sexuality also placed her in a problematic category of feminism, at least as far as others were concerned. *Playboy* magazine emerged in 1953 and offered men of her generation the pleasures of sex without the burden of family. Brown wanted to claim the same kind of sexual hedonism for women, and she always considered this claim a decidedly feminist one.[11] Single herself until age thirty-seven, Brown was well aware that contemporary social critics equated women's sexuality with danger and declared sexually active single women, or even all single women, misfits at best, sociopaths at worst. For Brown, the single woman's biggest problem was "coping with the people who want to marry her off!" According to Brown, the single girl had nothing to apologize for. While "indulging her libido, which she has plenty of," she could still be highly respected. "I did it," she writes in *Sex and the Single Girl*. "So have many of my friends."[12]

However progressive, though, Helen Gurley Brown's take on sexuality was not wholly compatible with that of many of her feminist peers. Like them, she rejected the double standard that had declared marriage monogamous for women but not for men, labeled sexually active women sluts and sexually active men studs, and deemed single women old maids but men simply bachelors. Unlike them, however, Brown celebrated rather than complained about women's compliance with the rules of femininity. She agreed that as women put on makeup or took off lingerie, they "performed" femininity rather than engaged in what other feminists might have considered an "authentic" self. Brown had no problem with such behavior; in fact, she considered it among the most delightful benefits of being female. She saw no reason for women to leave off dressing in sexy clothing, wearing makeup, and behaving seductively or even submissively as they simultaneously claimed an active, enjoyable, fulfilling sexuality. She claimed these rights not only for heterosexual women but for lesbians as well, although her attempts to make her own writings lesbian-friendly met opposition at every turn.

Finally, Brown's playful approach put off many serious-minded feminists of her generation and later. Ever the optimist, she chose to see pleasure where others saw danger, allies where others saw oppressors, and opportunity where others saw obstacles. If other feminists could be faulted for overemphasizing the ways in which women were victimized, Helen Gurley Brown can be faulted for underemphasizing women's workplace and personal challenges. *Sex and the Single Girl* and *Cosmopolitan* both preached the wonders of single life for women and refrained from much consideration of issues such as wage differentials, sexual violence, or the workings of divorce law. This breezy approach, combined with an equally breezy writing style filled with exclamation points and affectations ("I get goosebumpy thinking about what has happened to women") provided others the opportunity simply to dismiss her.[13] They shrugged her off based on misinterpretations and at their peril, however, because she more than anyone understood the emerging single-girl phenomenon and she more than many others captured the loyalties of women in the mainstream.

Throughout the women's liberation era, Brown recognized that large numbers of women wanted a role model rather than a movement, a friend rather than a political mentor. An early practitioner of self-help, she believed that women needed help both getting through the day, at work, and through the night, in their intimate relationships.[14] None of her attitudes or practices, as far as she was concerned, detracted from her feminist credentials. Further, Brown was savvy enough to know that not even the most liberated of women lived outside of the pressures of beauty culture or male-dictated cultural spheres, and she recognized that she had among her readers feminists who read her magazine on the sly. When Helen Gurley Brown left *Cosmopolitan* in 1997, after thirty-two years, her magazine ranked sixth at the newsstand and remained, for the sixteenth year, number one in college-campus bookstores.[15] With its assumption that women want their sexual, emotional, economic, and professional needs met, Brown's philosophy continues to resonate today, even for those generations of women raised in the aftermath of second-wave feminism's many successes.

Although this book is not an authorized biography, in that Helen Gurley Brown has not read it or given her stamp of approval to its contents or arguments, it benefits tremendously from her gracious permission to quote from any and all of her published and unpublished writings, which span from her childhood to her later years and fill nearly fifty boxes in the Sophia Smith archives at Smith College. And her story is by no means over, as she continues to amass papers and letters that will have to be added to that collection. At eighty-six, Helen Gurley Brown continues to work, now as editor in chief of Cosmopolitan International, and to espouse her very particular and still-relevant brand of feminism. Rather than granting Brown's form of feminism a new name, such as working-class feminism, mainstream feminism, or second/third-wave feminism, any one of which might be appropriate, I choose instead to consider her life and work an untold element of the second wave and a clear antecedent of the third. In fact, her work and life trajectories span even more time than these two waves. Brown herself was thirty-three years old and in the workplace for fifteen years before she met a woman who had her own secretary rather than worked as one. In the span of her long life, she has both witnessed and ushered in tremendous changes in women's lives, and this biography identifies the most salient and most lasting of her contributions.

The many boxes of papers that reveal at least parts of Helen Gurley Brown's life also reveal, not unexpectedly, the kinds of contradictions one encounters in the life of a real human being rather than an idol, feminist or otherwise. In the countless interviews she has granted, Brown has put forth a personal history that rendered her a young woman lacking in ambition—the product of a poor, "hillbilly" family—yet the documents relating to her childhood and adolescence reveal her to have been an ambitious, assertive presence among her peers. She has argued that she was satisfied with the life of a secretary and became a copywriter and then a successful writer only at the urging of others, yet her unpublished writings reveal that she envisioned herself a writer, with an audience, from an early age.

Other contradictions emerge as well. Helen Gurley Brown argues that sex is as basic a necessity as daily bread, but she herself barely eats.[16] She has long promoted a fairly libertine sexuality, particularly regarding sex outside of marriage, but she has practiced and expected fidelity in her own marital relationship. Certainly each of us rewrites elements of our own history; perhaps famous people simply have more opportunity than most to revisit and revise. The gift of biography is that it allows these various stories to tangle with each other. In the case of Helen Gurley Brown, her delightfully knotty life story suggests just how complicated issues of family, sexuality, femininity, ambition, success, and intimacy have been—and remain—in the lives of American women.

Helen Gurley Brown has never considered herself unique, but she does acknowledge her own uncanny ability to tap into the desires and struggles of American women of various identities. "I picked up a torch, I'd guess you'd say," she explains simply, but with her singular presence and singular philosophy, and through her many books and through *Cosmopolitan*, the magazine that will forever remain linked with her, Helen Gurley Brown not only picked up a torch but also brought her feisty feminist messages to generations of women.[17] She ushered in and has long continued to define the feminist mainstream: a place of challenge, comfort, self-realization, and change for American women. Helen Gurley Brown's feminism continues to have its appeal, its reach, and its power to intimidate or threaten both the status quo and her fellow feminists. Brown is fine with that. After all, as she declares and demonstrates, "living dangerously lengthens and strengthens your life."[18]

bad girls go everywhere

growing up gurley, and a girl

Before it became famous as the birthplace of Helen Gurley Brown, Green Forest, Arkansas, a tiny town in the Ozarks, was known principally for two things: its individualistic traditions and its bawdy folklore. It seems a fitting place, then, for Helen Marie Gurley to have entered the world on February 18, 1922. Years later, as a young adult struggling to survive financially on a secretary's salary and then, even later, as a successful writer and editor enjoying financial security, Brown largely denied any connection to the place of her birth. Green Forest lacked the cachet claimed by many of her equally successful contemporaries who hailed from cities like New York, Chicago, or Los Angeles. And her own Horatio Alger–like approach to success left little room or incentive for her to delve too deeply into the significance of her life as an Arkansan.

Nevertheless, reflective or not, in her appreciation for individual accomplishment and in her celebration of sexuality, Helen Gurley carried forward some of the traditions she hardly realized she had inherited. In her conscious mind she remained haunted by certain aspects of her young life: nagging poverty, the stark contrast she felt between the everyday life of her family and community and the widely publicized lives of the Hollywood stars with whom she was enamored, and the ways in which her family, in particular her mother, seemed perpetually to hang back from, rather than embrace, life. From an early age she envisioned herself on the run, and that metaphor would shape her decision making and her sense of her self, her family, and her past for her entire life.

In some ways and perhaps largely unwittingly, Helen's mother, Cleo, would plant the idea in Helen's mind that family and community held one back rather than provided a framework for success in life. Cleo Fred Sisco Gurley had been born in the tiny community of Alpena, Arkansas, the oldest of nine children and an intellectually promising child from the start. Saddled with family responsibilities from a young age, Cleo was delighted when her parents managed to let her move to Green Forest to live with an aunt and attend high school. One of her high school teachers convinced the family that Cleo was simply too bright not to attend college so, for what amounted to "one glorious semester," she enrolled at the University of Arkansas at Fayetteville. But her family called her back home to help out with her younger siblings for a time, and her promised return to college never materialized.

A young woman could obtain respectable employment as a teacher in rural Arkansas without a college degree, so to support the family Cleo settled in to riding three miles by horse each day to teach in a one-room schoolhouse in Reuhel. After four years of teaching, she met fellow teacher Ira Marvin Gurley, who attended the Cumberland Law School in Tennessee while teaching in Gardner, Arkansas. Cleo married Ira Gurley rather than her high school beau, Leigh Bryan, because Gurley was more in keeping with her family's expectations: he hunted, fished, exhibited a certain charm, and offered greater promise as a provider than did the bookish but, in her mind, more compatible Bryan. It was a decision she would long regret.

By the time of Helen's birth, Cleo had, at her husband's insistence but much to her chagrin, left her job to raise Helen and Helen's older sister, Mary.[1] Cleo subsequently, and even visibly, bore the burden of having relinquished rather than taken on significant life decisions, largely through a process of resignation. She resigned herself to leaving college to meet her family's needs, resigned herself to marrying Ira Gurley when she preferred another suitor, and resigned herself to giving up a meaningful career when her husband requested that she do so.

Helen discovered her mother's discontents in piecemeal fashion, as the family was unaccustomed to talking about such things. They knew or spoke little about their ancestors, whose life stories might have shed some light on female aspirations among the Ciscos. Prior to Cleo's death in 1980, Helen participated in an effort to recover some basic facts about the family, but overall they appeared satisfied with a mere sketch of who and what came before them. Believed to be of Spanish lineage, and descending from a colonial-era immigrant named DeSesco who settled first in the Carolinas, the Ciscos would migrate to Arkansas by way of Kentucky and Tennessee. On the Gurley side, Helen descended from a seemingly quite wealthy great-great-grandfather, whose will, probated on December 2, 1865, four days before the Thirteenth Amendment to the U.S. Constitution abolished slavery, bequeathed an abundance of land in addition to thirteen slaves to his wife and ten children. Little more is known of Helen's paternal roots or family, even those who lived closer to Helen's own time, as she grew up in closer contact with her mother's family than her father's. She spent her infancy near her mother's family, but in 1923 Ira Gurley completed law school and won election to the Arkansas state legislature. The family moved to Little Rock, the state capital, roughly 120 miles, and in some ways worlds away, from Green Forest.[2]

The Gurley family had been quite poor in the early days in Green Forest. Even though Ira held a respected position as a schoolteacher, the setting was rural and the pay minimal. The family's financial situation improved considerably when Ira assumed his position in the legislature. They moved to Pulaski Heights, now known as Hillcrest, which had been annexed to the city in 1916 and served, because of its streetcar service, as Little Rock's first suburb. Little Rock had shed its frontier image and, in the Gurleys' early years there, actively promoted itself as modern, an effort that succeeded in drawing new residents. Its population grew from forty thousand at the turn of the century to nearly eighty-two thousand by 1930. Visitors to Little Rock frequented the nearby Hot Springs National Park, which preceded Yellowstone by forty years to become the nation's first national park. The grand hotels and world-class bathhouses of Hot Springs attracted many luminaries during the 1920s—and even the 1930s, when there was a Depression-era Civilian Conservation Corps camp on the park's premises.[3] The ascendancy of Little Rock and its environs matched that of the Gurley family, particularly of Ira, who took on an increasingly visible and important role in state politics.

Little Rock itself would gain notoriety on two very different occasions, one cultural and one political, the first during and the second after the Gurley family's residency there. First, in 1925, the screenwriter and flapper archetype Anita Loos serialized *Gentlemen Prefer Blondes*, a saucy satire of Prohibition and of the relationship between the sexes, in *Harper's* magazine. The tale, which would eventually become a Broadway hit starring Carol Channing, and then a Hollywood film starring Marilyn Monroe, follows the escapades of its main character, the Little Rock native Lorelei Lee, a seemingly unintelligent woman who uses her abundant street smarts and feminine wiles to encourage men, married and single alike, to keep her in liquor, clothes, and even diamonds, without her having to marry them. After all, as Lorelei famously tells us, "Diamonds are a girl's best friend."

But *Gentlemen Prefer Blondes,* in addition to publicizing the varieties of modern choices available to young American women, appointed Little Rock the cultural capital of unsophisticated, humdrum American life, the kind of place any aspiring glamour girl would want to leave behind. Lorelei Lee and her best friend, Dorothy, "just two little girls from Little Rock," savvy to the reality that men in American culture often pay for relationships with their wallets and women with their bodies, head straight to New York, address such exchanges of sexuality head on, and come out on top, contrary to the abundant morality tales of their day. "A kiss may be grand but it won't pay the rental, on your humble flat, or help you at the automat," the lyrics to the song tell us; a working girl may need a sugar daddy to help with the basics in addition to the luxuries of life. Considered too crass, too working-class, too sensuous, and in many ways too honest by the monied classes whose ranks they wish to join, Lorelei and Dorothy do not, as many would argue they ought to at least know enough to do, slink away. Instead, they take on their so-called superiors, and most often win.[4]

Loos's tale of what Lorelei left behind in Little Rock, combined with descriptions of what she encountered once she became unhitched from small-town life, proved an enormous hit. H. L. Mencken called Anita Loos the first American writer who "made fun of sex," Edith Wharton called the book "the great American novel," and public figures as diverse as James Joyce, Winston Churchill, and William Faulkner sang the book's praises. Many women developed their approach to flapper fashions and behavior by studying Loos, who seemed to embody, physically and socially, a carefree, media-generated understanding of contemporary life. Many years later the story of Lorelei's exploits reemerged, providing the basis for Madonna's 1985 "Material Girl" music video, in which "the boy with the cold hard cash is always Mister Right." But two decades earlier, in a phrase that links Loos, Brown, and Madonna in a fascinating cultural triangle,

Helen Gurley Brown had stated in a *Time* magazine interview, "I am a materialist, and it is a materialistic world."[5]

Gentlemen Prefer Blondes doubled *Harper's* circulation, sold out halfway through its first day when published as a book, became a best-seller in thirteen languages, and ensured "gold digger" a secure place in the nation's vocabulary. Years later, when Helen Gurley Brown hosted a syndicated radio show, a caller asked her if diamonds really were a girl's best friend and, if so, how might one go about securing them. In response Brown made mention of Anita Loos, lamenting that the days of such gold-digger practices had ended decades earlier. "I think all the sugar daddies dissolved in their own sugar or something and chorus girls have to compete with all the other pretty girls there are nowadays," she stated. She did have advice to share: marry a rich man for big diamonds or a less wealthy man for smaller diamonds, or better yet, buy them for yourself.[6] In 1925 Lorelei Lee, savvy to the facts of working-class life and gender dynamics, knew this third option remained unavailable to her. Some things had changed by the time Helen Gurley Brown hit her stride.

Little Rock gained not only national but also international fame several decades later when, in 1957, it became the site of the first implementation of the 1954 *Brown v. Board of Education* decision desegregating the nation's schools and declaring the "separate but equal" doctrine unconstitutional. Little Rock's Central High School, which Helen Gurley would have attended had she remained in Little Rock for high school, came to symbolize the lengths to which white citizens would go to enforce racial segregation. As the black students who came to be known as the Little Rock Nine attempted to enter the school, the Arkansas National Guard, under the direction of Governor Orval E. Faubus, failed to protect them from angry and violent mobs. In response to the governor's recalcitrance, President Dwight D. Eisenhower took over the state National Guard and sent the U.S. Army's 101st Airborne to the school to enforce implementation of the ruling.[7]

Even though Helen Gurley would have been in her thirties by the time of the Little Rock Nine, race relations in Arkansas undoubtedly provided an important backdrop for her young life and a formative element of her adult views on American society. The young Helen attended segregated schools and was subject to racial segregation in most public spaces. At one point in her adult life, Helen Gurley Brown noted a lack of anti-Semitism in her home state by explaining "we were pretty busy with apartheid" and arguing that, although at least outside of her family she had been schooled in prejudice, she had "[come] around pretty well."[8] She maintained that her own parents, only a generation away from slavery themselves, abhorred racism and provided her a means of escaping the harsh perspectives of her immediate environment. Nevertheless, like many of her contemporaries, Helen Gurley makes few references to the issue of race in her early journals or later recollections, and although she crosses many boundaries in her writing, Helen Gurley Brown often assumes her readership to be white and their problems fairly universal. Little Rock provided Brown a lifelong metaphor for escape, a comfortable, comforting, and convenient perspective that, in leaving Little Rock, she also left behind intolerance and certain forms of privilege.[9]

The most immediate context for the Gurley family in Little Rock during Helen's early life was the Great Depression. Arkansas had been the hardest hit state during the Great Mississippi Flood of 1927, one of the nation's most destructive natural disasters. The state suffered agricultural losses in the millions of dollars, and tens of thousands of people lost their homes, some permanently. A drop in the price of cotton, unrelated to the flood, made things worse, and the state was as a consequence particularly ill prepared for the enormous economic downturn of the Depression. Helen's family fared better than many people in Little Rock and most in the Ozarks, white or black, during the early years of the crisis. Her father remained employed, even gaining appointment as the commissioner of the Arkansas Game and Fish Commission and earning as much as fifty dollars a week, at a time when many Arkansans had no income to speak of. Some relief for the state eventually came with the Roosevelt administration's Works Progress Administration, which employed many people in Arkansas. Little Rock, in particular, benefited from the construction of a series of long-lasting buildings made of native stone, including the Little Rock Zoo, many of the city's municipal buildings, and an art museum.[10]

Regardless of their improved financial status, or their residence in a city that was cosmopolitan by any measurable standards available to the Gurley family, Helen remembered their life together as anything but happy. Her mother, Cleo, had nearly died during the birth of each of her daughters and remained frail and tentative about the world, "terminally sad" as Helen would later describe her: "She was smart, gentle, sensitive to the point of dandelion fragility—you couldn't breathe on her without hurting her feelings—and totally frustrated."[11] As a teenager, Helen would discover that a significant source of Cleo's enormous disappointment with the world remained her decision years earlier to marry Ira Gurley rather than Leigh Bryan. Cleo seemed never to come to terms with herself—or with Ira—over a choice that felt coerced rather than free. Helen's best friend in Little Rock, Elizabeth Jessup, would remember Cleo in similar fashion, noting her "infrequent (and therefore surprising) smile." She recalled, "I never tried to figure out why she was so quiet."[12]

As children, Helen and her sister, Mary, with no sense of the complications of gender relations in general or of their parents' marital relationship in particular, and with a self-absorbed approach to adults and adult concerns, found their father loving, well liked among their friends, and fun to be around. He took them to the state fair each year and regularly took them to the local airport to watch the planes take off. Helen experienced Ira's playful and light personality as a positive counterpoint to Cleo's negativity and inertia.

As much as Cleo struggled in the marriage, her hardships would be compounded when, in the midst of the Depression, tragedy beset the family. Ira Gurley, forty years old and preparing to run for secretary of state, died in an elevator accident in the state capitol building in Little Rock on June 18, 1932. The tragedy brought the family some initial fame, with "acres of flowers" delivered to the house and the funeral, and Ira Gurley's picture featured on the front page of both major papers, the *Arkansas Gazette* and the *Arkansas Democrat*. Almost immediately, however, rumors abounded about the accident, complicating the family's grieving process. According to one, the monies had been appropriated for a new elevator to replace the old and dangerous one, but lawmakers had siphoned off the funding, using it for other projects or to line their pockets. Another rumor posited that Ira had tried to jump onto the elevator after it had left the floor because he spotted an attractive woman inside it.

Whatever the case, Cleo Gurley, then just thirty-eight years old, found herself widowed with only a small grant from the state and a minimal insurance settlement. Her small-town teaching experience, from which she was by now years removed, had done little to prepare her for life as the single parent of fourteen-year-old Mary and ten-year-old Helen during such lean times. She attended typing school and took in some sewing, but few economically viable opportunities presented themselves for women in general or for Cleo Gurley in particular in the early to mid-1930s. She lived in an era in which women had become subject to numerous policies of protective labor legislation, which simultaneously ensured that women would have safer working conditions than men and reserved for men the more hazardous and, not incidentally, more lucrative jobs. In the 1930s a combination of such "protective" attitudes about women, combined with the realities of the Depression, made gaining any form of employment difficult for women.[13] On top of that, as the adult Helen later came to believe, Cleo suffered doubly with Ira's loss, struggling economically but also feeling tremendous guilt for not having loved the husband who lost his life so tragically: "In the determined, irrational way of neurotics," Helen would explain about her mother, "she felt, from not loving him, she must somehow have caused him to die."[14]

Like many women of her day, Cleo viewed a second marriage as one potential avenue to greater financial stability, and in her case she had a definite prospect in mind. Years later Helen pieced together memories from two trips she and Cleo took following Ira's death and realized that her mother's hunt for Leigh Bryan, and the many things he represented, began soon after Ira's demise. During the first trip, in 1933, ostensibly made to attend the World's Fair in Chicago but actually designed so that Cleo could determine Leigh Bryan's location, Helen became enamored not only with the fair but also with the city, whose double-decker buses, huge billboards, and Marshall Field escalators dazzled the young girl. For the first time, she saw a world outside Arkansas, and Chicago, thereafter, remained in her dreams as a formative presence, a formidable and seductive promise of life beyond Little Rock.[15] Apparently, Cleo discovered during and after the trip that Leigh Bryan lived not in Chicago, as she had thought, but in Cleveland, where he worked as an ice cream salesman. The next year she invited Helen to travel to the World's Fair again, but this time she had a more elaborate, more deceptive, perhaps more desperate plan in mind.

When they arrived at the train station in Chicago, Cleo suggested that, because it was raining, they continue on and visit Cleveland, which they had never seen, then swing back to Chicago for the fair. Once in Cleveland, Cleo dropped Helen off at various movie theaters as she went in search of Bryan and then again after she had found him, as the two grown-ups caught up on their respective lives. After Helen informed her mother that a flasher had approached and then stalked her in a movie theater, Cleo cut the visit short. They did stop at the World's Fair on the way back. "I don't think things went that well with Leigh Bryan," Helen recalled later, "though she did marry him five years later."[16] One can imagine the difficulty for Cleo of reconciling the real Bryan with the long-imagined and much-romanticized one. Given her financial straits, which were soon to worsen considerably, one can also imagine the pressure she put on herself to marry and to hope that a long-held dream would somehow materialize into a comfortable reality.

Helen and her mother returned to Little Rock, Leigh Bryan stayed behind in Cleveland, and it was years before Helen heard about him again. In the meantime, she tried to carve out a satisfactory girlhood without her father, in far more constrained economic circumstances, and with her difficult and moody mother. She was close to her older sister, and the two girls considered themselves allies in the face of their mother's provocations. Before Ira's death, young Helen had dreamed of achieving a secure place in the loftiest social circles in Little Rock and beyond, and with her father's rapid ascendancy in Arkansas politics she seemed poised to do so. Even after he was gone, Helen's outgoing personality, combined with her mother's genteel manner and fine sewing skills, ensured Helen, dressed appropriately for all social occasions, occasional entry among the privileged in Little Rock. She enjoyed friendships with the few wealthy children in town; attended their parties, even though she could not reciprocate; and relished the attentions of their parents in the splendor of luxurious surroundings. She viewed in increasingly stark relief the differences between her life, which she later recalled as "ordinary, hillbilly and poor," and theirs, which she coveted with a fair degree of intensity.[17]

Gurley later recalled playing in the autumn leaves at a country club with some friends while the other children's parents played golf. She needed to use the restroom but was too embarrassed to ask where it was or how she might gain entrance. "Don't these damn children of the rich ever have to empty their bladders?" she jokingly remembered years later, revealing her ability, slowly acquired, to mock what had mattered most to her as a child. She managed to sneak into the leaf pile and "get on with it," but she knew that even ways of peeing signaled a chasm between her life and theirs. Essentially, Helen Gurley understood that class mattered.

A few years later, wading through a creek in the Ozarks on the way to a church revival with a group of extended family, her cousin Yvonne stopped to urinate right along the trail and in front of everybody. "Couldn't she wait until there was nobody around?" Helen demanded of Yvonne's sister. "Guess she had to go," was the straightforward and unaffected response that shamed Helen and illuminated again the class differences she had hoped to transcend. "I am definitely better than this, I decided," she wrote later, remembering that moment, "though I don't exactly know what I meant by better. They and I are different anyway and I want out."[18]

Helen's sister, Mary, would, in later years, take Helen to task for her repeated use of the pejorative "hillbilly" rather than the more respectful "mountain people" to describe their family.[19] Unlike Mary, however,

Helen never felt proud of the people or the places she came from, and once she left Arkansas, she never returned there to live. Like Lorelei Lee in *Gentlemen Prefer Blondes,* she saw Little Rock as a dead end. "I didn't like the look of the life that seemed to be programmed for me," she remembered. "It didn't look promising. Even as a teenager I was an achiever. I had a reasonably good brain, though it wasn't fashionable to do anything about it in those days. Even then I was aware that if you put effort into it you generally got something out of it."[20]

Interestingly, Helen Gurley held onto the belief that this pull-oneself-up-by-one's-bootstraps approach to life, which she maintained from an early age, emerged in reaction to rather than in concert with what she experienced at home or in her community. Her favorite quote, "I must go home periodically to renew my sense of horror," came from the pen of writer Carson McCullers, a contemporary of Helen Gurley Brown's who skillfully explored what Richard Wright dubbed the "bleak landscape of the American consciousness beneath the Mason-Dixon line."[21] In a draft of one of her books, *Having It All,* Brown would claim that the primary gift her family gave her was something concrete against which to strive: "If you have some daily anguish from some cause that's not really your fault—a rotten family, bad health, nowhere looks, serious money problems, nobody to help you, minority background (I didn't have that—a WASP—but I had other things), rejoice! These things are your fuel!"[22]

Only later would Helen Gurley come to understand and then appreciate her mother's position within her marriage, within the cultural setting of the South, and within the economic setting of the Depression. The truth is that years before the Great Depression took its toll or Ira lost his life, Cleo had performed an act of sacrifice hardly identified as such in that day, leaving her job as a schoolteacher to attend to her husband and children. Although she would later return to work out of necessity and, indeed, take on tremendous responsibilities as a single parent during the Depression, Cleo never forgot that early and deep sting of injustice. She had loved teaching and had wanted to continue to work, but her husband would have none of it. Ira was a "typical chauvinist," Brown came to understand, who had voted against women's suffrage and demanded his wife's presence in the home. Cleo had already experienced her share of sacrifices growing up, and as an adult she rejected, at least in her mind, the notion that she alone, as a woman, wife, or mother, should remain selfless. Having played a large role raising the eight younger children in her family, Cleo longed for a different formula in her own life but found no support for creating one.

Cleo never forgave her husband for holding her back and arguably never forgave her daughters for the central, albeit unwitting, role they played in ending their mother's career. "You should realize that I am no longer the Gurley 'doormat,'" she once wrote to Helen in a fit of anger, "and that I have feelings, a little bit of pride and dignity left, even if Cave-man Gurley and his offspring did make chattel property and a slave of me for many years." Here, Cleo Gurley put into words the bitterness she made evident silently for so many years. In an ideal life, Helen later argued with an understanding and empathy that took years to develop, her mother "wouldn't have had to give up teaching for one single year."[23]

After many years of resenting her mother's bitter, guarded approach to life, Helen eventually came to appreciate Cleo and even regard her as a feminist. "You know what some men are like now in terms of wanting their wives only to be wives and mothers and keep sparkling houses and cook unforgettable meals," she wrote in the 1980s. "Well, my mother was no cook and no housewife and didn't like her husband (my father) very well and it was 50 years ago, so you can imagine how many laughs she had from day to day!"[24] Gurley also came to appreciate that her mother differed from other mothers in ways beyond her incompatibility with traditional wifehood and motherhood. She had high expectations of Mary and Helen and always encouraged them—in fact, always expected them—to use their minds.

From Cleo, Helen learned that sacrificing for others proved a mixed, vexed experience with equally mixed, vexed results. From other role models in her young life, she learned something different but equally important and certainly equally formative: focusing on the self provided not simply an alternative to sacrifice but a positive approach to life, one that facilitated rather than detracted from one's ability to assist others. In one instance, one of her teachers at Pulaski Heights Junior High School in Arkansas invited the dean of a local women's college to the school. The guest shook hands with a few of the students, Helen among them, and the teacher later admonished Helen because the visitor had complained that her handshake felt like the "proverbial wet fish." This teacher taught her to shake hands deliberately and firmly and not to worry that a strong handshake conflicted with appropriate practices of femininity.

A second formative experience occurred when another teacher at the school posed a question to the class: who was the most important person in the world to them? The children offered the expected responses—mothers, fathers, God, grandmothers, and Franklin Roosevelt—but the teacher was having none of it. "She smiled," Gurley later recalled, "and said the southern, charming, Little Rock, Arkansas, equivalent of 'You are all full of shit. The most important person to any of you is yourself.'"[25]

Helen Gurley received conflicting messages about achievement, social class aspirations and limitations, and women's roles, but she also experienced a girlhood abundant in friendship and activity. Elizabeth Jessup later remembered many of their undertakings, including Saturdays at the movie theater or at Oaklawn racetrack, where the horse-loving Cleo would take the girls before the track imposed an age limit—and then dress them up to defy the age limit once it was established. Helen wrote and starred in dramatic performances, took and gave dance lessons, and spent countless hours reading Hollywood fan magazines or playing kick the can and other games on the street.[26] The childhood friend that Jessup remembered made the most of every opportunity and could in no way be overshadowed by other children's personalities or accomplishments. Yet, Helen arguably also felt herself "less" than others, in part because she had lost her father, in part because her family struggled financially, and in part because of her mother's understandably depressing assessment of their collective lives and future prospects.

The key elements of Helen Gurley's planned escape from her family's poverty, however genteel it was, merged through a deliberate combination of hard work, charm, and most importantly, residency almost anywhere but Arkansas. Years later the sense of panic she felt when she thought of being stuck there still resonated: "I always get out but what if some day I couldn't, they wouldn't let me go...hold me down...make me stay stone still." In the end Helen Gurley did escape Arkansas at an early age, but without simultaneously escaping the hold of her family or the dictates of poverty. In 1937, after many attempts at making it in Little Rock, and concerned that her nineteen-year-old daughter, Mary, might become pregnant and stuck in a life similar to the one she had lived, Cleo planned a temporary relocation to California, where Ira's brother lived. Mary balked at the idea and initially stayed behind, relenting after a few months and joining her mother and sister in the two-room apartment Cleo rented in Los Angeles.

Only a few months later, Mary contracted polio, a disease that would rob her of the use of her legs and, by and large, confine her to a life defined by her disability. Mary Gurley was hardly alone. This disease had killed thousands of Americans in the early twentieth century, with the 1916 outbreak in New York paralyzing twenty-seven thousand people and killing nine thousand more. There was little in the way of relief, as it was not until 1954, nearly twenty years after Mary contracted polio, that trials of the Salk vaccine would begin.

It became widely known that President Franklin Roosevelt suffered from polio, but the media respected his wish never to be photographed with his braces or his wheelchair visible. Public fear about polio, combined with a lack of understanding about disabilities in general, may have prompted Roosevelt to act in this fashion, but his actions did little to stem the tide of public terror of all things associated with the disease, including its many victims. Mary spent the rest of her life in a wheelchair, unable to move her legs at all. Her medical condition determined the family's residency for the next several years, as polio treatment in California surpassed that available almost anywhere else, and certainly that available in Arkansas.[27]

The family initially lived in a bungalow near Los Angeles's Orthopaedic Hospital so Mary could receive ongoing care. She underwent pool treatments and massage therapy, and then the more radical procedure of muscle transplants, but nothing her eminent physicians attempted could reverse the damage that had already occurred. Helen attended school but spent a great deal of time with Mary, accompanying her to the movies, to the track, and shopping. Helen later remembered how well Mary negotiated the streets and curbs in the days long before there was any real awareness of people's differing needs when using the streets or public transportation, and half a century before the passage of the Americans with Disabilities Act.[28] The family had few contacts and came to rely for emotional support on a wheelchair-bound woman next door who, along with her husband, had conquered what Helen remembered as "the depression and sads" that went along with polio.[29] Cleo, Mary, and Helen proved less successful in overcoming those feelings.

The paired afflictions of polio and poverty ensured, as Helen later remembered, that Cleo Gurley and her two daughters would remain locked "in a deadly embrace." Another time, she remembered those lonely and difficult times less dramatically but nevertheless poignantly: "We managed. We were close to each other, but we were so frightened. There wasn't much sympathy in the world."[30] There was indeed little sympathy and, for this family, little opportunity as the long years of the Great Depression continued unabated. And the move to Los Angeles, which might have seemed downright magical to a young girl who spent many hours flipping through dogeared copies of Hollywood magazines on her porch in Little Rock, signified additional responsibilities almost immediately as Helen took on the role of the healthy sister, competent daughter, and family decision maker.

Nevertheless, Helen's active involvement in the worlds available to an adolescent girl continued through the move to Los Angeles and through her high school years, regardless of economic woes, Mary's polio, Helen's related responsibilities, or Cleo's negativity. Helen Gurley was not simply involved in a myriad of school-related activities; she also stood out as a leader in many of them. One of her high school classmates wrote to tell Helen how she viewed her: "I can't tell you how I envy your popularity here at school. I don't believe anyone is known any better than yourself." Another girl wrote to explain that in the high school government structure, "any girl who runs for any office has a dream or a hope, that maybe someday she can be able to ask Helen Gurley to be her nominator." Yet another classmate declared Helen to be her vision of "an ideal high school girl," someone who stands up for what is right "when everyone else in the crowd doesn't."[31]

Gurley's high school admirers numbered more than the few who wrote her adoring letters. At John H. Francis Polytechnic High School in Los Angeles, she showed up again and again in the 1939 senior class lists of "best of" and "most likely." She tied for third-most-popular girl, lost "most likely to succeed" by two votes, came in third for "biggest apple polisher," and tied for fifth for "best girl dancer." On top of this, she was class valedictorian and served as president of the World Friendship Club and the Scholarship Society. She was interviewed in the student newspaper for an article about girls wearing pants to school, a new and controversial phenomenon at that time. "It lowers the respect of other fellows and girls for the one who comes to school in slacks," she argued in an expression of youthful conservatism that nonetheless reveals a characteristic self-assurance. "It is just as out of place as a playsuit at a formal affair." Gurley took charge of refreshments for the school prom, performed a monologue in a talent show, and was inducted into the Ephebian Society, which was reserved for students in the top 10 percent academically who also provided leadership, exercised character, and demonstrated citizenship.[32] In short, in a graduating class of 375 students, Helen Gurley stood out. She had developed what would have been, even in the years immediately preceding the Second World War, the ideal profile for getting into the college of her choice.

Many of the legion of articles published on Helen Gurley Brown refer to her as a "mouseburger," a term she invented to describe a young woman of average looks, with some intelligence, more likely working in a job than pursuing a career. The mouseburger receives little assistance in making her way through life but doggedly perseveres. She has been told repeatedly that beauty is a woman's greatest asset, but practical as she is, the mouseburger knows that a sufficient degree of that particular currency belongs to few women and certainly not to her. Nevertheless, the mouseburger demonstrates characteristics that bode well for success: an instinctive drive, a willingness to work hard at any task, and a determination to support herself and attain independence. Helen Gurley Brown would later claim that she had always been this kind of girl: a Depression-era child raised by a depressed mother, an acne-ridden teenager yearning for some of the traditional markers of beauty, a shy working girl who learned the ropes of single life and the work world slowly, a young woman who experienced a fair degree of emotional turmoil.

It remains difficult to assess the degree to which the mouseburger moniker applied to the young Helen Gurley herself or even provided an explicit link between her and the legions of working girls who eventually wanted to be like the grown-up Helen Gurley Brown. Did the young Helen Gurley, regardless of her outward demeanor, personality, charm, or accomplishments, actually consider herself utterly unattractive and, as she sometimes also argued, utterly lacking in potential? "I had no money, no college degree, I had wall-to-wall acne, and my family were hillbillies. I had an average IQ," Brown recalled in a newspaper interview in 1980. And in a 1985 interview with the feminist Gloria Steinem, she recalled that she had not attended college at all and that her highest ambition had been to keep herself from going "down the drain."[33] Her high school yearbook, however, portrays a well-respected, confident young woman who declared her dream to become successful one day as a businesswoman. Perhaps Helen Gurley, like many young American women, feared on some levels the profound power of her own personal aspirations.

Regardless of her accomplishments or popularity, there remained one area in which Gurley fully identified, publicly and privately, as inferior: in her "average" looks. In the end, after all, the graduating senior may have received scores of accolades, but she did not even find herself in the running for the designation of prettiest girl in the class. At the end of their senior year, one of her closest friends in high school, Florence Stanley, wrote her a letter outlining Helen's full range of personality traits. Helen had helped Florence gain self-confidence, provided an excellent role model for other students, and bore herself with equanimity and tact. Nevertheless, Stanley acknowledged in the letter, she fell short of perfection. "I think you care too much about money, though. And you really shouldn't be so sensitive.... And you used to be so very sensitive about your complexion. My goodness, a girl who has all that you have shouldn't mind that much." An honest friend, Stanley did not argue that Helen's concerns about her complexion rang false; instead, she argued that given everything else she had going for her, Helen Gurley should hardly have worried about something as trivial as pimples.[34]

And yet for Helen, her complexion was anything but trivial. After money, it proved her most significant insecurity. For many years her memories about the acne she suffered remained tangled with memories of herself, her mother, and her sister adrift in California. Her uncle, who struggled just to provide for his own two children, cousins Bob and Virginia Gurley, offered the family little support. The small family of Gurley women faced the nagging questions of how they would survive financially and ensure that Mary received the care she needed. "We didn't have those wonderful cozy sessions at home, where we cheered each other up," Brown later remembered, comparing her life to television programs that idealized family life. "We were just scared. Twice each week, after my mother would take me to the doctor to get all the pustules opened from my terminal acne...she and I would just drive around and cry in our old Pontiac. That was all she and I could think to do."[35]

Helen's obsession with her looks emerged from typical teenage angst, the culture of the day, and, to some degree, her mother's divided consciousness on matters of female beauty.[36] Cleo valued achievement and was not herself beautiful, but she had had a beautiful sister growing up and had wished for a beautiful daughter. As a result her messages about beauty came across almost as confused as did those about sacrifice and achievement. When Helen listened to her mother praise her academic accomplishments, she also heard, beneath the surface of Cleo's spoken words, the message that Helen had better work hard academically and use her brain because, after all, she could not rely on beauty to carry her through. The disappointment Cleo expressed about her daughter's lack of conventional beauty surely affected not only their relationship but also Helen's sense of self. But the result was not entirely negative; her mother's disapproval also promoted Helen Gurley's development of her influential philosophy, which provided not a rejection of female beauty but rather a curious, however pragmatic, acceptance of self in the face of such a lack.

Years later, after Cleo Gurley had read scores of interviews with her then-famous daughter in newspapers—local, national, and international—she remarked that Helen had exaggerated the negative elements of her childhood. Remarked Brown, "She thinks my version is not exactly the way it was, but, of course, it's not really about how it was that is important but how you felt about it."[37] Indeed, Helen's ordinary rather than exceptional looks, or at least her perception that she was simply ordinary, remained a largely unspoken but enormously significant deficit for her in her youth and then again in her work life. Praise from her friends for her intellectual or civic accomplishments compensated only in part. It is true that Helen Gurley Brown would never be referred to as beautiful, but as she gained confidence and maturity she developed a presence, a way of commanding people's attention with a demeanor that would grow increasingly strong and undeniably sexy. Like many women of her generation and after, she eventually came to realize that success and power produced their own beauty.

Similarly, her identity as a self-made woman became an enormously useful and seductive—if somewhat exaggerated—element of Helen Gurley Brown's persona. Its focus on the individual would exasperate her mother and sister, who saw her as part of a family that both nurtured and challenged her. It would also put her in conflict with many other feminists in the coming years whose political philosophy centered on the notion that women as a group faced oppression, and only as a group could they battle it. Brown's far more individualist approach to feminism allowed for, and even nurtured, the particular brand of self-help she offered other women over the years: "If I could make it, so, of course, can you." It is true that Brown would rewrite aspects of her life, to one degree or another, to fit this model. At the same time, she undoubtedly struggled inwardly, and sometimes outwardly, to figure out how a poor girl from Arkansas could make it in a wider world.

In the end, regardless of Helen Gurley's impressive accomplishments and high hopes, or her mother's expectations concerning her intellectual abilities, money proved the final arbiter in determining Helen's life immediately following high school. Soon after Helen's graduation, Cleo moved the family to Warm Springs, Georgia, so that Mary could receive polio treatment at a facility founded by Franklin Roosevelt. Like her mother, Helen had the opportunity to attend one semester of college, in her case at Texas State College for Women. Family finances would not support continuing there, however, so she returned to California and attended

Woodbury Business College, a secretarial school, graduating in 1941.[38] She worked her way through school, simultaneously studying and supporting her mother and sister, then put her secretarial training to work in the first of a series of seventeen secretarial positions in Los Angeles.

Like many other bright, academically engaged and accomplished young women of her generation, Helen Gurley forfeited the opportunity of a college education. Whether it was because they had to support their families, or because boys would be sent to college and girls kept home, or because it proved too difficult to work and attend college in the days before either reliable part-time work or student loans, many women entered the workplace with limited training and few opportunities for advancement. Clerical work for women appeared fairly glamorous but proved a decidedly low-paying, often temporary stopping point on the way to what most considered women's true vocation: marriage and family.[39] Gurley's experiences of family, however, complicated her ideas about marriage as a goal from an early age. Looking out for oneself, according to lessons she learned both negatively and positively, led not to sin but to salvation, and such a philosophy must have proven a welcome salve to someone who had ambitions but had received decidedly mixed messages about achieving them.

Helen Gurley's determination to avoid rather than embrace additional responsibilities, and to take care of herself, played a significant role in her marrying late in life, late at least for someone of her generation. "I tended to associate with people who were doing well," she later remembered. "I had enough responsibility with my sister without picking up any other strays along the way who needed to be nurtured, helped and protected. I was not Mother Teresa. I tried to do right by my sister, because there, by the grace of God, it could have been me. But it fell on her instead of me—she got polio and I didn't."[40] This remark might appear cavalier, even callous, but it suggests the practical side of Helen Gurley, the side that recognized that survival itself required both hard work and more than a smidgen of selfishness.

Gurley began working while she attended business school, typing up on-air announcements at radio station WKHJ in Los Angeles. She found her boss a "rather unpleasant fellow" but acknowledged that she made annoying errors on an almost daily basis. Once she had him announce fiftieth birthday greetings to a twelve-year-old child; another time she had him announce a fourth wedding anniversary to a couple of thirteen-year-olds. Gurley may have had ambition, but it took her some time to figure out how to make a go of things at work. As she remembered later, "The reason for all this lousing things up was partly because I couldn't type well yet and partly because I couldn't read the correspondents' writing and partly because when you start doing things wrong for a boss there is absolutely no end to the things you can do to upset him." She recalled how, on Pearl Harbor Day, when the other secretary in the department flew out of bed "like a greased mosquito" and showed up at the station "all ready to sting and serve," Helen went about her Sunday as usual, focusing on preparations for her evening date. "Mary Ellen got a big raise and the station sent her around town in a limousine for a month. So much for me being an early whiz."[41]

Another of Helen Gurley's early work memories both demonstrates her teenage insecurities and anticipates the ways in which her ideas about sexuality would later get her into trouble with other feminists. The "fellows" at the radio station—announcers, sound men, engineers, music clerks, and minor executives—played a game they called "scuttle," chasing the secretaries, receptionists, and file clerks, and pulling their panties off. Decades later, Helen Brown would, to the dismay of feminists across the country, describe scuttling as an example of the kinds of friendly sexual harassment women were beginning to take too seriously. The young Gurley never actually experienced the scuttling game herself but felt far more than a tinge of insecurity at not being considered pretty enough to be pursued during this dubious office practice. The men most likely considered her a "kid," someone whose age clearly demarcated the line between appropriate and inappropriate prey, but Gurley, insecure in her looks and ability to attract, interpreted their failure to include her a mark against her rather than a blessing.

Helen's home life continued to present significant challenges. She, Cleo, and Mary inhabited a less-than-glamorous Los Angeles, teeming with refugees from the South and Midwest, occupying an apartment next to the railroad tracks on Fifty-ninth Street and Western Avenue.[42] The building was so poorly constructed and maintained that gophers would tunnel up through the floor and into their rooms. Money always posed challenges for the family, even after Cleo married Leigh Bryan and he moved to California to live with them. Given Leigh Bryan's symbolic importance in Cleo's young life, and then his actual status as her second husband and Helen's stepfather, he assumes a remarkably minimal presence in Helen's life and recollections. In all of her writings over the years, published and unpublished, she has had little to say about Leigh Bryan, little of that positive. For someone of Helen's ambitious nature, a man whose only job had been as a Good Humor salesman hardly invited admiration. He was nice enough, she felt, but "embarrassing and ineffectual."[43]

Helen had assumed so significant a role as the family provider by this time that Leigh Bryan, too, seems to have become subject to and accepting of her authority. His presence appears to have had little impact on the three women with whom he lived, perhaps at least in part because the marriage lasted only five years, as Bryan died slowly and painfully of stomach cancer.[44] Regardless of Cleo's motivations for marrying him, it must have been a challenge for Bryan to integrate himself into the well-established relationship of Cleo and her daughters, one forged in pain and dependency. The marriage must also have been a significant blow for Cleo, whose resignation about other areas of her life may well have compounded her already high and decidedly unrealistic expectations of him.

After high school Helen started to lose what she considered her wallflower look. Her complexion cleared up, what she called her "thin and curveless" body began to develop curves, and she stopped feeling a need to pretend that dating failed to interest her. She realized that things had shifted significantly in her favor one night when she attended a party and encountered some former high school classmates. One young man from her graduating class, not recognizing her, asked to be introduced. Helen subsequently made the most of the possibilities of this new, attractive persona, and she began to put her own particular mark on single status in the late 1930s and early 1940s. "It was so much fun being popular," she recalled, "I didn't want it to end by settling down with one boy. So when anyone got serious about marriage or even suggested going steady I would just laugh and say there's plenty of time for that."[45] To some degree, of course, her reluctance to marry stemmed from a view of her mother's two problematic alliances, but it also suggests Helen's ability, even as a young woman, to question the status quo.

As much as she enjoyed her popularity in social circles, Helen Gurley remained haunted by what she considered the cruelties of her class position. She hungered for money and glamour, neither of which was immediately available to her as a secretary. Growing up in Los Angeles during the golden years of Hollywood, and having spent much of her adolescence attending the movies, she coveted what seemed "so unbelievably, indescribably glamorous."[46] Her family would drive up and down the Sunset Strip, feeling every bit the poor displaced Arkansans they were, but nevertheless experiencing a bit of the "sheer glittery beauty" rubbing off on them: "Yes, we had a right to be on that street, didn't we?" Helen wondered—and hoped.[47] Importantly, like Lorelei Lee in Little Rock and then in New York, Helen Gurley realized in Los Angeles that access to such glamour would result not from her making it in Hollywood, as she held neither discernible acting talent nor aspirations to become a starlet, but from relationships with men.

Clearly, men earned the money she lacked and would, given the way she saw things working around her, finance her entrée into new worlds. Gurley went out with many different kinds of men: soldiers, a doctor, a young man who became the president of the student body at Berkeley. She fell in love for the first time, with a man with an enviable Wilshire Boulevard penthouse. In this relationship she encountered what she would experience with other men for the next few decades: an enjoyment of what wealth provided but also the pain that resulted from emotionally distant, if not outright cruel, treatment.[48] To her credit, Gurley would most often move on when the going got rough, but she suffered her share of what she considered intense emotional pain in romantic relationships.

Helen Gurley's meandering nature applied not just to relationships with men but also to employment opportunities. Once she earned the top pay available at Radio Station WKHJ and completed her secretarial training, she began her characteristic practice of switching jobs to raise her pay by even the smallest amount. She got fired a few times along the way as well, the first time for sleeping at her desk and another time for not sleeping with her boss. Sex with the boss remained an option, however, and she engaged in the practice early in her career. She worked for a short time for Paul Ziffren, a struggling young tax attorney who would later become head of the Democratic Party in California. Gurley found legal secretarial work "beastly boring" but never forgot Ziffren. He had introduced her to Shakespeare and Emerson, offered to introduce her to wealthy men, and given her practical advice about the world. She wrote him decades later, upon learning that he was dying, to share her memories. "You were a lovely supportive friend when men weren't often friends of women in those days," she wrote. "Women adored you, of course. You gave me ten pounds of bacon—bacon!—when it was rationed and that was a treat for my family.... Just know what an influence you had on someone's life— and you were also good in bed though I only got to find out once—strong and ardent and caring."[49]

Helen Gurley Brown would speak proudly of such liaisons in *Sex and the Single Girl* and in her later writings, but mixed in with pride in these early years, undoubtedly, lay uncertainties about relationships outside of the bedroom, which contributed to Gurley's sex-friendly demeanor with men. In later years she stated that as a young woman she had no idea how to make a man happy "anywhere but in bed," and she stayed in a problematic relationship with a man who flaunted his cheating because at least in bed she was an equal. After years of therapy she attributed that openness, or insecurity, depending upon one's take, to having lost her father at such an early age.[50]

As she moved from secretarial position to secretarial position in the early to mid-1940s, Helen Gurley also continued to support her mother and sister. Things at home began to improve as they all secured steady, if not particularly lucrative, employment. Cleo worked at Sears Roebuck, marking tags for clothing, and Mary worked by phone for C. E. Hooper, a radio rating service, charting people's listening preferences. In 1947, though, Cleo and Mary decided to return to Arkansas to live with Cleo's parents in Osage, feeling that Helen had assumed too much responsibility and that they might have an easier time of things back home. Cleo worried that Helen would never marry if she continued to move from job to job every few months, and she knew that Helen's peripatetic employment resulted from concerns about supporting the family. Apparently, the question of whether or not Helen would return to Arkansas with her mother and sister did not emerge in discussions. Instead, they simply talked about where Helen would live once the others migrated home.

Years later Helen Gurley Brown reflected on what she realized had been yet another incredible sacrifice on Cleo's part: "It was kind of a gift she gave me . . . she figured I shouldn't be 'sacrificed' and, considering how unselfish parents can be, I have never gotten over this overwhelming thing that she did for me. She absolutely doted on me and yet chose to live away from me with my sister so I would be 'free.'"[51] Cleo and Mary packed up and left California, and Helen Gurley entered a new phase of life, significantly, or at least relatively, free of family burdens and doubly intent on making the most of what the workplace, and men, had to offer a single woman in Los Angeles.

2

work life, romantic entanglements

After Cleo and Mary returned to Arkansas, Helen Gurley moved in with a friend from work, at least until she entered into another phase of her single life—as a kept woman. "I've never worked anywhere…without being sexually involved with somebody in the office," she stated bluntly in an interview years later. Given that she was employed as a secretary in seventeen different offices before she began her career as an advertising copywriter, Gurley undoubtedly engaged in numerous sexual relationships and an even greater number of sexual liaisons. When asked, "What about the boss?" she replied flippantly, "Why discriminate against him?"[1]

Such attitudes would get her in trouble not only with her more conservative contemporaries but also with many among her feminist peers, who saw inherent inequities and exploitation, rather than fun and games, in such alliances. Although the more radical among them would argue that marriage itself was a form of prostitution, most feminists felt that altering rather than simply manipulating women's economic subservience to men was the correct path to take. Helen Gurley's approach to such gendered inequalities more closely approximated that of Lorelei Lee, who recommended, "Find a gentleman who's shy or bold or short or tall or young or old, as long as the guy's a millionaire."[2] Most of her searches to date had resulted in her dating men who paid for one thing or another; but when Cleo and Mary moved away, Helen could actually contemplate the more radical approach of being a "kept" woman. Her newfound freedom from family responsibilities facilitated an experimentation, albeit brief and unrewarding, with this more blatant economic give-and-take.

In the particular case that resulted in her being kept, Helen Gurley worked as a secretary for a man whose prejudices bothered her but whose financial status proved too tempting to resist. M., as she called him, worked as a film studio executive. He hoped to make it in Hollywood but was, as she recalled with appropriate irony years later, an anti-Semite who continually worked against his own best interests by avoiding Jews as working partners. Such bigotry would prove a fairly hopeless precondition for work life in a place where Hollywood dreams were also often Jewish realities, particularly in the prewar period.[3] As she recalled later, as early as the initial job interview with the man, the understanding that "we might Become Something to Each Other" floated in the air.[4] M. explained that Helen, like other women in what appeared to be a sequential entourage, could benefit tremendously by having a relationship with him. He intimated that she would receive clothing, cash, even a stock portfolio and property for making herself available sexually.

Envisioning a tremendous shift in her financial standing, Gurley accepted the position, understanding, she thought, all of what such employment entailed. "You'd have to say that I was not innocently swept into sin but, baby-browns wide open, was encouraged in; the strain of caring for Mother and Mary had become a bit of a drag," she wrote years later.[5] M. set Helen up in her own apartment, which she had long coveted, provided her money to furnish it as she wished, and then essentially kept her ensconced there. He taught her how to behave as a mistress: to shift from work clothes to lingerie, keep his favorite beverages on hand, collect tidbits of gossip and information with which to entertain him when they were not in bed together. M. also provided her access to petty cash at the office, sometimes as much as a thousand dollars—more than her annual salary.

Although she was enamored of the idea of living this way, surrounded by such tangible, material fruits of her labor, Gurley found the realities of the setup increasingly less appealing. "I had hoped the keeping would lead to permanent financial security for Mother and Mary and me," she later remembered. "The way the deal was outlined, that was exactly what was going to happen, but nearly everything went wrong!"[6] M. disapproved of her friends, particularly her Jewish friends, expected her complete fidelity, and demanded that she stay at home nights, ready at a moment's notice in case he happened to work himself loose from his wife. Gurley lasted at this for a while, getting the apartment furnished just right and using petty cash to purchase a *New Yorker* subscription for her sister, Elizabeth Arden treatments for her mother, and a trip to Palm Springs for herself and a friend. She felt certain he knew she was "stealing him blind," but he let it continue, at least for a time. In a recollection that calls to mind that other girl from Little Rock, Lorelei Lee, Helen remembered that he gave her a watch that was a bit understated for her taste—and all she could do was thank him for giving her a gift not crowded with diamonds.[7]

Although she loved the shopping opportunities and the apartment, Gurley, then only twenty-five, quickly felt more bored with than captivated by either the man or the situation. She grew to hate having sex with M. and increasingly dreamed up ways to untangle herself, at least from the rigidity of the situation. Her well-posed complaints to him went nowhere. When she needed more outlets for spending the money she had "earned," M. suggested she send more gifts to her family; when she complained she felt trapped at home, he suggested another trip to Arkansas; when she complained of spending too much time alone, he offered to put her mother and sister up in their own apartment if they returned to California. Each of his solutions to her increasing misery, however, meant possible or certain exposure of Helen's kept status to Cleo and Mary, which Helen was determined to avoid. She continued to find Cleo difficult to get along with, even though they no longer lived together, and she kept much of her personal life to herself.

To her growing dismay, Gurley found herself faking orgasm "often and well," acquiring sweater sets rather than a stock portfolio, and generally feeling disenchanted with this version of a relationship, which she realized had proven an utterly dependent form of achieving independence. When M. decided after about a year to sell his business and move away, she experienced, by and large, relief.[8] Gurley later claimed that her ineptitude as a kept woman forced her to have to make it on her own, but it seems unlikely, given her peripatetic approach to jobs and to relationships generally, that she would have lasted long in this combined job–relationship even if M. had hung on much longer.

The job in which she doubled as a kept woman was neither Helen Gurley's first nor her last job in Hollywood; she also worked at the William Morris, Music Corporation of America (MCA), and Jaffee talent agencies. But she appears to have quickly and effortlessly gotten over her youthful fascination with Hollywood rather than succumbing further to its seductions. Gurley recognized that she had no talent as an actress, and she found the professional rules in Hollywood frustrating. At MCA, for example, the company prohibited fraternization between talent agents and secretaries: the front stairs were designated for agents, the back for secretaries. Such a prohibition well nigh demanded a challenge from someone accustomed to dating men she met on the job, and Gurley managed to break the rule and date an agent whose clients included Frank Sinatra, Dean Martin, and Jerry Lewis. Although she worked in buildings frequented by Abbott and Costello, Ronald Reagan, Jules Stein, and other front-page personalities, she never met them and, by and large, found that secretarial jobs in Hollywood provided little in the way of access to the stars or their worlds. She readily moved on to employment opportunities outside of the film industry when they offered more money or more promising ways to enhance her social life. Helen Gurley climbed the secretarial ladder and continued to live a vibrant single life (although never again as a kept woman), until she landed a job she would hold for the remainder of her secretarial career, as executive secretary to Don Belding of Foote, Cone & Belding advertising agency in Los Angeles.

Don Belding, known as "Mr. Advertising of the West," managed the entire agency, brought in high-level clients, and attributed his success to having a loyal staff and encouraging everyone to work fairly independently.[9] He seems to have been as fond of Helen Gurley as she was of him, and the two refrained from making their relationship a sexual one. Helen Gurley Brown argued later that at the moment she began working with Belding and came to know his wife, Alice, she believed she had reached the height of her career. "I thought, boy, this is it! These people were wealthy, they sort of adopted me. I went to their home for dinner, I went out with General Bradley, whoever was in town that my boss associated with, and it was a big time for me and that I should ever be anything other than that didn't really occur to me."[10]

The Beldings became like family to Helen, "the strong group of relatives I never had," she recalled, or at least the strong group of wealthy relatives she never had.[11] Don and Alice provided her a direct and everyday connection to the world she had venerated since childhood. She took dictation in a limousine, brought Don Belding's dog to the phone to speak with his owner when Belding was traveling, learned which glass went with which kind of wine or spirits, and developed conversational skills in the company of a wide range of accomplished and well-heeled people.[12]

Helen Gurley's actions during these years make somewhat problematic her later recollections that she utterly lacked ambition as a young woman; in fact, they reveal the degree to which she always paired survival with ambition in her approach to life. "I never expected to be anything other than a secretary," she claimed years later, but Gurley clearly came to see herself, more and more, as a professional person, first as a professional secretary and then simply as a professional.[13] She became active in the Chamber of Commerce Women's Division and in the National Secretaries Association, both organizations of women who identified at least in part as professionals, even with all the limitations they faced in the workplace. For women of Gurley's generation, ambitious or not, gender continued to dictate when and where career paths might open up.

Men without college educations still found entry-level positions that led to professional success. One of Helen Gurley's employers, William Morris, became famous for the "mailroom concept" of career advancement for men.[14] Bright young men took jobs in the mailroom at the William Morris Agency, worked hard to prove themselves, and often found their efforts rewarded with promotions to professional positions. For women, few such opportunities existed. The mailroom system still operates at William Morris, and today women make up roughly half of its beneficiaries. But in Helen Gurley's day, a professional woman remained, by and large, a professional clerical worker for life.[15]

Nevertheless, the evidence suggests that Gurley, regardless of her lack of education in other academic or professional areas, did not simply envision herself working as a secretary for her entire career. In 1953 she participated, for the second time, in an annual competition in *Glamour* magazine, "Ten Girls with Taste," designed to select "ten women of average income who demonstrated good taste in every area of living." The winner would receive a two-week trip plus a new wardrobe. The thirty-nine thousand entrants revealed what they wanted out of life, and Helen Gurley wrote that she aspired to write copy rather than simply take dictation. Later she remembered, "I felt I better not say I just wanted to be a secretary, that wasn't what they were looking for, so I said 'I'd like to write copy.'"[16]

Certainly, savvy contestants tailor their responses to what they believe will gain them notice, but one has to wonder if there wasn't more than a grain of truth in Helen Gurley's stated ambitions. After all, by this time she had worked in innumerable offices and achieved considerable success herself, and she had also watched men with less experience or talent move into professional positions unavailable to her. Regardless of her intentions, she must have convinced the judges at *Glamour* that ambition ranked among her many impressive traits. Based on her photo and the eight-page questionnaire, Gurley became one of seventeen semifinalists, and then one of ten winners. She returned from the whirlwind trip to Hawaii a minor celebrity, mentioned in a newspaper gossip column in Los Angeles, and in a full article, "Miss Helen Gurley, Former Arkansan, Honored by *Glamour*," in Little Rock.[17]

During these years Helen Gurley also had an active, if not always emotionally rewarding, social life. As time went by she found herself one of the few women her age who remained unmarried. In that "long decade" of the 1950s, stretching from 1947 to the early 1960s, Americans married in greater and greater numbers and at younger and younger ages. Women were often married by age twenty-one, and unmarried women became rarer and seemingly more problematic.[18] For Helen Gurley, as a single woman in her late twenties and early to mid-thirties, not only most of the women but also most of the men she knew had married. However, for reasons Helen Gurley inherited rather than created, but certainly for reasons she felt comfortable exploiting, marital status alone would not stop many of those same men from expressing interest in her. Men's infidelities, which Hugh Hefner would immortalize in the pages of *Playboy*, starting in 1953, existed uneasily beside this postwar passion for marriage and family.[19] In an unpublished piece about her single life, Gurley put it this way:

> As the only extant single female of my generation, I am often called on by friends to see an evening through with visiting males from other cities…usually business associates of my girlfriends' husbands. We all pretend we don't know the associate is married and [that] the outing with or without the presence of the friends who arranged it is conducted on a moral, high-level basis.… [My friends] don't approve of single women dating married men as a rule and neither do I, of course. Any more than I approve of tipping or Xmas cards.…They're just nasty habits that have sprung up and are hard to stamp out. Particularly if you love to eat and

frequently find yourself with only peanut butter and chocolate covered graham crackers in the house and a married man on the phone.[20]

One can imagine how difficult it was for a heterosexual woman interested in men to remain single amid all the nuptials and childbirths of these pro-marriage, pro-children years. Many women in the nineteenth century had remained single and childless, among them such notables as Catherine Beecher, Susan B. Anthony, and Louisa May Alcott, but this history was lost to the coming generations, replaced with a definition of woman by and large as wife and mother. And Helen Gurley not only rejected the notion that she had to marry but she also defined herself, married or not, as permanently childless. In this she must have seemed an aberration at best. American women of her generation, born in the 1920s and 1930s and of childbearing age during the postwar baby boom, would cut the rate of childlessness in the United States in half.

Women deemed worthy of having children, that is, white and at least somewhat educated women, were also expected to do so within the confines of marriage. Mothers actually became popular-culture sex symbols, and mothers and babies featured prominently both in the national consciousness and in the ways in which the nation depicted itself. Wherever Gurley turned, including, increasingly, to her own mother, who entreated her to conform, she encountered the message that she ought to pair up with a man, with the end goal of marriage, children, and a predictable, if enervating, suburban lifestyle.[21]

Socially, women and men of Gurley's day spent time together, but they did so in curious, ritualistically segregated patterns. Women and men might arrive at a party together, but they soon split into separate encampments and engaged in equally separate conversations. For a single woman this posed difficulties, as she found herself neither at home in the women's camp nor entirely welcome in the men's. One night, relegated to the women's group and feeling deadened by the requisite trading of recipes and comparing of brands of appliances, Gurley broke in. "I threw in a recipe for London Fog—take one quart of vanilla ice cream, six cups of coffee, one quart of Gordon's gin, serve, get—, pass out. Nobody took any notes to speak of."[22] Whether apocryphal or true, the story is indicative of the challenges Helen Gurley faced in everyday life. As the years went by, she would find fewer and fewer single women her age, fewer unmarried men her age, and seemingly no shortage of married men eager to engage in extramarital relationships. She navigated these waters with no role models, little social support, and virtually no venue for honestly discussing the state of relationships during these years.

Because of her personality and wit, Gurley continued at least to receive social invitations. She also looked for opportunities to meet men on her own. During World War II, she danced at USO dances at various Army, Navy and Marine camps along the coast of Southern California and later jokingly claimed to have danced with "approximately three thousand, four hundred and seventy-five GI's."[23] She dated men she met at work, went on blind dates arranged by friends, and provided married men company at social events and sometimes in bed. She found that the stated rules provided little actual guidance for her, so she made up a new set of rules as she went along. She continued to view each man as someone to date, someone to have fun with, and someone whose better-paying job could subsidize her pleasures, rather than as someone to settle down with in a marriage that she could predict would most likely remain monogamous for her but not for him.

Unlike other feminists, Helen Gurley would advocate working the system rather than changing it, manipulating the rules men wrote rather than attempting to rewrite the rules altogether. As she saw it, marriage, rather than constituting the best years of one's life, was "insurance for the worst years of your life." After all, she suggested, "During your best years you don't need a husband." That did not mean, of course, that men did not factor greatly into the equation for single happiness: "You do need a man, of course, every step of the way," she explained, "and they are often cheaper emotionally and a lot more fun by the dozen."[24]

Helen Gurley's best girlfriend during her Foote, Cone & Belding years, and then for the rest of her life, was Charlotte Kelly, later Charlotte Kelly Veal. As executive secretary, Gurley was responsible for hiring Kelly into Belding's office. When Gurley was promoted to copywriting, Kelly replaced her as executive secretary. Over the years, they gossiped about their personal lives and kept track of each other's dating lives: "what was working what was not…there was considerably more in column B than in column A." They may have been best friends, but Gurley could not convince Kelly to share what might be called her somewhat mercenary attitude toward men and money. At one point, she attempted to convince Charlotte to go out to lunch as a foursome with Bill Wilkinson, who was Helen's date, and Jim Brodgon, a coworker. Charlotte ought to have gone, Helen felt, because she made one hundred dollars less than Helen and owed on a bank loan. Helen knew Brodgon could help Charlotte out; after all, she herself had had a relationship with him for a few months four years earlier, and he still gave her gifts. Admittedly, she revealed, the gifts, like fruitcake and pralines, did fail to inspire or sustain.

Helen actually toyed with the idea of asking Brodgon for gifts of money instead. "They [pralines] probably cost about $2.75 a box and this would keep me in Kotex two or three months," she mused, again fantasizing about manipulating the rules set by men rather than rejecting either the rules or the men outright. Charlotte, however, had no interest in a man whom Helen herself described as utterly unappealing: he was over seventy years old, and everything seemed to have sunk to his "rear end." Nevertheless, Helen found Charlotte's steadfast refusal troubling: "It seems to me that Charlotte might get down off her high horse inasmuch as one lunch hour can only take at the outside three hours and seven martinis can smooth just about anything out." Charlotte's response: "She'd rather eat peanut butter and raisin bread from here to eternity than be with the likes of these slobs."[25]

One of Helen Gurley's most longstanding relationships, with a man she refers to in her journal as W.G., lasted on and off for nine years. A well-paid copywriter at Warwick & Legler advertising agency, W.G. treated Helen both lavishly and shabbily. She never paid for anything during their years together, including the hundreds of bottles of champagne they drank, the sumptuous meals they enjoyed at fine restaurants, or the luxury vacations they took to Hawaii and Mexico. However generous, W.G. was also pathologically unfaithful, and as much as Gurley might condone such infidelities in her future writings, she had a great deal of difficulty living with this arrangement in her own life. The list of W.G.'s offenses grew over time. At first newly divorced, he kept in what Gurley considered too intimate contact with his ex-wife; he later flirted with Gurley's girlfriends, bought gifts for other women while vacationing with her, and kept letters from other women in full view in his apartment. She would repeatedly leave him for his offenses, only to make her way back again. One senses that had W.G. asked, Helen just might have married him. It was not that she was particularly happy. Instead, at that point in her life she, too, had internalized to some degree the message about an imperative to marry; on top of that, she was not entirely convinced that she could find better.[26]

With some distance, Helen Gurley could better analyze the situation. "The worst struggle you can have is being madly in love with someone who is not madly in love with you. That's a bitter experience," she said years later. "He was addicted to me because I could be depended upon to be very upset when he was having an affair with someone else."[27] It is difficult to reconcile Helen Gurley's reaction to W.G., and her ultimate decision that such a life was unsuitable for her, with the pro-infidelity advice she would become known for. One could argue that Brown would always advocate the necessity of secrecy when it came to infidelity, and W.G. flaunted his relationships. To be fair, Gurley, too, dated others during these years, including the prizefighter Jack Dempsey, but she seems to have done so in response to, rather than in tandem with, W.G.'s approaches to conducting a relationship.[28] The relationship between Gurley and W.G. remained ill-defined until the end, and she played the subordinate, insecure partner.

At the same time that Helen Gurley attempted to figure out her long-term relationship with W.G., she tried to sort out her professional life. She had written on the *Glamour* magazine entry form that she hoped to write advertising copy. Although she later claimed that she did it for the sake of winning the contest rather than to communicate her true ambitions, she must have made a persuasive case on paper and in person. After all, a staff member at *Glamour,* Mary Campbell, subsequently telephoned Gurley's boss and asked him why he didn't provide her the opportunity to write copy. Around the same time, Alice Belding, the boss's wife, also advocated on Helen's behalf with her husband. In Foote, Cone & Belding, as in the advertising industry generally, women were most often considered too emotional to write advertising copy or to take the criticism that inevitably accompanied this line of work. Women had, in fact, been writing advertising copy for half a century by this time, but that was another history that remained buried to many, Helen Gurley among them.[29]

Don Belding's objection to Helen's writing copy, however, proved far more pedestrian than concerns about her suitability as a woman: how, he wondered, would he replace such a talented and proficient secretary? Nevertheless, he gave in to his wife's requests and a stranger's prodding, and Gurley took as her first client Sunkist, writing radio commercials for the navel-orange crop that came out each January. For three years she literally left her desk temporarily to write these ads and then return to her job as secretary. When she finally moved to copywriting full-time, she garnered immediate success, adding Catalina swimsuits and clothing, the Stauffer Home Reducing Plan, Breast O'Chicken, Lockheed, and other, smaller, accounts to her lineup.

In 1957 Foote, Cone & Belding hired an outside agency to evaluate Helen Gurley's work. In the report she is described as bright and engaged but exhibiting the kinds of trouble one might expect from a career woman. Gurley is said to be successful on the job not in spite of her sex, as one might expect women in traditionally male fields to be described, but because of it. Like her target audience, female consumers, she is depicted as less than rational. Gurley approaches work with a "subjective, feminine, intuitive sensitivity," the report states, "most certainly not with rational, objective, or even very communicable logic." She is "all Woman," and needs to belong "intimately somewhere to someone." The need for belonging, for which most career women compensate with "brisk efficiency or brittle scorn," the report continues, remains acutely visible in Gurley, who is overly demanding of others and harbors inflated expectations of her professional potential. One has to wonder about the evaluation: does it adequately describe Helen Gurley's strengths and weaknesses in the workplace, or simply demonstrate the kinds of inherent sexism she regularly encountered? In the evaluator's opinion, it seems, any normal woman would have, by Gurley's age, transferred her intellectual and personal energies to husband, home, and children.[30]

Writing advertising copy prepared Helen Gurley well for her later work writing for popular audiences. For Max Factor eye makeup, she wrote advertising titles like "Wild Irish Eyes," "Siren Eyes," and "Eyes in the Limelight," each of which was provocative in its day. One of these ads, "Devil Eyes," evokes images of a woman in charge: "It's nice to be an angel most of the time—but tonight—let your eyes reveal the daredevil side of you! Let them go deep, dark and devilish…suggesting, just suggesting, the wanton and wicked." For Pan-Cake, another cosmetic, she described a woman purposefully taking a man's phone call after telling him she did not want him to call: "Tonight you must be more beautiful than you really are…you must be beautiful, period, when your mirror has been telling you for years the most extravagant adjective that can ever apply to you is…attractive. Poof to that! Tonight you will be beautiful!" These ads, like her later attempts at writing female sexuality into a central position in American culture, proved successful, and in a short time Helen Gurley became the most highly paid female copywriter on the West Coast. In the course of her advertising career she received three prestigious advertising awards, the Lulus.[31]

Helen Gurley had several opportunities to marry during these years, but she always held off. In the years since, she has offered several reasons for what was, by all accounts, a radical life choice for a heterosexual woman in the 1940s and 1950s. In one version of her story, the men she wanted to marry did not want to marry her, and the men who proposed marriage held little interest for her. In another version, she identified marriage with children, and since she had no interest in children she felt no compulsion to marry. In yet another version, almost every man she met and dated was already married. "At thirty-one I have a coterie of followers," she wrote in an unpublished autobiographical piece, "quite as ardent and devoted and twice as vocal as ever I had at twenty-one....A few of them prosperous— quite a few of them still with hair—all of them pursuing the Medusa of love and every last one of them married!" As a single woman wrestling with social expectations and her own desires, and finding little guidance in the lives of those around her, Gurley entered therapy, which she would find enormously helpful, intermittently, for the rest of her life. Her initial years of therapy provided her with yet another explanation for her longstanding single status. "I found out I didn't like myself very well," she revealed, which might account for her making the wrong kinds of choices about men—repeatedly.[32]

Regardless of her reasons for staying single, Gurley undoubtedly pursued an independent, sexually active, socially active life. She tended to date wealthy men but maintained an affinity toward those who knew what it was like to make their own way in the world. About the prizefighter Jack Dempsey, whom she dated for a year during the W.G. years, she wrote, "Some people thought we probably used an interpreter to get through to each other, and I must admit we were rather an unlikely couple, but our philosophies were the same. He said perhaps there were people who could take shortcuts and get what they wanted, but he was, and obviously I was, too stupid to work it out that way so we had to go right through the tunnel...chug chug chug chug until we came out at the other side."[33]

In the years before she met the man she would marry, David Brown, Helen Gurley kept a diary of musings about men, relationships, and dating.[34] Some of these entries are clear attempts, written in more than one draft, to put in writing the experience of the single girl; they certainly suggest that Helen Gurley, from early on, had an audience in mind. In one such musing, "How to Get Men to Give You Presents," Gurley offers scheme after scheme about how to get money from men, including regular dates, bosses, and even men women meet on a night out. The "out of town guy," for example, will readily pay for cab fare home for a woman. Let him give you, rather than the cabbie, the money, she suggests, then have the cab pull over immediately, but out of sight, so you can jump out, keep the cab fare, and take the bus or return to your own car.

Gurley's wit comes through in another entry, in which she discusses the naive woman who might think that if a man asks her to drinks, she can respond to the invitation for a second or third drink with "No, I think I'll just take the money instead." Any "lady of the evening," she argues, "knows it doesn't even pay to say I'd like some nourishment instead. An offer for a drink is an offer of a drink and don't ever think otherwise." She continues: "If you're going to start torturing yourself with that old line about what you could have bought with the money that bought 25 martinis between you the evening before, you are just asking for trouble." She extends humorous but practical advice to the neophyte who is just learning the exchange nature of contemporary sexuality in such transactions: "Go to a bar that offers pretzels or crackers and cheese dip. Get there before six. Other hungry ladies may have gotten there first."

Helen Gurley's diary reveals how she, like many other women of her generation, remained underpaid in the workplace and therefore vulnerable to the dictates of men's wallets, regardless of their accomplishments. Tricky business, that. Gurley remembered how she once casually mentioned to a man she was seeing that she hoped to get a watch for Christmas. Tipped off to her blatantly economic take on the relationship, the man not only failed to give her a watch but also canceled the magazine subscriptions he had bought her. Gurley provided other kinds of flagrantly commercial advice to her potential or imagined readers, developing a straightforward approach to the economic side of relationships that few women or men of her generation would address head on. But when men proved unwilling or too dense to provide the money women needed, women had to look elsewhere, and in a few journal entries she explores the benefits of raiding the office purse.

Several of Gurley's writings provide elaborate schemes about how to use company funds for personal needs. In one case, she advises, a secretary can invite another secretary to lunch with the company's approval, then institute this plan: talk about dieting, forgo the cocktail, order first and choose the cheapest item on the menu, and generally give the guest the impression that less lunch is more. At the end of lunch, submit a petty cash voucher for $5.00 for the cheap $2.25 lunch, and with the remainder buy two pairs of stockings. In another case she suggests that secretaries arrange to purchase items for the office as an additional means of lining their own pockets. One time, for example, her boss asked her to purchase a fever thermometer. She found one in the office, gave him that, and submitted a receipt for a pint of gin she bought to share with her girlfriends that night.

Helen Gurley's aspirations as a writer became apparent in these entertaining diary entries and then confirmed in those articles she submitted, however unsuccessfully, to *Glamour, Playboy,* and *Esquire* in the late 1950s and early 1960s. The *Glamour* piece addresses women's travel and the need to pack lightly and accessorize, and provides an apt example of the Depression-era attitude that would stay with Helen Gurley Brown in almost all of her future writings, regardless of how wealthy she would become. "Throw out what's really wrong and makes you unhappy every time you wear it. Keep what's good," she instructs. "Then buy right things—relentlessly and stoically only what's lovely and right, no matter how few. It will be harder on you even than [on] the salesgirls. But you will feel like a princess when you go to a party."[35]

Another article, rejected by both *Playboy* and *Esquire,* titled "How to Have an Affair and Live" and submitted with the androgynous byline "HG," lays out a set of rules for married men who might wish to become involved with single women. Never assume the sex is as good for her as it is for you, she cautions ("Many attractive females don't consider sex much of an offering inasmuch as it is available to them from most of the men they know"). Don't fail to give her presents, even money, even if she insists she does not need anything. Keep her in liquor ("Never, repeat never, drink up her booze without replacing it. Bring more than you consume"). The final piece of advice: don't lie about the little things. As she explains, "The big lie you may be inadvertently building, that the two of you will be married, is going to be hard enough to deal with at the time of her divorce-or-departure ultimatum. Make sure she can trust *you* in less serious matters along the way."[36]

This kind of tale, of a single woman initiating, experiencing, even celebrating affairs with married men, would become Helen Gurley Brown's stock in trade and eventually make her something of an anachronism. Yet this single woman–married man arrangement, so readily available and hardly invented by women, seemed one means of making things work for the struggling single woman. For Helen Gurley, it offered up a way of living that remained, for a long time, more palatable than marriage. As much as she wished for the right man to marry, she knew that the wrong men existed in abundance, and it seemed practical for her to enjoy what they had to offer. In the end, Helen Gurley Brown developed and maintained a fairly libertarian stance on sexuality: whoever can keep the man keeps the man. Sometimes you win; sometimes you lose.

In another early, unpublished piece, Gurley compares the kept woman and the wife, idealizing the single woman and pitying, if not vilifying, the married: "You are the one who stays custodian of the heart while she keeps only his name, his money if there is any, and occasionally gets to have another child. For her there is no glory," she states. "She is dull and comfortable and there you are, a cup of wine drunk at the moment of perfection."[37] She expresses disdain for married women, much as we might expect married women to have expressed disdain for her. In an unpublished short story, Gurley introduces the semi-autobiographical character Dana, who works in advertising and succumbs to various romantic temptations. One night she engages in a surprising conversation with a married woman who asks if she is a career girl and then announces that she, too, wishes she had pursued a career rather than simply getting married. Dana becomes suspicious at this point, knowing that this is what married women often say just before going in for the kill. Surprisingly, though, this woman seems sincere. "I sometimes think a husband and three children aren't enough," she states, revealing a truth Dana believes but finds most wives loath to confess.[38] Gurley views married women simultaneously as victims of social choices and as individuals who sold out for security, such as it is. She feels little affinity with these women, yet in a curious way she hopes one day to join their ranks. Both her astute observation and her naïveté about married life include the notion that, in her case, becomes a reality—that things could actually be different for her.

One of Helen Gurley's proudest moments as a young, single woman occurred when she bought a Mercedes Benz sports car for five thousand dollars in cash. She had been waiting for a telephone call that would offer her a copywriting position in New York. When the much-anticipated job did not materialize, she decided that if she was to stay in Los Angeles she needed a new car. She had long been lusting after a Thunderbird, so she decided to change her life in one significant way if it were not destined to change in another. Hoping to use some of what had proven to be successful tactics in other arenas, Gurley dressed in a short skirt and paraded around car lots in the greater Los Angeles area. "Well, sir, I would just like to tell you," she recalled, "I could have shown up in a grass skirt and have been an aboriginal Zulu from New Zealand and it wouldn't have influenced anybody. A $3,400 Thunderbird costs $3,400."

Although she did examine Thunderbirds, she found herself drawn to a Mercedes 190 SL sports car. She ended up impulsively spending much of her life savings on the car, then taking it home and promptly hiding it, too embarrassed to show it to her mother, who believed in purchasing only American cars, or her boss, who knew how much money he paid her. When she finally drove the car to a work-related event, she drew quite a crowd. "Maybe you think this doesn't get to somebody who could only have attracted a crowd in her old car by running down three pedestrians," she joked.[39]

Saving more than five thousand dollars on a secretary's salary was no mean feat and demonstrates the ways in which a philosophy like Gurley's, in an era like the 1940s and 1950s, worked for a woman. Well-paid men, given what feminists might have labeled their unearned privileges in the workplace, literally paid to keep the company of women. Whether it was a drink after work, a dinner date, or a long-term liaison, men financed Helen Gurley's social life. Lorelei Lee had proclaimed, "For a kid from a small street, I did very well on Wall Street."[40] Equally astute, Helen Gurley put her savings in the bank.

Helen Gurley Brown would later attribute her success in luring her husband David Brown as a mate not to her feminine wiles but to this car, which she had purchased shortly before she met him. "Never having been married to or involved with a woman who bought her own bobby pins, let alone paid cash for a car, this acquisition had to seriously impress my new friend," she joked.[41] When he walked her to her car for the first time, she did not see love in his eyes, but she did see respect. Given what she had been through with W.G. and others in a long string of boyfriends and lovers, respect seemed a perfectly good place to start.

Helen Gurley's spontaneous splurge on the car seemed also to be justified by an almost immediate and immensely promising career move. Although she felt tremendous loyalty to the Beldings personally and professionally, when the Kenyon & Eckhardt agency attempted to lure her away with double the salary and increased responsibilities, she accepted the offer.[42] Gurley had truly come into her own professionally. Kenyon & Eckhardt, the eleventh-largest advertising agency in the world at that time, billed almost one hundred million dollars annually. She worked with three others on the Max Factor cosmetics account, which alone totaled five million dollars. Almost immediately upon assuming the new position, however, she found that her employers took her and the other two female copywriters less seriously than they did the male copywriters.

Management troubles brewed, and Gurley watched fifteen male copy chiefs come and go. "Sometimes they were flown in from the New York office, sometimes they were local recruits," she recalled, "but nobody ever supposed Marilyn, Mary Louise, or I was capable of promotion to such an exalted spot."[43] Years later, when she recalled the Kenyon & Eckhardt years, she equated the marginalization she felt to what she had experienced in unrewarding intimate relationships. "Many men feel you're nothing after they get you. They wanted me desperately, but when you belong to them, you're nobody."[44]

At one point during her trying employment at Kenyon & Eckhardt, Helen Gurley met with the West Coast manager of the firm, who informed her that her salary would most likely be cut in half. She asked if the agency was dissatisfied with her work. He reported that it was not. She asked if this was Kenyon's way of asking her to quit. He argued that it was not. They had, simply, concluded that she was overpaid. Even after the agency implemented the salary reduction, Gurley decided to stay on while she explored how to move out of what had once seemed the unattainable world of advertising. But as her supervisors gave her less and less work to do, her frustrations grew more acute. Her first acts of revenge were petty: using work time to attend to personal needs, or using the company mail service to send packages to her mother, sister, or friends overseas. She would use idle time at work to focus on other writing opportunities. In the meantime, she plugged away at work, considered new professional opportunities, and focused on her personal life, which had begun to include that "difficult, complex paragon," David Brown.[45]

3

David Brown

Through her late twenties and early thirties, and assisted by her single and married friends, Helen Gurley dated widely, keeping a sharp eye on the pool of eligible bachelors in Los Angeles. By thirty-five, she determined she was ready not just for another affair but, she hoped, for a long-term commitment. But while age may have compromised her embrace of single life, by no means had it compromised her desire or determination to marry someone of substance. She considered only men of means, successful men, and stayed clear of "ordinary men [she] might have to help support" along with her family.[1] One morning, as she walked for exercise with her friend Ruth Shandorf, Gurley listened intently as her companion described David Brown, a film studio executive and former New Yorker. Shandorf explained that Brown's second marriage had recently ended and that he was "on the market," and Gurley felt an immediate compatibility, not simply for an affair but for marriage: "It wasn't love at first sight for me. It was love before first sight. I had fallen in love with his credentials: forty-two, brainy (people said he was brilliant), glamorous movie executive, good looking, terrific personality."[2] Believing she understood marriage better than most people engaged in the practice, and keenly aware of her own priorities, Gurley was undeterred by Brown's two failed marriages. She asked Ruth for an introduction.

Helen Gurley had time to sit with a description of David for some time before she encountered the real thing. Following their initial conversation, Shandorf warned Gurley that she ought to postpone the proposed blind date for a while as David was in a "starlet phase," dating widely and not ready for a sensible (that is, marriage-bound) woman like Helen. Helen continued to go out with other men but kept thinking about meeting David. A year later, Shandorf let her know that the time seemed right. After one evening's introduction at a dinner party at Shandorf's house, and the promise of a date to follow, Helen considered David close enough to the ideal for her liking: "Having him [be] a turn-off would have screwed everything up," she wrote years later.[3]

But meeting David Brown and marrying him proved two different things. Having just ended a marriage and with a teenage son in his custody, David himself was in no hurry to fit into anyone's, never mind Helen Gurley's, marriage plan. The maturity she was drawn to, and that would enable their relationship to begin on a level far more sophisticated than those relationships Gurley had already walked or crawled away from, also ensured that David would think hard about marriage before he would act, regardless of Helen Gurley's seductive charm or talents of persuasion. In addition, he quickly and apprehensively sized up her agenda. By the time he came along, he later joked, Helen was determined to marry, and he fit the bill as well as anyone might have. "It's just that she was looking for a husband. There's no bones about that," he recalled in a tone that reveals his customary wit but also, perhaps, more than a tinge of truth. "So she decided to pick on me."[4]

Born into an affluent New York family on July 29, 1916, David Brown could not have come from a background more different than Helen Gurley's, although each had grown up without a father at home. David's father, Edward Fischer Brown, a financially successful public relations executive for the milk industry, left the family to marry his mistress when David was a toddler. His mother, Lillian, remarried, this time to a wealthy man thirty years her senior, Isador Freundlich, who moved the family from the then-affluent community of Sheepshead Bay, Brooklyn, to Woodmere, Long Island. They lived there until 1933, when they relocated to New York City amid tremendous financial losses suffered during the Great Depression. Brown's memories of this early wave of New York suburbanization remained positive decades later: "The Island, as we called it then, was young and dewy and we were Robinson Crusoes venturing to every brook and forest."

His mother and stepfather, part of the country club set on the South Shore of Long Island, traveled by ship to Europe every summer, and Brown had fairly free reign to indulge in his passions for inventiveness (he would watch Charles Lindbergh take off for Paris in the *Spirit of St. Louis,* and build shortwave radio receivers and transmitters with friends) and indulgence (he would smoke cigarettes and drink alcohol with friends). "Our parents were awash in the hedonism of the period," he recalled. "They were at the country club breaking the 18th Amendment and one or more of the Ten Commandments, no doubt."[5] He remembered one of his parents' returns from Europe, in the middle of Prohibition, when they disembarked with crates filled with fine wines and spirits disguised as grandfather clocks. Incidentally, during his Long Island years, David caddied at Woodmere Country Club for William Fox, the motion picture executive for whose company Brown would, forty years later, become an officer and director.[6]

David Brown's early youth was a mixture of economic privilege and emotional deprivation, as his father had literally abandoned the family, avoiding contact with his first family and keeping David's existence a secret from his second, which included his wife, the well-known violinist Nathalie Bosko, and their children, Edward and Natasha. Brown would not see his father again until he turned seventeen and needed money for college. David graduated from high school just as the family lost its Long Island home because of delinquent taxes. "As General Motors went, so did we—down, down, down," Brown would write, recalling how the Depression struck the wealthy as well as the poor.[7] His mother, who had never sought alimony or child support from David's father, now decided, as he later recalled, to "put the arm on the old boy" to send their son to college. Had his father declined, he knew, his mother would have scrubbed floors to allow him to go: "She was that kind of woman."[8]

The intermediary in David's reintroduction to his father was George Wolf, the husband of David's maternal aunt, and an attorney for the Mafia chieftain Frank Costello. "His background was quite different from the Southampton and Fifth Avenue set in which my father traveled," Brown recalled. With this imposing but out-of-place escort, David arrived at his father's office on East 40th Street, saw a view that "could only be surpassed on an airplane," and began a somewhat clandestine relationship with his father, who put David through college, paid him a sizable allowance, and kept his existence secret from his second family for another twenty years.[9]

Brown's father indulged in the kind of hedonism available to men of his day and invited David to join in. Once they rekindled their relationship, they saw each other one evening a week at swank New York locales, including the Murray Hill Hotel and the New York Athletic Club. They also frequented places like the renowned nightclub, Russian Bear, where his father was less likely to be spotted in the company of the women they inevitably included on their soirees: "Sometimes he would provide a date for both of us and sometimes I would provide a girl for him."[10] Their relationship was more like that of brothers than that of father and son, but the elder Brown made no fuss about sending David to Stanford University, where as a self-described "very average student" he majored in psychology. His father also provided him an allowance so generous that Brown had to work for five years following college to earn a salary that surpassed it.

Nevertheless, the elder Brown kept his son a secret from his second family until David decided, in 1951, to stop in at his father's house in Southampton, where David and his second wife, Wayne, were to spend a summer weekend. In the fifteen minutes between David's phone call and their arrival at the house, his father explained this entire history to his wife, telling her of his former wife, twice-married son, and grandson. Once the ice was broken, David developed a relationship with his new family, one that would last beyond his father's death in 1973. "I never loved my father," Brown wrote, remembering their relationship, "but I admired his cool and his courage."[11]

In addition to splintered family lives, David Brown and Helen Gurley shared peripatetic work histories. Over the years, Helen has taken every opportunity to publicize the number of secretarial jobs she held before she switched from mouseburger to career-woman status. David has not chosen to provide his audiences with any such careful accounting, but a quick glance at his work history suggests that he can nearly, if not clearly, rival his wife's numbers. He started his professional life after college, working as a newspaper copy editor in San Francisco. He soon relocated to New York, where he pursued a master's degree in journalism at Columbia University and found employment at *Women's Wear Daily*, working on the copy desk and filling in as a third-string theater critic. His boss, the celebrated Broadway personality Kelcey Allen, was, as Brown later recalled, "no highbrow." Not only content but eager to cover musicals and "leg shows," Allen left the more sophisticated theater, the Shakespeare and Eugene O'Neill productions, to David Brown. The bright and engaged Brown cut his critical teeth on first-rate theater and at a young age established a name for himself as a serious critic.[12]

Brown left *Women's Wear Daily* to pair up with his friend Ernest Lehman, who would become one of Hollywood's most successful screenwriters, in a freelance partnership. He founded David Brown Associates, with Lehman, as they joked, as his only associate. During the Depression years of the later 1930s, their main source of income was horoscopes, which they wrote for the Peerless Weighing and Vending Company's subway scales. They also composed radio scripts, which led Brown to a job on the staff of *Pic,* an early picture magazine. His first significant break occurred in 1942, when he became the nonfiction editor of *Liberty,* a blue-collar weekly that attracted a large but less highbrow audience than *Collier's* or the *Saturday Evening Post.*

After a successful year on the *Liberty* staff, Brown was drafted into the army and entered military intelligence. At the conclusion of the war, he hoped to return immediately to civilian life rather than linger in the military. He was, coincidentally, aided in this endeavor by the well-known Washington journalist Drew Pearson, who exposed the waste of taxpayer dollars on idle soldiers by focusing specifically on the base at which Brown served. Overnight, the base was closed and David Brown was out of the army and back at *Liberty,* now as fiction editor, a post that would provide him the opportunity to critically review fiction. That skill would become his professional mainstay in Hollywood.[13] By thirty-one, Brown had become editor in chief of *Liberty* and was widely respected in the publishing world.[14]

David Brown's next break, after a brief detour to Chicago to work for the American Medical Association, came with his appointment as managing editor at *Cosmopolitan* magazine, the same magazine Helen Gurley Brown would take over and transform almost twenty years later. Brown, too, attempted to transform the magazine, with far different results. He worked for Herbert R. Mayes, whom he considered the best magazine editor of the day. Mayes held the same high opinion of himself. Ironically, they turned out a brilliant magazine, "so brilliant that it dipped to the lowest circulation in its history," Brown recalled. As a team, Brown and Mayes failed to read or adequately respond to postwar changes in American cultural life. First and foremost, by 1949 television posed a significant challenge to magazines, as it increasingly drew in not only magazine readers but previously loyal magazine advertisers as well. As Mayes remarked, they edited for a general magazine audience "that no longer existed, and we were not smart enough to be aware of it. Nobody knew what to do with *Cosmopolitan* until Helen Gurley Brown came along."[15]

Even though David Brown's work produced less than stellar results at *Cosmopolitan,* the magazine's owner, the family-run Hearst organization, proved loath to see him quit, and when he received an offer from Darryl Zanuck to head the story department at Twentieth Century Fox in Hollywood, Hearst offered to match the salary. Brown found the courting process an ego boost, as Twentieth Century Fox announced it sought "the best editor in New York," a moniker Brown relished for himself. The combination of professional and personal draws finally prompted him to accept the offer: "I thanked Berlin [Richard E. Berlin, the president of Hearst], but my mind was set on California." Having just married his second wife, Brown felt "desperate to leave New York and start a new life with a new wife." His first wife would retain official custody of their then nine-year-old son, Bruce, but David would later share custody. So off he went to California, reading about movies during the cross-country train trip, a necessity, given that he had, to date, seen tremendous amounts of live theater but few films.

Brown would experience tremendous success in Hollywood, but he never relinquished the native New Yorker's sense of East Coast superiority over the West Coast. Wayne shared his disdain for all things Californian, and because he moved to Los Angeles for a promising job and she moved simply to accompany him, the relocation spelled trouble from the start. A "brilliant working lady" whom David had met at Hearst, where she worked at *Good Housekeeping* magazine, Wayne Brown found the Hollywood Hills in 1951 a form of exile. Vassar-educated and a longtime resident of Greenwich Village, Wayne felt desperate for something more "real" than Hollywood. David Brown sought help from his growing body of associates, and one of them, Maggie Ettinger, one of Hollywood's most successful press agents, hired Wayne. On the job Wayne Brown met and fell in love with Robert Healy, the head of the advertising agency Interpublic, Inc., and she left David to marry Healy and take a copywriting job in New York. "In writing Margaret Ettinger to save my marriage by giving my wife a job," he explained, "I ended my marriage by giving my wife her next husband."[16]

Professional challenges accompanied personal challenges. Brown entered Hollywood just as television began to complicate matters for film, much as it had done earlier for popular magazines. For Twentieth Century Fox the solution to half-empty movie houses was CinemaScope, a wide-screen film process that used newly designed lenses that replicated the closeness of 3-D films without necessitating that audiences wear glasses. David Brown's boss, Darryl Zanuck, purchased world rights to the lenses (which had been patented by a French inventor), renamed them CinemaScope, and ushered in a critical new development in film. After that, as Brown half-joked, "I was asked to find movies with width, instead of depth." Twentieth Century Fox stopped production of the 1953 release *The Robe* halfway through, switched from the traditional film format to CinemaScope, and never looked back. The studio reaped enormous profits with every wide-screen film it produced, its efforts assisted by Marilyn Monroe who, shooting *How to Marry a Millionaire*, Fox's second CinemaScope release, specifically promoted the lenses and the format.

Twentieth Century Fox's innovation proved a serendipitous development for David Brown, whose success then paralleled that of Cinema-Scope: he quickly rose to the top of the Twentieth Century Fox ladder, eventually being named vice president and director. But before he would reach his greatest professional successes, or even be elevated to producer, he would meet Helen Gurley, and his world would once again change.[17] "I was saved not by CinemaScope but by a lady in a narrow chic frame topped by pepper-and-salt hair," he would write later. "Her name was Helen Gurley. She was brown-eyed, smart, striking-looking, slight, and nervous. Also very sexy, and knew it. I would have died without her."[18]

Helen Gurley's journal entries and unpublished writings bear witness to her growing excitement about David Brown, even before they had their first date. "Wouldn't you have fallen in love with him?" she asks. She hoped that he would have been equally intrigued by the profile of her that Ruth Shandorf provided David: "Successful but not driven career girl, no debts of any kind, no ex-husbands (and believe it or not, some men consider them a worse talisman of emotional disturbance than the absence of them), no children, no relatives in the city (maybe that sounds cut off to you, but to a bachelor it can sound quiet and peaceful), occupant of a chic apartment, owner of a small but good portfolio of stocks and a 190 Mercedes Benz sports car which I had paid $5,000 all in cash for, three weeks before. Doesn't that sound attractive to you?"[19]

Their first meeting at Ruth Shandorf's house prompted another, and soon they were dating. David found Helen refreshing for California, which he considered an intellectually vapid place generally and a veritable "wasteland" with regard to women of intelligence and sense.[20] At the same time, having just ended a marriage, he was in no hurry to become overly serious. "I was on a kick of dating geisha and peasant types. I had only just shed a working wife, and for a while I wanted girls who had absolutely no rights," he recalled later.[21] Other differences emerged, too: he liked to drink before, during, and after supper; she did not. She liked sweets, which he considered gauche. He appeared brilliant compared to her—and hers was not an insignificant intellect. She characterized his mind as one that "girls can get into but don't have much fun inside of because they're bumping up against Schopenhauer and Bacon." Nevertheless, they continued dating, Helen with her mind ever more steadily on marriage, and David wanting to take things slowly. "I had gone through boys like popcorn," Helen later recalled. "I was ready to be true. I was grateful for someone like David." They worked through their differences with a maturity about relationships seemingly new to both of them. Each of them had been through traumatic romances and breakups. Like Helen, David had undergone therapy. Each took pleasure in becoming involved with someone who was, as Helen put it, "a loving, non-exploitative kind of human being who, amazingly, could be as much fun as the other kind."[22]

For her part, Helen began to devise and then enact a plan to shed her single status and marry David. After they had been dating a few months, a fabulous opportunity came up for Helen: after three years on a waiting list, and a process that had included letters of recommendation from civic leaders, prominent businessmen, and current tenants, she was offered an apartment at Park La Brea, one of Los Angeles's most coveted residential buildings. Residence at Park La Brea would have fit into Helen Gurley's earlier single life quite advantageously because the complex housed the kinds of people with whom she wanted to mingle, but with marriage on her mind she readily turned it down. Instead, she rented an apartment only fifteen minutes from David's house in the Pacific Palisades and hunkered down for the long haul. Soon afterward, David and his son, Bruce, departed for New York City, where they would spend Christmas with Bruce's mother, Tibbi. Although she also traveled for the holidays, to visit her family in Arkansas, Helen felt abandoned. Her feelings of desertion, partly alleviated when David gave her a string of pearls for Christmas, became even more intense when she took the pearls to get them insured and discovered they were worth less than fifty dollars.

This experience confounded Helen. What was more significant: that he gave her a gift, or that the gift had little monetary value? Did David value her at fifty dollars? She consulted her psychiatrist, whose care she had left some time earlier. Neither Helen nor her doctor could work through whether David was literally stringing her along. In an uncharacteristic move, when David returned Helen said nothing about the gift, indicating either her insecurity in this particular relationship or her acceptance of her psychiatrist's suggestion that David was simply a man who did not give expensive gifts to girlfriends. Whatever the case, Helen found him generous in other ways and decided she could let this lapse go. "After all," she rationalized, "what are inexpensive pearls when you are getting the number one booth at Romanoff's without a reservation any night you stroll in?"[23]

After a year of dating, Helen and David fell into a routine of spending much of their free time together in what Helen called David's "Elsinore-type house," with its beautiful view of the Pacific Ocean, but they appeared no closer to marriage. Helen recorded her feelings during this period in a diary written on Warwick & Legler advertising agency letterhead, which must have served as a continuous reminder of her highly unfulfilling relationship with W.G. Helen's writings convey mixed feelings. She was, in many ways, in awe of David and his intellect, yet she felt uncertain about what life with a man more cerebral than most would mean for her. "I love David," she writes, "but I don't know whether I will marry him. He makes me feel like a nothing though he loves me too. I feel much more like a something with other people—smarter, cleverer, funnier and prettier— but feeling like that with other people just about equals feeling like nothing with David because he is so much smarter than they are."

Helen notes David's insecurities in addition to his strengths, and in the balance decides that their relationship falls into the realm of the mutual. He supports her, and she allays his fears that he has not made significant enough a contribution. "He doesn't want to make an Albert Schweitzer–type contribution," she explains in a journal entry. "He would rather have written *South Pacific*." David's lifestyle is far from the Hollywood type, and Helen largely seems content with dinners out and occasional special events in a life otherwise lived, by and large, in his rambling house with his teenage son, Bruce; middle-aged housekeeper, Mrs. Neale; and dog, Duncan.[24]

Such domesticity was new for Helen, who by this point had lived away from her own family for nearly twenty years. At first she had difficulty keeping the names of the boy and the dog straight, and she found relating to a teenager fairly vexing. She initially considered herself and Bruce "distant friends"; he was probably used to having women around and did not care much for or about her one way or another, but he became increasingly morose as he grew older and she spent more time at the house. The connection between Helen's presence and Bruce's sullenness proved difficult for either Helen or David to parse. Mrs. Neale, an Englishwoman who looked "somewhat like one of those people who goes charging around in armor and breastplate in a Wagnerian opera," seemed to consider Helen suspect, simply by virtue of her never having been married.[25] In an environment in which she exercised little influence, never mind control, Helen read small gestures on David's part as indicative of a growing relationship. It meant a great deal to her, for example, when David gave her his private number at home rather than having her rely solely on the answering service she had used to contact him for many months. Helen settled in fairly agreeably to spending her time learning "geisha ways," cooking for and waiting on David. Waiting, that is, for marriage.[26]

Helen's wait would prove lengthy and frustrating. She later wrote that most men prove reluctant to marry and that this reluctance can be confounding to women operating under the standard rules of behavior. "We were taught that boys chase girls," she writes, "so how is it that things become switched around so completely that here you are laying down the law—'I will give you until February to make up your mind, and if you can't, then it's goodbye.'"[27] She herself performed this dance with David, leaving the relationship defining to him as long as she could stand it. After a year and a half of dating failed to produce a marriage proposal, she laid down an ultimatum. In the end, this approach worked out for her, although she acted spontaneously rather than in the ideal, elaborately planned manner she would later write about.

One night Mrs. Neale interrupted David and Helen to explain to David that she had been examining fabrics for redecorating. She showed them her favorite samples, which, she explained, also happened to be the dog's favorites. Helen nearly lost her temper, finding herself outranked not only by the housekeeper but also by the dog. If David did not want to marry her and allow her to redecorate the house, she informed him, he ought to let her know right then and there because she would go home, redecorate her own apartment, and never see him again. David responded to Helen's tirade casually and calmly: she was the nicest girl he had ever known, but he was not ready to commit to marriage. He hoped she would think it over, take back the stipulation, and continue in the relationship.[28]

Helen stormed off, arranged to spend the weekend at the ranch of her former employer, Don Belding, and waited for David to submit. He did as much that same evening, at least so she thought. David came over to her apartment, pleading with her to stay in the relationship and not to redecorate her own apartment. Helen took this as a proposal but wanted him to sweat it out a bit, so she kept to her weekend plans. She also kept a blind date she had arranged earlier, with Ron Getty, the son of the oil tycoon J. Paul Getty. But his wealth was no match for what she considered his social limitations, and by the end of the weekend her longing for David, and marriage, had only increased. When they saw each other again, David informed her that his entreaty was not actually a marriage proposal; he had not, after all, said the word "marriage," had he? Ready to skewer him with the shish kabob on her dinner plate, Helen nevertheless pulled back. She let David know, this time calmly but firmly, that she had no interest in living with him outside of marriage, and she left.

The next morning David did officially propose, but the next several months amounted to an on-again, off-again betrothal. Helen refrained from telling people outside her family that they were engaged, which proved particularly painful for someone who was finally taking a path she knew others would heartily endorse. Her mother came to visit, and, patient as she was through the confirmations and cancellations, Cleo one day asked Helen bluntly, "Do you think maybe David doesn't really want to get married?"[29] Helen was terrified that this was true. She revealed her uncertainty about marriage in general and her own marriage in particular in a May 1959 newspaper article titled "Marriage? Three Modern Misses Discuss an Up-to-Date Dilemma!" which featured Helen Gurley and two other single women. Gurley must certainly have felt flattered to be profiled as an enormously successful career woman. At the same time, the article went to press as she was pressuring David Brown to marry her. In the article, she made several contradictory claims, reporting that marriage was the best state for a woman, arguing that she had no regrets about remaining unmarried at age thirty-seven, stating that all women wanted to marry, and making the case that she personally relished her freedom.[30]

Following a summer in which the wedding was on and off the calendar about five times, Helen Gurley and David Brown did marry, on September 25, 1959, in a quiet ceremony in Beverly Hills. Helen would have preferred a slightly more elaborate affair, but she prioritized the marriage over the wedding and went along with David's wishes. Ruth Shandorf, who had introduced the couple; David's son, Bruce; and Pamela Hedley, David's secretary, served as their witnesses. Helen later wrote about their reception, claiming perhaps sincerely that she was fully on board with its nontraditional elements: "Went to dinner at Perino's then the Largo on Sunset Strip to see stripper Candy Barr. Candy is a damned fine stripper and I thought it a perfectly fine place to spend our wedding night."[31] Helen moved into David's house at 515 Radcliffe Avenue, Pacific Palisades, and they began to figure out how to live a married life. They had high hopes but no role models for living out a marriage in which both partners sought full professional and personal fulfillment. Seemingly countless issues posed potential roadblocks, including money, work, sex, domestic life, and the changing realities of their resident adolescent.

The house, rather than offering immediate conjugal bliss, became Helen's preoccupation. However much occupied by an astute and eligible bachelor during the *Playboy* era, David's rambling house was no bachelor pad. For starters, David slept in a single bed, so sex during those first nights of married life proved pedestrian rather than risqué. But the truth is that Helen's preoccupation for their first days of marriage was far from amorous: she determined to make David's house her home. Taking a week off from work to set things right, she assumed the role of wife right from the start. Helen suggested she use her salary to decorate the house; David deferred. She sent Mrs. Neale on vacation, hired her previous housekeeper, and began what she assumed were her tasks as a wife. Each room required significant cleaning and showed the limitations both of Mrs. Neale's expertise and of her energies. Helen suggested they fire Mrs. Neale and hire someone competent, someone who would accept Helen rather than David as the boss; David again deferred. The bottom line, as Helen put it, was that if she did not hire someone who could handle the job, she would have to quit her own job and take over as resident housekeeper. David deferred to this line of reasoning as well.

A second, although perhaps less desirable, element of moving in to David's house was dealing with his son, who at sixteen had descended into what Helen and David increasingly considered juvenile delinquency. "There has never been the slightest question in my mind that it's him or us, him against us and we would need at least two more of us to make any decent kind of showing," Helen confided in her journal.[32] One night when Bruce had permission to invite six friends over, and Helen and David had gone out, David received a call from the police informing him that nearly all of Santa Monica High School was partying at the house. Bruce's friends regularly slept and ate there, and their habits, sleeping most of the day and eating everything in sight, caused David and Helen, newlyweds regardless of their maturity, considerable consternation. Bruce's gang of boys had occasional run-ins with the law over alcohol and committed other petty offenses, and then one day David learned that Bruce had been kicked out of his school, Los Angeles's Harvard Military School, for his inability to get along with teachers and other students. David enrolled Bruce in another private school, the Rexford School, but he was eventually asked not to return there either.

Bruce ran away from home during Helen's first month in residence after she audaciously interrupted him in his room to ask if he planned to join them for breakfast the next morning. He soon returned home but then ran away again, generally refused to eat with them when he was there, and rebuffed any and all friendly or parental advances. David and Helen recommended that he see a therapist. Bruce rejected the idea, protesting that many of his friends had seen psychiatrists and seemed worse off for it. Eventually, David reached a point of such frustration and emotional uncertainty that he let Helen take the lead. And in the end, perhaps because of simple developmental changes or perhaps because Helen seemed increasingly less of a threat to the bachelor relationship Bruce had had with his father, he began to come around. He started by returning home at mealtimes and allowing himself to be talked into eating with them rather than carrying his plate to his room.

Finally, the family fell into a routine. Helen would go to Bruce's room to announce the meal, and he would come out and join them. Life as a stepparent, never easy for Helen, began at last to feel less disruptive and more a part of married life with David.[33] Both Helen and David began to feel they could develop relationships with Bruce based on trust rather than discipline. Unfortunately, things would never improve sufficiently. Bruce went to college and established himself in a career in journalism, but he never gave up the use of drugs and eventually died from the complications of substance abuse. In their later years, David and Helen both would consider the loss of Bruce, and their inability to help him end his years of self-abuse, the one painful shadow in their otherwise satisfying and undoubtedly successful lives.[34]

One of the most vexing elements of Helen and David's early married life, money, would remain thorny even as their wealth expanded exponentially. Helen got what she considered a handsome personal allowance from David, plus money for food and household expenses. On top of that, her own salary was hers to do with as she pleased. Although she could by no means complain about a lack of money, she did take issue with one thing: she had no idea how much money they had, where it went, or the degree to which they lived within their means. For a woman who had spent twenty years supporting herself through careful if not miserly budgeting, the seeming abundance went only so far in alleviating her concerns about the economic details of their life together. David explained that he knew little more than she: the bills went directly to his business manager, who met with him once a month for a check-signing session. Helen challenged this arrangement. "What's a wife for?" she demanded, carving out for herself yet another element of married life.

David agreed to hand the finances over to Helen, who grew more indignant when she learned the full scope of his spendthrift ways. Determined to put David on a budget regardless of his earned income, she identified problem areas and began to cut him off. She felt they spent too much money on restaurants and wanted, in particular, to regulate his spending at the Red Lion, a restaurant in the Beverly Hills Hotel that refused service to women—"if you can imagine in our time," she wrote indignantly in her notes.[35] David would eventually resume control of their finances, but by that point the couple had so much income that Helen, too, considered David the more astute money manager.

Helen grew even more irate when she discovered that David had spent more than eight thousand dollars on furniture for Wayne, his former wife, who had moved back to New York. David explained that rather than divide what they had in the California house and ship half of it to New York, he agreed to buy Wayne new furniture. No fan of the Pacific Palisade house's furnishings, Helen argued that he had already spent more on her furnishings than his own were worth.[36]

They would continue to differ over money issues throughout their marriage, with Helen playing the role of the Depression-schooled skinflint and David the role of the affable, generous-to-a-fault fellow. Helen never let go of the scrimp-and-save mentality that had allowed her to purchase that Mercedes Benz with cash. Years later she would impress upon her *Cosmopolitan* employees the need to live within their means by bringing their lunches to work in paper bags and forgoing trips to restaurants. David would continue, over the years, to over-tip wait staff and taxi drivers, and the couple would complain about, but tolerate, what they perceived as the other's excesses.

The marital arrangement between Helen Gurley Brown and David Brown proved both typical and atypical for the postwar period in which it was launched. David did earn the larger share of the family money, but Helen earned and managed money with skills born of studied experience. They came together to parent an almost-grown son, one who would only reluctantly be convinced that he needed another adult woman in his life. Helen took responsibility for the house, but she inherited both the house and the weighty furnishings that David and his previous wife had accumulated. Their marriage provides a fascinating case study of the ways in which couples in their day, and for decades afterward, would negotiate grown-up relationships, outdated rules about women's and men's roles, and the economic realities of the workplace, which favored and rewarded men more than women.[37]

Work remained central to Helen, who probably only briefly toyed with the idea of quitting her job and taking on the housewife role assumed by the other movie executives' wives with whom they socialized. In fact, work played such a critical role in her self-identification and everyday life, and took up so much of her time, that she had to figure out how to deal with David's now more frequent objections to her devotion to work generally and to her weekend work schedule in particular.[38] They arrived at what appears to have been a middle ground, with Helen working hard on the job but assuming, right from the start, a fairly traditional, "wifely" role at home.

David enjoyed Helen's nurturing at home but fully supported her work outside as well. "She's too smart to be a nothing, a satellite with that 'dreadful wife' feeling," he explained. "Besides, a woman with achievement is exciting. She brings a man's talents into play."[39] Helen seconded this thought; David, she said, "couldn't imagine having anything to say to someone who did nothing but housework all day."[40] David understood that not all men felt this way but argued that it was the alpha man rather than the inferior man who thrived in such circumstances: "Only highly superior men can stand the ego assault of a successful working wife," he wrote. "Perhaps you can be one of these men—or, more important, perhaps your wife can be one of these women. If she is, can you measure up to the challenge?" David considered himself just such a specimen. "I'm very confident," he stated. "I don't believe in false modesty. And because I'm very well-known in my field, I have no necessity to prove myself to anybody."[41] According to David, his own undiluted masculinity allowed for Helen's unconventional femininity.

Consciously or not, Helen and David Brown found a workable formula for their marriage: he would support her, unequivocally, in her professional life, and she in turn would serve him, unequivocally, in their domestic world. She would cook his breakfast and dinner even when she herself refrained from eating. She would pick up his dirty towels from the bathroom floor, wash the dishes, and tidy up the house. She would take care of him during his intermittent bouts of depression. In exchange for his acceptance of her independent working life, she would offer a high level of caretaking, and she considered it a balanced arrangement. "I've always been a loyal company girl. If they're good to me, I always try to be good back. Same thing applies with a husband," she explained.[42] Helen's professional life contradicted cultural expectations, and even she believed she was fortunate to remain in the game as a married woman. Even though David had been married twice before, both times to working women, his masculinity seemingly depended on some degree of subservience on her part, at least in her mind.

Several journalists who interviewed the couple noted that David Brown hardly seemed the type of man to make Helen Gurley Brown swoon. Writers repeatedly described David with such adjectives as genial, courtly, mature, and cerebral, but none seemed compelled to use sexy as a descriptor. For Helen, though, what always made David so enormously sexy was that he supported her financially and emotionally, promoting her full self within the marriage. "Men who help women with their careers are sexier than men with flat stomachs, large biceps, and other remarkable assets," she asserted.[43] "So many women have got all this 'stuff' in them—a book or a play. Or they may have fabulous business or other talent. I want every woman to have a husband like mine, a husband who can be a real friend and companion, who knows how to bring out that secret gift or talent so many women have, but never put to use."[44]

Helen Gurley Brown's long-held libertarian approach to men—she who keeps the man happy keeps the man—applied to her relationship with David much as it had applied to her relationships with men married and single in her younger days. But in this case, Helen attempted to care so thoroughly for David in order to keep him loyal that she at times began to mirror not so much the independent woman but the cloying spouse she had long vilified. In his mind, she actually began to morph into his mother. David recalls in his memoir that no woman was as attuned to his needs as his mother; that is, until the day that Helen, who he described as "in all respects save carnal desire" to be "the reincarnation" of his mother, came along. "Is she my mother?" he asks problematically in one of the book's discussions of his relationship with Helen.[45] Helen attempted to make up for her strong emphasis on her career by maintaining a similarly strong emphasis on homemaking. And as much as David supported and even facilitated Helen's career decisions and moves, he, too, relied on occasional traditional, staid juxtapositions, comparing her with that "other" career woman, the one who cannot keep her man happy. "She is not a typical, emasculating, obsessive career woman," he stated admiringly, if problematically, at one point.[46] In a generation of change, such things proved difficult to sort out.

In forging new ground, Helen Gurley Brown and David Brown had to figure out how to respond to traditional and changing definitions of masculinity and femininity, traditional definitions of a wife and a husband. In some ways, they fell into well-worn rather than radically new roles, with Helen starring as David's mother and David starring as Helen's father. Nevertheless, they also forged a new path by manipulating rather than negating the old norms of masculinity and femininity. Helen played the housewife, but she pursued paid work, holding significant and rewarding positions. David played the husband, accepting her caregiving but also pushing her to new professional heights. One close friend offers yet another perspective: "My theory is that their marriage is all a fantasy. But they believe this fantasy; it's the perfect love affair." She continues: "Some time ago Helen figured out she was supposed to be playacting this perfect marriage—that she was supposed to make David's breakfast, even though they have help. But it works for them."[47] Whatever the case, these two individuals would, through their marriage, form a productive professional and personal partnership, and nowhere would the results of that partnership be more apparent than in the planning, writing, editing, marketing, and publication of Helen Gurley Brown's 1962 smash hit, *Sex and the Single Girl*.

4

sex and the single girl

At the 2001 opening of the Prada flagship store in Manhattan, Candace Bushnell announced to the press, "If you want to know the truth about it, I'm hoping to get laid tonight."[1] She made visible, in what seemed her singularly radical and direct manner, the enormous sexual agency single women of her generation exercised in New York City. A newspaper columnist, Bushnell had published a collection of her popular columns as *Sex and the City,* and HBO purchased and then masterfully transformed the book into what became an overnight sensation. The series ran from 1998 to 2004 and echoed the aspirations and frustrations of millions of single women intent on experiencing sexuality on their own terms. After six seasons, viewers blogged and wept their way through the final episodes, intent on continuing to exercise the permission the series gave them to stay single in style. As one viewer put it, "Thank you for showing me that there's nothing wrong with waiting for what I want and for wanting a relationship on my terms."[2] *Sex and the City* was undoubtedly a phenomenon, but credit for first introducing the unmarried woman to instructions on how to live "irresistibly, irrepressibly, confidently, enviably single" belongs not to Candace Bushnell but to her predecessor, Helen Gurley Brown.[3]

Sex and the Single Girl, Brown's little book of advice for sex-friendly single girls, hit the bookstores in May 1962 and became an overnight success. In three weeks it sold more than two million copies.[4] By July it had reached the *New York Times* best-seller list, entering at number eleven and moving up to number six within three months. It reached the number-three slot on the *Los Angeles Times* and *Time* magazine best-seller lists and was condensed in *American Weekly* and serialized in the *New York Post.* The book's immediately famous author made appearances on some thirty-odd television and radio shows, including the *Mike Wallace Show* and the *Today Show,* in the summer of 1962. *Sex and the Single Girl* became an international best-seller as well and was published in twenty-eight countries and half that many languages.[5] Reviewers loved it or hated it, with the naysayers snarling that Brown's work was part of the general "breaking down of moral values" that was "leading Western civilization into a decline." Conversely, supporters considered *Sex and the Single Girl* a modern-day Bible, as one reviewer put it, "candidly voicing a set of mores that are accepted in the metropolitan cities of our new Space Age."[6] Whether they praised or pilloried, the nation's readers and pundits could barely stop talking about *Sex and the Single Girl.*

With chapter titles like "How to Be Sexy," and "The Affair: From Beginning to End," this roughly 250-page volume, written in Helen Gurley Brown's signature style—personal, chatty, enthusiastic, and direct—exposed the reality that many unmarried American women liked men, money, work, and sex, and wanted to feel good about rather than ashamed of the life choices they made or contemplated. For those who had longed to see these issues emerge in public, Brown's authoritative voice provided assurance that modern liberated behaviors belonged not to the few but to the many. For those who recoiled at this exposé of what they considered the underbelly of American sexual and social behaviors, Brown had on hand another, equally authoritative but somewhat more defensive and less convincing, voice, that of the reporter who simply recorded, rather than instigated, changing social mores.

Regardless of her multiple approaches, however, how was it that Helen Gurley Brown, by now quite happily married to David Brown, became the spokesperson for single women nationally and internationally? Had she not fully joined the ranks of the group the book seemingly left behind, married women? Certainly, by 1960, when she began to write the book, Helen Gurley Brown could have readily moved forward into a somewhat conventional married life rather than begun to chronicle the singles world. She had proven herself as a career woman. She had had an exciting single life, populated by scores of men, married and single, and by now she had married the kind of man she had always envisioned pairing up with—charming, smart, and wealthy. At this point Brown could have finally begun to play by the rules: she could have quit her job, taken on volunteer work, and settled into the life of a Beverly Hills matron. David Brown might well have favored such a move himself, as he had been married to—and been walked out on by—two career women.

Yet Brown continued to develop rather than abandon her professional aspirations, even though quitting paid employment was for someone of her age and someone of the social class she now found herself part of, she realized, "the thing to do." She stayed on at Kenyon & Eckhardt even though she had a difficult commute and a difficult work situation, and even though she and David together had more than enough money to support her at home. "You weren't supposed to want to work anymore," Brown recalled years later, remembering the tenor of the postwar period, but by then her life had been so defined by work, for so many years, that she could not extract herself from its grasp. "For me it didn't happen," she stated, revealing that the decision did not even merit a great deal of consideration. Brown's rising dissatisfaction at work might have prompted the emergence of a domestic self, a wife who abandoned the miseries of the work world, but instead it prompted the resurrection of her peripatetic self, and she began to dream once again about doing something else, about moving on.[7]

Each Sunday Helen and David took a five-mile walk in Will Rogers State Park in west Los Angeles. They used the time to process work-related concerns and to enjoy being outdoors together. On one such walk, Helen again raised the issue of her ongoing tribulations at Kenyon & Eckhardt. At thirty-eight, she had been working for twenty years but felt herself in a new kind of bind, one that resulted from the as-yet-unnamed issue of the glass ceiling. Few clear job tracks existed for female professionals of any kind, and no new opportunities loomed for her as a copywriter, so Brown had, by and large, reached the pinnacle of her professional life in advertising. She wondered with good reason whether she had a professional future anywhere. She had been thinking that she would like to try her hand at writing professionally. Perhaps David could help. "You've helped lots of other people do some extracurricular writing—how about me? Maybe I could write a book. Do you think so?" she asked. David did. He knew Helen had a lot to say, and he believed she had a knack for writing.[8] If others could do it, why not Helen?

In the course of his work, David received hundreds of story line ideas, screenplay starters, many of which he passed on to writers who might want to explore their potential. That day in the park he recalled that he had recently seen an outline about a woman having an affair, with chapters about the apartment and about cooking. Did that seem like the kind of project Helen would want to take on? In fact, the description sounded uncannily similar to the pieces she had been composing, in one form or another, for years. David retrieved the outline, and Helen went straight to work, discovering how readily it came together. The project seemed made for her because it had been her life for so many years. "I guess nobody really believed that a girl could deliberately decide to have an affair and clean the decks for action," Brown recalled with the same incredulity about the American public that many readers would express about her. With the utterly familiar contours of the sexually active single girl's world feeling fairly mundane to her, Brown wondered at first if there was enough to say either to or about single women. "But as I got going," she recalled years later, "I found that there really was some stuff to be said about the single girl that nobody had written before. Here I was full of it."[9]

David Brown looms large, legitimately, in narratives of the origins of Helen Gurley Brown's blockbuster book. He assured Helen she could write a book and provided her the initial storyline for this text. He offered Helen the controversial and highly successful title and "produced" the book as much as he produced any of his Hollywood films. Helen and David's partnership is nowhere more apparent than it is in the execution and success of *Sex and the Single Girl*. Yet this telling, truthful as it is, also distorts, as Helen's agency in the process becomes underestimated. "Two or three people actually said they wrote *Sex and the Single Girl*," she explained a few years after the book's publication, "and it took years before a large portion of the country didn't think that David wrote it, but those things don't hurt, they really don't."[10] Whether "these things" hurt or not, and one guesses they would have, they distort the fact that Helen Gurley Brown wrote *Sex and the Single Girl* in her own voice, exploring the issues she knew and had lived, and did so in a style that was purposefully and singularly her own.

Although it was her first published work, *Sex and the Single Girl* continued a tradition of writing Helen Gurley had started years earlier: a variety of short written pieces, fiction and nonfiction, that explore single life and contain frank discussions of sex, pregnancy, married men, work, and money. These unpublished works provide evidence that, regardless of the degree of partnership evident in *Sex and the Single Girl*, and contrary to the ambitionless persona Brown crafted to represent her past in the aftermath of the book's extraordinary success, making it as a writer outside of the world of advertising was undoubtedly one of Helen Gurley's single-girl aspirations.

Many, if not most, of Helen Gurley's unpublished works depict the trials, tribulations, and joys of the single woman. One storyline, written with customary Gurley humor and typed on company letterhead, concerns a girl who, in the days before the *Roe v. Wade* decision legalized abortion, thinks she has become pregnant and tries to miscarry by hanging off doorjambs and piling furniture on top of her body.[11] Another highlights the adventures of Charlotte, who, fearful of revealing her sexual experience to her boyfriend, George, and thereby losing his respect, appears destined as a consequence to remain stuck in an exceedingly boring sexual relationship. A nonfiction piece argues that women's relationships with each other have more depth than their relationships with men. Other pieces describe the intricacies of dating married men.

Of varied lengths and in various stages of editing, these works together provide a clear sense that, during her single life, Helen Gurley enjoyed the craft of writing and hoped to see her name and work in print. She attempted, unsuccessfully, to publish a few of these pieces in popular magazines. Regardless of her own efforts, however, even the link between Gurley's early, unpublished writings, her dreams of reaching publication, and *Sex and the Single Girl* benefited enormously from, if not required, David's intervention. He had connections in the publishing world and a knack for knowing what might resonate with a reading public. He saw her as a communicator and a potential spokesperson and knew about her passion for writing. In fact, David's first and most lasting inspiration to encourage Helen to write *Sex and the Single Girl* came from a stack of letters he encountered, quite by accident, among Helen's things at home.

One day soon after they married, Helen flew to Arkansas to visit Cleo and Mary, and David, as was his custom, stayed home. Rummaging around in a room that contained much of what Helen had brought along with her when she moved into his house, David found a stack of letters, an extensive correspondence between Helen and a married man from Chicago. He sat down and read the entire collection of letters, and rather than emerge from his reading jealous, or even wondering why she had held onto letters from a man he had known nothing about, David Brown emerged inspired: Helen could write. He told her so then, enthusiastically, but the idea would take far greater shape when Helen later asked him specifically about writing a book. Nevertheless, these early letters—and the romance recorded in the letters—have a particularly prescient relationship to *Sex and the Single Girl*.

On her first airplane flight, from Los Angeles to New York, sexy, single, twenty-seven-year-old Helen Gurley met an attractive "boy," the account executive Bill Peters, twenty-nine, who worked at the J. Walter Thompson advertising agency in Chicago. Married, with two children, Peters fell for Gurley quickly—and she for him. For nearly two years, from May 1949 to January 1951, they maintained a correspondence filled with flirtations, book discussions, sexual innuendoes, political jibes, and revelations about daily life. Helen arguably found the correspondence as valuable as she did the relationship, evidenced by the fact that she photocopied her letters to Bill and kept them along with his letters to her. "Evidently I liked them and him," she noted on a page she attached to the stack of letters years later. This series of letters, as much as the relationship itself, provided Helen Gurley an important avenue in which to practice her writing and perfect the style she would utilize so effectively in *Sex and the Single Girl*: a direct, confessional, sexy, humorous, singularly Gurley mode of written expression about single life, about her own life.

Since they had seen each other only that once, on the flight, the letters between Helen Gurley and Bill Peters start out informally but with some distance, continuing the discussion they had begun on their hours-long flight. Peters describes his job and the house he is having built in the suburbs; Gurley reveals her literary tastes, which range from *True Story* magazine to the *Wall Street Journal*. They argue politics, a realm in which Bill falls far further to the left than Helen does: he complains of having to make his living in "this capitalist world," while she tells him that when she sees him she'll reduce him "to a reactionary state in no time." The letter writers soon establish a greater degree of intimacy, engaging in suggestive discussions of how they might spend time together dancing in a club, lying on the beach along the Pacific coast, or cozying up in Helen's apartment.[12]

The letters continue apace, with Peters writing Gurley even while she visits Osage, Arkansas, on a vacation with Cleo and Mary. Helen and Bill enjoy not only the connection they establish but also the expressive freedom that letter writing affords, and they seem to try out writing approaches on each other, engaging in mundane descriptions of daily life supplemented with humor and an occasional element of hyperbole. At times Peters comes across as the quintessential postwar male, constructing a new home in the Chicago suburbs to provide his family an escape from the tiny, urban apartment they occupy. He describes the building process in detail in several letters, telling Gurley, one imagines, more than she needs to know about the roof, the stain, and the foundation's placement, "ready for back-filling, sewer connected, ready for basement concrete to be poured." In fifties style, he describes a do-it-yourself project planned for his upcoming vacation, the laying of a cork-tile floor in several areas of the house.

Peters often presents himself as an exemplar of postwar family relations, yet neither he nor Gurley appears inclined to note the somewhat jarring transitions from the prosaic—"the roof is on the house"—to the passionate—"I'm as excited as a schoolboy at the thought of seeing you." At other times, Peters poses as the beleaguered postwar husband Hugh Hefner would liberate in *Playboy* magazine just a few years later. "I eat in silence, with the exception of the strange abdominal protestations of my ulcerous stomach," he writes in one letter. "My wife glares at me. I glare back, pushing a half grapefruit into her smirking face." Well experienced in the realm of married men who lament their fallen state with no real intention of altering it, Gurley responds with what can be interpreted as either a simple acknowledgment or a more serious challenge: "You're happily married."

Helen Gurley, too, writes playfully about her life, at times posing, perhaps, as the single girl bereft of meaningful relationships. At the start of the correspondence she teases Bill that she will have little to say to him: "Yes, it would be fun to write you occasionally but I'm perplexed about subject matter. You don't know anybody I know—and vice versa. I like cats—you probably hate cats." The prospect of their relationship is "fraught with problems," Gurley declares, but she clearly enjoys crafting each letter. She describes a party she had given for some girlfriends, "a miserable affair at which everyone was bored to tears," particularly herself. She recalls, "They all ate, and drank gin, and two of them got extremely ill and I kept thinking what an intolerable waste of gin it was." Helen intimates at every turn how much more exciting her days would be if Bill were part of them in person and not just on paper, but she admits that their actual meeting might be the death of the relationship. "If it isn't like that, it will be some kind of miracle—people are always so different," she laments.

In his missives, and for the most part with her encouragement, Bill Peters increasingly reveals the degree to which he is falling for Helen Gurley. She appears to be in synch with him emotionally—that is, until he ends a letter with "Honest to God, I think I'm in love." At that point Helen becomes quite direct: "One word to you who are already wise," she writes, "You are NOT in love and I shall personally be responsible for your strangling if the subject comes up again! I consider married men anathema second only to mice…and you could easily scare me half to death." Bill's married state disallows serious discussions of a "love" relationship between them, but it does little to preclude some fun on and off the page. In virtually every letter, Helen encourages Bill to travel to Los Angeles to visit, writing at one point that if he wasn't coming out, she would prefer he "just drop dead—immediately!" Peters eventually manufactures reasons for a work-related trip to Los Angeles, and he and Gurley scheme about how to sequester themselves away during most of his time there, regardless of his need to go into the office or visit with his in-laws. Peters can simply claim he has to spend all of his time with a client, Gurley advises: "And it isn't unconventional at all to practically live with a client if they have problems." At the last moment the visit falls through, but the two correspondents keep the relationship alive through fairly regular dispatches filled with increasing familiarity, witty repartee, and lively sexual tension.

Helen eventually pens a "Dear John" letter, revealing that she and Bill had finally had a visit together, during which he had revealed himself to be just another married man looking for something other than what she sought. Love, she suggests, seems to mean something different to her than to him, and his marriage, regardless of his conflicted feelings about it, poses an insurmountable barrier for Helen. "So be a good boy and leave me alone," she implores, and the trail of their correspondence ends there. No lovers' quarrels, no entreaties, no tears. Relationships with as little basis as this one certainly do tend to come and go, but one has to wonder about what remains unstated in this stack of letters generally and in the "Dear John" letter in particular. Had Gurley found herself once again falling into the clutches of a married man, this time refusing to play the role of the other woman? Or, perhaps, did Gurley find Peters less appealing in person than on paper and employ the excuse of what might be called "his love and hers" because it provided a simple, effective means of ridding herself of a married suitor who no longer held her interest? To what degree was Gurley—or Peters, for that matter—enamored primarily with the freedom the correspondence allowed but their actual lives precluded?

When Helen Gurley Brown later asked her husband if he thought she could write a book, he remembered that stack of letters, recalled how strong and entertaining Helen's written voice could be, and encouraged his wife to start writing immediately. If anyone was full of experience, advice, and passion about women's single lives, he felt, it was Helen. With that encouragement, Brown dove into the project, using whatever time she could pilfer from her uneventful workdays, the whole day on Saturdays, and much of Sundays writing the book that would eventually be published as *Sex and the Single Girl*. She resisted David's suggested title at first, finding it too clinical: she favored a more personal, more subjective, less sociological approach to the life of the single girl. At his continued urging, though, she accepted the title, recognizing as she went along one important reality of the marketplace: a controversial book title might well boost sales.

From the start, Brown's aim, in addition to writing a successful book, was twofold: to defend the "real-life" sexually active single girl against her detractors, and to give that same woman the ammunition to stand firm against those who wanted to marry her off. "The reigning philosophy at the time was that if you were female and not married by age thirty, you might as well go to the Grand Canyon and throw yourself in," she recalled years later. "If you were having sex and not married, don't bother with the Grand Canyon, just go to the kitchen, put your head in the oven, and turn on the gas." As Brown saw it, "I knew these ideas were cuckoo."[13] She knew that her single life, the lives of single women friends, and even the lives of the married men and women she knew differed in significant ways from the prescribed behaviors.

Helen Gurley Brown believed an honest, direct approach was the best way to create solidarity with and among a readership of women who actively sought or inwardly desired fulfilling, unapologetically sexy single lives. She considered her own married state no deterrent: she had many long years of experience to remember and draw on. As the back cover of *Sex and the Single Girl* put it, "Marriage has in no way diminished the author's almost fanatical interest in the problems of single women, whom she considers undoubtedly the least understood and most maligned minority group of all time."[14] Although people would occasionally comment that a married woman wrote *the* guide for single women, few questioned Brown's credibility as a chronicler of single life.

In thirteen breezy chapters, starting with "Women Alone? Oh Come Now!" and concluding with "The Rich, Full Life," Brown disabuses her readers of the idea that single women constitute a defective species, arguing instead that the single woman, the "newest glamour girl of our times," needs no one's pity and deserves no one's scorn. Brown's single girl likes men, single and married; enjoys sex, considering it as natural a practice for women as for men; aims for financial independence, including her own savings account, apartment, and stock portfolio; and enjoys her body and the various sexual choices available to her, which might include sexual initiation in addition to surrender. What Brown's single girl does not like, above all else, is the message that somehow she ranks inferior to the married woman, or presents a social problem. This single girl is to be envied, not pitied; admired, not despised. "She is engaging because she lives by her wits," Brown tells her readers. "She supports herself. She has to sharpen her personality and mental resources to a glitter in order to survive in a competitive world, and the sharpening looks good." She continues: "Economically she is a dream. She is not a parasite, a dependent, a scrounger, a sponger or a bum. She is a giver, not a taker, a winner and not a loser."[15]

In the first few chapters of *Sex and the Single Girl*, Helen Gurley Brown tackles several of the shibboleths of postwar culture, without apology and in style. For starters, she argues that singleness is a perfectly wonderful state for a woman, for any length of time, rather than simply a prelude to marriage. "Real" life is available to single women every day; it is not something they must anticipate experiencing only with the arrival of matrimony. When women are young, Brown argues, they not only can but actually should actively eschew marriage and experience the liberating potential of the single state. "Although many's the time I was sure I would die alone in my spinster's bed," she confesses in the first chapter, "I could never bring myself to marry just to get married." She notes, "I would have missed a great deal of misery along the way, no doubt, but also a great deal of fun." In only a few pages, Brown begins to shatter the common wisdom of the postwar period, which increasingly and rigorously dictated early marriage for women.[16]

Intent on shoring up the positive attributes of the single woman, Brown juxtaposes the single and the married woman and finds not the single but the married woman lacking. Although she has joined the ranks of married women, Brown clearly continues to identify with the single set. Brown told a reporter, "I cannot identify with the professional wife—the girl who lives in the suburbs looking after other people and taking care of their house, any more than I would identify with a frogman or a rock-and-roll band. I am not saying that I am right and they are wrong—just that I feel that way."[17] To another reporter she declared wives "dull and hypocritical" and married people generally not her "cup of tea."[18]

Helen Gurley Brown's own longevity as a single woman, she seemed to believe, transformed her into an entirely different species, something in between the single and the married woman, and certainly not a "wife," regardless of her matrimonial status. Helen Gurley got her hands on a man as desirable as David Brown not in spite of but because of her seventeen years living the single life, learning to take care of herself, developing independent attitudes and practices, and becoming the kind of woman he would be attracted to. "He wouldn't have looked at me when I was twenty, and I wouldn't have known what to do with him," she announces in *Sex and the Single Girl*, criticizing the practice of early marriage so common in her day.

In such a rule-abiding, domestically defined era as the postwar period, who would Helen Gurley Brown attract as her audience? As children of the Great Depression, coming of age during World War II and entering adulthood during the Cold War, Helen Gurley Brown's peer group of white, working-class, and middle-class women by and large followed a set of rules laid out for them: they sought the security of marriage at an early age; initiated what became known as the baby boom, by having babies early and often in their marriages; and hunkered down in the suburbs to live out their lives. Many sought the serenity and stability unavailable to their parents.[19] Prescriptive literature of the day, and the reported beliefs of American women and men, suggested that Americans feared any alternatives to marriage. World War II had briefly provided women with improved opportunities in the workplace and more authority in the family, but many Americans hoped such changes would prove temporary. As one wartime pamphlet put it, "The war in general has given women new status, new recognition....Yet it is essential that women avoid arrogance and retain their femininity in the face of their own new status." The pamphlet warned women that they ought not to pass up what might prove a fleeting opportunity to marry: "She may be the woman of the moment," it threatened, "but she must watch her moments."[20]

Wartime ideologies continued through the long decade of the 1950s. Marriage was simply a given. "What else was this stupid war for?" asked a reader of *Mademoiselle* magazine. One clear result of the increasing insularity of the postwar period was early marriage. In 1945 the average age of marriage for women was twenty-three, and by 1951 one in three women married by age eighteen. In 1958, a year before the then thirty-seven-year-old

Helen Gurley married David Brown, the rate of American women marrying between ages fifteen and nineteen exceeded that of any other age group. This promotion of early marriage went hand in hand with a developing paranoia about single life for women. A collection of essays published in 1949 entitled *Why Are You Single?* considered single life a form of social delinquency. One essay describes the litany of maladies the unmarried woman living across the hall from the reader (the book hesitates to fully implicate the reader herself) may harbor: coitophobia ("morbid fear of marital relations"), gymnophobia ("dread of the sight of a naked body"), apheophobia ("dreads to be touched"). "There may even be a morbid obsession against household duties," the text warns, in what today's reader could almost only understand as satire, "a dread or intense dislike for housekeeping."[21]

Young women seemed to agree with their advisers, both in philosophy and in practice. A 1956 magazine poll shared the opinions of more than two thousand high school girls on the plight of single women. Ninety-nine percent of the respondents agreed with the statement that "single career women [had]...so thoroughly misunderstood their central role and identity that they had failed to achieve even the most basic task of establishing a household."[22] This association, of women and the home, progressed swiftly during the decade, so that in 1959, when Vice President Richard Nixon traveled to the Soviet Union and engaged with the Soviet premier Nikita Khrushchev in the so-called Kitchen Debate, the equation of femininity, domesticity, and nation seemed wholly American and superior to any definition of womanhood available elsewhere.

One teenage girl spitefully provided a label for American women who, in the face of such a cultural tide, chose single status: "misfits." By choice, as she put it bewilderedly, they were "out there alone." She explained, "It's crazy. And hard to understand....They're not in the normal range."[23] Things got to the point that "[an unmarried woman] as young as twenty-one might worry that she would end up an 'old maid.'"[24] In some ways, then, one might have thought that Helen Gurley Brown would simply be swimming upstream, her ideas resonating little with a generation as dedicated to marriage and steeped in domestic ideology as this postwar generation was.

Even Helen Gurley Brown herself seems, at first glance, a likely candidate for the kind of hunkering down common among her peer group. In his classic work *Children of the Great Depression,* the sociologist Glen Elder studied a sample of white, largely Protestant, working- and middle-class individuals who were youths during the Depression. In his findings, children whose traditional home lives were most disrupted by the Depression most actively aspired to live out those same traditions in their adult lives. In this reading, Helen Gurley Brown, having lost her father and experienced the difficulties inherent in living in a female-headed household during the Depression, would have been a likely candidate for a traditional marriage, children, and suburban living. For a time during her youth, she did hunger for such gender conformity. "During the Depression, when we were having a rough time scraping along," Brown later remembered about her relationship with her widowed and struggling mother, "I told her I didn't think she should take in sewing. She wanted to put a sign out in front of the house that said sewing and alterations, and that absolutely offended my ten-year-old sensibilities."[25]

But Helen Gurley Brown's own life choices, coupled with the enormous success of *Sex and the Single Girl*, suggest not that she became transformed into an entirely unique woman, living a life "before her time" and carrying others along with her, but rather that the fissures in the postwar domestic formula always existed side by side with the formula. The young Helen may have wished her mother did not have to work, but for herself she saw no future but work. Marriage in the 1950s may well have been considered the "be-all and end-all of life," and those who remained single by choice deemed "sick," "neurotic," or "immoral," but as Brown herself put it, quite simply, she did not invent the single girl, nor did she become a stereotypical housewife once she married. In *Sex and the Single Girl*, she both reported on and encouraged what she and others lived, what remained remarkably silenced in the culture, what she and her legions of fans believed had to be made visible.[26]

Once Brown establishes, in the first few pages of *Sex and the Single Girl*, that single women have almost everything going over married women—they have more time and money to spend on themselves, they move more freely in the world of men, they never become drudges—she moves to the topic everyone who bought, borrowed, or sneaked a copy of the book anticipated: sex. "Theoretically, a 'nice' single girl has no sex life," she starts off, already making somewhat redundant her second sentence, "What nonsense!" Brown goes on to explain that single women actually have better sex lives than married women, and for the most practical set of reasons: the single woman need not be bored with one partner ("Men never come to her bed duty bound"); she is free to engage in sex, or not ("A flirtatious married woman is expected to Go Through With Things"); she and her partner can more likely linger over sex ("A married woman and her husband have precious little time and energy for romance after they've put the house, animals and children to bed"); and she can still be a lady while "indulging her libido" ("I did it. So have many of my friends").[27] Sex, according to Brown, may result in intercourse, but it is more than that: "It begins with the delicious feeling of attraction between two people," she writes. "It may never go further, but sex it is."[28] Although she does not use the word "desire," the truth is that, for Brown, sex is desire, and desire is altogether natural and healthy. "You inherited your proclivity for it," she writes about women's interest in sex. "It isn't some random piece of mischief you dreamed up because you're a bad, wicked girl."[29]

Helen Gurley Brown puts into everyday, even sexy, language the realities that Alfred Kinsey, in *Sexual Behavior in the Human Female*, otherwise known as the Kinsey Report, revealed in 1953, nearly a decade before the publication of *Sex and the Single Girl*. Kinsey surveyed the sexual practices of almost six thousand women and encountered evidence of widespread premarital intercourse. When *Time* and *Look* magazines offered their readers summaries of Kinsey's findings, appreciative and indignant readers alike responded. "Any man who could get that much straightforward information from one, let alone nearly 6,000 women, should be *Time*'s Man of the Year," wrote one respondent, while another reported that she read the article with disgust. "He takes a so-called survey of a few American women with bad morals and sets them up as an example of typical American womanhood."[30]

Brown would experience similar reactions from readers a decade later when her lack of moral outrage over single women's sexual lives, particularly in regard to married men, led many to see her not as a reporter but as a promoter of promiscuity. Brown defended herself thoroughly. "No, I'm not promoting promiscuity," she argued after the book's publication. "I'm not for promiscuity. I simply said that most single women of my acquaintance have had, or are having, something to do with a man—by that I mean an affair. And I say that it isn't the end of the world. Now a lot of moralists would like to think that it is, and they still keep pretending that it is, and that a girl is ruined when this has happened to her. But it really isn't so."[31]

Brown, too, had some data to back her up, although far less than that employed by Alfred Kinsey.[32] The U.S. Census revealed surprising numbers of unwed women and woman-headed households in 1960, the same year that the birth control pill reached the market. Within two years, at least 750,000 women were on the pill, and an estimated 500 more began taking it every day.[33] Within a few more years, singles bars would begin to open on Manhattan's Upper East Side, and Americans would describe their relationships, heterosexual and homosexual, married and single, using nouns such as "lifestyle" and adjectives such as "single."[34] Helen Gurley Brown lay on the cusp of these changes, reporting on the phenomenon of sexual liberation as it emerged. She stood on far more shaky ground than did Kinsey in her claims of objectivity, however. Unlike Kinsey, she relied on her friends and her own experience for most of her primary source materials, and unlike Kinsey, she offered advice on "how to" do anything from flirting effectively to meeting men on vacations, on business trips, or at political gatherings.

Kinsey's earlier evidence, arriving on the scene as it did during the maturation of Cold War thinking, had resulted in renewed efforts to reign in female sexuality. Many people feared that women, as the sociologist Willard Waller put it, had "gotten out of hand" during the war. Even when the cultural moralists refrained from mentioning sex as the danger, one could read between the lines. A marriage and family textbook published during the war anticipated the risks: "When women work, earn, and spend as much as men do, they are going to ask for equal rights with men. But the right to behave like a man [means] also the right to misbehave as he does. The decay of established moralities [comes] about as a by-product."[35] Women's increased promiscuity, evident during the war and documented afterward in the Kinsey Report, became aligned in the national imagination with other postwar threats, namely homosexuality and Communism. A strong nation required strong families, and strong families required both monogamy and women's subordination.[36] If women were somehow inherently sexual, and sexuality was inherently dangerous, women would have to be rushed into marriage, the only safe place to contain all of that incipient sexuality.[37]

Kinsey had discovered that Americans had contradictory beliefs about and practices of sexuality. Eighty percent of the women he surveyed reported that premarital intercourse was unacceptable, yet 50 percent of those same women engaged in it themselves.[38] Helen Gurley Brown instinctively understood and directly confronted such discrepancies. She understood that women were instructed not to enjoy sex, but she also knew that she and many of her friends took enormous pleasure in sexual activity. She knew that single women's dalliances with married men violated many social codes, yet she also knew that such things happened, and on a regular basis. She had suffered the injustices of sexual hypocrisy, which would have labeled her and her peers deviant, and she knew that she was not alone in adapting actual practices, not simply cultural beliefs, to her own liking.

If Brown's acknowledgment that single women had sex without ill consequence proved controversial, her argument that single women had sex with married men went over the top for many readers. In her defense, Brown simply reported on what she and so many other unmarried women found to be true: married men were always available, and they sometimes even proved appealing. "He is as available for observation as the common housefly and about as welcome to many single girls as the common cold," she notes about the married man, suggesting that few single women could avoid them but most would do well to do so.[39] She outlines reasons not to become involved with married men with at least as much passion as she conjures when describing the benefits of such involvement. The married man, regardless of his promises, almost never gets a divorce, and if he does there is no guarantee that he will marry the single girl who has been waiting for him. The married man is unavailable at most times one wants him, including weekends and holidays. He may be jealous of a woman's other relationships (if a woman does get involved with a married man, Brown instructs, he should not be her only beau), he often lies, and most importantly, a single woman may actually fall in love with him.[40]

Brown also lists the positive elements of such liaisons. The married man often proves generous with gifts and money, and if he does not, she suggests, "You can explain the economic facts of life."[41] He is frequently good in bed, careful not to get a woman pregnant, and faithful. Lacking the fear of commitment so common to single men, even in the era of domesticity, the married man is also generous with praise and able to connect emotionally, unafraid that a woman will interpret such practices as a marriage proposal. In the nature versus nurture argument about marital infidelity, Brown views men as biologically unable to help themselves. "Man is not monogamous no matter how much religion and social writ tell him he is," she states matter-of-factly. "You don't like your adorable Persian kitty dragging a maimed, half-alive pigeon into your living room but that's the nature of Persian kitties."[42]

It may sound as though Brown's intention is simply to let men off the hook, to excuse their behavior. Instead, her goal is to acknowledge what she sees as dependable if deplorable behaviors and encourage women to make the most of the realities of contemporary life. "It seems to me the solution is not to rule out married men but to keep them as pets," she states. "While they are 'using' you to varnish their egos, you 'use' them to add spice to your life."[43] Women hardly invented men's infidelity, Brown rightly argues, and married men rarely prove to be satisfactory partners, but reality is reality. Single women in 1962 were likely to encounter interested and interesting married men at every turn, and although perhaps they should have, they were unlikely always to resist temptation. Given that situation, savvy women could actively anticipate and then benefit from these liaisons, unbalanced in the men's favor though they most often proved to be.

If Americans in general wrestled with the contradictions between their stated beliefs and actual practices of sexuality, often practicing more than they preached, Helen Gurley Brown seems to have suffered from the opposite affliction, preaching more than she practiced. It is true that during her single days, married men proved fair game for her romantic desires. She found them exasperating in some ways, as she outlines in her book, but she also found them not only acceptable but sometimes highly desirable sexual partners. In *Sex and the Single Girl* and elsewhere, she admits to having what she calls a "rather cavalier" attitude toward the wives of the husbands she and all these other single women were having affairs with. "A wife, if she is loving and smart, will get her husband back every time," she writes. "He doesn't really want her not to. He's only playing."[44]

But when she writes this book, she herself has already married David Brown. Do the same rules apply when she, and not some other, easily stereotyped woman, plays the role of the wife at home? It seems not. The married man/single woman trope becomes, in a sense, Helen Gurley Brown's stock in trade, part of what she would carry into her tenure at *Cosmopolitan* magazine and throughout many, if not most, of her future writings. Yet she and David explain, in a number of interviews and writings, that infidelity has no place in their marriage. "David is convinced," his work partner Dick Zanuck stated two decades into the marriage, "that if Helen caught him having an affair, she'd kill him. I mean really kill him."[45] As Zanuck suggests, two separate Helens exist, one the perpetual single girl who cares not a whit for that unfortunate character, the wife, and the other the grown-up married woman who is that wife and could no better than anyone else weather the storm of marital infidelity. The issue for Helen Gurley Brown was not so much that her life changed after marriage but rather that she seemed trapped afterward, culturally, by the figure she cultivated so carefully and defended so vigorously in and after *Sex and the Single Girl.*

Sex and the Single Girl offers women practical advice about getting and staying sexy in order to attract these men, single or otherwise. And on matters of nutrition and exercise, for which Brown would maintain a life-long passion, she does not hesitate to lecture. "You are the world's dumbest about nutrition!" she rants. When she had been feeling "lower than an earthworm" herself in her early thirties, friends suggested she visit a health food store for a consultation. Diagnosed with chronic fatigue and a vitamin deficiency, Brown went home with the makings of a high-protein Serenity Cocktail (whose recipe is included in the book), an assortment of vitamins and minerals, soy pancake mix, and a determination to get healthy. Eventually, she combined good nutrition with a consistent exercise program, and *Sex and the Single Girl* gave her the opportunity—in an era in which exercise for women drew little support—to encourage her readers to do the same. "This shape business is important—inside and out—if you're not going to take singleness lying down—except when you want to."[46]

If support for women remaining single forms the first significant part of Brown's argument in *Sex and the Single Girl,* and honest discussions of sex and sexual desire form the second part, money and work together form the third element of Helen Gurley Brown's recipe for single success. In fact, Brown's reader is single and sexy precisely because she is economically independent. "Being smart about money is sexy," Brown proposes in a chapter titled "Money Money Money," and she admonishes readers who might use the excuse of insufficient funds for a lack of independence or style.[47] Nobody has enough money, she says, but those who follow her principles can make it on their own. And no one, she intimates, would have been a less likely candidate for financial success than she: "No matter how little money you make, you can live on it...attractively. I know. I was poor nearly always."[48] Young women who want the glamorous single lifestyle Brown so seductively describes have to maintain her three-part approach to money, exercising effective money management at home, professional assertiveness on the job market, and studied femininity on the dating/relationship front.

Money management for the legions of women in her imagined audience, most of whom are working-class or middle-class women lacking higher education or much professional training, means penny pinching. Brown admits that some of her rules (do not buy a thing you do not absolutely need; negotiate with doctors' offices about bills) may prove difficult to follow, but she wants her working-class working girl to be fully independent. One of Brown's primary rules is to economize on the utilitarian so that things that bring extra happiness, or an additional dose of sexiness, come within reach of the working girl's purse. In this scenario, needs and wants all prove negotiable, but the sexy single girl occasionally favors the wants over the needs, for it is the sexy dress rather than the brand-name shampoo that keeps one sexy in addition to viably single.

Over time the *Sex and the Single Girl* reader will develop a financial sensibility, and she can then support herself for as long as she remains single, either by choice or by chance. Brown admits that some of her suggestions for money management border on miserly, but she shares them nevertheless, as a girl never knows when she might need to increase her economy. Exchange gifts you receive from others when you don't really need them, she advises. Make your own Christmas cards, do your own hair, go without stockings as long as you can, wear old clothes or no clothes at all at home, welcome hand-me-downs, and go in with other girls on shower gifts. If the single woman follows these guidelines, she will not only be able to support herself but also save money, building not only a savings account but also a stock portfolio for her future needs. Behaving like this, according to Brown, increases the single woman's sex appeal and also her sense of personal responsibility. In important respects, *Sex and the Single Girl* is an early money-management guide, a precursor of the books that would become increasingly popular in the aftermath of decades of feminist activism about financial matters.

Too many women, Brown fears, indulge in impractical money practices that do them harm. One of her favorite examples is the retail sale. Conventional wisdom would encourage the thrifty girl to purchase items on sale, yet Brown considers this a poor approach to money management. The sale-seeking woman ends up with items that truly belong in a sale and not adorning her sexy body. "Some of my girl friends bring back their two-dollar blouses and shoes from the sales with the comment, 'For two dollars, how could you go wrong?'" she explains. "My notion is, 'For two dollars, how could you go right?'"[49] Such advice seems utterly practical rather than revolutionary. But today's women are accustomed to encountering financial advice for women in newspapers and women's magazines; such counsel was far less common in the early 1960s. Financial security for women, in the minds of most of Helen Gurley Brown's contemporaries, arrived only with, and remained entirely dependent upon, marriage. In this regard Brown's tips proved noteworthy, if not radical.

In *Sex and the Single Girl,* wise spending pertains to all areas of savvy women's lives, except one; that is, when she is in the company of men, the single woman should refrain from spending at all. Never go Dutch treat, Brown admonishes, and never entertain deadbeats. Let men know when they drink more of your liquor than they supply, never buy your own cocktails, and encourage gifts from men, as gifts "are part of the spoils of being single."[50] Expensive items, particularly when they come from a married lover, can ease the pain of the inequity the single woman inevitably experiences. In *Gentlemen Prefer Blondes,* Lorelei posits that girls ought to try to get their hands on some diamonds because, after all, those "louses" inevitably go back to their "spouses." Helen Gurley Brown puts it this way: "A lady's love should pay for all trips, most restaurant tabs, and all liquor." In *Sex and the Single Girl,* Brown explains what she had explored in her unpublished writings for years: all relationships, including sexual ones, come down to exchanges of one sort or another.[51]

In the world Helen Gurley Brown and her readers inhabited, men both earned more money and crafted the rules about relations between men and women; as a consequence the least they could do was pay for the company in addition to whatever else it is that women, by their own choice, contributed. *Sex and the Single Girl's* reader should be able to handle a checkbook and have sufficient funds in her account to be able to pay her own way, but as far as actually paying her way, Brown has three words of advice: "Don't you dare!"[52] Helen Gurley Brown certainly offended middle-class sensibilities by acknowledging this reality. She threatened further by assessing, not wholly in negative terms, the inherent value of such exchanges.[53]

Knowing what we know about Helen Gurley Brown's own life, it comes as no surprise that work forms a central component of her definition of a singularly sexy and successful single life. In a chapter titled "Nine to Five," Brown explains that work is, by all means, a place to meet men, but more than that it is a central element of a single woman's identity. It gives her money that she needs to support herself. It helps her furnish an apartment, to which Brown dedicates an entire chapter and much significance. Most importantly, though, "a job gives a single woman something to be." She explains, "A married woman already is something....Whatever hardships she endures in marriage, one of them is not that she doesn't have a place in life."[54] Adrift culturally and often socially, the single woman finds tremendous meaning in her workaday world. Brown's readers may long to marry, she admits, but that issue remains in some ways irrelevant to the question of work: "While you're waiting to marry, or if you never marry, a job can be your love, your happy pill, your means of finding out who you are and what you can do, your playpen, your family, your entrée to a good social life, men and money, the most reliable escape from loneliness, and your means of participating."[55]

Brown argues the merits of attitudes that feminists only a few years later would condemn as inherently sexist and oppressive. But the working-class realities of Helen Gurley Brown's 1940s and 1950s would not disappear overnight. Women found that employers designated certain jobs for women and others for men, saving for women the lower-paying positions and denying them the training that would enable them to enter or move up a career ladder. When women did secure the same jobs as men, they were paid substantially less. Banks denied women credit, further mandating their dependence on men.[56] It would prove enormously difficult for single women to exercise the kinds of independence Helen Gurley Brown advocated, even allowing for some "treating" by men. And the same advice givers who promoted early marriage, and who denigrated single women, also argued that work could prove a woman's ultimate undoing. "The Single Career Woman...may find satisfaction in her job," warned *Life* magazine in a special report on women in 1956. "But the chances are that she will suffer psychological damage. Should she marry and reproduce her husband and children will be profoundly unhappy."[57]

Brown's approach to living in a world that worried to distraction about women in the workplace differed from that of the feminists whose voices emerged almost immediately after hers. While they determined to battle attitudes men generally and employers specifically held about women, Brown instead attempted to shore up women's confidence. In 1962 great numbers of women believed that a career would "spoil" them for marriage. Brown anticipates such reactions in *Sex and the Single Girl* and counters with the argument that a career is "the greatest preparation for marriage." Acknowledging that many women fear that men prefer women whose intellects remained hidden, Brown argues, "I never met one who did." She explains: "Never in my life! If they do, it must be because they have so little on the ball themselves they need a moron around to make them feel superior."[58] Recognizing that other women fear that a loss of femininity inevitably accompanies success on the job, Brown provides another argument. "We owe the 'battle axes' of another era more than we can ever pay. They had to be hard as nails and drive themselves in like nails to compete with men. Not you, magnolia blossom!"[59] Finally, Brown understands that many women worry that they almost have to become men themselves to succeed in a man's world. For those women, Brown offers specific career advice: "Publishing and advertising are both wonderful fields for women because you are paid handsomely not to think like a man."[60]

A realist, Helen Gurley Brown understood that her contemporaries lived in a world they neither fashioned nor controlled. According to her philosophy, however, that reality ought not to have deterred them from living fulfilling personal and professional lives, being sexy, making choices, making money, or having sexual relationships. Carrie Bradshaw and her friends in *Sex and the City* would follow a hauntingly similar path three decades later. In *Sex and the Single Girl*, single women can refuse to marry if it isn't right for them, refrain from buying into outmoded definitions of female sexuality, find work they feel passionate about and find meaning in, enliven their domestic surroundings to meet their needs, and enjoy being women under what Brown would consider fairly liberated conditions.

Doggedly optimistic, *Sex and the Single Girl,* like its author, has little room for the victim. But this approach to a male-dominated world would meet tremendous resistance in the aftermath of the book's publication, not only from the moralists but also from the feminists, many of whom who had little tolerance for Brown's particular stance on womanhood. Some would find her celebration of heterosexual relationships sexist, her reliance on men cloyingly dependent, her feminine behaviors self-deprecating, her solutions to an oppressive work world insufficiently collective, and her "girl" insufferably immature. But Helen Gurley Brown never doubted that she, too, was a feminist, a believer in the inherent potential of women deemed by many to be undesirable spinsters, priggish old maids, or unethical temptresses. *Sex and the Single Girl*'s publishing history reveals, however, that selling the message of female independence, sexual and economic, was for Brown a complicated, contested, and profitable enterprise.

5

sensationalist literature
and expert advice

SELLING *SEX AND THE SINGLE GIRL*

Regardless of Helen Gurley Brown's flair for writing or David Brown's connections in the publishing industry, *Sex and the Single Girl* would prove a difficult sell. None of the large publishing houses would touch it. One requested a "toned-down" version, but when the revised version also proved too controversial, David advised Helen that they should submit only the original and not give in until they secured a contract for the manuscript as written. He felt certain that anything short of that would damage both the book's and the author's integrity. David's close friend Oscar Dystel, the head of the paperback publisher Bantam Books, kept the manuscript for several weeks, then turned Helen down over dinner. "I nearly choked on my lasagna," she wrote about the experience years later. "You must never turn anybody down at dinner."[1] Both Helen's mother and David's father read the manuscript and requested that she abandon the idea of publishing it. "It may be a sensation and get a great deal of publicity," Cleo wrote. "So do murder and rape!"

Helen and David would not be deterred by any of their critics. Several people advised them that Helen needed just the right kind of publisher, someone unafraid of challenging what was, in many ways, a traditional publishing world. After Helen and David heard the publisher Bernard Geis's name in several different contexts, they mailed him a copy of the manuscript. Ten days later Geis responded, offering the Browns most welcome news: he agreed to publish the book. Geis included with his letter a six-thousand-dollar advance, and Helen, during her otherwise fairly moribund days at Kenyon & Eckhardt, eagerly returned to the as-yet-unfinished manuscript. Neither the astute Berney Geis nor the clever Browns anticipated the phenomenal success of *Sex and the Single Girl*, however, and they agreed on a fairly conservative contract, with terms specifying that Helen could not receive more than fifteen thousand dollars a year in earnings; anything above that would be credited to her account for future years. It was a contract they would have to revisit, and quite soon.[2]

The Chicago-born Bernard Geis, the son of a cigar maker whose business survived the Depression and financed the younger Geis's college education, started his New York publishing career working for the prestigious *Esquire* and *Coronet* magazines. He moved into the book world, securing a position as an editor at Grosset & Dunlap, the publisher of several tremendously successful children's book series, including Nancy Drew, the Hardy Boys, and the Bobbsey Twins. In the early 1940s, when Grosset's president John O'Connor helped launch a new paperback publishing company designed to challenge the sovereignty of Pocket Books, Berney Geis was on hand to offer a name for the new "major house," as they confidently described themselves. He suggested a cocky rooster to rival the already existing paperback icons of the albatross, penguin, pelican, and kangaroo, and Bantam Books, the house that would later turn down Helen Gurley Brown, was born. By 1950 the Bantam ad "Rooster or Capon?" would claim, demonstrating one way in which sexuality could be infused into popular media of the day, that all of its books were uncut, not condensed, as had been typical of paperback publishing.[3]

In his next position, as an editor and publisher at Prentice Hall, Berney Geis worked on the television host Art Linkletter's companion book to his popular show *Kids Say the Darndest Things*. The book achieved modest success, but when Linkletter mentioned the book on his show, sales skyrocketed. The lesson was clear to Geis, who already considered himself media savvy: crossovers resulted in increased sales. He promoted book reading as on a par with watching movies or television and harbored few fears about the ways in which "mass" was, rightly or wrongly, associated with "crass." In short, he reveled in appeals to a mass rather than class audience.

The unconventional Geis decided to start his own press and immediately recruited several celebrities, including Groucho Marx, to help finance the endeavor. Bernard Geis Associates was founded in 1958. By the time the Browns first learned of him, Geis had achieved considerable success. A few years later, in 1966, he would reach the pinnacle of his career with the publication of Jacqueline Susann's *Valley of the Dolls,* but in the meantime he would do well by Helen Gurley Brown, and she by him.

Housed on East 56th Street in New York, the Geis offices, like Geis himself, would become known for inviting controversy. A brass firefighter's pole connected the two floors of the suite of offices, and staff and visitors alike would use the pole to access the lower floor. The pole gained some notoriety during the miniskirt period of the 1960s, and Geis himself became notorious for his maverick ways in a conventional industry.[4] The writer Joan Didion quipped that Geis developed a reputation as a publisher "who seems to like his authors to fit their typewriter time around *The Tonight Show*'s schedule." Another critic called him "the non-publisher of non-books for non-readers." But many people watched admiringly rather than disparagingly as Geis pioneered the multimedia approach to book publishing.[5] He also championed a strategy that recognized working-class readers, targeting smaller cities, giving special attention to bookstore owners, contacting small-town newspaper reporters, and even involving the teamsters who shipped the books. Through a combination of promoting the risqué, often by quite costly means, developing new strategies for meeting the masses where they lived and worked, and pushing his authors into the limelight at every chance, Bernard Geis Associates would, in its twelve-year lifespan, put seventeen books, close to a quarter of its total output, on the *New York Times* best-seller list.[6] Because of her working-class background, eagerness to engage in the marketplace, and affinity for working girls, Helen Gurley Brown would respond positively to Geis's philosophy and approach.

Helen Gurley Brown's *Sex and the Single Girl* fits somewhat curiously into the history of publishing in the 1950s and early 1960s, claiming a niche in both the sensationalist and the expert-advice genres. By no means was Brown the first to discuss sex in a mass-market publication. Pulp fiction, printed on inexpensive newsprint (pulp), originated in the late nineteenth century in magazine form and gained a large readership from the 1920s through the 1950s. Pulp magazines spawned such literary forms as detective, adventure, and science fiction novels, in addition to the lesbian pulp novels of the fifties and sixties. Many pulp magazines featured tantalizing covers of flesh-baring women, but the actual content was most often less explicit than those covers suggested. *Sex and the Single Girl* provided a tantalizing title and a cover that argued it was time to "torpedo the myth" that single women refrained from sex, thus copying elements of the pulps that preceded it, but the book adheres more closely to the paperback tradition of the late 1950s and early 1960s than it does to the earlier pulp genre.

Mass-market paperbacks emerged on the publishing scene in 1939, introduced by Pocket Books and sold principally through periodical distributors. Distributed widely, and sold in "mass" locations such as airports, bus stations, drug stores, and chain stores, paperbacks democratized reading in America. Before paperback books, most consumers could not afford to purchase books, and most books did not sell widely. Modeled on the earlier success of Albatross and Penguin books in Europe, Pocket Books sold cheaply, at 25 cents a copy, and were an easy sell at a time when Americans began to have and spend more disposable income.[7] The first million-copy seller, Dale Carnegie's *How to Win Friends and Influence People,* anticipated *Sex and the Single Girl* in important ways: it promoted a Horatio Alger approach to life, located success in the worlds of work and money, and argued that its author, regardless of his own achievements, shared a set of values with his readers. And Brown's success would depend not just on Bernard Geis but also on Pocket Books, which would pick up her contract when *Sex and the Single Girl* moved from hardcover to paperback.

The paperback industry, well under way when Helen Gurley Brown wrote *Sex and the Single Girl,* revolutionized reading in general but also transformed the reading practices of women and men. The paperback in its early days appealed primarily to men. Men, after all, had both the funds to purchase paperback books and greater access to them, as they were the ones who frequented newsstands and then airport terminals. Many of the first best-selling titles—Westerns, adventure novels, and hardboiled mysteries—targeted men by featuring unappealing if not downright misogynist portrayals of female characters. As paperbacks began to seek supermarket distribution, and then particularly as women broke the barrier to editorial positions in publishing houses, many more books directed at women reached publication. Women eventually would equal and then surpass men as paperback purchasers. By the time Brown published *Sex and the Single Girl,* many paperback titles, including cookbooks, gardening books, house and home books, and primers on marriage, family, and children had become enormously popular among women readers. More importantly, however, in terms of setting the stage for *Sex and the Single Girl*, several successful "women's novels" of the 1950s provided readily accessible and frank, however fictionalized, discussions of female sexuality.[8]

In the mid- to late 1950s, two of those fictionalized accounts of single women's lives, Grace Metalious's *Peyton Place* and Rona Jaffe's *The Best of Everything*, became overnight successes. Like *Sex and the Single Girl*, both of these books featured single female protagonists (assuming we can agree that Helen Gurley Brown serves as the protagonist of her nonfiction title), explored female sexuality, and acknowledged single women's relationships with married men. Like *Sex and the Single Girl*, *Peyton Place* and *The Best of Everything* reached the *New York Times* best-seller lists and were made into popular films. Brown's book would cross the line between the fictional and the real, making the case that real-life, rather than imagined, women lived such lives. Nevertheless, the similarities among the three texts, and their reception among women readers, prove striking.[9]

Grace Metalious's *Peyton Place* was the surprise best-seller of 1956. It was inexpensive, sensationalist and, to many, immoral. It was also a quick read and was straightforward about issues of sex, child abuse, alcoholism, and incest; readers loved it. *Peyton Place* sold sixty thousand copies in the first ten days of its release as a Julian Messner hardcover and stayed at the top of the *New York Times* best-seller list for more than a year. Released after that first year as a Dell paperback, it sold three million copies in 1957 and had sold ten million copies by 1966.[10] *Peyton Place* might seem tame by today's standards, and in fact it contained few explicit references to sex, but sexuality infused the novel, as did the radical notion that sexuality was of interest—and purposefully pursued—not only by boys and men but also by girls and women. Like Helen Gurley Brown, Grace Metalious deserves credit for introducing feminist themes to a mass audience. But even before Brown, Metalious began to create an active female readership for sexually suggestive if not explicit reading material.[11]

Rona Jaffe's debut novel, *The Best of Everything*, was published in 1958, just two years after *Peyton Place* and four years before *Sex and the Single Girl*. It focuses on the work and romantic lives of four young women employed as stenographers in New York's publishing industry. Drawing on her experience as an editor at Fawcett Publications, and on her own single life and the lives of several of her friends, Jaffe drew a picture of single life in Manhattan that rankled critics, many of whom lamented its lack of literary sophistication. Regardless of its lowbrow style, however, *The Best of Everything* pleased readers everywhere with its unaffected, straightforward approach. The book's opening sentence invited actual and aspiring urban sophisticates into the heady setting of New York City in the bustling postwar years: "You see them every morning at a quarter to nine, rushing out of the maw of the subway tunnel, filing out of Grand Central Station, crossing Lexington and Park and Madison and Fifth avenues, the hundreds and hundreds of girls." These young women may be dressed in recently purchased, chic black suits or faded, five-year-old black ankle strap sandals, but they all share their youth along with one other thing: "None of them has enough money." Solidarity among women emerges from an awareness of what would, only a few short years later, be labeled sexism, or male dominance, rather than, simply, everyday life.

Rona Jaffe, a Radcliffe graduate and lifelong single woman who argued once that she preferred her single status to what she described as her peers' "rat race to the altar," achieved immediate celebrity status with the publication of *The Best of Everything*. Jaffe provided for most of her main characters far less professional success than she herself achieved. Whether her characters also had less good fortune in relationships with men we cannot say, as we know little of Jaffe's romantic life, but the women in *The Best of Everything* definitely struggle with men, "cads," who by and large charm the female characters at the same time that they repulse the book's omniscient readers. The *New York Times* reviewer Martin Levin, expressing sentiments with which many, if not most, reviewers agreed, deemed the book and its characters overly formulaic. "Before very many coffee breaks one is a stretcher case, one is pregnant and the third is off to Las Vegas with a notorious lounge lizard," he wrote. "But that's the life of a working girl, at least as seen through Miss Jaffe's wide eyes."[12]

Jaffe's eyes must have grown wider still when *The Best of Everything* hit the *New York Times* best-seller list within two weeks of publication and remained there for five months. As with *Peyton Place*, readers loved the drama, often sexual in nature, that these young women worked through. Jaffe's mother, like Cleo Bryan a few years later, shared the consternation of the critics, but for her own reasons. When the book made money, she feared, in keeping with the pathological reasoning about women that Jaffe explores explicitly in the novel, that her daughter had become less rather than more marriageable because of her success. When *The Best of Everything* became a film, generating even more fame, one of her mother's friends empathized: "Poor Rona!" she lamented. "With the film sale...all that money, now she'll never get married!"[13]

Brown's book both deviates from and depends on these earlier blockbusters. It provides a nonfiction and far more upbeat approach to women's sexuality than do *Peyton Place* or *The Best of Everything*. For Brown, the "rich, full life" for women includes sex, and plenty of it.[14] Brown largely avoids the sordid elements of emerging female sexuality that Metalious and Jaffe explore, including sexual harassment, rape, incest, pregnancy, and abortion, and instead celebrates women's potential for financial and sexual autonomy.[15] Nevertheless, the enormous success of these earlier works helped create a readership for Brown by introducing characters who pursued sexuality, avoiding or abandoning feelings of guilt along the way.[16] One of Peyton Place's central contributions to women's lives was the suggestion that women wanted sex and enjoyed it, that sex was not something men really wanted and women simply acquiesced to."[17] Helen Gurley Brown would take that a step further, promoting such messages in a form that spoke from the realm of reality rather than simply imagination.

Arguably, *Peyton Place* and *The Best of Everything* primed the American female readership for *Sex and the Single Girl*. By 1962 women were poised not only for the content of Brown's work but also for her approach, dispensing practical, however risqué, advice about young women's sexual and workplace concerns. The teenager who tore the cover off *Peyton Place* and hid it inside her school textbook, the babysitter who combed her employer's shelves hoping to find the book available for late-night reading, the young woman who read it on the sly at work, the grateful woman who did not have to ask for it by name because it was displayed so prominently in her local bookstore—all of these readers and many more were ready to move beyond the imagined world of sex and money and hear about women's actual experiences.[18] In short, they were ready for an "expert" like Helen Gurley Brown to tell them how to live the singularly sexy single woman's life.

In writing *Sex and the Single Girl* in the postwar period, Brown engaged in what had become by then a traditional practice: dispensing advice. At various times and in various ways, Americans have turned to others for guidance about daily living. These advice givers might be clergy, educators, politicians, family members, popular magazines, or self-appointed experts on one subject or another. Americans in the postwar period certainly sought out a great deal of guidance. The inherited wisdom of parents and families seemed increasingly less viable in this period of change, and many Americans welcomed the advice of a new range of advisers.[19] Among these, single women would encounter and welcome Brown, who fit into the expert category comfortably—and then not. Like many of the reigning advice givers of the day, she spoke to her readers in an authoritative yet not unfriendly manner. In her first-person, "in my opinion," "I decided long ago" fashion, Brown offered a voice both humble and authoritative, light and serious—an approach that helped people consider her both expert and friend.

In other ways Brown did not fit comfortably within the expert camp. Her claim to fame was neither a degree nor a pedigree; she simply spoke from experience. In fact, she opens the book by citing her lack of credentials. "I am not beautiful, or even pretty. I once had the world's worst case of acne. I am not bosomy or brilliant. I grew up in a small town. I didn't go to college. My family was, and is, desperately poor, and I have always helped support them. I'm an introvert, and I am sometimes mean and cranky."[20] Unlike Dr. Benjamin Spock, who relied on his medical credentials in his best-selling advice book, *Baby and Child Care,* or Norman Vincent Peale, whose significant theological clout provided the authority for his own best-seller, *The Power of Positive Thinking,* Helen Gurley Brown relied solely on experience and observation in voicing her opinions and dispensing her advice. Such an approach gained Brown many detractors but won her even more admirers. In calling things as she saw them, Brown demonstrated an uncanny ability to tap into the minds of single women, a group of people most other American experts either ignored or maligned.

Brown differed from her advice-giving peers in another significant way. Unlike them, she offered counsel that challenged rather than supported social conventions. Most advice givers of the time saw the nuclear family as the central unit of the society; Brown argued that single women could exist on their own. Contrary to the mainstream advice givers, Brown exposed as inherently flawed the reigning set of rules about intimate relationships that its proponents touted as uniquely American, valuable, and suited to all. Most experts saw women as subordinate to men; Brown argued that women could and ought to make choices independent of the needs or opinions of men. Most advice givers viewed women as mothers first and foremost, and from an early age; Brown fractured that connection culturally and then biologically, arguing that women could, if they decided eventually to take that path, have babies into their forties. With her guidance, Brown's single women made a range of unpopular choices, sex with married men standing out most vividly among those.[21]

Young women of the early 1960s encountered plenty of advice, much of it encouraging them to marry. Respondents to a 1962 *Ladies' Home Journal*–Gallup poll largely embraced that advice. They reported that, as women, they, rather than men, had to draw the line when it came to sex. They used sex to keep men interested, but with the goal of actually having intercourse only after marriage. What the man got, in the resulting social arrangement, was a virgin bride. What the woman got, according to these seemingly quite eager takers, was the split-level house, built-in oven and range, and living room with exposed beams. In other words, throughout the 1950s and regardless of the Kinsey Report's findings, men continued to be defined as wanting sex, women as resisting it; men as providing for things domestic, women as coveting them.[22]

Brown provided a different message, and from a different frame of reference. In her writing, readers encountered an older confidante who celebrated rather than attempted to contain female sexuality. "It was as though my book and newspaper readers had found a friend. I was the sophisticated older sister in whom they could confide," she remembered years later. "In 1962, most of the advice givers were still pretty puritanical—Abigail Van Buren, Joyce Brothers, churches, teachers. Unless a girl could afford to go to a psychiatrist, which I had done, there really wasn't anybody terribly hip who would be responsive to questions she would not dare ask anybody else."[23]

The advice proffered in *Sex and the Single Girl* recognized the inequalities young working women of Brown's day experienced. Many women's employment histories, even by the early 1960s and with a new and more educated generation of women, continued to match Brown's own in significant ways. When *Sex and the Single Girl* was released, almost one of every three women was employed in a clerical or secretarial job. By 1974, women held four of five jobs in that category. Even though Brown's readers, at least as single women, never fully realized the upper- or even middle-class identity to which they aspired, with her advice they could dress the part, speak the part, and furnish their homes accordingly.[24] It is no surprise that, in filling this particular advice-giving niche, Helen Gurley Brown would so effectively reach young, working, and ambitious single women, however professionally limited.

Brown's supporters often praised her by equating her form of advice with that of mental health practitioners. An article in *Rogue*, a men's magazine, reported that a "well-known Beverly Hills psychiatrist" touted *Sex and the Single Girl*'s therapeutic effects. "Beset by familial and community pressures but driven nearly frantic by biological need, the single girl has been caught between two powerful opposing forces," the article explains. "*Sex and the Single Girl* helps to resolve this conflict, and should release her to the involvement and enjoyment of a satisfactory adjustment to her role as a female."[25] Bernard Geis claimed that many readers wrote letters insisting that Helen Gurley Brown served them even better than did a psychiatrist, offering them pride in their single status and the means of talking back to those who wanted to marry them off.[26] Brown, who had benefited enormously from therapy, and who would in *Sex and the Single Girl* and all subsequent instances praise psychological and psychiatric practitioners, could not have received much higher praise than that.

Letty Cottin (later Letty Cottin Pogrebin), the director of promotion and publicity at Bernard Geis Associates, would make her mark as a writer and then as a well-known feminist and editor at *Ms.* magazine. In 1962, though, she had one claim to fame: her mastery at marketing books like Helen Gurley Brown's. For the release of *Sex and the Single Girl,* Cottin arranged multiple tours for Brown, each with appointments with press columnists, appearances in bookstores, and interviews on television and radio. Cottin put into practice Bernard Geis's early understanding that marketing a book must, by necessity, be a multimedia event. The list of publications carrying ads for the book was extensive, including the daily *New York Times* and *New York Times Book Review, Esquire,* the *Village Voice, Cosmopolitan,* the *Chicago Sunday Tribune,* and *Redbook.* Smaller ads appeared in other newspapers in Chicago, San Francisco, Los Angeles, and New York. Advertising expenditures in the first month and a half after publication reached thirty thousand dollars.[27]

Brown, herself quite actively interested in strategies around the book's promotion, kept in close contact with Letty Cottin. Given her years-long experience in advertising, it made sense for Geis Associates to involve her. She and Cottin discussed a variety of related issues, including the need to keep the book visible, feeling that it was far easier for women to pick up a copy from a display than to ask for the title by name; making the book available in department stores and the Playboy Club; and the ethical issues involved in Brown's naming actual former boyfriends in her public appearances. Since some television stations would not allow Brown or her interviewer to utter the word "sex," Berney Geis advised Brown to hold the book up for a close-up shot.[28]

Geis Associates solicited quotes for the book's jacket from the actress Joan Crawford and the burlesque dancer Gypsy Rose Lee. Brown sent Cottin a list of the top thirty-six national advertising agencies, along with the names of women who worked in them. She also responded to every request she herself received concerning the book.[29] Brown wrote Berney Geis, outlining some of her efforts including sending an autographed copy to her former boss, requesting that he pass it on to the former president Dwight Eisenhower. "I think Mr. Belding is quite proud of the book because he comes off nicely in it," Brown explained in her letter. "He probably also knows that Eisenhower, at times in his life, has liked single girls. I don't think we can use this for publicity."[30]

Publicity prompted further publicity, and stories, some perhaps apocryphal, began to appear in the press, as did cartoons about the book and its readers. One such story told of a secretary at the Library of Congress who got a notice about a book she had borrowed. "Madam, please return the book you borrowed immediately," the notice read. "This book is urgently needed by a member of Congress." The book was, of course, *Sex and the Single Girl.* A *New Yorker* item featured a teenager who attempted to purchase the book from a "tired, circumspect middle-aged male clerk" and was told that she was much too young to buy it. "Don't worry. It's not for me," the girl assured the sales clerk. "It's for my mother."[31]

Both Letty Cottin and Helen Gurley Brown proved relentless in their efforts and conspired on another strategy to capitalize on the controversial sexiness of the book and its title: a book ban. Many readers of *Sex and the Single Girl* felt the book ought to have been censored, and the publisher would have been only too happy to see that occur. Had Geis published the book only a few years earlier, it might have happened. In the early years of the twentieth century, would-be censors had relied on the Comstock laws, which made it illegal to send "obscene, lewd, lascivious, or filthy" materials in the mails.[32] The advent of paperback publishing had brought on a renewed wave of censorship. Critics targeted books that had reached publication as uncensored hardcover editions. The issue, as they saw it, was the democratic potential of paperbacks, which were available to a far wider range of people.

In May 1952, the House of Representatives authorized a probe of the paperback, magazine, and comic book industries to determine the extent of "immoral, obscene or otherwise offensive matter." In what seem in retrospect fairly biased hearings, during which committee members went on the attack and few industry representatives had an opportunity to speak, a congressional advisory board issued recommendations that, although not legally binding, had a chilling effect on the paperback industry. By the early 1960s, though, when *Sex and the Single Girl* reached publication, fewer and fewer censorship cases arose, and when they did, publishers generally prevailed.[33]

Regardless of the changing tide, however, Letty Cottin and Helen Gurley Brown colluded to get *Sex and the Single Girl* censored, with Cottin sending out advance copies to people she felt might take the bait. The resulting media exposure, she knew, would only promote sales. Cottin hoped, prepublication, to get the book censored by the main public library in Little Rock, but to no avail. Brown argued that a religious ban might be easiest to incite, "since the book promotes sex out of marriage and extramarital sex," which all sects would hate. She mused, "Maybe a Catholic ban!" Brown was unsure how to accomplish it but, like Cottin, she had no doubts about its efficacy. "Letty, dear," she wrote, "I don't know how to get a public denunciation—a nice, strong, snarly, vocal one—from some religious leader, but it is a possibility." Eventually, Cottin suggested they abandon the banned-book approach, but Brown was loath to relinquish such a brilliant marketing appeal. "I know how hard you've tried with the banning thing," she wrote. "Would the D.A.R. ban it? They're objecting because Tarzan and Jane weren't married, but of course that was to protect school-children readers." When Brown received a speaking invitation from a Catholic women's group, the two schemers dropped their efforts to get the book banned. Geis concurred.[34] The book would eventually meet the censor's gaze abroad and be banned in both Spain and Ireland, but those actions had no influence on domestic sales.

Indeed, as early feminists, Helen Gurley Brown and Letty Cottin understood that they had to manipulate media outlets, tap into sensationalist publicity efforts, and generally play the system in order to get Brown's messages to mass audiences of women. The serendipitous combination of the book's particular message and this particular messenger, Geis Associates' creative marketing approaches, a healthy publicity budget, and auspicious timing ensured the immediate and enormous success of *Sex and the Single Girl.* Released on May 23, 1962, the book sold more than fifty thousand copies in its first four months. By October, Geis was on his sixth printing, and the book had not yet been released in paperback. By September, rights had been extended to Britain, France, Australia, Sweden, and Japan. By 1965, publication had extended to Portugal, Norway, Holland, Italy, and Denmark. In the end, the book sold—and sold well—in thirty-five countries. Young women, single women, married women, and men of all stripes had spoken. Sex was no longer a taboo subject for the adult reading public.

Sales figures attest to the popularity of *Sex and the Single Girl,* but by no means did all the reviewers speak favorably about the book. In fact, few reviews proved casual in their response to the book. Most were either highly complimentary, applauding the book's liberating effect on readers, or highly negative, deeming both the book's content and the author's writing style pedestrian at best. "*Sex and the Single Girl* by Helen Gurley Brown is about as tasteless a book as I have read this year," wrote one reviewer. Norman Vincent Peale, in "Where Do You Draw the Line?" worried about the harmful influence of American public figures, including in his list of offenders Ernest Hemingway and Helen Gurley Brown, whose book he called "one long glorification of indiscriminate sex." Letters to the editors of many of the nation's newspapers took the same tack, as typified by this piece in the *San Francisco Chronicle:* "Helen Brown's attempt to break down girls' chastity by commercializing sex in degrading book form is a libel against American womanhood. The affairs, methods and advice she describes may have root in the small promiscuous circles in which she moves, but I have faith in the higher standards of most American women." Brown's mother agreed, considering the appearance of such troubling practices to be isolated among Brown and her friends in Hollywood, which was "highly contaminated with carnal lust."[35]

Dismissals of Brown's writing style emerged in several of the reviews, including a *Los Angeles Times* review that stated that *Sex and the Single Girl* was, in fact, "hardly a book at all but a collection of burblings, printed, bound and provided with a dust jacket." Other reviewers praised the book's realism and straightforward approach. Some simply suggested that the book invited highly disparate readings. "This is a fabulous book that will do wild or wonderful things for the systolic pressure of the American Woman, depending on her circumstances," wrote a reviewer. "Blood will boil, simmer, run cold, or effervesce."[36]

Once the reviews began to come in, Brown paid a great deal of attention to the positive reviews and largely avoided the negative. David quickly moved into producer mode when sales grew so quickly that the agreement that Helen would receive fifteen thousand dollars a year became utterly unsatisfactory. He began to write letters to Bernard Geis, challenging the current terms and offering alternatives. "You are hearing from me rather than Helen," he explained in the first of these letters, "because Helen prefers to address you solely on creative matters—and besides, she says that I should take an interest in her affairs as this is a community property state! What a dowry!" David acknowledged that he wrote as a husband but gradually made it clear that he alone would manage the money end of things. "I shall try not to burden you with further correspondence as I know that authors' husbands can be a bore," he wrote in July, and in August he stated, "I promised not to stick my nose into Helen's affairs but she keeps egging me on inasmuch as she claims to be only a lover!" Thereafter, David left off the justifications and simply wrote "Helen would prefer," "Helen would like," and "Helen's first concern." He negotiated a new agreement, in which Helen received flat sum payments of $105,000, $45,000, and finally $60,000, in order to bring down the balance, which would eventually exceed $250,000.

While David handled the business end of things, Helen continued her practice of relentless book promotion, appearing in cities nationwide. For the most part, she encountered welcoming, enthusiastic audiences. While on a trip through the Midwest, however, Helen met up with a less-than-enthusiastic response, and she remembered the experience years later with continued incredulity. "I would be rather astonished," she remarked, "at how puritanical people were and how terrified they were that sex could be pleasurable." For the most part, she avoided any of the negative reviews or publicity. "When I got critical mail and phone calls, I chucked those," she remembered later. "I never read critical articles. I was pretty much insulated from real criticism, and I knew right was on my side, so I didn't feel too lonely."[37] Helen relied on David, on Letty Cottin, on Berney Geis, and on the strong internal sense that she was contributing something to others through her honesty.

In 1971, after Jacqueline Susann had published her two enormous hits, *Valley of the Dolls* and *The Love Machine*, she and Helen Gurley Brown had a conversation about what had made them so successful. They agreed that their particular strengths included acknowledging and celebrating the realities of average women and understanding the most effective, everyday means of communicating with those readers. They believed that they knew and understood their readers because they had lived those lives themselves. Brown and Susann talked, Brown told her mother afterward, about the difference college educations would have made in their lives. "We both think they would have destroyed us!"

With *Sex and the Single Girl*, Helen Gurley Brown capitalized on the era's social schizophrenia and brought a series of arguably feminist messages to a mainstream audience. She was, as Joan Didion said about her at the time, just the person to communicate to an audience of quintessentially American "lonely spirits" who wanted a sister, a friend, and a confirmation that the world was changing—and they were entitled to grab a piece of it while the taking was good.[38]

6

sexy from the start

THE EARLY YEARS OF SECOND-WAVE FEMINISM

When people think about the early years of the second wave of feminism, many believe, simply, that "Betty Friedan did it all, with maybe a little help from Gloria Steinem."[1] Until Betty Friedan wrote *The Feminine Mystique,* the story goes, no one, not even women themselves, understood that sexism existed or that women could make a variety of choices about their lives.[2] In recent years historians have begun to unravel the complexities of the feminists and feminisms that circulated in the 1960s and 1970s, but few acknowledge—never mind consider— Helen Gurley Brown. Yet *Sex and the Single Girl,* like Betty Friedan's *The Feminine Mystique,* introduced feminist thinking to millions of readers, documented both women's aspirations and their discontents, and refused to apologize for its bold demands for women. On top of that, *Sex and the Single Girl,* which came out a year before *The Feminine Mystique,* shifts not only the date of popular feminism's emergence but also broadens the movement's message and its audience. Helen Gurley Brown sought to liberate not the married woman but the single woman, not the suburban but the urban dweller, not the college-educated victim but the working-class survivor. "I had no idea what I was doing," Brown remembered about the time, demonstrating the ways she could at times buy into the narrative that erased her influential and deliberate contribution. "Feminism was nowhere then....And what I was saying—that single girls, nice single girls, had sex lives—really caused a great ruckus." A ruckus, yes, and in hindsight, an indisputably feminist ruckus at that.[3]

Helen Gurley Brown and Betty Friedan shared more than the experience of seeing their books reach publication in the early 1960s. They had been born almost exactly a year apart, Bettye (she dropped the "e" when she graduated from college) Goldstein on February 4, 1921, and Helen Gurley on February 18, 1922.[4] Each spoke from personal experience and with an internal confidence that millions of other women could relate to their own stories. Each responded passionately to the postwar obsession with domesticity and the resulting tension experienced by women who pursued any interests outside of marriage and family. As young girls and women, Helen and Bettye saw firsthand the damaging price of the domesticity-is-all agenda, having been raised by somewhat embittered, somewhat broken women whose husbands had demanded that they abandon meaningful work to raise their children. As adults, neither Brown nor Friedan believed that women could be satisfied by the options contemporary life afforded them, even as their generation concretely replaced that of their parents. With long work histories themselves, they held an inordinate faith in the value of work, paired with a stubborn and healthy skepticism about women's supposedly nurturing dispositions. Each believed that she, through her particular brand of self-help, could assist other women in their search for a more rewarding way of living a woman's life. Finally, contrary to what they might always have voiced publicly, Helen Gurley Brown and Betty Friedan shared another significant characteristic: the desire to achieve not only fame but fortune as popular, even populist writers.

The parallels between the Goldstein and the Gurley families provide insight into the ways in which discontent in mothers could produce feminist responses in daughters. Friedan's mother, Miriam Goldstein, had worked as the society-page editor of a Peoria, Illinois, newspaper until her marriage. She then raised three children, assisted her husband in the family business, and participated in community work. Although the Goldstein family was better off financially than was the Gurley family, Bettye's parents fought frequently over money, particularly when their jewelry store, like most other businesses of its kind, suffered a decline during the Great Depression. Had her husband supported her in continuing employment outside the confines of the family, Miriam could have contributed more financially than she was able to do by simply helping out at the store. Her marginal position in the business did little to improve her status in the family or her sense of herself as a working person. Engaging and remunerative work would certainly have staved off some of the dissatisfaction underemployment bred in this bright, college-educated woman. Years later, Betty Friedan singled out Miriam's discontent over leaving paid employment as the impetus for her own feminism. "I sometimes think that what really motivated me was a gut awareness of my mother's frustration," she argued. "I wanted women to be able to feel better about being women than my mother was able to." This gut awareness readily translated to extended investigations, in *The Feminine Mystique*, of women's numerous dissatisfactions.[5]

As with Helen Gurley Brown, the women's movement, along with therapy, would enable the adult Betty Friedan to see her mother in a more sympathetic light than she had as a youngster, when her mother's bitterness simply wore her down. "Nothing my father did, nothing he bought her, nothing we ever did seemed to satisfy her," she remembered. "I didn't want to be like my mother." She viewed women's dependence on men as harmful not only to women themselves but to their entire families, men included. Wanting more independence herself, and also identifying with her father and his more public world of work, Bettye Goldstein, like Helen Gurley, came to identify paid employment as a necessary component not only of women's independence but also of their positive identity as women and as citizens. Likewise, Betty Friedan only gradually came to realize that as a child she had preferred her father's company in part because he was emotionally free of the burdens that continually haunted her mother.[6]

As children, and in significant ways, each of these girls resisted identifying with her mother, and the chasm between mother and daughter grew as adolescence progressed into early adulthood. Ironically, both Miriam Goldstein and Cleo Gurley promoted their daughters' intellectual interests and accomplishments at the same time that they expressed regret that the girls lacked conventional beauty. They offered conflicting messages about womanhood, alienating the daughters they attempted to educate about the mixed and ultimately burdensome realities of women's lives. Later in life, however, by experiencing for themselves and by exploring with others what it meant to live in the world as an adult woman, Betty and Helen each eventually came to feel solidarity with the woman she had long viewed as the antithesis of a role model. Each understood what her mother had sacrificed, not only for her husband but also for her children, and each came to appreciate the complicated nature of these legacies.

Helen Gurley Brown directly and repeatedly referred to her mother as a feminist who, though often by negative example, had shown Helen that another way of life was possible. Betty Friedan sent her mother a copy of *The Feminine Mystique* with a note that read, "With all the troubles we have had, you gave me the power to break through the feminine mystique....I hope you will accept the book for what it is, an affirmation of the values of your life and mine."[7] Although Friedan would raise three children, and Brown would remain childless, they nevertheless shared a lifelong aversion to the motherhood-is-personhood philosophy that seemed to reemerge and haunt their generation just as surely as it had haunted that of their overburdened and disgruntled mothers.

Friedan and Brown shared some family characteristics and family dynamics, but their lives differed in significant ways as well. Friedan's Jewish identity, coupled with her early radicalism, had resulted in her advocacy of working-class and African American women long before she wrote *The Feminine Mystique*. Both her earlier writings and her post–*Feminine Mystique* works demonstrate a collective consciousness that complicates the individualist approach of *The Feminine Mystique*. Nevertheless, in this, her most famous publication, if not in her entire life picture, Betty Friedan shared with Helen Gurley Brown a commitment to an individualist ethos. Each believed that even though women received countless messages about how they ought to behave, they retained the capacity and the responsibility to shape their own lives. The secretarial school–educated Brown approached this philosophy from a working-class perspective and following years of financial independence as a single woman: no one but an individual woman could ensure her own survival, let alone happiness. Work was the key to autonomy for Brown and her working-class cohort.

The Smith College–educated and professionally employed Friedan approached the question of individual autonomy somewhat differently, and from a middle-class perspective. Speaking from a place in which survival was more or less a given, Friedan promoted the idea of life plans for women, with which women would purposefully shape their futures, planning so that education and meaningful work always accompanied decisions about marriage and family. Friedan's tools for female autonomy included, in addition to paid employment, education and the arts. She relied on the work of the popular humanistic psychologist Abraham H. Maslow and others who argued that the individual self becomes whole by engaging in creative activity that "carries forward human society." The two women would agree that circumstances of birth mattered in the overall scheme of things. However, they would argue, each in somewhat different terms, that the individual had terrifically significant choices to make. In their books, Brown and Friedan would demonstrate and promote the incipient power of an early second-wave feminist agenda for crafting a new female self.[8]

Sex and the Single Girl and *The Feminine Mystique* were, by all accounts, projects designed to assist women along their paths to self-improvement. In this sense they functioned as conduct books, similar in important ways to the nineteenth- and early-twentieth-century conduct books aimed at middle-class women that had provided instructions in how to conduct oneself as a lady, how to mother children, how to provide a cozy domestic environment for one's husband. What differed was that in these new manuals women would learn to provide not so much for others as for themselves. Their conduct resulted in self-improvement, which would only incidentally, but nevertheless decidedly, improve the lives of others.

To put it simply, Brown and Friedan believed that traditional advice diminished rather than enhanced women's sense of self. For daughters of mothers like their own, and for all women who absorbed the culture's messages about womanly sacrifice and subordination, self-improvement was admittedly a narcissistic but just as likely a benevolent practice. Friedan became famous for using the language of personal growth to advocate for married women's emergence from the confines of the home. Hers was an individual process that resulted in collective change. "As if they were waking from a coma," she writes about women in *The Feminine Mystique,* "they ask, 'Where am I... what am I doing here?" The awakening in which she invited her readers to participate required that women move into a maturity unknown in contemporary practices of femininity, which effectively precluded a growing up "to full human identity."[9]

For Friedan, the healthy feminine self would have to reject a host of contemporary notions. She repeatedly cited studies that demonstrated that women increasingly understood femininity as the antithesis of achievement and subsequently exercised a femininity that infantilized their intellects. One study suggested that with few exceptions even college-educated women ended their personal and intellectual growth long before they reached maturity. Encouraged to choose domesticity over productivity, a passive life over a life actively lived, many women complied but few benefited. Women learned that only mannish women pursued careers, but they grew increasingly unhappy with their lack of responsibility to the world outside of the home. They learned that public success would spoil their lives, but they found little to celebrate in their mundane domestic accomplishments. They learned they had been freed by technology not to fret about the onerous nature of housework, but they felt debilitated by the ever-increasing standards of household cleanliness and super-attentive childrearing. With Friedan's guidance, women would reject this "feminine monster" as they worked toward full human identity.[10]

Important differences emerge in the works of Brown and Friedan, and one of these concerns women's paths to success. *The Feminine Mystique* does not elaborate on the methods women use to attract and seduce men. After all, the women Friedan speaks to and for have already met, married, and moved to the suburbs with their love interests. One imagines, nonetheless, that Freidan would have considered advice such as that Brown proffered (look sexy, dress sexy, act sexy, and use your femininity, accompanied by all the smarts you can muster, all the way to the top of your professional and personal life) anathema in works aimed at women who took themselves seriously. Even though Betty Friedan employed many, if not most, of these approaches in her personal life, her professional, public, feminist persona more often negated such practices.[11] One imagines Friedan would deem Brown's studied performances, with some cause, little more than a prelude to dreary domesticity.

For Helen Gurley Brown, however, one of most enjoyable things about being a woman was having the freedom to play, to perform. Where the married woman's lifestyle seemed old and made her old, the single girl's was novel and kept her sexy; one threatened, whereas the other offered promises.[12] However, Brown's notions of human growth and self-worth, admittedly less academic than Betty Friedan's, could not simply be reduced to women deceiving men and themselves by acting feminine. Brown, too, argued that women never ought to present themselves as less able, intellectually, than they were, but she would not as a consequence deny them any of the playful elements of femininity. According to Brown, women could, using their bodies in addition to their brains, manipulate the system that manipulated them. And they could further, she argued emphatically, maintain rather than relinquish a healthy self-esteem along the way.

Helen Gurley Brown would also rely on the human growth approach, even if hers was a somewhat more narrow exploration of the concept than Friedan's. *Sex and the Single Girl* "isn't really about sex," she argued. "It's more along the lines of self-improvement."[13] Many would accuse Brown of making her definition of full humanity, or self-esteem, overly dependent on sexualized behaviors, or what Brown herself might call sexual allure. However, she never actually reduced women to their bodily charms, as much as she celebrated those charms. Brown's mantra, expressed repeatedly in one form or another, was that self-improvement and its accompaniment, self-esteem, belonged to women who sought independence and pursued paid employment. It did not hurt to groom oneself to be sexy along the way, but the key to a good life was developing the self through work. "There are wonderfully good-looking women who are intelligent and charming and interesting," she argued. "Yet, they don't have great self-esteem. My advice is to get involved in some kind of work that brings recognition. That can build more self-esteem than any psychiatrist, self-help book or lecture."[14]

Brown's working girls, who held jobs in office buildings, beauty parlors, airlines, and other working-class settings, could improve their sense of self regardless of the status of their jobs or the size of their paychecks. In other words, even without Friedan's life plans, which included education and cultural enrichment, women could enhance their lives. Those who had arguably felt the worst effects of the feminine mystique, divorced women, might enter Brown's self-esteem-through-employment project at a certain disadvantage, having been away from the world of work for some time and having failed at something considered critical in life, but they could enter all the same, and then make the best of it. "Sometimes I think it's a blessing when you have to work—when there is no other way out," Brown told a group of single parents, "because then you don't have to apologize to your kids about the steps you're taking."[15]

In Brown's experience, then, it was work, not social causes, not volunteer opportunities, not museum visits or adult education classes, that provided women with self-identity. Work also provided the always-needed, never-sufficient commodity, money, and it provided access to men. "A job is where the men are—you meet an awful lot more of them there than you do at the Laundromat," she writes, but Brown is never content to leave it at that, adding that "most importantly a job is where you have to be at a certain time, where people are depending on you to do certain things—it's great great discipline and gets you out of you."[16] For Brown, it would prove virtually impossible to separate out work, an active social and sexual life, economic survival, and women's self-satisfaction. Work provided women money; it also enhanced their sex appeal. Work provided women self-esteem; it also provided them access to men. Helen Gurley Brown could be faulted for accepting some of the inequities of the work world rather than encouraging women to fight them, but there is no doubt that she urged women to engage fully in whatever occupation they pursued.

Although both Brown and Friedan extolled the virtues of work, important differences emerge in their treatment of women's employment. Friedan, in *The Feminine Mystique,* if not in other of her writings, has long been considered the spokesperson for one type of emergent 1960s feminist: the college-educated housewife who clamored for paid work to alleviate some of the burdens of her vapid suburban existence. Younger feminists who emerged from the Civil Rights and New Left political arenas, and who promoted a more radical philosophy, have been considered representative of the second significant feminist cohort, that of college- and movement-educated women coming of age angry with the costs of sexism in their lives and in the lives of their mothers. Helen Gurley Brown, who herself fits comfortably in neither category, invited in to feminism another important but often invisible group, working-class women, largely but by no means exclusively white, whose goals included financial independence, the freedom to engage in sexual activity outside of marriage, and the enjoyment of, rather than a rejection of, the fruits of capitalism. Hers was no insignificant agenda, nor was her audience insignificant in number.[17]

In *Sex and the Single Girl,* Brown encourages women to scrape away at whatever job they find themselves in and to look for opportunities to improve their positions, all the while acknowledging that the world remains unfair to the working girl. She also invites readers, without apology, to indulge in some of the narcissism that capitalism allows. Rather than simply avoiding what Friedan calls, in *The Feminine Mystique,* the "sex sell" of contemporary advertising, Brown's working women use their consumer dollars wisely but well, adorning their bodies and their apartments while they simultaneously put away a few dollars for the future.[18] Friedan portrays work as critical to women's sense of self, although she views it as less critical to survival. "Men no longer need to work all day to eat," she writes. Her readers face additional expectations in the service of their identity as workers: they should work not to pay the rent but to improve the lives of others, not by punching the clock but by contributing creatively to work that "carries forward human society." Friedan worries about her peers accepting unfulfilling jobs in bleak suburban environments. "Women who do not look for jobs equal to their capacity, who do not let themselves develop the lifetime interests and goals which require serious education and training," she writes, "who take a job at twenty or thirty or forty to 'help out at home' or just to kill extra time, are walking, almost as surely as the one who stay inside the housewife trap, to a non-existent future."

This notion of domesticity's "trap," the element of *The Feminine Mystique* that has garnered Friedan the most attention, points to a significant difference between these competing forms of early second-wave feminism. Betty Friedan's exposure of the "problem that has no name" relies primarily on a juxtaposition of family life and personhood, while Brown's celebration of the single woman defines the home as a site of potential liberation rather than oppression. *The Feminine Mystique* relies heavily on Friedan's reading of women's magazines, in which marriage, motherhood, and suburban living are promoted as the only acceptable paths to adult womanhood. Friedan introduces the beleaguered middle-class housewife into the feminist lexicon, where she resides virtually unchanged for the remainder of the second wave of feminism. Having bought into the magazines' messages, Friedan argues, women increasingly become imprisoned in their homes. This second-wave employment of the lost housewife needing liberation, introduced by Friedan and refined by others, would make it exceedingly difficult to imagine the home as a site of fabulous or even fun feminist activity.[19]

In this regard, *The Feminine Mystique* played an enormously formative role in defining feminism among its fans and its critics, and in the popular imagination, as an anti-housewife phenomenon. Rhetorically, certainly, Friedan's argument aligned nicely with that of many white male intellectuals of the time who similarly equated the home with women and therefore characterized women as inferior.[20] Friedan set up the opposition between feminist and housewife, arguing as vociferously as anyone that the public world, the male world, the work of paid rather than unpaid work, trumped women's work in the home to such a degree that little further discussion of domestic life's ups or downs was warranted. Housewives who claimed to get any pleasure out of their roles would simply have been operating with what Friedan, during her years of involvement in leftist politics, might have labeled false consciousness.[21]

Friedan's reluctance to consider alternative arguments about women's home lives provided her detractors with evidence that she was not one of the women she purported to speak for. To some degree, they were right. Friedan had lived in the suburbs raising children for ten years, but during that time she both relied on hired help and worked as a freelance writer for women's magazines, neither of those a typical suburban housewife's practice, particularly in this era. Even she admitted, with no small measure of pride, that she was not one of the bored housewives whose grievances she documented. "As for me, I'm very unbored," she confessed right after the book's publication. "I'm nasty, I'm bitchy, I get mad, but by God, I'm absorbed in what I'm doing."[22]

Not everyone agreed that women had to be liberated entirely from their homemaking responsibilities. The chef Julia Child, to provide one example, also critiqued women's traditional roles and sought to improve their sense of self, but her vision did not include a directive to leave the home or even, for that matter, the kitchen. From her enormously popular television program *The French Chef,* which debuted the same year as *The Feminine Mystique,* through her subsequent book publications, Child acknowledged that cooking had been designated women's work, but she never considered it a deterrent to women's creativity. "This is a book for the servantless cook," she explained in the opening of *Mastering the Art of French Cooking,* "who can be unconcerned on occasion with budgets, waistlines, timetables, children's meals, or anything else which might interfere with the enjoyment of producing something wonderful to eat."[23] For Child, a refusal of elements of the housewife role did not necessitate a refusal of domesticity altogether.

Helen Gurley Brown's take on women's household responsibilities also differed from that of Betty Friedan. In part because Brown spoke in *Sex and the Single Girl* neither to nor for housewives, her arguments about the home received less attention as the second wave progressed. They proved formative, however, for young women readers who remained enamored of creating an independent and cozy space for themselves. They also proved lasting, more recently becoming recycled in third-wave feminist explorations of women's lives in which practices such as sewing and knitting become understood as feminist endeavors. Like Friedan, Brown subscribed to male cultural values in her dismissal of women's concerns about housework and children. She repeatedly referred to her single women as "superlative" and hence superior. She repeatedly mocked married women's suburban lifestyles and their dinner-party conversations. She found housewives decidedly not sexy, easily threatened, and often disingenuous. Nevertheless, although she disapproved of what she considered the drab and tiresome women who filled the ranks of housewives, Helen Gurley Brown believed her sexy single woman could reclaim the home and liberate herself within its walls.

Brown introduces the apartment in *Sex and the Single Girl,* for example, not as a deadened or deadening environment but rather as a vibrant, inspiring space, filled with touches unique to the singular single girl. "If you are to be a glamorous, sophisticated woman that exciting things happen to," she advises, "you need an apartment and you need to live in it alone!" Like the *Playboy* magazine bachelor invited to craft a private sphere free of women, Gurley's single woman is free to craft a space free of the debilitated spirit of the housewife. Brown states that the apartment, in the grand scheme of things, trumps even the man whose presence one occasionally hopes for in that space. "When your name comes up in conversation," she writes, "people will say with far more glowing admiration, 'That girl has the most divine apartment!' than they will ever say 'That girl has the most divine husband!'" Far from being awful because it belongs to a woman, the apartment draws status from the equation between femininity and domesticity and from the ownership women exercise. "One is something she created!" Brown says, again juxtaposing the apartment, which the woman can craft, and the husband, which she sadly enough cannot. "Think of yourself as a star sapphire," she instructs. "Your apartment is your setting."[24]

Betty Friedan complains in *The Feminine Mystique* about the "thing-ridden" houses in which postwar women feel isolated and trapped, but for Helen Gurley Brown, single women rightly focus on decorating, which makes their homes anything but alienating. They should stock their kitchens, purchase a few glamorous pieces of furniture, and paint their walls, preferably off-white ("Everything, including you, looks divine in them"). A woman may decorate her apartment or adorn her body with others, namely men, in mind, but the decision about whom she invites into the apartment and when remains entirely at her discretion. With lovers, for example, women should not feel compelled to use their home to "pay back" dinners out with dinners in: the "correct ratio," she writes, between dining on the town and in one's apartment, "is about twenty to one!" For a woman not engaged to the man in question, she continues, readily admitting that the notion of engagement itself is already a bit passé, "you don't really have to pay back dinner ever."

Bachelors must recognize that part of the price of their freedom and privilege is, quite simply, paying for women. "No use making their bachelorhood easy by feeding them like little mother," she admonishes. This kind of understated sexual reciprocity, which infuriated so many feminists, including Betty Friedan, was simply reality as far as Brown was concerned.

Taking it one step further and really cementing the notion that home life can be both blissful and blissfully female, Brown argues that the single girl, so singularly spectacular that she would enhance any environment into which she entered, can routinely if not permanently accept rather than extend invitations. As Brown puts it, cheering on her domestic but hardly domesticated reader, "Feel free to be America's guest!"[25]

Sex and the Single Girl also instructs the apartment dweller, who realizes or perhaps hopes that sex and not just sexual attraction may be among the activities that take place in the apartment, to decorate her abode with a man or prospective man in mind. Keep cigarettes and ashtrays on hand, she advises, and have a good but not great television set ("or you'll never get him out of your apartment"). Again, however, although she may have a man in mind, the apartment's occupant formulates the rules about any and all activities, including when and where sexual activity might occur. Negotiating this is not always easy, so Brown provides some specific advice. The apartment should be inviting, but not so much so that the woman loses control to a male guest and finds herself in danger: she discourages women from leaving lingerie strewn about or from placing mirrors on the bedroom ceiling. In *Sex and the Single Girl*, the home that validates women's independence and sensuality rather than threatens it is decidedly private rather than public space, inherently feminine rather than masculine, and well taken care of. In short, Helen Gurley Brown sees no reason for women to abandon the home. Her readers have the freedom to seek liberation from outdated ideas about womanhood without simultaneously giving up the notion of home or even the work that goes along with maintaining it. Brown's readers, of course, clean up after themselves.[26]

Helen Gurley Brown stands less clear about how her young, single, sexy women, should they wed, will translate this freedom of the hearth into something lasting. Brown would encourage women to find ways to keep not only creativity but also sensuality alive, to resist the creeping presence of boredom in the marital kitchen, living room, or bedroom. But would her liberated single women realistically or perhaps inevitably morph into Friedan's miserable marrieds, assuming the glum reality that ultimately unsatisfying housework portends? Brown, writing her advice before the release of Friedan's, and catering to a different audience, does not pretend to solve the "problem that has no name." She does, however, suggest that many women's dreams, contrary to Friedan's messages about a postwar uniformity of womanhood, include alternative, potentially liberating lifestyles. She also suggests that women who follow her formula for living a single life—that is, pursuing their work with a passion akin to the passion of romance; not waiting for marriage to enjoy sex; marrying later, if at all; and enjoying the freedoms femininity allows—will not end up as bored housewives in need of rescue. "Those who glom on to men so that they can collapse with relief, spend the rest of their days shining up their status symbol and figure they never have to reach, stretch, learn, grow, face dragons or make a living again are the ones to be pitied," she writes in the conclusion to *Sex and the Single Girl*. "They, in my opinion, are the unfulfilled ones."[27]

Another significant difference between the feminism of Helen Gurley Brown and that of Betty Friedan has to do with their conceptions of female agency and female victimization. Brown would express little tolerance for the victim position either imposed on or claimed by women, whom she saw as equal to men in the most fundamental ways: equally sexed, equally competent, equally capable of making decisions good and bad. Quite simply, as she saw it, women had responsibility for their own lives. "I am messianic on the subject," she writes. "Use your own guts and energy to improve yourself, your job, your intellect, and every other possible thing. You can't sleep your way to the top or even to the middle, and there is no such thing as a free lunch. You have to do it yourself, so you might as well get started." For all her advice about the joys of having men in women's lives, and for all the suggestions she offers about how to lure them there, Brown never considers men a substitute for truly living one's own independent life, even in marriage. No matter their humble circumstances or trying daily lives, she repeatedly encourages her readers to see themselves as capable and to reject wholesale well- or ill-meaning attempts to be cast as victims.[28]

Betty Friedan also encourages her readers to take charge, to make changes in their lives, to reject the rules under which women labor, and to construct life plans so they can live more independent and healthy lives. At the same time, however, in *The Feminine Mystique* and later, she promotes the woman-as-victim argument as much as or more than her ideology of self-help. For her, and then later for many other feminists influenced by her, women's victimization results from having been sold a lie, a duplicitous argument that femininity "is so mysterious and intuitive and close to the creation of life that man-made science may never be able to understand it." Following the directives that accompany such a narrow exploration of the possibilities of the female self, women come to believe that they can find fulfillment "only in sexual passivity, male domination, and nurturing maternal love."[29]

For Friedan, contemporary femininity proved little more than a trick, a lie that effectively infantilized women, making them prisoners inside their homes, marriages, and families. Friedan would highlight the notion of victimization and imprisonment, extending the metaphor as far as death and claiming that the economically comfortable American housewife could be compared with the millions of people exterminated in concentration camps in Europe during the Holocaust. Like other American Jewish writers in the 1950s and 1960s, she would employ Holocaust imagery to gain a popular hearing and further a liberal cause. In Friedan's case, she argued that the feminine mystique was a form of genocide, a mass burial of American women.[30] Only women who listened to her advice, who gave Betty Friedan rather than others this level of influence over their lives, could escape such dire futures and live autonomously.

Although Betty Friedan's notion of female victimization would prove lasting in its influence in the American feminist consciousness and feminist literature, it has not been without its critics. Nor was it uncontested when first published. Since the inception of the second wave of feminism, in fact, a variety of women, including working-class women and women of color, have rejected the notion that women are primarily victims. Helen Gurley Brown was in good, if somewhat ignored, company when she rallied against the victimization model. Resourceful and self-reliant working-class women, for example, could hardly sit back and weep while the world passed them by. Similarly, African American women and other women of color have steadfastly resisted not only oppression but also the victim label, however harsh their life circumstances.[31] More recently, young feminists have also rejected that label. One contemporary feminist describes herself and her peers this way: "Not anti-feminist at all, but also not: my body, myself / my lover left me and I am so sad / all my problems are caused by men / but watch me roar / what's happened to me is deadly serious / SOCIETY HAS GIVEN ME AN EATING DISORDER / A poor self esteem / A victim's perpetual fear / ...therefore I'm not responsible for my actions."[32] For many feminists, then, the victim position claimed by and for Friedan's class- and race-privileged readers would seem worthy of derision.

Sex and the Single Girl and *The Feminine Mystique* also differed in their discussions of female sexuality and sexual desire. Helen Gurley Brown was unequivocal in her argument that the pleasures of sex belonged to all women, single and married, and on terms of their choosing. At the insistence of her publisher, her focus was on heterosexual women, but she believed adamantly that sexual freedom applied to all women and located a disturbingly similar hypocrisy at work in the denial of lesbian desire and of single heterosexual women's desire.[33] In *Sex and the Single Girl,* sexy and sexually satisfied women are those who support themselves, enjoy men and male company but do not depend on it for survival, and enjoy sex, sexual desire, and, to some degree, being objectified sexually. Brown encouraged women to explore on their own and then present themselves to men as independent, desirous, sexual adults. "There are plenty of differences in the sexes," she argues, "but I don't think basic desire would be one of them."[34]

Brown acknowledges that what she considers natural and appropriate expressions of that desire, others would consider an ascendancy of the "sluttish element" in women. Always ready to point out sexual duplicity, she agrees that perhaps previously unknown levels of sexual purposefulness among women had come to the fore. "However," she stated in an interview, "is there a husband moving among you who does not secretly like the 'sluttish element' in women?"[35] In *The Feminine Mystique,* Friedan would prove far less sex-friendly, viewing sex as one of the elements of a deadened life, a practice pathologically unrewarding for women. Hardly a source of their liberation, sexual practices in the postwar period, as far as Friedan could tell, reduced women to "sex creatures, sex-seekers," who participated not in erotic and autonomous adventures but rather in a "strangely joyless national compulsion."[36]

In *The Feminine Mystique,* what begins as an attack on Freudian notions of womanhood and the cult of femininity turns into a general attack on female sexuality. Female promiscuity, as defined in her day, emerges in the book as a sign of unhealthy repression, twisted to the point of a self-damaging practice, rather than as a potential solution to female oppression. The woman who in *Sex and the Single Girl* finds sexual engagement rewarding may be the same woman who, in *The Feminine Mystique,* desperately and unsuccessfully attempts to meet other, unfulfilled needs through sex. Helen Gurley Brown asks her readers, "Would it surprise you to know that your most wicked and base thoughts—secret fantasies—even leanings to homosexuality, are not unusual, and should not alarm you?"[37] Betty Friedan would likely have disagreed. The real answer for Friedan is female identity, not sexuality, and unlike Brown, Friedan effectively severs sexuality from identity.[38] What Friedan identifies as the "American preoccupation" with sex is, arguably, the same acknowledgment of female sexuality that Helen Gurley Brown both relishes and promotes. Friedan imagines an opposition between the mind and the libido and views sex as an obstacle to women's full development.[39]

One issue that raised the ire of many second-wave feminists was that of woman as sexual object. Too many women dressed in uncomfortable clothing and impossibly high shoes, wore makeup, and behaved in seemingly narcissistic but arguably self-denigrating ways in order to attract men. All of this appeared particularly disempowering to many feminists, who actively attempted to discourage women from such practices. As Helen Gurley Brown and her working-class readers would have been quick to realize, however, castigating women for dressing for success in a male world denied the realities, if not also the desires, of the women who had no choice but to wear makeup and dresses, do their hair, and shave their legs for work. To be fair, Betty Friedan would have little to say about such practices specifically in *The Feminine Mystique,* and she did engage in such practices in her own life, but she would certainly complain about Helen Gurley Brown's objectification of women in *Cosmopolitan,* considering it obscene. "Instead of urging women to live a broader life," she argued about the magazine and, by extension, about Brown, "it is an immature teenage-level sexual fantasy. It is the idea that woman is nothing but a sex object, that [she] is nothing without a man, and there is nothing in life but bed, bed, bed." For Friedan, what Helen Gurley Brown actually expressed for or about women was not respectful or celebratory but was instead suffused with "utter contempt."[40]

For her part, Brown expressed little tolerance for the anti-sex-object position some second-wave feminists promoted. "If you're not a sex object," she stated plainly, "you're in trouble." Among the best things in life, she maintained, is having someone want you sexually. "You can't get anybody to bed unless you are the object of sexual desire," she writes, "so there is nothing wrong with being a sex object. He is your sex object. It works both ways."[41] If a woman used cosmetics, or clothing, or a particular way of walking to make herself the object of desire, all the better. Naturalness, according to Brown, was highly overrated. In the end, Friedan saw danger where Brown saw fun. Trapped in an immature sexual state, Friedan's housewives never fully reached maturity. Voicing an argument that would become popular among feminists, Friedan would state that sexual desire could not actually be claimed or experienced by women living in conditions such as those faced by her contemporaries. Incapable of managing their desire, women instead became managed by it. For Brown, sex and identity could not be disentangled within the human female; for Friedan, they seemingly could not be joined.[42] Sex, in all its guises, appealed to Helen Gurley Brown. Sex, in any of its guises, seemed to frighten rather than inspire Betty Friedan.

After the publication of *The Feminine Mystique,* it was inevitable that journalists would ask Helen Gurley Brown to comment on it. In one instance, "It's very sound" formed the extent of Brown's tepid response. This reporter then pushed Brown to comment on *Playboy* magazine, and her tone changed as she declared *Playboy* "terrific, absolutely first-rate."[43] In part Brown may have been responding to what she saw as the dour feminist response to her own celebrations of female sexuality. In part, too, she preferred to see women as sexual actors rather than as sexually acted upon, even if they acted in a venue like *Playboy,* and she would repeatedly refuse a feminism that demanded victims. Many would argue that *Playboy* simply made women sexual victims, but Brown would not see it that way. Any discussion of women that failed to acknowledge sexuality, in all its subtle or loud dimensions, provided its own form of victimization. In short, where Friedan saw empowerment through identity, and identity as intellectual rather than sexual, Brown saw empowerment, first and foremost, through a connection with the body and its naturally sexual existence.

Brown would publicly and then privately attempt to find commonalities with Friedan, particularly around the issue of work. "Frankly, I haven't been able to convince anybody so far but Betty Friedan that women should have jobs," she wrote, "and you know every time she says roughly the same thing in her own way she gets her head chopped off."[44] Friedan would prove less desirous of seeing herself in the same category as Brown, and her denial of Brown's feminism would prove instrumental in fostering a cultural dismissal of Brown's sex-friendly, performance-friendly, capitalist-friendly philosophy for many years. Nevertheless, Brown's agenda continued to exist side by side with more radical forms of feminism, only to reemerge in full force, decades later, as something called the third wave.

Although they rarely shared a platform either physically or metaphorically, and they were constantly contrasted in the media and in interpretations of feminist history, Brown and Friedan would privately and tentatively court each other. "Dear Mrs. Friedan," Brown wrote in 1963, "I wanted you to know how much I admire you and your work." She told Friedan that she incessantly promoted *The Feminine Mystique* while on tour for her own book, saying, "I know my publisher wonders sometimes whose book I'm selling." Perhaps because Helen Gurley Brown broke the ice, or perhaps because she had already been planning to do so, Betty Friedan wrote back and attempted to further secure a relationship. She refrained from extending the same level of praise for *Sex and the Single Girl* that Brown had offered for *The Feminine Mystique*, but she thanked Brown for her kind words and then got to her point: did Brown have any suggestions for how she might interest someone in a movie dramatization of *The Feminine Mystique?* "If you have any thoughts as to someone who might be helpful to talk to about this....I would certainly appreciate your dropping me a line at the Beverly Hills." Brown responded immediately, providing contact information for a literary agent in Beverly Hills who was a good friend of the Browns.[45] Like Helen Gurley Brown, Betty Friedan, feminist, hoped not only for liberation for women but also for a bit of fame and fortune for herself. And just as Friedan attempted to cast a wider net, in the aftermath of the publication of *The Feminine Mystique*, Brown, too, wasted no time, in the wake of her success with *Sex and the Single Girl*, in looking for additional opportunities to keep her own name, face, and written work in the public eye.

7

packaging a message—
and a messenger

elen Gurley Brown's youthful longing for money, plenty of it, matured
into an adult yearning for even more of it. "Work is where the money
is—and money is lovely," she wrote in an outline of her second book,
Sex and the Office. "[I] am getting annoyed," she continued, "with people
who try to shush me about money. They're making excuses for not having worked to hit the jackpot or are terribly rich already!" David Brown,
encouraged by the phenomenal success of *Sex and the Single Girl,* equally
desirous of seeing Helen earn tremendous amounts of money, and savvy
to the commercial worlds in which they operated, set to work immediately
to sell the message (single girls are sexy and wonderful) and the messenger
(Helen Gurley Brown). "In a sense," Helen would claim about David, "I'm
a product of his imagination." And David's imaginings, when it came to
branding Helen or the "Sex and the..." theme, appeared limitless.[1]

With Bernard Geis's support, David urged Helen to explore every commercial venue he could think of: additional books, record albums, a film,
a syndicated newspaper column, television sit-coms, television talk shows,
even an adult board game. The only offer Helen seemed to reject outright

was that she host a nightclub act.[2] *Sex and the Single Girl* had become, David Brown wrote to an executive at the toy manufacturer Milton Bradley, "an industry in itself," one that could spawn an adult game without too much difficulty. "While I am not a game specialist," he asserted, "it seems to me that something along the order of Monopoly could be devised. The promotion opportunities are fabulous." Although that project never got off the ground, the possibilities nevertheless appeared limitless. Financially lucrative opportunities implicit in the "sex and the...." theme became obvious to others as well, including the psychologist Albert Ellis, who took advantage of the brand and published *Sex and the Single Man* in 1963. The Browns immediately sued him, with some success. David Brown kept one eye out for commercial opportunities and another for what he considered trademark transgressions. It was a busy time.[3]

Perhaps the most lucrative project, or at least the one that ensured the most profit for the least effort, occurred when the Brown–Brown–Geis trio sold the film rights for *Sex and the Single Girl* to Warner Brothers for two hundred thousand dollars. Saul David, a producer and friend of the Browns, brokered the deal, but it became vastly complicated as studio executives realized the difficulty of turning that particular book into a film. Saul David ran into one studio executive who complained that the book had no plot. "I told you that a hundred thousand dollars ago," David quipped, reminding his colleague that they had purchased a sexy title more than anything else. The lack of plot led to a string of screenwriters who failed, until Joseph Heller, of *Catch-22* fame, eventually wrote a workable screenplay. His work, however, was based not on *Sex and the Single Girl* but on another book entirely, Joseph Hoffman's *How to Make Love and Like It,* the tale of a thirty-five-year-old virgin anthropologist who had written a best-seller on sex. Things grew increasingly complicated because the writer David Schwartz had already tried this tack, so when the film was released, the publicity read, somewhat convolutedly, "Based on the book *Sex and the Single Girl* by Helen Gurley Brown. Screenplay by David R. Schwartz and Joseph Heller. Story by Joseph Hoffman."

In the end, other than its title and the fact that the main character was called Helen Gurley Brown, the film had nothing in common with the book. For her part, the real Helen Gurley Brown graciously stayed out of all film-related issues once she received her royalty payment. "They paid me a fantastic sum for my book," she told *Cosmopolitan*. "You should leave movies in the hands of people who know what they are doing." With an all-star cast including Natalie Wood, Tony Curtis, Henry Fonda, and

Lauren Bacall, the film succeeded in keeping Helen's book title in public view for the next several years. It also, as people continued to joke years later, netted Helen Gurley Brown forty thousand dollars a word, one clear result of successful branding.[4]

Still employed at Kenyon & Eckhardt in the immediate aftermath of *Sex and the Single Girl,* Brown found herself drawn to projects she could fit into her workaday world. A record album invitation promised another significant payoff and appealed to her right away—well, almost right away. When Gene Norman of Crescendo Records asked Brown to consider reading *Sex and the Single Girl* aloud for an album, her first reaction was incredulity. Who would listen, she wondered, when the book was already widely available in print? "People who don't like to read," he answered frankly, and Brown agreeably signed on. But the Browns discovered that Warner Brothers retained recording rights to *Sex and the Single Girl,* even though the company had not exploited them, so Helen had to draft new material for the album. The end result was *Lessons in Love,* with *How to Love a Girl* on Side A, and *How to Love a Man* on Side B. Brown seems to have dumbed things down for a prospective male audience. "I'm a lucky girl, that's who *I* am," the cover blurb begins. "Last year I wrote a book called *Sex and the Single Girl* (a girlish, gurgling, non-literary kind of thing) which became a best-seller." She conspiringly admits that she did not intentionally write a best-seller, but since people seem to agree with her views she has emerged again, with a great many opinions "and almost unlimited nerve."[5]

The material in *Lessons in Love* may be new, but the advice to women on Side B is largely reminiscent of the advice Brown had proffered only months earlier in *Sex and the Single Girl.* She describes how to talk to a man in bed, how to love a boss (platonically, preferably), how to say no to a man ("who looked great on the cruise but awful ashore") and how to say yes to a married lover (carefully, so as not to get caught). She hones right in on the gender inequities that keep women vulnerable and advises women to seize control of their sexuality, and her words and tone maintain her characteristically odd mixture of strength and coquettishness. "We're supposed to have lost our femininity and robbed men of their masculinity," she states emphatically. "It's so silly!" Either having grown a bit more comfortable with married life herself, or understanding that her target audience had come to include both married and single women, Brown includes as a finale "How to Love Your Husband and Nobody Else," in which she advises married women, all of whom have paired up with imperfect men, to make one of two choices: divorce, or better, accept that her mate won't be meeting all her needs and that ultimately only she can do that.

The most significant difference between *Sex and the Single Girl* and *Lessons in Love,* and perhaps what marked the record as a failed endeavor from the start, is that this time Helen Gurley Brown deliberately targeted a male audience. Much of the material on the album cover seems addressed specifically to men, and the advice to women is relegated to Side B. On Side A, Brown instructs men how to have an affair "and live happily ever after," how to behave at home if "misbehaving away from home," how to get the most from their secretary (keep it platonic), and how to say no to a girl (their mother, a girl who wants to marry them, etc.). An odd piece called "Little Man, You'll Have a Busy Day," addresses short men and their supposed insecurities, encouraging them to act big even if they do not stand tall. The most interesting elements of Side A, however, explore women's continued economic vulnerability in relationships, which Helen Gurley Brown's honesty can do only so much to mitigate and which men as an audience may have been loath to hear about, particularly on an album that promised salacious rather than serious fare.

Brown takes the opportunity of having secured a male audience to state directly what she could only muse about hopefully to her female audience in *Sex and the Single Girl*. She advised a man having an affair, for example, to give his lover gifts, lots of them. "Money is a perfectly wonderful present," she says, "not half as insulting as you'd like to think." The authoritative voice she gained through the success of *Sex and the Single Girl* provides Brown the confidence to speak directly about matters she could only half-joke about earlier: "A readily negotiable share of General Motors or U.S. E Bond tucked in with a bottle of Arpège is something few girls will find offensive." Unlike other feminists among her peers, who would attempt to eliminate such sexual and economic exchanges between the sexes, Brown views the imbalance as one that requires a recalibration rather than a rejection. In her view, men who earn the wealth ought to share it, and who better to partake of such benefits than the women who share their sexual pleasures. Given the blinding nature of their privilege, men, she believes, will not arrive at such a practical stance without explicit guidance.

The album contains another piece that seems incongruous, given its adults-only labeling and seemingly sex-driven definition of the "love" requiring "lessons." The final address to men, "How to Love Your Wife and Nobody Else," encourages men who love their wives to foster in those women personal growth, the pursuit of higher education, and work outside the home. She anticipates their concerns or objections and rallies them to her cause. "About the children," she instructs, "they need a mother's love…not necessarily a mother's care 24 hours a day." Brown praises available childcare options and argues that even if a woman's salary pays only for childcare and housekeeping support, it is money well spent. "You won't lose her by letting her go," she counsels. "So encourage her to be the smartest, sexiest, wittiest, brightest person she can be…and that means to other men, too. She'll worship you for it."

In retrospect, such unquestionably feminist messages, targeted at men who may well have expected something far more sexy, and certainly something far less pedantic, may have been responsible for the decidedly poor album sales for *Lessons in Love*. When Brown subsequently proposed writing an entire book called *How to Love a Girl*, Letty Cottin nixed the idea, arguing explicitly that men did not view themselves as needing advice about courting women. Women, she agreed, would purchase a book with *How to Love a Man* as a title.[6] This proved a hard lesson for Helen Gurley Brown, who felt she had the answers for men and women both, but this reality ultimately resonated with her own internal sensibilities. Men remained in decision-making positions in relationships, in part at least because of financial inequalities between the sexes. Women could not change that overnight, if they could change it at all, but they could address it with deliberation. *Lessons in Love* attempted, with limited success, to inculcate men with new ways of behaving through a mix of sexiness and sermon. Most men apparently felt less than enamored with Helen Gurley Brown's sermonizing.

Lessons in Love netted only $376 in royalties for the first three months of 1963, and $88 for the second three months. In all, the album sold more than ten thousand copies and netted Helen a few thousand dollars. The Browns acknowledged that the project had not met expectations, but they considered it a "working formula" and hoped to follow it up with a more lucrative successor. "We have done quite a bit of soul-searching about the last album," David wrote to Gene Norman a year later, pushing the idea of a second album. "With your help and guidance, we are sure we can come up with a winner."[7] They worked for some time on David's proposed *Helen Gurley Brown's Vacation Kit for Lovers*, but this album stalled somewhere in production. Helen did eventually produce a second album, *Helen Gurley Brown at Town Hall*, a recording of one of her popular talks, but it generated little attention. As a result, having learned their lesson about identifying and pursuing a clear audience, Helen and David decided that with Helen's next big venture, a syndicated newspaper column, they would turn once again to women, a more certain audience for her unique and uniquely delivered messages. As we will see, they achieved far more substantial success.

Through all of this, the Brown–Brown–Geis trio found other ways to keep Helen in the spotlight, and these included the exhausting cross-country and international book tours Letty Cottin organized through Geis Associates. In addition to such deliberate publicity efforts, Helen received innumerable invitations to give talks, write magazine pieces, and make guest appearances on television. Many who extended invitations requested the standard Helen Gurley Brown pitch, with which she grew increasingly comfortable onstage. She delivered her sex-friendly, singles-friendly message at the first annual Summer Singles Rendezvous at Grossinger's resort in the Catskills, at several Parents without Partners meetings, at women's club meetings, even at Catholic women's organization gatherings. She provided snippets of her philosophy in innumerable magazine and newspaper interviews.

At other times she had to respond to unnerving requests that she modify her message to suit the needs of different audiences. *McCall's* magazine invited her to slant a piece toward accelerating husband hunting for those who had begun to feel desperate. Brown declined. "I'm not sure how I feel about giving advice to girls about getting married because I so fervently feel they shouldn't try," she wrote, "and they should concentrate on everything but and then it may happen."[8] Similarly, the *Saturday Evening Post* invited her to write a piece titled "Sex and the Married Woman." Again, Brown demurred: "I don't think married women are sexy, per se—at least not to their husbands—and I couldn't begin to take the same approach for them that I would for single girls, but I do think there are certain efforts they should make along this line toward remaining sexy, period."[9] Brown tried to maintain the integrity of a position that others saw as inherently contradictory. Yes, women wanted to get married; yes, men featured prominently on the list of desirable things in life; yes, women should seek out men's attentions, using their feminine wiles as needed. Nevertheless, she always asserted, adamantly, the best way to do that was to focus first on the self and only second on the man.

Helen's scores of appearances helped keep sales of *Sex and the Single Girl* steady, but she and her publicity team recognized that they had to do more both to keep her engaged and to keep the money coming in. Most of her appearances netted money only indirectly, through sales of her book, and Helen, who quit her job at Kenyon & Eckhardt in November 1962 in order to go on extended book tours, desired a more direct source of income. The idea of a syndicated newspaper column appealed both to Helen and to David, who saw her as increasingly overburdened by the cultural responsibilities inherent in being the author of *Sex and the Single Girl*. Helen had become inundated with fan mail from readers, who not only sang her praises but also solicited her advice on specific issues and problems. Between answering fan mail and traveling, she was beginning to feel quite fatigued. She had signed a three-book contract with Bernard Geis but struggled to find the energy or the time to explore potential book ideas for a significant writing project.

If she had her own newspaper column, the Browns reasoned, Helen could answer fans' questions far more efficiently and profitably than she could by staying home and writing each individual a letter, and she could keep her name in the public consciousness until she turned out that second book. She might also, they realized, earn as much as a hundred thousand dollars a year from syndication rights. Admittedly, this new project promised far less than the forty thousand dollars per word Helen netted from selling the title of *Sex and the Single Girl* to Warner Brothers, but the steady publicity and the equally steady income proved too tempting to resist. The timing proved beneficial in unexpected ways as well, as Helen and David, who had taken a job at New American Library, moved to New York City soon after she signed the contract. A newspaper column was, after all, portable employment.

With David's assistance, Helen secured a generous contract with the Times-Mirror Corporation, publisher of the *Los Angeles Times*. Signed in January 1963, the contract specified that Helen would write a column three times a week and retain all rights to any commercial ventures that emerged from the project. The *Times* secured the right to publish the columns as a book if it so wished. Brown earned 50 percent of the gross revenue from syndication sales, and she soon appeared in about fifty newspapers nationwide. In the end, she earned about a thousand dollars a month on the column, far less than initially anticipated.

Helen had initially proposed *Frankly Female* as the column's title, but they eventually agreed on *Woman Alone*. Helen limited her intended audience with a column specifically targeting single women, but she realized that many divorced and widowed women, in addition to the legions of never-married, sought her advice, and together these women numbered twenty-four million, a sizable reading public. And after all, she had never quite fit in with the married crowd, even if she attempted to reach them with *Lessons in Love*. She was now back in familiar territory. Playing with the slogan of the staid *Ladies' Home Journal*, "Never Underestimate the Power of a Woman!" Brown suggested that her slogan ought to be "Never Underestimate the Power of a Woman Alone!"[10]

Brown's first column, "Calling All Widows, Divorcées, Bachelor Girls," and the second, "New Glamour Girl of Our Time," defined with clarity her intended audience, her admiration for this group, and the seriousness with which she approached her cause. As the publicity charged, no single voice for single women, save "the undisputed champion," Helen Gurley Brown, had emerged in recent years. She would continue the work she had started in *Sex and the Single Girl*, now with a personal approach and a loyal devotion to her equally loyal followers. Relying on a familiar formula, Brown immediately appointed not predatory or noncommittal men but married women as the sorry counterpoint to her sexy girls. As early as the second column, she suggested that single women of all stripes, a sophisticated set, head out into the world to charm. From their mouths, thankfully, one could expect "not one syllable about a new recipe for banana bread and tricks for getting candle wax out of table linens or that perennial favorite, toilet training." Brown went a step further than insulting married women, labeling them disingenuous in their negative sentiments about their single sisters. "These detractors are often women themselves who are trying to justify a different way of life—suburbia and domesticity—with which they possibly have become disenchanted. They criticize single women because they're just a little bit jealous," Brown opined, incorporating some of Betty Friedan's rhetoric and inviting controversy in her first week on the job.[11]

Over the course of the next two years, Helen Gurley Brown wrote this thrice-weekly column, focusing on issues such as vacationing alone, the importance of good nutrition, the value of volunteer work, the necessity of paid work, how to deal with people who pity your single state, the trials of obtaining child support, enjoying being forty and older, raising children alone, the value of psychiatry, women and alcoholism, stretching meager incomes, the value of raw ambition, and of course, meeting men.[12] She expanded the range of her audience beyond the fairly young crowd she had addressed in *Sex and the Single Girl*, noting that "a girl of 35, 45 or older shouldn't worry about getting married." In one column she defends a sixty-two-year old woman who, contrary to the wishes of her children, refuses to marry her suitor and wants only to "stay friends." Good for her, says Brown, and too bad for her children, who "will have no choice but to have their teeth recapped when they grind them down over this mother who may sound frivolous but who very much knows her own mind." In another column a fifty-four-year-old woman involved with a twenty-nine-year-old man similarly receives Helen Gurley Brown's blessing. If he isn't marriage material, the woman isn't wasting her time. Instead, "she's getting an adventure out of her system that may make her better able to make a happy marriage when the right man arrives!"[13]

Brown used the column to acknowledge the realities of divorced women, particularly single mothers, whom she realized were trying to raise their children in emotionally and often economically challenging circumstances. In living without a man, she states encouragingly in one column, women can learn to meet their own emotional needs and grow more than they had within their obviously problematic relationships. Identifying with these women's often meager financial circumstances, Brown urges them to hold their heads high. Single mothers ought not worry too much about their children, who will get by without the money fathers all too often withhold. "When we don't have a husband to depend on and to support us, we are forced to become more dynamic and self-sufficient," she writes. "As for your children, money to burn never built a child's character or even made him any happier, so far as we know." In another column Brown provides practical advice for actively dating single mothers that resonates with the financial schemes in her earlier, unpublished writings: she explains that women should always find a way to make their dates pay for babysitters. Be sure to invite the man in at the end of the night, she instructs, and then in his presence say, "How much do I owe you, Mrs. Clompkins?" While you rummage around in your purse, Brown explains, "any gentleman who is one will take care of the bill." Following that, of course, he can give the babysitter a lift home.[14]

All women, divorced or widowed, young or old, working girl or professional career woman, Brown states repeatedly, must put their energies into their work and their selves—and occasionally shake things up—in order to live rewarding lives. Given the shortage of eligible men (a theme Brown repeats throughout her career, often citing statistics), the most often appropriate but sometimes excessively high standards of women, simple bad luck, or deliberate choice, some women may never marry, but single status, when lived out by ambitious, hardworking, and positively selfish women, can be blissful. And single life, in Brown's world, inevitably includes rather than excludes men. In fact, she repeatedly intimates, if she does not state it outright, that men will flock to just those women who follow her advice for superlative living, single-style.

A great many of the columns explore how this works for women of a range of different identities. In "A Shade of Difference," Brown reports on her interview with Marilyn Hainsworth, an African American woman who lives alone, has pursued an exciting career in private philanthropy, and either fends off or welcomes those in her surfeit of admirers. In an early example of second-wave feminist analysis that equates the "woman question" with the "Negro question," Brown argues that neither group stands in society only as victims. "No more than Negroes can be lumped into one miserable, pitiable, downtrodden collection can women alone be either," she writes. "Many of both colors do superlatively well, thank you." Brown continues her individualist approach to life, arguing vehemently that race, class, and age distinctions aside, the single American woman has got it all going on. "You can have almost anything," she states emphatically in her final *Woman Alone* column, "anything you want out of life if you work like a wharf-rat at everything you take on."[15]

Helen Gurley Brown's contract with the *Times Mirror* stipulated that if ever, for four consecutive weeks, her income from the column amounted to less than three hundred dollars a week, either party could terminate the agreement. By the beginning of 1965, Brown was averaging less than five hundred dollars a month, and she decided to quit. Not surprisingly, given the relatively short run of the column, the Times Mirror Corporation chose not to reprint the *Woman Alone* collection as a book. Initially a wildly controversial endeavor, defending the single woman grew increasingly mainstream following the publication of *Sex and the Single Girl* and other events of the early 1960s, including the introduction of the birth control pill and the launch of singles bars, clubs, and vacations designed especially for singles.

Nevertheless, Berney Geis did have that three-book contract with Brown, and collecting the columns seemed a relatively effortless publishing task with potentially strong returns, given the enormous success of *Sex and the Single Girl*. The result, *Outrageous Opinions*, featured roughly half of the published columns and a book cover that promoted Helen Gurley Brown, once again, as a renegade author. "Helen Gurley Brown's new book should be required reading for every female over the age of consent," claimed Jacqueline Susann in bold print on the back cover, linking Brown with Berney Geis's other female blockbuster author. Susann, who would become most famous for *Valley of the Dolls* a few years later, had already established a reputation with *Every Night, Josephine!*, a nonfiction book about her beloved pet poodle.[16]

Subtitled "The Games Men and Women Play," and inviting in "career girls," "maiden aunts," "go-go girls," "plain Janes," "spring chickens," and "sprung chickens," *Outrageous Opinions* offers Helen Gurley Brown's opinions on the "Single State," which she considers "a nice place to love if you live every minute of it," but the book also provides "some zingy, swingy tips on what to do—and how to do it—if you're ready to quit paddling your own canoe." Unlike the *Woman Alone* column as a whole, which emphasized work, leisure time, children, dating, feminism, and women's bodies, all with an eye toward female life satisfaction, and featuring a secondary if significantly present subtext about attracting men, the published collection is more focused on a "ways to get a man" rubric. Even her opening columns, which argue that single women are just fine "as is," thank you, are provided a peculiar subheading here: "How to Get with It (and Him)."

Other themes Brown emphasized in the syndicated column, most conspicuously work and money, became less pressing in the published collection, and some compelling columns from the series were simply excised. In one *Woman Alone* column, "Make Your Job Bring More Happiness Units," Brown had encouraged all working women to envision themselves eventually moving into better-paying jobs. No one, she stated, including elevator operators, hotel maids, or house maids, should see herself as existing outside of a framework in which she might climb some kind of job ladder. In "The Proper Attitude about Money," Brown had described how a male reader had stopped her on the street to complain about her "mercenary" approach to women, men, and money. "I do plead guilty," she explained, "to encouraging girls to respect money and try to get their share of it sometime in their lives."[17] Brown appears, for commercial reasons, or perhaps simply for the ease of attributing a theme to the somewhat disparate collection of newspaper columns, to have succumbed to the invitation to put the snaring of and caring for men in an even more central position than she had in the column. She continued to struggle with the dilemma she set up for herself: how to argue that women ought to live their lives for themselves and not worry about marriage while simultaneously acknowledging and celebrating the importance men hold in women's lives.

After some back and forth about a third book, to be titled *Sex and Marriage,* Helen and Berney Geis agreed that Helen would instead write a book on the second topic with which she could claim significant expertise:

the work world. It was true, of course, that marriage and domesticity remained strong goals for young women coming of age in the early 1960s and reading *Sex and the Single Girl*. Many, if not most, of them could have used advice about how to have sexually satisfying married lives. The same could be said of their older, already married sisters. It is equally true, however, that more and more of these women were projected to remain employed not only after marriage but also after having children. Married women's employment rose by 42 percent in the 1950s, so that by 1960 the majority of working women were married. Forty percent of those workers were also mothers. Most were employed in office jobs, the workplace most familiar to Helen Gurley Brown.[18]

The office, then, seemed an appropriate setting for Brown's next "sex and the..." undertaking. "We are beginning to get fervent letters addressed to you from single girls who consider your book the answer to a maiden's prayer," Geis wrote Brown, just after the release of *Sex and the Single Girl*, counseling her to start another book right away. "While not all your fans are office girls, most of them are. We should strike while the ardor is hot— like in April or May of 1963, not wait until 1964."[19] Helen, with her self-proclaimed "suicidal, masochistic, nihilistic streak," agreed, even though she was writing her syndicated column in addition to giving talks and making talk-show appearances to sell *Sex and the Single Girl*.[20]

Ingeniously, Brown used her many appearances both to hawk *Sex and the Single Girl* and to invite audience members to prepare themselves for her next big hit. "I really picked one hell of a subject," she argued about her upcoming book during one talk, "suggesting not only that women have a better life when they work in a job they get paid for but also that they are sexier." Sex and the office was not, in fact, a new topic, since Brown covered it deliberately and well in *Sex and the Single Girl*, in her syndicated column, and in virtually every live appearance she made, but she found a way to differentiate between the first book project and the second. "For two years beating the drum about 'single girls are wonderful,'" read the notes for this same speech. "Have a new drum...women who work are wonderful—even includes some married women, whom I usually consider maybe the dullest girls God ever put down anywhere."[21]

With her second book, Helen Gurley Brown went right to the heart of office dynamics, including sexual politics. In the early days of the corporate world, in the late nineteenth and early twentieth centuries, the metaphor for the secretary–boss relationship was that of father and son: the fatherly boss would both mentor and lean on the younger employee.

By Helen Gurley Brown's day, when secretaries were almost exclusively women, many working women replicated their relationships with their husbands, acting like office wives to their bosses.[22] Supposedly, these virtuous working women hardly had to fend off predatory bosses, as gentlemen populated one employment rank and ladies the other, but those women would have done so if conditions had warranted. After all, women, everyone agreed, ultimately held the reins where sexual activity was concerned. Both the world of the corporate office and that of women changed significantly in the postwar period, however, as women teemed out of bus and train stations everywhere, much as they teemed out of Grand Central Station in the opening pages of Rona Jaffe's *As Good As It Gets,* into the thousands of offices in midtown Manhattan and elsewhere.

Given her interests in sex, money, and work, and the ways in which women negotiated the three, the office provided more than adequate fodder for Brown's second book. The glamour of the working girl, after all, resulted in large part from her proximity to the men who had power, and married or not, as Brown well knew, those powerful men and those aspiring and sexy women often entered into flirtations, if not actual sexual relationships. Stating plainly that she documented rather than invented, Brown shifted the boss–secretary metaphor, substantially and irrevocably, from husband–wife to lover–lover. Whether or not bosses and secretaries actually acted out the sexual element of their relationships, sexual energy charged through all of the workplaces in which Helen Gurley Brown had resided. With her guidance, astute bosses and equally astute employees could both recognize and learn to negotiate the energy that was arguably more dangerous when ignored than when acknowledged.[23]

Other social commentators who recognized and called attention to the same shift in office dynamics most often did so in one of two ways, neither of which appealed to Brown. On the one hand, the moralists among them attempted to control women's sexuality by frightening or shaming women into behaving appropriately. Conversely, the celebrants among them most often, through lurid language and misogynistic images, and in such venues as pornographic magazines or *Playboy* magazine, mocked the working girl, depicting the sex-starved, seductive secretary and the hapless married boss in one set of scenarios or the lecherous old man and the innocent, bosomy young woman in another.[24] What made Brown's take unique was not only that she stated the terms of the game explicitly but also that she argued that sex often made for improved rather than degraded workplaces not only for men but for women. More, not less, work would be done by more generally satisfied, or perhaps satiated, employees. As she had argued in *Sex and the Single Girl*, "Managements who think romances lower the work output are right out of their skulls. A girl in love with her boss will knock herself out seven days a week and wish there were more days. Tough on her but fabulous for business!"[25]

In *Sex and the Office*, Helen Gurley Brown elaborates on many of the themes she had introduced earlier: openness about women's sexuality is healthy and necessary, the office is a decidedly sexy environment, and women can work the system there, as they do in the world of dating, by using their sexual seductiveness and even prowess to get ahead. "You see, I don't think it's wrong to use your sex appeal and femininity to get ahead on a job," she writes. "In fact, I can't think of a better way to do it!"[26] But as sexual as Brown's secretary may have been, she made her own decisions about her sexual activity. She was not the "sexretary" of bawdy humor but, instead, a sexually curious female worker.

Given her goals, Brown attempts in *Sex and the Office* to address the easy questions in quick order so that she can get to more complicated fare. In a draft of the book, she explains that her first purpose is to speak to and then move beyond those people who believe women should not work. She requests that her response, "Bullshit," be placed in bold type in the text. For Brown, the realities about women's need to work for pay are so clear that they hardly require justification. Work is where men, money, satisfaction, recognition, fame, sanity, and exposure to new worlds reside. "You never know when lightning might strike," she explains, but it is far more likely to strike in the workplace than it is in the shelter of the home. In the published version, which leaves out the "bullshit" in favor of a more extended analysis, Brown states that, rather than "harangue" those women at home who have come to believe the standard nonsense about women and work, she will allow working mothers to speak for themselves.

In two of the book's case studies, "Christine" and "Sally" reveal the struggles but also the myriad benefits available not only to working women themselves but also to their families. Remarkably prescient, Brown's Sally reveals that it is not "the amount of time you spend with your children that counts, it's the quality of the time." Neither woman apologizes for her selfishness, but each is well aware that people expect her to. Work provides a grounding and a sense of self, Brown believes, which prove necessary for all women "married or single, mothers or childless, grandmothers or ingénues." As she writes in the conclusion to *Sex and the Office*, "Whether their job is good or bad, women in offices never have to search for their identity and wonder who they are."[27]

Sex and the Office was, regardless of its similarities to *Sex and the Single Girl*, a new book, and Brown attempted to use her recently gained commercial clout to include controversial material that had been excised from the previous volume. When he edited *Sex and the Single Girl*, Bernard Geis convinced her to take out several references to abortion that she had included in the manuscript. Abortion remained illegal in the United States throughout the 1960s, and a virtual endorsement of an illegal practice as early as 1962 could arguably have created problems for the book, its author, and its publisher. Strongly pro-choice and keenly aware of the double standard in place about men's and women's sexual behavior and sexual responsibilities, Brown never forgot the sting of injustice she felt in making those excisions.

When she undertook her second book project, she attempted again to be true to her own inclinations about matters sexual, and her drafts of *Sex and the Office*, and a series of letters between Helen and Berney Geis, reveal that in this case the distance between Brown's predilections and Geis's directives had widened even more. Left to her own devices with *Sex and the Office*, Helen Gurley Brown would have crafted a far more radical exploration of the nature of female ambition, female sexuality, and the hazards of dating life in the early 1960s. The book offered, as its cover blurb stated, "more outrageous, practical and challenging advice from the author of *Sex and the Single Girl*," but it also offered, unbeknownst to readers, far less outrageous advice than Helen Gurley Brown had wanted to dish out.[28]

First there was the issue of female ambition. Although "secretary" actually encompassed many different job titles and many different job descriptions, the term and its accompanying limitations often came to stand in not only for women's job possibilities but also for women's career aspirations. Helen Gurley Brown, having herself moved from secretary to executive secretary to copywriter, wanted her readers to know that job or career advancement was available to women in all sorts of occupations. In a draft of the book, she tackles this question in the first chapter. "Men like having us in their offices, of course, but some of them (not all but quite a few) poor darlings, are not about to let us get rich and successful under their very noses if they can help it, so we have to sneak past them." She continues: "These wistful lambs think we ought to do only the housekeeping chores (emptying ashtrays, making coffee, all that sort of thing just like their wives do at home). That's okay to begin with, but then we want to go on with our success."

At Geis's request, Brown shifted much of this material on getting ahead out of the beginning of the book. "Most girls—probably 90 percent—who work in an office are not pyramid-climbers," he suggested. "I would put the three self-improvement chapters…in the middle of the book, in the back as sort of an appendix or save them for a future manual for girls who want to get ahead."[29] Brown's compromise includes mentioning getting ahead several times in the opening pages but then promising more about that later: "Before you start marching," she writes about women with ambition, and preceding a chapter on fashion, "we'd better make sure you're dressed for the parade."[30] Chapters on dressing for success and on makeup now precede chapters on getting ahead, but Brown did manage to place "Sneaking Up on the Boys" and "The Keys to the Men's Room" before the two chapters of recipes for workplace luncheons.

A second theme present in the notes and drafts of *Sex and the Office,* but absent in the published version, is lesbian life and sexuality. One of Brown's earliest sets of notes about the proposed book lays out her goals: "To write a book saying that offices are fun—that they are more fun if you work hard…that they offer a grown-up the only guilt-free, healthy, un-criticizable way to have warm relationships, occasionally verging on the sexy and romantic, with other grown-ups." One element of acknowledging actual grown-up sex, for Brown, was acknowledging lesbian sexuality, which she saw as integral to office politics. "I must dwell on sexier stuff," she explains to Berney Geis as she lays out a chapter outline on homosexuality. "I plan to put in a chapter on lesbians and their male counterpart. Some companies, of course, are notorious for being flocked to by this group—probably top management is queer—and this I don't think has ever been written about entertainingly." Geis, though at first encouraging, eventually advised and then more or less demanded that she back off. Even the often irreverent and risk-prone Geis had his limits.[31]

One draft chapter of *Sex and the Office,* which became "Three Little Bedtime Stories," contains six short stories, the first of which, "The Seduction…with a Difference," opens with these lines: "I'd been approached once before in my life…while I was still married…by a girl." The narrator had declined that girl's invitation, but two years later, following her divorce, she responded positively to the advances of Claudia, a woman with "crazy green eyes that slanted like almonds, and practically alabaster skin," who wore silk suits and appeared to be incredibly wealthy. The narrator describes, in steamy detail, not merely the first kiss but the entire lovemaking scene between the two women, often explaining how Claudia understood the narrator's body and sexual needs in a way she had not before experienced with men. And contrary to the narrator's own expectations, things felt right rather than wrong throughout the experience. "You just don't have the least concern about 'is this right...what on Earth am I doing...this is another woman,'" she writes. "You just think 'This is how it should be.'" At the end of this erotic workplace tale, Brown reverts to form by having the narrator assure not only the reader, but surely also herself, of her innate heterosexuality. "What happened will never happen again," she argues, "but I'm glad it happened."[32]

Another proposed chapter, "Boys Will Be Girls...and Vice Versa," includes "the personal recollections of Laura, who went over to their side, and what her physical and mental reactions were after having loved only men all her life."[33] The vehemence with which Geis rejected both the "little bedtime story" and the chapter on homosexuality in the office, instigated by the steamy case history but nonetheless eventually including all references to homosexuality, is telling. "I agree that I've never read anything like that case history," he wrote to Helen when she persisted in including it in the book against his wishes. "I agree that it's done with explicit frankness and yet in the most deft style. I agree that this would sell an extra 50,000 copies of the book—and I insist on cutting it from this book." Ever on the lookout for a sensationalist publishing opportunity, Geis suggested that she publish the piece as a work of fiction, and under a pseudonym. "When I okayed a chapter on 'Boys Will Be Girls,'" he explained, "I thought it was going to be about how to handle temperamental homosexuals in the office, plus some of the complications resulting from the domination of certain kinds of business by homosexuals. I got a lot more than I bargained for." Geis expected that Helen would expose homosexuality as an aberration, not include it as a normal and expected element of either everyday life in the office or everyday women's lives.[34]

On this point Brown proved less willing to compromise. "Now for the fight," she retorted. "Will you consider some more about whacking the lesbian part out?...The lesbian thing just seems part of the office to me."[35] She offered to insert a caveat stating that lesbianism is, at least in our culture, considered sick, but Geis failed to pick up on that. All along he clearly preferred that she write a separate book on the subject. "Almost everyone has the same curiosity you express in your letter," he advised early on, "how did they get that way and what goes on. As you point out, there are many books on male homosexuals but not too many on the female." After much back and forth, Brown allowed Berney Geis to exercise editorial control, and all of this material disappeared from the text, but she could not help but let him know that she failed to see the subject as so utterly controversial. "Whereas there is no material on abortion, etc., anywhere that I know of and you probably wisely took it out of the first book, this subject, in its way, is not all that taboo," she wrote with frustration and, one senses, resignation.[36]

After minimizing Brown's discussion of female ambition, and removing all references to lesbianism, Geis banned a third element of women's lives that Brown had included in the manuscript: sexual violence. Fully exploring grown-up sexual relations in and outside of the office, for Helen Gurley Brown, included acknowledging what would only in the coming decades be named date or acquaintance rape. In the second of her little bedtime stories, titled "Rape—More or Less," a narrator describes the experience of being raped in the front seat of an automobile by a man she had known through her work and had trusted. Al was a musician with a big-name band, and "all the fellows and girls in the store knew him," the narrator explains, justifying her decision to go off for drinks alone with this man. After a few drinks, he suggested they get in his car so they could stop for a bite to eat before heading home. Soon after, he pulled over and assaulted her inside the car. "I know it's hard to believe," she writes, "but, you see, the space in a car front seat is so small—you can't run anywhere— and if the guy is bigger than you...."[37]

The victim of this rape never told her parents, but she did confront her accuser, who told her he would pay for an abortion if she needed one. In the end, she recognizes she is not alone in her experience. "I've talked to other girls who have had almost the same thing happen," she writes, "somebody who they thought was pretty nice turned into an absolute monster." Helen Gurley Brown's fellow feminists might have criticized this narrator's conclusion, which was simply that women needed to be more careful about who they dated, but, to her credit, Brown included in a sexy grouping of stories this example of what was an all too common, if yet insufficiently named or discussed, outcome of office-related romance. This piece, however, never made it to publication.

In her drafts of *Sex and the Office* Brown also included other sexual experiences outside of the mainstream—or at least outside of early 1960s mainstream explorations of female sexuality: discussions of contraception, an older woman and younger man coupling, a woman partially disrobing and participating deliberately in sexual activity in a moving car, and some tame S&M sexual activity, in which a woman enjoys being beaten, lightly, with a whip. She also included a whole chapter on call girls, exploring their lives as working women and their value as stand-ins for those working girls who did not want to engage in sexual activities with their bosses or their bosses' out-of-town friends. Geis placed these discussions in the category of publishable material, even as he objected vehemently to the piece on lesbian sexuality. "No objection was made by me to the rape scene, the gal driving bare-chested in an open car, or the man beating his girlfriend lightly with a whip. I just happen to feel," he wrote, "that a literal description of a homosexual act between two girls would ruin your reputation if you were to publish it."[38] In the end, much that proved controversial was dropped, including the story about date rape, all of the lesbian material, and descriptions of what was considered kinky heterosexual sexual activity. Even the material on contraception, four years after the advent of the birth control pill, disappeared from the text of *Sex and the Office*.[39]

Decisions about what stayed in the book and what simply had to go provide an interesting glimpse not only at the possibilities of an unleashed Helen Gurley Brown but also at the meanings of women's sexuality in postwar American life. Lesbians were often used to contrast inappropriate female behavior (homosexual, independent, assertive) with appropriate female behavior (heterosexual, subordinate, passive). Lesbians, as a consequence, were considered a direct and significant threat to the nuclear family. For Bernard Geis, definitions of "normal" heterosexual sexual activity, contained in marriage, could be tested in *Sex and the Office* as long as the woman remained heterosexual. Tales of more daring sexual exploits, including lesbianism, had to go. Interestingly and tellingly, however, that other threat to the family, the prostitute, remains in the book, rating an entire chapter. Presumably, because she catered to men and did little to change the ways in which "normal" heterosexual women enacted their sexual lives, the prostitute remained a fairly safe character for Berney Geis and for the American public.[40]

In July 1964, Bernard Geis Associates released seventy-five thousand copies of *Sex and the Office*, and the book garnered reviews that ranged from enthusiastic to warm to lukewarm to icy. "Helen Gurley Brown has done it again!" exclaimed one reviewer, and another predicted, "*Sex and the Office* is sure to be one of the best read, most-talked-about books of the year." *Psychiatric Quarterly* applauded Brown's frankness on matters of female sexuality. Gloria Steinem, writing in the *New York Herald-Tribune*, however, found the book a mixed reading experience. "In a writing style that is an ingenious combination of woman's-magazine-bad and advertising-agency-bad," she argued, Brown had somehow buried a great deal of valuable information. *Life* magazine called the book "a silly shallow thing, very much a symptom of this, the Age of the Gland." Reviewers could not help but compare *Sex and the Office* with *Sex and the Single Girl,* but by no means were they in agreement about which was the better written or more successful endeavor. Some called the book sexier than *Sex and the Single Girl,* while others considered it less so. Still others argued that neither one, ultimately, was about sex at all.[41]

Sex and the Office sold and caused controversy internationally as well, as the West German government sued the magazine that excerpted it for publishing "youth-endangering literature." Eventually, the magazine prevailed, and *Sex and the Office* continued to be sold in Germany.[42] Most reviewers had to admit that, whether or not they liked or admired the book, its author had again exhibited a singular flair for packaging both herself and her message. One reviewer offered a backhanded compliment: "One cannot blame Mrs. Brown, of course, for capitalizing on the popular fancy for books of degradation, disaster and illicit sex. After all, we all like money. It is regrettable that she has to be so amusing about it."[43]

Amusing, yes, and equally entrepreneurial, Helen Gurley Brown launched *Sex and the Office* and then moved on, barely taking a glance back, remaining continually on the prowl for opportunities to make money and keep her name in public view. However, one cannot help but wonder: if she had retained control of *Sex and the Office* and put into print the material her publisher took out, would her next attempt, to move into the world of television, have been more successful? Helen Gurley Brown was poised and ready to bring more honest and open discussions of female sexuality into the realm of popular culture. It is not difficult, after all, to imagine a 1960s version of *Sex and the City,* starring a youthful version of Helen Gurley Brown, preceding and even outshining Mary Tyler Moore's Mary Richards as television's maverick single girl.

8

normal like me

THE SINGLE GIRL ON TELEVISION

In 1970 CBS introduced *The Mary Tyler Moore Show* and with it, television's first independent career woman. "The world is awfully big," Sonny Curtis sang as the show opened, "and girl, this time you're all alone." By the time *The Mary Tyler Moore Show* had entered its second season, the opening lyrics had been changed from the tentative, "You might just make it after all," to the confident, "You're gonna make it after all."[1] This not so subtle shift reflected the producers' confidence that their character, Mary Richards, the first independent single female lead of a situation comedy, would actually make it on her own in urban Minneapolis. The more assertive lyrics also reflected a shift in the American viewing public, which, long resistant to televisual images of female independence, had truly embraced rather than simply tolerated this representation of womanhood.

True, Marlo Thomas's sitcom, *That Girl*, had preceded *Mary Tyler Moore* by four years, but Ann Marie, who moved out of her parents' home to pursue an acting career in New York City, relied on her parents or her boyfriend, Donald, to bail her out of her many misadventures. Mary Tyler Moore's character, a jilted thirty-something woman who moved to

Minneapolis determined to support herself both emotionally and financially, provided viewers with television's first single woman truly attempting to "make it on her own." In a piece of television history lost until now, the prescient Helen Gurley Brown had proposed her own version of Mary Richards, Sandra Sloan, eight years earlier, and had been rebuffed at every turn. In the early 1960s, much to her chagrin, neither the industry nor the viewing public was ready for the independent, sexy, and self-deprecatingly funny television character Helen Gurley Brown was poised to unleash.

As a means of packaging both Helen Gurley Brown and her single girl, television seemed to offer enormous promise. David Brown had felt television's sting when he entered film production in the 1950s, a decade that would prove monumental in defining Americans' relationships to popular media. In 1950, more than four million families in the United States owned television sets, but a short decade later fifty million sets had been sold, some of those as multiple purchases to single households. The statistics for 1960 sound closer to today's than they do to those of 1950; almost 90 percent of American homes had television sets, and the average person watched television roughly five hours a day. Quite simply, television had become part and parcel of American life, threatening the success of radio, print media, and Hollywood film. Helen Gurley Brown, along with her supporters David Brown and Berney Geis, realized that television was a medium well worth exploring. They had tapped into it immediately to promote *Sex and the Single Girl* and its author, and Helen and David hoped to explore it in other ways, including through a proposed situation comedy, *The Single Girl Sandra*, based loosely on Helen Gurley's single life.[2]

As they were to discover, 1962 was a conservative year for television. The main theme of television continued to be family life, and female characters continued to exist almost solely within those families. The most popular shows featured women who had either achieved middle-class status and moved to the suburbs or those who aspired to do so. Female characters could be funny, but their comic adventures relied on the steadying influences of husbands and children. Television humor emerged, by and large, from parents' relationships with their children.[3] Even as social changes outside of television would increasingly disrupt this model of the family ensemble, television would steadfastly hang on to the model, with a great deal of success.[4]

There was little room for single women in such representations of American life. When Lucille Ball filed for divorce from Desi Arnaz in

1960, the public reacted as though their *I Love Lucy* television characters, Lucy and Ricky, were also splitting up. The producers believed they could hardly bring Lucy back to the screen as a divorcée once she and Ricky Ricardo would no longer work together, so they created a new show featuring her as a widow. Widowhood on television became the first means of representing a degree of autonomy among women, who could not, at that moment, remain single by choice. *The Brady Bunch,* in which a widow and widower married and merged families, would prove one of the most successful of these somewhat revised depictions of the family.[5] More-significant changes taking place in the world outside of television, including, of course, the ascendancy of divorce, would take some time to be reflected onscreen.

Helen Gurley Brown's untelevised heroine, Sandra Sloan, and Mary Tyler Moore's successful protagonist, Mary Richards, had more than single status in common; they also worked for a living. The televised work world included a few women, but they differed from the more likable, more attractive homemakers whom men and children ultimately depended on and viewers applauded. Mary Tyler Moore had earlier played just that kind of character, the homemaker uninterested in the world of work, on the long-running *Dick Van Dyke Show. Dick Van Dyke* also featured the career girl Sally, who, though talented and funny, never came across as appealingly feminine.[6] The few single women on television through the 1960s included not a single desirable, or even particularly likable, never-married woman. Instead, in addition to the plain and unappealing Sally on *The Dick Van Dyke Show,* they featured the widowed and daffy Lucy in *The Lucy Show,* the eager spinster Miss Brooks in *Our Miss Brooks,* and the unmarried but always boyfriend-accompanied Ann Marie in *That Girl.* Television producers had not yet begun to think of single women either as credible characters or as an advertising demographic worth pitching programs to.[7]

Presumably, Helen Gurley Brown might have had more luck had she introduced her sitcom just a few years later. The early 1970s marked an era of more analytical approaches to television, in which single and working women would become significant because of their buying power. The seventies would also be marked by greater television risk-taking, more network collaborations with independent studios, more internal pressure from the increasing numbers of women working in positions of power in the industry, and more external pressure from the women's liberation movement.[8] As things stood in 1962, however, no one dared sign on to *The*

Single Girl Sandra. Brown enlisted the literary agent Lucy Kroll to send the proposal to a variety of producers. Screen Gems, one of several to reject the proposal, let Helen know that they simply did not believe that "female heroines can carry a show."[9] ABC executives concurred, stating that the history of television suggested that the female lead had proven "uniformly unsuccessful."[10] They also deemed Sandra's workplace setting, an advertising agency, an unlikely backdrop for viewer identification. In 1962, neither the convincing Helen Gurley Brown, the widely respected David Brown, nor the media savvy Bernard Geis could sell their idea to network television. Helen Gurley Brown was, as far as television was concerned, ahead of her time.

Brown's proposal for *The Single Girl Sandra* remains fresh today. It introduces a heroine whose character resonates with the long line of independent female television characters who have followed Mary Richards and whose numbers include Phyllis, Alice, Kate and Allie, Murphy Brown, Ally McBeal, and more recently, Carrie Bradshaw, Charlotte York, Samantha Jones, and Miranda Hobbes. Sandra Sloan, protagonist, works as a copywriter in an advertising agency, is in her late twenties, and earns a good living. No great beauty (a mouseburger, perhaps), Sandra relies on her innate wit, charm, and survival skills to "make it on her own" in and outside of work. She is, as Brown envisions her, "old enough to make quite a good salary and afford the pretty clothes she will wear and the delightful apartment she will live in, young enough to have lots of beaux and lots of delectable-looking girlfriends and sometimes be caught up in the follies of the young."

Although "funny things" happen to Sandra, she is far from a brainless beauty comically at the mercy of men in general or coworkers in particular. Throughout the series, Brown intended for Sandra to come across as intelligent and responsible. Brown felt confident she could make Sandra not only a credible character but also a highly entertaining one, through episodes highlighting her work life, romantic entanglements, and friendships with both women and men. She knew that significant humor resided in singles life, and she wanted to see that richness translated to television. For Helen Gurley Brown, single women were to be admired, not pitied; celebrated, not chastised. They could be laughed with, not at. Where better to do that than in a situation comedy?[11]

Helen Gurley Brown pursued this project with her customary intensity, drawing up a proposal in addition to a series of segment outlines. At work in the ad agency, Sandra Sloane takes responsibility for several accounts, including the Happy Tail Dog and Cat Food Company, Little Dynamo Raisin Growers, an unnamed firm that makes mortuary equipment, and another unnamed company that makes padded bras. While many of the episodes deal with Sandra's life outside of work, quite a few of the comedic elements of the series draw on her professional life and concerns about her accounts and clients. The padded-bra client, for example, considers branching out into padded fannies and "other alluring areas." The raisin account requires that Sandra travel to an international beauty pageant, where she finds the beauties boring and the process corrupt. Miss Australia is caught wearing falsies and the press bets on the girls as though they are racehorses.

Like Brown's workplace settings in *Sex and the Single Girl,* and *Sex and the Office,* the setting in *The Single Girl Sandra* is critical to the story. Employment here provides women with much-needed money, professional work with which to engage, and a valuable sense of community and identity. "The ad agency will not be peopled with monsters and imbeciles," Brown writes in her proposal, "but with the kind of folk who actually work there. Maybe it will be refreshing to see ad agencies depicted realistically (with the accent on comedy) as it was when *Dragnet* depicted cops as intelligent and *The Defenders* decided to depict lawyers as sometimes fallible and confused."

The advertising agency, an important setting for female aspiration, is complemented here by the setting of Sandra's "just-short-of-smashing" poolside apartment, an equally important space for exploring Sandra's passions for fashion and home decorating.[12] For Brown, work in and of itself is essential, but work also, importantly, allows the single girl to showcase the fruits of her labor at home. In *Mary Tyler Moore* the producers would take that doubled setting a step further: the workplace setting and the workplace "family" stand in for Mary Richard's traditional but absent family, and the home conversely becomes a haven for a motley crew of unrelated friends and coworkers. This not only proved a winning formula in the 1970s—a decade more accepting of family diversity—but also provided a powerful template for situation comedy for decades to come. The boundaries of public and private were toppled, not only by placing women in the public sphere of the workplace but also by amplifying the role of the home as a prime site of female activity.[13]

In Helen Gurley Brown's imagined world, the home also becomes a site of sexual activity for the willing single woman, and one imagines that Brown's Sandra Sloan would have, more directly than Mary Richards, dealt with that reality onscreen. In fact, one can imagine that Sandra Sloan's apartment would have, had this proposal actually been developed into a situation comedy lasting several seasons, visually and experientially resembled something between that of the virginal Mary Richards and the sexually experienced *Playboy* bachelor. The apartment would have provided space for a traditionally outcast group, in this case the single girl, but it would do so with a bit more explicit sexuality than that offered by the often hilarious but nevertheless demure Mary Richards. "We should give them a show about sexy girls and men who are not murdering, or shaping up the prairie," Brown writes, "but doing exciting things girls and men do now."[14]

In one letter, Helen Gurley Brown describes her protagonist: "This girl is my heroine and I know to a fare-thee-well what she would be like...who she'd know...where she'd go...what she'd do and say."[15] In fact, the prototype for Sandra does have a great deal in common with the younger, single, working Helen Gurley. In love with a jazz musician both she and the audience know she will never marry, Sandra dates a host of eligible or seemingly eligible bachelors, including a newly divorced psychiatrist, a dull engineer, and a boy who has a glamorous mother and who himself is "probably queer." Brown elaborates on the gay male character, casting him eventually as a steady friend rather than a potential lover. As she explains about Sandra, "There isn't any end to the characters who move in, then out, of her life."[16]

Brown introduces her rather relentless man-shortage theme in one proposed episode of *The Single Girl Sandra*. "Carol, why aren't I married?" Sandra asks her girlfriend. "You were just too busy being smart and writing and having a career," Carol answers supportively. It's more complicated than that, Sandra complains. Part of the problem is that among the few eligible men reside "the people in prison, and the lepers and the morons who'll never leave mama and the ones who are professional Don Juans and people like, Oh, him...he'll never get married." Through Sandra, Brown explores the angst many actual or aspiring career women of her generation and since have felt. "I don't have all that much of a career for heaven's sake....It shouldn't have kept me from getting married. I think I just never was in a hurry to get married...and then suddenly I woke up and realized everybody else was married and I'd better be, too, but there wasn't anybody left."[17] In Brown's case, she found David; in Sandra's, Brown directs her to move on, with humor, to another potential relationship, workplace crisis, or amusing adventure with friends.

Like Brown's Sandra, Mary Richards and the host of television heroines who followed her also wondered at times if their quests for self-improvement, or even survival, ultimately placed them in the category of the unmarriageable. "Well, I just wanted to let you know that sometimes I get concerned about being a career woman," Mary Richards laments to her coworkers in one episode of *Mary Tyler Moore*. "I get to thinking that my job is too important to me," she adds. But in words that Helen Gurley Brown would have applauded, Mary Richards continues: "And I tell myself that the people I work with are just the people I work with. But last night I thought what is family anyway? It's the people who make you feel less alone and really loved."[18] Mary Richards would remain single, engage in meaningful relationships with others, and make it on her own. Sandra Sloan would have done the same.

Even though ABC rejected Brown's proposal, she did not give up on television without a fight. David Brown twice sent the proposal for *The Single Girl Sandra* to Warner Brothers for consideration, but he was rebuffed. Helen wrote several additional proposals for programs in a variety of formats, including situation comedy, reality television, talk show, and game show. *That Tully Girl*, her second proposed sit-com, introduced Lois Ledbetter, a temporary office worker or "Tully Girl," who takes on a different job in each episode. Shortly after she arrives in a new position, Brown writes, "all hell breaks loose," but things work out eventually, and at the end of every episode Lois heads off to a new temporary position. Another proposed sitcom, *Normal Like Me*, exploited the popularity of psychoanalysis. The main characters' encounters with therapists and with each other in group therapy would provide the comic relief, as a group session might include people and their dogs, or role-playing that somehow got out of hand.[19]

Brown proved equally prescient with some of her other proposals. One, *Personal and Confidential*, anticipates Dr. Phil's "get real" approach to problem solving four decades later. In Brown's concept, during each episode a female guest would air her personal problems, getting the full attention of Helen Gurley Brown, who would then offer her advice. "I have no compunction about giving advice because I did it for twelve chapters in a book and many people think it's good advice," Brown states. To further stress her credentials in the proposal, Brown cites other experts—psychiatrists and physicians: "Several psychiatrists and internists have written that they are giving a copy of *Sex and the Single Girl* to all their single women patients and some of the married ones...that it is a constructive, definitive work on the subject of single women and sexuality." Another proposed program Brown would host, *What Is Your Problem?,* would introduce an issue such as homosexuality or a problem such as alcoholism, weight gain, loneliness, or unemployment, and invite experts to offer advice to viewers dealing with that topic.[20]

In Brown's proposed *Making Marriage Work,* a spinoff of the *Ladies' Home Journal* feature *Can This Marriage Be Saved?,* couples would air their problems live on the show. First the husband would describe his grievances to the panel of experts, including Helen Gurley Brown, then his wife would reveal hers. Following that, with neither spouse present, members of the panel would evaluate the case. Yet another proposed program, *Behind the Scenes,* would present an in-depth look at "personality at work in a glamorous occupation." One of the most well-developed proposals was for *Frankly Female;* it positioned Helen Gurley Brown as an "immoderator," accompanied by an equally irreverent male co-host who would "represent" men. One segment of the show would feature women's complaints, voiced by Brown, which might include how mass-circulation magazines, edited by men, "assume women have no interests other than kitchen and nursery"; how wives at parties bore people to death with relentless discussions of their children; the "absurdity" of hiring men to do jobs women can do better; and the issue of "Mrs. Finkbine going to Sweden for an abortion (although HGB would never [criticize] that)" or "Mrs. Finkbine not being able to get one here." Brown and her co-host would participate in lively and straightforward repartee in each segment, keeping things on the "light, controversial side."[21]

Helen Gurley Brown's notes include several proposals that were not as well developed, too, one of which seems more akin to twenty-first-century reality programs like *The Osbournes* or *The Anna Nicole Show,* or perhaps *The Girls Next Door,* which stars Hugh Hefner's girlfriends, than it does to *Candid Camera,* these reality shows' earliest predecessor. Brown suggests *Sex: Female,* in which a camera, sometimes hidden, would follow a woman around for twenty-four hours. The film would then be edited down to a thirty- or sixty-minute segment for airing. Attempting yet another genre, Brown proposed *Cook's on the Fire,* a game show in which each contestant would answer questions about and undertake demonstrations of recipes, table settings, and entertaining "while she gathers in prizes both modest and lavish." Participants might be asked to name the four kinds of glasses for wines then pour the correct liquid into the correct glass. They might be given a table full of ingredients and asked to make, separately, an ice cream soda, a sundae, a parfait, and a banana split.[22]

In the end, Helen Gurley Brown had a great deal more success appearing on other people's television shows than she did airing her own. She served as a regular guest, or perhaps regular prey, on the *Pyne Show,* hosted by the conservative talk-show pundit Joe Pyne. Every time she went on the show and faced his abuse, she explained afterward, people called her on the phone to offer their condolences as though there had been a death in the family. But Brown knew Joe Pyne helped rather than hindered her career, so she willingly put up with the abuse. "Joe will hold up a copy of my latest book and say 'look at this trash,'" she told a reporter, "and bingo, that sells an extra thousand copies. The more disgusting he makes a thing sound, the more eager people are to buy it."[23]

Helen Gurley Brown eventually became a television regular, even obtaining a contract with *Good Morning America,* where she served as a commentator one morning a week for more than two years.[24] She also found supportive audiences, and obtained many repeat invitations, on shows that included the *Mike Wallace Show,* the *Phil Donahue Show, Larry King Live, Nightline, Geraldo,* the *Joan Rivers Show, Celebrity Chefs,* and *Crossfire.* She was the tenth-most-frequent guest on the *Tonight Show,* most often with Joan Rivers or Burt Reynolds, and had a standing invitation to appear on the *Merv Griffin Show.* She appeared on *Oprah, 20/20,* and *60 Minutes.* On these varied programs Brown repeated, in a lively and gracious manner, her singular message: single girls have lots to live for and no apologies to deliver.

Although she never achieved the level of television success she had hoped for, Helen Gurley Brown briefly hosted *Outrageous Opinions,* a talk show that featured an impressive guest list but never became successful enough to move out of its assigned daytime slot. The irony of Brown hosting a program geared only toward homemakers, who formed daytime television's primary audience, was not lost on Brown: "I'm not sure I'm the great all-fired buddy of the housewife," she admitted, curious herself about the program's potential. "I've never been one myself." The guests on *Outrageous Opinions* included Woody Allen, Erica Jong, Bella Abzug, Barbara Walters, David Susskind, Shere Hite, and Norman Mailer, and the topic was—every week—sex. As much as that topic proved comfortable for Brown, it seemed that she had difficulty relating to her guests. The show was one of Brown's rare failures.[25] The failure might also be attributed to the limits of sex as a sole topic of conversation for anyone, even with prodding from Brown. Guests appeared eager to talk about sex, but they often did so in roundabout rather than direct ways. "I have a compulsion to kiss a mailman," Woody Allen confessed; Otto Preminger spoke about the phallic nature of the saxophone. *Outrageous Opinions* aired in a cultural in-between time: television was not as confessional as it would rapidly become, but neither was sex so forbidden as to sustain a nation's interest as a mere topic of conversation. As Brown herself once confessed, "I like sex, but I feel people who go around yapping about it too much— or those who are absolutely preoccupied with sex and talk about nothing else—may have a problem."[26]

Brown admitted that she fared far better as a television guest than host. And as much as she relished the opportunity to hawk her wares in a commercial context, she particularly enjoyed her opportunities to appear on public television, most memorably with Charlie Rose and Richard Heffner, where the lack of commercial interruption allowed for extended conversation and analysis. Interestingly, in what may or may not be an attempt to justify her lack of success in this genre, she stated that television was the one arena in which she did not respond positively to the demand for hard work. Talking about herself was always easy, she felt, but asking people about their lives required preparation. At any rate, regardless of her failure in hosting or producing television shows for herself, Brown understood that television played an enormous role in her success. "I'm grateful to my toes to those television hosts and producers who let me talk, sell product, and become famous," she wrote, "yes, television is how it happens." There is no question that Brown craved the spotlight and would have been thrilled to find success on the screen, but she was also content with the level of fame she achieved. "I'm not a big celebrity," she admitted comfortably, "just well known enough so that people sometimes come up and say hello and tell me they like me...I like that."[27] Brown maintained certain mouseburger qualities straight through on her own particular path to celebrity.

Someone less driven than Helen Gurley Brown might have been exhausted by the early failures she experienced, as her proposals for TV shows met with repeated rejections. During those same years, though, she also experienced intermittent successes, including a syndicated radio program in Canada that was never picked up in the United States, continually strong royalties from sales of *Sex and the Single Girl,* and less strong royalties from *Sex and the Office.* Even so, the Brown–Brown–Geis team would not relax until Helen had another project, something strong and steady to occupy her days. Helen and David, her "agent husband," as he had come to call himself, gravitated in the direction of magazines, where Helen would eventually both reach unparalleled success and revolutionize the genre of women's magazines in the United States and globally. As David explained to Berney Geis, once they began to float the idea of a women's magazine more seriously, "With Helen's acceptance in the advertising business plus her secure reputation as a spokeswoman for women on their own, we have here a potential bonanza with profit possibilities greater than anything we have undertaken thus far."[28]

If only he, or she, or Geis, knew just how true that was. With this project, a magazine aimed at the sexy and unapologetic single woman, Helen Gurley Brown would again be ahead of her time. But because her proposal landed on the desk of executives at Hearst just as they struggled to determine the fate of the longstanding but fairly moribund *Cosmopolitan* magazine, the outcome was different than it had been with her attempts to make it on television. *Cosmopolitan* was due for just the kind of lift Helen Gurley Brown had in mind. Hard work and serendipity—a most auspicious combination.

Helen Gurley lamented the loss of her father, Ira Gurley, who died when she was ten. "His death probably turned me into the great little man pleaser I am to this day," she later remarked. *Sophia Smith Collection, Smith College*

Gurley's mother, Cleo, and sister, Mary. Mary's life was in many ways defined by the polio she contracted at age nineteen. *Courtesy Helen Gurley Brown*

Gurley considered herself a "mouseburger," but her high school yearbook reveals just how popular and respected she was among her friends. *Sophia Smith Collection, Smith College*

With the training she received at Woodbury College, a secretarial school in Los Angeles, Helen Gurley acquired the skills to land innumerable jobs. *Courtesy Helen Gurley Brown*

Don Belding hired Gurley at Smith, Cone & Belding, the advertising agency he ran, giving her great professional and personal encouragement. *Courtesy Helen Gurley Brown*

David and Helen Gurley Brown in a family snapshot taken on their wedding day, September 25, 1959. *Courtesy Helen Gurley Brown*

With the publication of *Sex and the Single Girl* in 1962, Helen Gurley Brown became an immediate—and international—sensation. The store window of Lamston's, a five-and-dime, advertised one of her book signings. *Sophia Smith Collection, Smith College*

Sex and the Single Girl promoted the controversial message that men enriched the lives of young working women in a variety of ways. *Hearst Corporation, Courtesy Sophia Smith Collection, Smith College*

Brown eagerly provided readers worldwide with opportunities to listen to her message; here, a hopeful fan in New York gets her book autographed. *Sophia Smith Collection, Smith College*

Helen Gurley Brown's ability to tap into the minds and influence the behavior of single women made her a cultural icon, as this *Look* magazine cartoon demonstrated. *Courtesy The Charles Martin Trust*

The New Yorker took a more sardonic view of Brown's perspective, but its attention in 1968 was in any case a sign of arrival. © *2003 The New Yorker Collection from cartoonbank.com. All rights reserved*

Helen Gurley Brown in the *Cosmopolitan* art department soon after she took over as editor in 1965. *Sophia Smith Collection, Smith College*

Countless women relied on Brown as they navigated the challenges of single life: work, money, fashion, men, and, of course, sex. Her advice, in the form of a comic strip, was syndicated by King Features in newspapers nationwide. *Helen Gurley Brown, Courtesy Sophia Smith Collection, Smith College*

Helen Gurley Brown's first (1965) and last (1997) issues of *Cosmopolitan*, thirty-two years apart, are hardly distinguishable by their content. *Hearst Corporation*

The media frequently contrasted Helen Gurley Brown's *Cosmo* with Gloria Steinem's *Ms.* magazine. Contrary to media analyses and to the opinions of many in the women's movement, however, the second wave of feminism included both approaches to women's liberation. © 1974 *The New York Times Company. Reprinted with permission*

When No Nonsense named Brown its American Woman of the Month in 1993, she donated the $5,000 fee to the National Abortion Rights Action League (NARAL). *Kayser-Roth Corporation, Courtesy Sophia Smith Collection, Smith College*

Throughout her career, Brown has been steadfast in her support of abortion rights. She commissioned magazine articles on the topic and has marched in pro-choice demonstrations. *Courtesy Helen Gurley Brown*

Brown's relationship with her husband, David Brown, has been a crucial element in her life story. Throughout their marriage she has prided herself on personally preparing his meals. *Courtesy Helen Gurley Brown*

John Mack Carter, president of Hearst Magazines, dances with Brown, still rail-thin at age sixty-eight, at the party celebrating her twenty-fifth anniversary as *Cosmopolitan's* editor. *Courtesy Helen Gurley Brown*

On her departure as editor of *Cosmopolitan* in 1997, Absolut Vodka paid Brown this tribute. *© 1997 Absolut®Vodka. Reprinted with permission of V&S Vin and Spirit AB. All rights reserved*

good girls go to heaven—bad girls go everywhere

HELEN GURLEY BROWN'S *COSMOPOLITAN*

In the aftermath of the 1962 publication of *Sex and the Single Girl,* Helen Gurley Brown's fans sent her so much mail that the post office in Pacific Palisades, California, informed Brown that they would no longer deliver it to her home. If she wanted her mail, she would have to pick it up. Helen's fan mail followed her on her move to New York City in 1963 and continued to arrive even into 1964. "It seemed to me that Helen was developing a constituency, if not a cult," David remembered with appropriate awe years later, adding, "The women who read her stuff felt they knew her personally." For her part, Helen, too, felt a personal connection with each correspondent and pounded out individual responses on her trusty Royal 440 typewriter. Although she had taken on the newspaper column hoping to reach her audience collectively rather than individually, she still received a great deal of mail—and felt a need to respond to it. Eventually, though, even the intrepid Helen Gurley Brown became exhausted by the volume of the mail and the effort required to reply in anything other than routine fashion. Desperately wanting to maintain contact with her fan base, who not only pumped her ego but also provided a market base for her books, newspaper column, and other money-making projects, Brown needed to devise a more efficient means of connecting with her constituency.[1]

Ever on the lookout for new business opportunities, Helen and David kicked around a number of ideas and continued to pursue television opportunities, but the project that started to take for both of them was a magazine. Helen, they decided, would edit a women's magazine. They sat down at the kitchen table to brainstorm, alone at first and then with Helen's dear friend and former coworker at Foote, Cone & Belding, Charlotte Kelly. David had secured Charlotte a position as executive secretary to David O. Selznick, who was working on a Broadway musical version of *Gone with the Wind,* and she moved to New York from her native Los Angeles. The three friends began to toss around ideas for a new magazine format, one to rival longstanding publications aimed specifically at women. Unlike traditional service magazines such as the so-called Seven Sisters (*Ladies' Home Journal, Family Circle, Woman's Day, Good Housekeeping, McCall's, Redbook,* and *Better Homes and Gardens*), which largely addressed married women by highlighting their domestic and family obligations, Brown's magazine would appeal to the young, unmarried, even unsettled "girl," helping her mark her territory in the modern world.

Unlike *Mademoiselle* or *Glamour,* part-fashion and part-lifestyle magazines aimed primarily at young women, this magazine would acknowledge that many women would remain on their own not just until age twenty-five or so but after they had launched their professional lives and through their relationships with a variety of men. The new magazine would capture the allure of magazines like *Vogue* and *Harper's Bazaar,* but unlike those strictly fashion publications it would focus on women's emotional lives and provide supportive advice. It would, in short, introduce a fresh format for a women's magazine, redefining what it meant to provide service. "We decided it would appeal to single girls, somewhat alienated young married women who were tired of PTA meetings and women's service magazines, and others addicted to Helen's frank, feminist views," David remembered later.

With this initial approach, and *Femme* as a working title, Helen began to develop the format for a magazine that would address the sexually curious if not sexually experienced young American woman.[2] In a twenty-one-page proposal, she explained that *Femme: For the Woman on Her Own,* a *New Yorker*–sized monthly with a minimum of sixty-six pages, would target a potential audience of thirteen million single women, including unmarried women, women with absent husbands, divorcees, legally separated women, and widows. Additionally, it would draw on some of the twenty-three million working women who, although married, formed what Brown called the "Betty Friedan set," intellectually curious women who remained, "because of their independent attitude," likely customers for the magazine and its advertisers.[3] The proposed publisher of the initial venture, David Brown, was credited in the proposal as originating the ideas for *Sex and the Single Girl* and *Sex and the Office* and being responsible for "other facets of his wife's career." Certainly, the Browns hoped to capitalize on David's name recognition in the industry, but the proposal makes clear that Helen retains her place as the couple's central commodity. "It would probably cost well over a million dollars in advertising and promotion," the proposal reads, "to create a spokeswoman who is so automatically identified with the cause of modern women alone as Helen Gurley Brown."

Incredibly enough, even today the initial description of *Femme* could, with few changes, describe the magazine Brown eventually did edit: *Cosmopolitan*. "*Femme* is for women who like men," she writes in the proposal. "*Femme* is for women who like themselves; *Femme* is optimistic, affirmative, upbeat; *Femme* is bold; *Femme* is entertaining and humorous."[4] *Femme* was, and *Cosmopolitan* remains, a singularly Helen Gurley Brown creation.

Ideas for articles and titles included "U.S. Presidents Who Liked Girls," "Where the Men Are," "A Divorcee's Diary," "I Married for the First Time at Forty," "Finance," "How Do You Do That?" (change a tire, for example), "I'm Not Married to the Baby's Father," "Alcoholism," "Are Psychiatrists Crazy?," "Nose Jobs," "Fighting Off a Rapist," and "Jealousy." The twin issues of abortion and homosexuality, which had been struck from her earlier writing ventures, found their way once again into Brown's work and emerge again in the core of the proposal. The would-be article on abortion—titled simply "Abortion!"—characterized her determination that the magazine would explore "the way women live on their own and not merely the way arbiters of society would have them live."

One proposed piece was titled "I Love Girls Like You Love Men"; another, which she planned to solicit from the psychologist Albert Ellis, would discuss how a woman could tell if she was dating a homosexual—and what to do about it if she was. Anticipating the age-old homophobia that would link all independent women with homosexuality, Brown carefully acknowledged the heterosexuality of what she imagined would be the majority of her readers. "If we have a woman doing some of the things in our pages that were once only done by men," she wrote, "paying the restaurant tab on a date, changing her own tire, running an insurance company, well, it is not because our Femme doesn't like men or isn't feminine to the core but only because that is how things are in the world today...and our Femme doesn't mind it."[5]

Arguing in favor of equality between men and women, but also securing a space for her magazine as a mainstream publication, Brown wrote that although the magazine would treat women as men's mental, physical, and emotional equals, "*Femme* sees no reason to dwell on this subject—the equality of women with men—but only to acknowledge it by the selection of editorial material."[6] In other words, *Femme* would appeal to women who wanted to live independently but not dwell on the politics of their decisions or their lives. Brown would, with *Cosmopolitan*, take a largely apolitical stance by claiming that, as in *Sex and the Single Girl* and *Sex and the Office*, she was simply reporting on rather than advocating certain behaviors of women.

Ironically, though, however much *Cosmopolitan* would become known as the magazine about women and sex, honest discussions of the full picture of women's sexuality, which for Brown did not exclude considerations of homosexuality, abortion, or sexual violence, would only rarely find their way into the magazine. Brown herself later explained that she had to kill certain articles because of what her employers at *Cosmopolitan* dubbed "taste." Once again, her own inclinations in terms of sexuality would prove more radical and less publishable than those of her colleagues in the publishing world. Helen Gurley Brown could push the limits of "taste," it seems, only so far. Cleavage, yes; lesbian sexuality, no.

David Brown shopped the proposal around, but the initial responses proved discouraging. It was tremendously expensive to start a new magazine, everyone cautioned, and although unmarried women had begun to gain recognition as a consumer group requiring attention, and the advertising-savvy Helen had listed in her proposal the products she believed they could solicit advertisements for, no financial backers came forward. The Browns shared the proposal with Bernard Geis, who sent it out to members of his circle, again without success. Nevertheless, the more they worked on it, the more determined the Browns became about the viability of the project. They would not give up.

Helen Gurley Brown would later be plagued by people who compared *Cosmopolitan* to *Playboy*, but, in fact, the initial comparison came directly from David, who, in a letter to Berney Geis, compared *Femme* with *Playboy*. "Hugh Hefner started *Playboy* with $11,000 and an idea which, in my opinion, is less promising than ours," he wrote, suggesting that *Femme* would surpass *Playboy* not only in originality but also in sales.[7] Geis, of course, concurred, and attempted again to market the idea, sending out query letters that identified himself and David Brown as the new magazine's consultants. Interestingly, given Geis's careful cultivation of Helen's image as the brazen spokesperson for the sexually active American woman, he toned down the rhetoric when he hawked this particular business venture. Unlike Brown's books, he stated with conviction, the magazine would "stay well within the limits of propriety at all times." As he had earlier with *Sex and the Single Girl,* Geis struck the articles on abortion and homosexuality from the proposal. Still, there were no bites.[8]

Finally, someone mentioned to the Browns that the Hearst Corporation was considering reorienting or closing down *Cosmopolitan,* an eighty-year-old publication aimed largely at women. A few people at *Cosmopolitan* had already determined that, in an attempt to reverse a disturbing pattern of increasingly languishing sales and advertising, the magazine ought to more purposefully and carefully target career women. David, certainly in part because he had served as a managing editor at *Cosmopolitan* in the 1940s, secured an invitation to introduce Helen's proposal to management, and his presentation piqued their interest. Hearst executives tentatively moved forward, but the truth is that they wished Helen Gurley Brown were less notorious a character. "Hearst is very conservative," Helen explained later. "They were not pleased that I had written that scarlet book."[9] Nevertheless, they suggested that Brown develop a mockup for several issues. She eagerly modified her proposal for *Femme* to make it specific to *Cosmopolitan,* critiquing the last eight issues of the existing magazine and providing a stronger sense of the difference her imprint would make.

In Brown's critique, some elements of the old magazine, including world news and much of the fashion and home material, would go, and the new magazine would never, as the old magazine had, wax sentimental about the good old days. Instead, in keeping with Brown's confident outlook for the future of women, it would communicate an optimism designed to encourage, even enable, readers to feel better about themselves and the world around them. Brown's extended analysis demonstrates the degree to which her personal philosophy would effectively become *Cosmopolitan*'s philosophy, one of support for women, a dedication to each and every reader, and a celebration of social changes already under way, including, of course, changes in the cultural definition of female sexuality:

> Everything in *Cosmopolitan* should be upward and onward, not in a goody-goody sense but in a realistic sense. I personally don't feel that the world is going to the dogs or that young people are inferior to their counterparts of a previous generation. Our moral codes have changed slightly, but what we have now is a lot better than the days of stricter moral codes when there was child labor, no equality for women, no federal aid for destitute people, plenty of robber barons and lynching. If we point out wrongs in *Cosmopolitan,* and I think there should be a minimum of preachment and sermonizing, we should say specifically every time what people can do about those wrongs.... When one puts down a copy of *Cosmopolitan,* he or she should feel better, if not downright wonderful. There should be lots of self-help, specific advice on how to do things; not so many global and cosmic pieces. The magazine should be closer to where modern women live than it is now. We should take cognizance of the fact that our nation is undergoing a cultural as well as a social revolution, but even an article on pop art can have a lot of you in it.[10]

Helen Gurley Brown's proposal had the effect she desired, and Hearst offered her a two-year, renewable contract to edit *Cosmopolitan.* As she put it later, "I sort of fell into their hands and they fell into mine." Indeed, it is remarkable that a woman with no editorial experience, actually with no magazine experience at all, marched into the Manhattan offices of *Cosmopolitan* in March 1965 and took over. "I wasn't absolutely sure that I ought to be a magazine editor," she recalled later. "It's like someone telling you to be an astronaut or a brain surgeon—something you simply had never done before."[11] To be sure, Helen Gurley Brown had a long and rich background working in advertising. She had David as an ally and professional mentor. Perhaps most importantly, she had an incredibly astute sensibility when it came to the modern, young, single woman. No one knew this woman, or girl, like she did, and no one spoke to her in quite the same voice that Brown used.

For one thing, she always related to her audience on a personal level. From the proposal through to the implementation of the magazine, and then on to its enormous success, Brown would attempt to make each reader feel as though she were being addressed as an individual. She convincingly assured each reader, or at least each woman who became a loyal reader, that the magazine was all about her, regardless of the variety of issues addressed and regardless of the images of female perfection that graced each month's cover. Brown also brought to *Cosmopolitan*, right from the start, an unshakable and contagious optimism about women's place in the world. This singular editorial style obviously worked, not only for Brown but for many thousands of women who frequented newsstands on their way to and from their workplaces, college or secretarial school classrooms, and homes.[12] In this way, Helen Gurley Brown fully established her feminist base—her readers.

Cosmopolitan so quickly and thoroughly became associated with Helen Gurley Brown that within a few years most readers assumed that the magazine had begun publication with Brown, never imagining it had been around for eighty years. The magazine itself fell prey to a similar amnesia, dedicating its November 1985 issue to a celebration of its twentieth anniversary with Helen Gurley Brown at the helm and largely ignoring its own centenary the following year. Yet *Cosmopolitan* had a storied past, one that Brown appreciated and respected but felt little compunction to replicate. Founded in 1866 in Rochester, New York, the magazine belonged to or was edited by the likes of Ulysses S. Grant Jr., William Dean Howells, and William Randolph Hearst. In 1906 *Cosmopolitan* published David Graham Phillips's series, "Treason in the Senate," which led President Theodore Roosevelt to coin this brand of expository journalism "muckraking."

Abandoning muckraking in 1914, *Cosmopolitan* began to focus on short stories and serialized novels and became known primarily for its fiction. The magazine published John Steinbeck, Ernest Hemingway, John Dos Passos, and Edna Ferber, among others. By the 1950s, after David Brown had left his position as managing editor to respond to the invitations of Hollywood, competition from television threatened the magazine's existence, and the Hearst Corporation began to go through editors quickly, once firing or losing eight in a single year. The magazine lost money as well, and although it had long been a favorite of William Randolph Hearst, rumors spread that the magazine might well close down. Helen Gurley Brown's entry could not, in the end, have been more serendipitous.[13]

On March 15, 1965, Helen Gurley Brown entered the Hearst building in midtown Manhattan as its newest magazine editor. Insofar as the April, May, and June issues were already sufficiently planned out or in production, she concentrated on July, her debut issue. Brown began to work on what became her trademark editor's column, "Step into My Parlor," offering the seductive message that the magazine simultaneously belonged to her and to each and every reader. "I've had the pleasure of meeting many of you before through my books and newspaper column," she wrote in her first column. "Now, honor of honors, I'll get to visit with you every month through the pages of *Cosmo*." Brown's philosophy, developed largely intuitively, deemed that she would pay little heed to existing *Cosmopolitan* readers, concentrating instead on the women she knew she could talk to. And she let them know right away that she favored them. Brown selected the stories she did for her inaugural issue for one reason only: "I thought they'd interest you…knowing you're a grown-up girl, interested in whatever can give you a richer, more exciting, fun-filled, friend-filled, man-loved kind of life!"

Brown herself had enormously high expectations of this inaugural issue: it had to promise something provocatively different from the fare offered by other women's magazines, and it had to stand out visually at the newsstands. The June 1965 issue was slated to feature a uniformed nurse on the cover and some interesting but uncontroversial material inside. The July, inaugural, issue had to differ in appearance in addition to content. Brown convinced Rona Jaffe to condense her latest novel, *Mr. Right Is Dead*, for the July issue. She accompanied that with a short story by Nadine Gordimer, an article about the birth control pill, a cover image of a very sexy woman, and a series of provocative cover blurbs penned by David Brown.[14]

Although the birth control pill had had its own debut five years earlier, in 1960, Helen Gurley Brown's particular sex-positive spin on women's lives reactivated the controversy about the impact of the birth control pill on American culture. Like nothing else before or since, the pill had given women freedom, including the ability to control their reproduction effectively for the first time. It changed the sex lives of women so that they approached sexuality with as much excitement as fear. It also had a tremendous impact outside the bedroom, as women gained more freedom to pursue careers, limit their family size, postpone childbirth, and think in terms of lifelong careers. The pill had encouraged *Esquire* magazine to claim, in 1961, "We appear to be living through a sexual revolution."[15] It was fitting that Brown's tenure at *Cosmopolitan* begin with a frank discussion of how the pill had improved women's sex lives. After all, for Brown, sex without fear ranked right up there with many other fundamental human rights.

In truth, the birth control piece had been commissioned before Brown took over the editorship of *Cosmopolitan*, but its inclusion in her inaugural issue lent further credence to the notion that things had truly changed at the magazine. Word about a transformed *Cosmopolitan* spread quickly, and July saw an increase of more than a quarter of a million copies in newsstand sales over June. As Brown predicted, the alluring blond woman on the cover added significantly to the new mix. "I got the sexiest picture I could find," she recalled later, explaining her philosophy that women no less than men longed for images of beautiful women. As she saw it, *Cosmo*'s cover image, and frank discussions of sexuality, provided a space for hundreds of thousands of women to see themselves. For Brown, readers did not have to resemble the cover girl in order to be moved by her sensuality, in large part because she came across as approachable rather than haughty, as an ally for the reader rather than an icon. The response was tremendous. In no time at all, as one fellow journalist put it admiringly, Helen Gurley Brown "took the sex out of girlie magazines and put it in a magazine for girls." Some, her own mother among them, would lament the changes and long for the staid old *Cosmopolitan*, but Brown and her editorial team never looked back.[16]

Brown's move from solitary writer to magazine editor, however smooth the transition, was not without its challenges. For one thing, aside from Diana Vreeland at *Vogue*, who had all her life traveled in the highest social circles, Brown was the only woman editing a major magazine. As Gloria Steinem recalled years later, all the women's magazines she herself had written for in the 1950s and 1960s had male editors. The overall culture at Hearst was male, and the combination of Helen Gurley Brown's gender, immediate success, and upfront ideas about sexuality produced in her employers and publishing peers a mixture of awe and confusion. To the dismay of many and the surprise of more, it became evident within months that she actually knew what she was doing. For one thing, even though or perhaps in part because she raised the newsstand price from thirty-five to fifty cents almost immediately, circulation and advertising pages skyrocketed. "We're so excited over here we don't know what to do," exclaimed *Cosmopolitan*'s publisher, Frank Dupuy Jr., as early as the fall of 1965.

At the same time that they praised Brown, however, Hearst executives did not know quite how to handle a "lady editor." They overlooked her when they made decisions that affected her magazine; they even overlooked her when they celebrated successes she had helped usher in. For example, when in 1969 they feted Hearst president Richard Berlin on his fiftieth anniversary with the company, they left Brown off the guest list simply because she was a woman. Berlin wrote to Brown afterward, telling her how lovely the party was and describing the taped messages he had received from President Richard Nixon, former president Lyndon Johnson, J. Edgar Hoover, and the Duke of Windsor. "I was sorry none of our gal executives were invited but yet they wanted to keep it strictly a stag affair," he explained with a candor that must have frustrated the by now firmly entrenched Helen Gurley Brown.[17]

In other instances, Brown squabbled with her direct boss, Dick Deems, who often worried that the magazine was "too sexy." She felt patronized by her managing editor, George Walsh, whom she felt repeatedly contrasted his superior intellect with her more plebian sensibilities. Indeed, Brown would faithfully remain committed to formulating a message of success for working-class women that, in its honesty and forthrightness, would prove troubling to many. One element of that message, carried over from *Sex and the Single Girl* and *Sex and the Office*, was that working women could target men above their social and economic stations, use all the tips the magazine offered to enlist these men as lovers, and benefit from the social and economic results of this approach. Some of her critics in the magazine world were troubled by the success and seeming social climbing of an unrefined editor and now a seemingly lowbrow magazine.

Nevertheless, as circulation rates rose and advertisers took greater notice, *Cosmopolitan*'s reputation shifted; it was increasingly viewed not just as sexy but as sophisticated, classy in its own inimitable way. Because much of this was attributable to Brown's personal vision and approach, she also gained a sizable number of supporters in the male world of publishing. Walter Meade, who worked as an articles editor for Brown, put her editorship alongside that of the editors who built New York's literary superstar, the *New Yorker*. "She edits a magazine the ways magazines used to be edited before all this committee crap," he stated in print just a year after Brown took over *Cosmopolitan*. "The *New Yorker* grew up that way. She knows what the girl who reads the magazine responds to, because she was that girl."[18]

Early on, it was not just the male leadership of Hearst that questioned Helen Gurley Brown's place at *Cosmopolitan*, and from her very first day on the job Brown sensed from her employees subtle or direct suggestions about just how out of place she was. She recognized that many of the people around her openly wondered why she, without "a whit of experience," had been put into the editorship of an ailing but beloved magazine. Clearly, and not unexpectedly, some of the people who now worked for her felt the situation should have been reversed, with one of them in charge and Brown arriving on the scene as an apprentice.

The new editor went home after her first day on the job feeling completely overwhelmed and justifiably confused. Some time after they had gone to sleep, David woke up to find her missing from the bed. He finally found her huddled under her desk "in a state of almost catatonic shock." In the days that followed, finding herself in a powerful but vulnerable position, Helen relied on her husband's unrelenting support. They developed a pattern: David would arrive in front of the Hearst building in the middle of the day and whisk Helen away in a cab to drive around Manhattan and discuss work. Before he dropped her back at work, he would have offered advice about everything from how much to pay for a particular article to how to deal with challenging personnel issues.[19]

David played the role of mentor well, but he also took on a concrete task at the magazine, one he would not give up for the duration of Helen's editorship: writing the cover blurbs that introduced readers to the article topics and, importantly, invited them in to the magazine. The Browns learned the importance of the blurb during production of her inaugural issue of *Cosmopolitan,* and the lesson they learned may well have played a part in David's retaining ownership of the process for so long. For the cover blurb on the birth control pill piece, David wrote, "The pill that makes women more responsive to men." When the company president Richard Berlin balked, Helen argued with him until he finally hung up on her. David suggested they take off the last two words, and Berlin okayed it. If this seems a small difference to today's reader, it reveals much about the environment Helen Gurley Brown had to negotiate: sexuality, particularly women's sexuality, retained an aura of mystery few felt comfortable exploring outright. And it demonstrates how, with David's help, she made many inroads, some incremental, some monumental. If a cover is a magazine's most important advertisement—an advertisement for itself—*Cosmopolitan*'s success in this department ultimately hinged on the winning combination of Helen's directives about ample and inviting cleavage and David's witty and cogent blurbs.[20]

After a few months of professional uncertainty and insecurity, paired with chutzpah and sheer determination, Brown began to feel more comfortable in her role and with her responsibilities. She more confidently implemented her own management style. The new editor did not fire anybody during her first three months on the job; this in itself was an unusual approach in the world of management, in which employee sweeps often accompany changes in leadership. In fact, thanks to her immediate success, she instead soon doubled her staff from twenty-five to fifty. Although she attempted to avoid conflicts with others, she had no qualms about telling people what she wanted.

Continual increases in sales contributed to Brown's sense that no one knew her targeted readership the way she did. Ultimately, she exercised a great deal of say in what ended up in each issue of the magazine. Unlike other magazines, where writers submitted story ideas, in Brown's *Cosmopolitan* she and the senior editors, meeting each Friday, hashed out article ideas themselves. Each of the sixty or seventy potential pieces they discussed would be judged based on its potential reader appeal and then contracted out to a writer. Brown knew that her real power lay in this process. As she described it, "You get to promulgate your own ideas onto a public. It's a lovely kind of power."[21]

One of the few elements of the old *Cosmopolitan* that Brown maintained was a commitment to fiction, although she immediately placed more commercial authors like Danielle Steel alongside literary writers such as Joyce Carol Oates. Brown added health and beauty columns, among others, but never retreated from what she saw as women's two most important concerns: love, including sex, and work, including money. She hired Francesco Scavullo, who had made a name for himself at *Harper's Bazaar,* to photograph what became the signature *Cosmo* cover shots—and then left him alone to work. As she honed her editorial skills and relied on instinctive ideas about what her readers wanted, Brown continued to draw on her core themes: love, sex, work, and money. She began with this somewhat narrow agenda, rarely deviated from it, made it the signature *Cosmopolitan* formula, and watched sales rise and rise and then rise again.[22]

Helen Gurley Brown reinvented the women's service magazine by addressing the needs of the thousands of women who grappled with outdated definitions of womanhood, femininity, sensuality, and sex. Until her magazine came along and provided this strikingly modern and cosmopolitan definition of womanhood, substantial numbers of women found little validation of their lives in women's magazines. The many women who would become loyal *Cosmopolitan* readers wanted someone to preach not *to* them but *for* them. "There are a lot of women out there who need help and they are $100 and 50 miles away from a psychiatrist," Brown explained. "What we are trying to do is absolve them of guilt by letting them know they are not alone."[23] She forcefully brought to a halt a long-standing magazine formula that stated that women who made independent choices about their lives, including sex outside of marriage, or even divorce, had to come to a bad end.

Brown also made money central to the concerns of the sexy and modern woman and replaced negative stories and statements with upbeat if sometimes unrealistic pieces like "How to Marry a Millionaire," or "The Non-Disastrous Divorce." She celebrated rather than worried over women's increasingly assertive sexual, professional, and financial practices, and readers could not get enough. "What women want is the same thing that men want," she explained. "We want love and sex and a place to live and warmth and food and clothing—all the creature stuff. But we also want the power, the glory, the money, the recognition, the achievement, the success." For Brown, whose own rags-to-riches story seemed to prove the potency of American capitalism, success included both a sex life and a bank account. *Cosmopolitan*'s features followed suit, and as Brown put it, this editor "didn't even seem to have to breathe hard" to make circulation rates rise. With the exception of only two months during her first dozen years, sales went up every single month.[24]

Few people criticized Brown as a boss, at least publicly. Many of her employees appreciated her direct approach, which freed them from trying to second-guess their employer. As Francesco Scavullo put it, "Helen isn't vague. She's instant, like the click of a camera." Likewise, others developed an allegiance with Helen Gurley Brown, because they knew what they were in for. "She was a great boss," said Myra Appleton, who worked for Brown for twenty years before she left to become the editor of *Lear's*. "Very straightforward, and she played fair. She didn't brood about things and she didn't keep score." Judith Krantz, a frequent contributor to *Cosmopolitan,* appreciated Brown's clear directives, and Rona Jaffe, another regular contributor, concurred. "I work so damned hard on these articles and it's heartening to know how much you care," she wrote Brown. "I don't think other editors are as sweet and thoughtful to their writers as you are, and that's too bad for them, but good for you and good for me."[25]

Brown regularly wrote comments on people's first and later drafts of material, and it was not uncommon to find her actually writing more in her comments than the writer had contributed in a written piece. Surprisingly to some, who tired of Brown's excessive use of quotation marks and exclamation points in her books, Brown herself played the role of grammar master over the pieces that appeared in the magazine and regularly supplied copies of Strunk & White's *Elements of Style,* a writer's manual, to her contributors, before eventually writing her own guide, *The Writer's Rules,* which emanated from a photocopied set of guidelines she developed at *Cosmopolitan.* Her work notes are filled with complaints about the quality of the writing her editors drew out of people. When Brown later reflected on the most significant challenges in her tenure at *Cosmo,* she lamented that the paucity of talented writers was one of the most significant drawbacks of the magazine business.[26]

Part of the reason Helen Gurley Brown had difficulty with writers was her longstanding reluctance to pay at the same rates as other publications. "You had to beg to get office supplies," one of her employees complained, and others felt she was willing to give plenty of feedback but little compensation to the writers upon whom the magazine depended. Her reputation as a miser was legendary in both her personal and professional life. She and David achieved a modicum of understanding at home: he would be labeled the wastrel and she the magpie whether they were vacationing or just spending time out in New York. She had no qualms about imposing her thrifty ways on the office staff and developed a reputation for recycling gifts. On one occasion an employee received a gift from Helen and opened it to find a gift Brown had herself received, chocolates imprinted with her initials. Her miserliness extended to food, and she admonished employees for going out to lunch rather than saving their pennies. She rarely went out for lunch herself, with the exception of the weekly advertising lunches that she hosted. Regardless of how much money she earned, or the wealth she and David accumulated collectively, Helen never let go of her Depression-era scrutiny of spending. At age eighty-six, working as the editor of Cosmopolitan International, she still carried to work homemade tuna salad, in a used yogurt container, inside a well-worn brown paper bag.[27]

One of the employee rumblings in the *Cosmopolitan* offices concerned what some considered Brown's sappy optimism, or what she might instead call her determination to put a positive spin on everything the magazine covered. She refused to criticize, never mind sensationalize, the lives or work of others. One of her lifelong friends, the famed New York gossip columnist Liz Smith, the "grande dame of dish," worked as the *Cosmopolitan* entertainment editor for eleven years. On staff when Helen arrived, Smith soon moved on, but she always laughed and teased about Helen's compulsion for the positive. "She destroyed my credibility as a film critic," she explained. "If the movie was awful, she just wouldn't let me write about it." Others suggested more directly and critically that this approach compromised editorial integrity. Some alleged that, as was commonplace in comparable magazines, quotations in *Cosmopolitan* were altered, case histories were made up, and letters to the editor were rewritten. By and large, though, the criticisms failed to stick, or at least failed to harm. Arguably, few readers of women's magazines would find any of these tactics, used on occasion, particularly surprising or particularly troubling, and Brown herself could attribute some of the changes in the text of an article to her zeal for well-written prose, no matter how short or seemingly trivial a piece might be.[28]

There was no doubt that *Cosmopolitan* was Helen Gurley Brown, and some of the magazine's employees responded to this particular work environment more positively than others. One editor felt that the *Cosmo* workplace contrasted favorably with other magazines, where "all the men sat by the windows and had their coffee brought to them...[and t]he women sat in the middle." *Cosmopolitan* differed not simply because there were no "macho carryings-on" but also because the hierarchy was singular and transparent. At *Cosmo,* as she put it, "there was Helen and then there was everybody else." Helen participated in—or interfered with, depending on one's point of view—so many aspects of production of the magazine. The senior staff, for example, kept a big book in which they jotted down story ideas. Helen regularly penciled in her own comments, and as one editor put it, the book eventually read "like her autobiography—her dream life, her sex life." Some found their boss's presence oppressive, and one former employee complained that Brown was "highly neurotic, high-strung and emotional." Nevertheless, she cultivated a remarkably loyal staff, with some top editors and her personal assistant staying with her for more than twenty years. "I think it's fascinating that all of your senior ladies feel loved and special and none of us feels jealous," the executive editor Roberta Ashley wrote in 1972.[29]

Given the widely recognized and, especially in the field of publishing, unusually low employee turnover at *Cosmopolitan, Fortune* magazine profiled Helen Gurley Brown in 1996, inviting her to share her insights about successful management. Some of Brown's suggestions seem in keeping with those of a fairly controlling boss: spending money is good, wasting it is dumb; don't lose your temper, as you already have control; listen to ideas but have your vision in place and stay loyal to it; leave your door open but try to visit others so you can control the time spent together. Others of her directives, however, demonstrate an awareness of delegating responsibility in order to promote professional growth: do not show off good people, just give them responsibilities; give credit to employees, sometimes even when it was your initial idea; put up with employees who need to deal with family issues on the workplace clock; fraternize with the staff when it feels right, as some may become close friends. Not surprisingly, Helen's final advice in the *Fortune* piece rings true for her in any setting and accounts in part for her own success: work harder than everyone else.[30]

When Brown took over *Cosmopolitan,* she introduced a layout that would remain largely unchanged for decades. One of her most important innovations was the magazine's cover format, which demanded that Brown push the limits of propriety without appearing to be crude. As she envisioned it, the cover would feature a different, attractive background color each month so a reader would recognize the new month's publication immediately on the newsstand. In contrast to the background would be the cover model, each featuring a novel look, including dress, hair color, and hairstyle. The cover blurbs, which would not serve as a simple table of contents but rather as a series of emotionally charged messages about the kinds of content the reader could expect to encounter inside, would also advertise that a new month signified new adventures for the reader.

The cover photograph would show cleavage at least once every three months, and every cover model, including those whose cleavage was kept under wraps, would appear sensual in a grown-up way. The model would always appear sexy. But in keeping with Brown's optimistic take on women's sexuality, paired with her determination to make sexually active women socially respectable, the model would never appear "moody or sad or dirty or lewd." As the magazine's "goodwill ambassador," the cover model would offer unspoken promises about the opportunities and the options available to those who identified, in one way or another, with the Cosmo Girl.[31]

It caused Helen Gurley Brown no end of irritation when her detractors complained about the unrealistic look, bodily proportions, or overall beauty of the *Cosmopolitan* cover model. For Brown, the woman on the cover could never be confused with the reader, who might be a working-class mouseburger like the young Helen Gurley, a confident career woman, or even a beauty in the most traditional sense, but who would virtually never be a perfect specimen of femininity. When others found it necessary to equate the cover girl and the reader and to point out the discrepancies between the two, Brown almost pitied their literal take. "Many people think she's the girl on the cover," she explained about her readers. "Well, that's one kind of Cosmo Girl, but there are only about thirteen of those in the whole world. Millions of other Cosmo women also look nice but they can be a doctor, lawyer, librarian, computer programmer, lab technician, TV-show coordinator, flight attendant."[32] Brown believed, and her readers confirmed through their loyalty, that the beauty of the cover girl did not preclude the average woman's identification with the magazine.

One of Brown's most ingenious inventions was in fact this Cosmo Girl, the imaginary stand-in for the magazine reader.[33] The Cosmo Girl, importantly, could be readily associated with the magazine but not hemmed in by one narrow profile or look. A 1970 survey of *Cosmopolitan*'s demographics showed the range of women who responded to Helen Gurley Brown's unique approach. Fewer than half of *Cosmopolitan*'s readers fell into the eighteen-to-thirty-four age group, so Brown did in fact reach not only young women but also that older group of women to whom she felt devoted. Fewer than half attended or had graduated from college, which means that Brown reached both her loyal working-class constituency and a growing number of more educated women. Just half of her readers worked for a living, which might have surprised Brown, who did little to cultivate relationships with the women she had long disparaged as housewives. Only half of the readership was single. In only one area could the readership be considered homogenous: the vast majority of *Cosmopolitan*'s readers lived in large metropolitan areas.[34] Regardless of the diversity of readership, Helen Gurley Brown, and seemingly everyone else, came to call the *Cosmopolitan* reader the "Cosmo Girl." This label provided a brilliant marketing tool and strategy for the magazine, an equally compelling means of identification for its readers, and a process by which a fairly broad readership with differing lifestyles, sexual practices, racial and ethnic backgrounds, and income levels could ally themselves with a single publication.

Brown used her years of advertising experience to her best advantage in creating and promoting this symbol of contemporary womanhood and of her magazine. She relied on this same experience to court advertisers as well, and as an editor she ignored what many considered the mandatory wall between the editorial and advertising departments. Many in the business argued that editors, by paying too much attention to advertisers' desires or complaints, unduly compromised a publication's integrity. But Brown, always attentive to the bottom line, felt she could hardly maintain such a stance. "I've heard of editors who want nothing to do with advertising," she argued. "They must be nuts. Advertising pays the bills." For her entire career at *Cosmopolitan*, she hosted a weekly luncheon for advertising clients and for the companies they represented. When speaking with advertisers, she relied on her depiction of the Cosmo Girl to convince them of *Cosmopolitan*'s eminent suitability for ads targeting female consumers. She would describe various aspects of the Cosmo Girl's life: the kinds of careers she was pursuing; her feelings about men and relationships; her health and diet concerns and practices; her definitions of beauty; her ideas about decorating, sex, divorce and housework; and her worries about sexual harassment, rape, and environmental degradation. And, of course, she would weave in discussions about the kinds of products the Cosmo Girl might purchase to assist her in her many undertakings. On the one hand, Brown collapsed all readers into the Cosmo Girl; on the other, using the Cosmo Girl, she had the opportunity to describe, to a larger audience, women's changing attitudes and desires.

Brown updated her pitch each year, acknowledging new trends in women's lives, but the Cosmo Girl remained fairly consistent in the most significant areas of her life for thirty years: she was lively, determined, sexually aware if not sexually active, hardworking, and, importantly, acquisitive. She relied on her magazine to help her make decisions about purchasing items ranging from breakfast foods to automobiles. These weekly presentations helped keep *Cosmopolitan* in the top rankings of magazine advertising pages and in the minds of people in affiliated professions. Remarkably, Brown pulled this off year after year, most often with little in the way of market research to back her up. Her sources for defining the Cosmo Girl remained, by and large, her own life, discussions with her employees, observations of New York City's working women on the buses Brown herself rode to work, and her conversations with flight attendants, receptionists, and other women she met while traveling.[35]

One of the most consistent ways in which Brown described the Cosmo Girl to advertisers was, not surprisingly, as someone who valued her work life. She believed *Cosmopolitan* had to remain "messianic" about the centrality of work in women's lives. "We were the first people to tell women that work can be—and ought to be—just about as thrilling as a love affair," Brown claimed. At one luncheon she put it this way: "Young Cosmo girls have finally got it through their heads you have to start small to get big. You don't enter as the CEO, but secretary is no longer a dirty word—though she may call herself an assistant." No matter how wealthy she or her readership became, Brown never lost her affinity for the working girl, and she took great pride when evidence revealed that secretaries continued to purchase the magazine. She instructed her employees to feature fashions that would prove affordable to modestly paid working women. This was no easy task, she acknowledged, as more expensive clothing generally looked best on the magazine's models, but she wanted her employees to make the effort. "Don't sell her down the river with a $5,000 Armani evening gown," she instructed.

Brown felt her magazine ought to make promises that remained within the reach of the reader who "lives in the real world," rather than in a real or fantasy world of wealth and privilege. She held to a consistent formula of two pieces, one major and one minor, about work in each issue of the magazine. This constituted her "whether they like it or not" stance, her big-sister approach writ large when it came to elbow-grease achievement, and on this she remained steadfast. "These subjects are not as riveting as emotional, man/woman, sex articles or even celebrity profiles," she explained, "but *Cosmo* readers are working women, must be encouraged to do their best and succeed, and be given information and advice to help them do so . . . we want to instruct and inspire."[36]

Helen Gurley Brown enjoyed being the well-paid editor of *Cosmopolitan* and relished the increasing celebrity accorded her. The Hearst Corporation paid her fabulously well, and she happily admitted, "I love money." But although it seems she could have made even more money for herself and for Hearst by lightening up on the career and money elements of the magazine, she repeatedly refused. In the 1980s, following the first slump in *Cosmo* sales and advertising pages during her tenure, Brown relented, somewhat reluctantly, and conducted a reader survey to ascertain more about the actual Cosmo Girl. Until this point, incredibly enough, Brown's instincts and observations had never been wrong. More than twelve thousand readers responded to the invitation to give feedback, and the results may have struck her as somewhat worrisome. Readers favored the emotional-content material, the pieces about men and friendships and love and loss. They felt far less enamored of the pieces on careers and money. Brown responded positively to some of the requests, such as those for more celebrity profiles, more quizzes, a greater inclusion of women of color as models, and more articles on older women and single parents. She would not, however, budge on the money and career columns; they would stay, regardless of what her readers said they wanted.[37]

At a 1991 advertising luncheon, Brown described how the Cosmo Girl had not changed all that much in twenty-five years. "She's still the one who loves men and loves children but doesn't want to live through other people—she wants to achieve on her own—to be known for what she does."[38] The Cosmo Girl had changed little in twenty-five years because, for the most part, she continued to match Brown's own profile as a working woman coming of age in the 1940s and 1950s. Whether or not the profile matched her actual readers is an open question, as Brown proved largely disinclined to conduct further reader surveys to determine who her readers were or what they most liked in the magazine. By creating the Cosmo Girl, Helen Gurley Brown had packaged herself yet again, providing a template for the independent and sexy American woman. Had she sought to trademark the Cosmo Girl, she would have had to present herself as evidence. She had a remarkable, even uncanny ability to simultaneously move forward with the times and hearken back to her own youth and personal proclivities—and to make magazine history along the way.

A passion for the single girl, which ran through all of Helen Gurley Brown's writings, would drive much of the content of the magazine throughout her tenure. "The Cosmo Girl doesn't need to get married for prestige or a meal ticket," she explained. "She can supply those things herself, so she is marrying a friend and a lover."[39] By maintaining this stance, that all women could have sexual and romantic relationships with men, the magazine suggested that marriage was often desirable but that single status remained perfectly acceptable. This stance allowed the magazine to avoid the antifeminist backlash that emerged in women's magazines in the 1980s and then again in the 1990s. One of the biggest elements of the backlash was a baby mania, in which magazine covers and articles featured celebrity women whose lives seemed to be centered around their children rather than their careers. *Cosmopolitan* steered clear of the mania, to its advantage. The Cosmo Girl might have children, but they did not define her life and, for the most part, had no place in her magazine.

Even for a special issue on working mothers, *Cosmopolitan* held to its tradition of featuring a lone woman on the cover. Helen Gurley Brown could not allow a baby to trump a woman either on the cover or inside the magazine—in part because the Cosmo Girl was Brown herself, and in part because Brown was adamant that the magazine maintain a singular identity. Brown also refused to give in to the simultaneous celebration of domesticity in so many women's magazines, where women were pictured not just with babies but with men, husbands in particular. A new celebration of traditional roles made opting out of the work world appear irresistible, even to women who had pursued careers rather than just jobs. Brown would have none of it. "As one Cosmo Girl said," she explained, "there's more to life than a hunk with a hammer."[40]

In addition to hosting advertising lunches, Brown crossed the advertising/editorial divide by writing ads for *Cosmo,* including many in a series of full-page advertisements placed on the back page of the financial section of the *New York Times* between 1965 and 1990. Many people found troubling the disjuncture between the photographs of the models, who could have been *Cosmopolitan* cover girls, and the text, which talked about things like Aunt Pauline's desire to know why "I," Beverly, haven't married. With *Cosmopolitan* repeatedly number one in sales and advertising pages among women's magazines, however, few quarreled too strongly with the campaign. Another series of ads ran in the *New York Times,* these between 1978 and 1984. Each ad introduced a different Cosmo Girl telling her story and featured a line at the bottom of the page, stating in large print, "If you want to catch me, you'll find me reading *Cosmopolitan,*" or "I guess you could say I'm that *Cosmopolitan* girl."

This series of advertisements, which read like pages from her diary, provides a fascinating and fairly concise chronology of the ways in which Helen Gurley Brown viewed and depicted women during the height of the second wave of the feminist movement. In the first, she celebrates women's brains and their bodies:

> People have been telling me I looked good in a bikini for about nineteen years (I was two when I wore my first one) and I think that's a nifty compliment! Of course, I also like it when they notice my *brain.* I did graduate magna cum laude from Ohio State, made Phi Beta Kappa and right now I do ecological research at a foundation. Are sexy bodies and nifty brains incompatible? Not according to my favorite magazine. They say a girl who has *both* can rule the world... and they help you develop each of these assets! I love that magazine. I guess you could say I'm That COSMOPOLITAN Girl.

In the second, Brown stands up for those smart women who also like to sex it up:

> Why can't we be loved for our goodness and forget about looks, especially when we'll probably never get all the way to gorgeous? Well, we *are* loved for our inside goodness by people who *know* us, but also judged on appearance by others... it isn't yet a perfect world. My favorite magazine says a brain and good disposition

are major assets for a woman, but don't feel guilty if you highlight your hair and are still hunting for the perfect lip gloss. You can care about looks *and* all the "important" things. I love that magazine. I guess you could say I'm that COSMOPOLITAN girl.

In the third, she offers the advice she gave out first in *Sex and the Single Girl*—have a fabulous life, and men will appear:

I suppose I shouldn't still be hung up on finding Mr. Right. After all, I'm 27 now (and past the boy-crazy years), successful at my job (brand manager at a big package goods company) and I just closed on my co-op on the Upper East Side. And yet, life's pretty empty without someone special to share the most important times with. Fortunately, there's a magazine that helps me keep things in perspective. It's okay to *still* want to meet the right guy. But my favorite magazine says to fill up my life with other pursuits—learn to cook, take French lessons, volunteer one day a week—while working on developing that special relationship. I still need that kind of advice, and I love that magazine! I guess you could say I'm *still* THAT COSMOPOLITAN GIRL![41]

The success of the Cosmo Girl was bound to have an impact on the larger world of women's magazines. As early as the late 1960s, not even five years into Helen Gurley Brown's reign, *Cosmopolitan*'s upfront and positive discussions of female sexuality began to drive the industry in new directions. It was not that women's magazines had avoided the topic of sex altogether before Helen Gurley Brown came along. For years, women's magazines had featured columns about sexuality, generally in the form of cautionary tales written by psychiatrists, physicians, or marriage counselors. The magazines relied on the theme to draw in readers but approached the realities of female sexuality with trepidation. A 1957 *Playboy* magazine article, describing the ways in which women's magazines would suggest the importance of and then readily contain female sexuality, had dubbed them "pious pornographers." Brown considered *Playboy* the "success story of our time," largely because the magazine recognized how important sex was in selling not only magazines but also consumer goods. She also called women's magazines on their problematic stance on sexuality, in a *Sex and the Single Girl* speech years before she took over at *Cosmopolitan*. "And let us not forget that *Ladies' Home Journal, McCall's,* and the *Reader's*

Digest have their own sexy contents that pull in readers," she asserted. "They may claim to be against sex, but they manage to print a great deal of rather salacious, exciting material before they come out and tell you that you aren't supposed to enjoy it."[42]

One of the best examples of this back-door approach to female sexuality was the well-known *Ladies' Home Journal* column "Can This Marriage Be Saved?" which located the solution to marital problems, including sexual ones, in women's accommodation to men's wishes and practices. Some readers certainly would have paid as much attention to the column's discussions of sexuality, which mentioned women's dissatisfactions, as they did to the pat solutions offered by the advice givers. But Brown took the discussion of female sexuality away from the twin designations of "grime or crime" and simply made it fun. Following her immense success in this department, other magazines fell in line; even *Mademoiselle*, long considered a fashion magazine for proper young ladies, began to feature articles about female sexuality. Nevertheless, as much as Helen Gurley Brown liberated women to engage in sex without guilt, she, too, maintained the perspective that women more than men would take greater responsibility for making relationships work. Nora Ephron, who wrote short fiction for *Cosmopolitan*, explained the problematic but real formula in this way: "Women think that if they could just understand men, they could do something. Women are always trying to do something. There are entire industries based on this premise, the most obvious one being women's magazines."[43]

Advertisers, who had long relied on toned-down but nevertheless fairly suggestive images and descriptions of female sexuality, felt liberated by Helen Gurley Brown and *Cosmopolitan* to explore the appeal of the sexual with greater deliberation. By the mid- to late 1960s, automobile manufacturers such as Ford, with its Mustang, began to create advertisements that directly acknowledged young women's market power and their sexuality. The famous Virginia Slims series, "You've come a long way, baby," always suggestive of women's power, including sexual power, made its debut in 1968. In truth, however, many advertising agencies and their clients occasionally worried that *Cosmopolitan* took the whole discussion of women's sexuality too far.

Although Brown would maintain that she virtually never considered whether or not advertisers would approve of something she printed, she was not averse to writing letters assuaging advertisers' fears. In one instance she wrote to Kroger Foods in Cincinnati, apologizing for the magazine covers that had offended them. She explained that she never intended to be "excessively sexy" and that the upcoming covers would be more in keeping with the *Cosmopolitan* genre they felt comfortable with. "Naturally, I want you to like them and believe that you will. I have no wish to lose or displease our very valued client," she explained. In another case, when Clairol, the magazine's biggest advertiser, threatened to pull out because they felt *Cosmopolitan* had become "too gamey," Brown actually pulled back. "Now . . . if they didn't represent one million bucks of revenue you'd tell them to go f— themselves," she wrote in an office memo, "and after considerable pain and soul-probing I know I'm not going to do much to get less gamey, but I'm also not going to do anything too flagrantly gamey for awhile."[44]

Complaints by advertisers provided an opportunity for the conservatives in Hearst management to voice their own concerns about the upfront presence of women's sexuality in *Cosmopolitan,* so at times Brown felt criticisms coming at her from several angles simultaneously. She fielded requests for the less frequent use of the word "orgasm," the elimination of the verb "come" in its sexual connotation, and discussions of sexuality limited to those that labeled sex as strictly heterosexual, connected with love, and not "self-induced." Brown responded, asserting that she had no difficulty connecting sex with love but found the anti-gay and anti-masturbation requests troubling and unrealistic. Her general response to management directives was to tone things down a bit for a month or two, then engage again in business as usual. Left to her own devices, one imagines that the magazine would have been, at the very least, far more lesbian-friendly than it ever was.

But Brown was not one to fight with management, whom she saw as largely indulgent of, rather than restrictive of, her imprint on the magazine. "I've used their magazine," she explained in an interview with Gloria Steinem, who attempted to get Brown to complain about the gendered treatment she received at *Cosmopolitan.* "I didn't put up a penny. I've got this instrument in which I can say what I want to. Everybody thinks it's mine. I have to remind myself, it's not mine, it's theirs."[45] The magazine was Brown's, though, in so many ways, and executives at Hearst were largely fine with keeping it that way. Over the ensuing decades, while other magazines struggled with sales, *Cosmopolitan* remained strong, often providing critical support to the Hearst Corporation's other less financially successful initiatives. Brown exercised the degree of freedom she did for a very good reason: her magazine reaped enormous profits.

Helen Gurley Brown knew the score. When Tina Brown served as editor of the *New Yorker,* a journalist asked Helen to compare herself to that other Brown. Calling Tina Brown the "most brilliant editor in the world," Helen said she "couldn't begin to do" what Tina Brown did. But Brown did not leave it at that. "She's just formidable," she praised, with sincerity. "But there's something I do that she doesn't do, which is make money for her publisher.... That doesn't mean she's a bad editor, but when you're toting up the qualifications of a successful editor, that would be one of them, and *Cosmo*'s a little gold mine. I think that's just super."[46] The Brown of *Cosmopolitan* magazine succeeded on a number of fronts; proud capitalist that she was, Helen Gurley Brown found the economic front particularly rewarding. In this and so many other ways, in fact, when Brown had her Cosmo Girls claim repeatedly, in advertisements for the magazine, "One of my most satisfying relationships is with a magazine," they could have been reading aloud from her diary.

10

sexual liberation on whose terms?

DEFINING THE SECOND WAVE

When most other feminists considered Helen Gurley Brown at all, they found her brand of liberation vexing. For one thing, she was an enormous proponent of the free market. Implicit in much feminist ideology and prominent within most women's liberation groups was a critique of the ways in which capitalism bolstered male supremacy. Employers offered women fewer opportunities than it offered men and paid women less than men because they continued to define women as domestic beings tied to the private rather than the public world. And women's continued dependency was more or less guaranteed in a world in which the wheels of industry depended on complementary unpaid labor, virtually all of that female, in the home. Confronting these realities, many feminists perceived capitalism as an impediment rather than an ally in their quest for equality. A lifelong proponent of the free market, however, Helen Gurley Brown would prove loath to attack with too much venom the very system that had ensured not simply her visibility but her very viability as a single woman in pre- and postwar America.

Brown never considered herself particularly partisan politically, but her leanings were from the start conservative if not libertarian in their favoring the free market. "I believe so devoutly in the private enterprise system," she stated, but ultimately feminism complicated her relationship to the American political system. She voted in every election but felt free, for much of her adult life, to swing her vote from Republican to Democratic candidate as issues moved her. In the end, though, her political leanings were socially liberal and fiscally conservative, so as the Republican Party moved further to the right she found herself, somewhat to her surprise, moving further toward the Democratic Party. The abortion question in particular piqued her, and although she initially voted for Ronald Reagan because of his adherence to strict definitions of the free market, she found it difficult to fathom how someone so enamored of liberty came out against abortion rights. Her own stance on abortion, among the most liberal in circulation, would steer her so clearly toward the Democrats that in later life she would be more likely, regardless of her feelings on other issues, to vote Democratic. By 2007, when Helen Gurley Brown was asked by *Vanity Fair* magazine to name the living person she admired most, she would, without hesitation, choose Bill Clinton.[1]

In other ways, too, Brown's philosophy would rankle. While many others in the second wave viewed women as inherently different from men, Brown espoused their similarities. In some cases, differences between women and men were ranked, with women considered morally superior to men, more in touch with the needs of their communities, families, and the world.[2] Brown would have none of that. She viewed men and women as equally competent but also equally bloodthirsty. As one journalist described it, Helen Gurley Brown's contribution was to reveal that young single women, "it turned out, were not as innocent and pure as we were led to believe—in fact—and this was what hit home—young unmarried females had many of the same urges and desires that young unmarried males had. In the home, in the office, and in love, the career girl wanted her piece of the pie, too."[3] Although she always defended the employment and personal dignity of those women who worked in traditionally female jobs, Brown never believed that certain jobs were biologically more suited to women or to men. She believed that women would compete in the workplace quite well alongside men, and that American women lusted for money as much as any entrepreneurial or competitive American male did. Brown believed women ought to be drafted just as men were and argued that she would willingly die for her country.

Sometimes those leanings became evident in her lectures or presentations. In the early 1980s, at a weekly *Cosmopolitan* luncheon for advertisers, she explained that the Cosmo Girl rarely worked just to pass the time. She wanted to be in on the capitalist system, and she wanted to earn as much as she could. "Feminists—of which I am one—think we deserve to have it all just as much as men do," she informed the male group surrounding her at the 21 Club. "Nobody asks you to give up your high-powered career to have a child or a beautifully run home," she said. The Cosmo Girl hoped to find a man who earned significant money, just as women had traditionally been trained to do. But she also expected to spend her days with a partner whose success and earning power she could at least attempt to match.[4]

For Helen Gurley Brown, capitalism was the system women could count on for increasingly diverse employment and earning opportunities. She contrasted her life, and even more so the lives of women in the generations that followed hers, with that of her mother, Cleo, who had raised her children in meager circumstances because she had little opportunity for remunerative work. Brown felt that women, like men, hungered for and had a responsibility to secure the full benefits of engagement in the capitalist system: savings accounts, retirement stock portfolios, and plenty of discretionary income. Brown would always see herself in agreement with other, more publicly identifiable feminists on the fundamental importance of work in women's psychic lives: women gained not only money but also their professional identity and social status through work. "But no feminist—not Gloria Steinem, not Betty Friedan," she stated vehemently, "ever inculcated me with that idea. I came up with that myself, and it's on every page of *Cosmo*."[5] Even so, an unrepentant capitalist, Brown had difficulty with feminists' practice of fighting for equal employment opportunities while condemning the system that provided those same opportunities.

Brown's loyalty to the free market extended beyond the workplace and into the far more intimate arena of sexuality. She viewed women's sexuality in the context of capitalist exchanges, where those with the money had certain degrees of power and those without tried to negotiate as best they could. For Brown, feminism could improve women's bargaining position, but it would not ultimately take sexuality, any more than it would take work, outside of capitalism's reaches. With *Cosmopolitan*, Brown would create, market, and further a female sexual marketplace in which both the inequities and the pleasures of a liberated sexuality within a capitalist system would become apparent and open to negotiation. She offered readers articles such as "Never Be Faithful to a Married Man," and "What

If?" a piece about what sexual relationships would be like if there were no bartering system in place, "with women trying to get the highest possible price for their wares (marriage, a continuing annuity) and men working for bargains."[6] The acquisition of sexual freedom for women was, as far as Brown was concerned, tied to the marketplace for better or worse.

Many critics of *Cosmopolitan* concluded that Brown's cavalier attitude about women trading sexual favors for dinners or nights out promoted the prostitution of women. Brown herself then fell into line with the most radical of feminists, who were considering the ways in which marriage itself mirrored prostitution. "Many a woman who is married is in a sense a prostitute," she claimed, "in that she accepts presents, money, automobiles, country-club memberships, trips to Europe and the good life from a man she can barely tolerate in bed." As for women who accepted things from men they were not married to, Brown wrote, "I feel she's less of a prostitute than the married woman who hates the bed relationship." Brown refused to call her "girl" a prostitute. Her lover was simply "making her life better" than it was. As Brown saw it, "In a way, we're all prostitutes."[7] Helen Gurley Brown's politics was steeped in political and economic understandings of sexuality, steeped in personal observation and experience, and it made many people, including many feminists, uneasy.

Legions of people would criticize *Cosmopolitan* for furthering the capitalist exploitation of women's bodies. For Brown, though, drawing a clear line between celebrating female sexuality within a system already in place and exploiting that same sexuality was a problematic enterprise. The libertarian in her would ask, simply, who was to decide which constituted celebration and which ran to exploitation? Brown believed that, ultimately, the market would rule; if she stayed on one side of the line, and met their needs, women would purchase her magazine. If she overstepped, and exploited her readers, they would switch their loyalties and purchase another magazine. That is not to say that either Brown or her readers always agreed about whether a particular image of a female body, an admittedly sexual female body, was healthy or unhealthy for women.[8]

In the end, in their quest to reject what they viewed as objectified depictions, many feminists focused on the negative elements of sexuality, including rape, pornography, and prostitution, positing women most often as victims of male sexuality rather than as people in control of and relishing their own.[9] For Brown, this would not do. She felt an obligation to focus primarily on the good in female sexuality, and for her it was enough that she herself believed that the representations in *Cosmopolitan* were positive. She maintained that she had a fairly good track record both as a feminist and as a bellwether of single women's desires. And further, in the marketplace, she firmly believed, other women, not men, would decide for themselves and in doing so determine the fate of her magazine.

Even though she regarded women and men as inherently more alike than different, Helen Gurley Brown regarded the feminist attempt at full equality in matters sexual as nothing if not naive, particularly for working-class women and within the capitalist framework they all inhabited. Brown's editorial notes on one short story submitted to *Cosmopolitan* reveal her lingering sense of the limitations of any hard-line feminism in the world as it was. The story's protagonist, Jennifer, commented Brown, needed to let her readers know her career was important, but additionally she could reveal just how hard it all is when the man "has more things in his life than you do," such as a wife, a fabulous job, money, or fame. Feminism, in this case, would get Jennifer only so far: "It's all very well," Brown asserted, "to say 'be equal'...but then he goes off to his fantastic house and family in Rye and you go off to your rye sandwich alone in your one-bedroom apartment."[10] This protagonist, according to Brown, could hardly afford not to play the sexual and economic system in her quest for the good life. Whether she ever put it in these terms or not, Brown was likely fairly frustrated by the ways she became boxed in, criticized for suggesting that women, because of the inherent inequities in the system, accept financial gifts from men, then criticized again for suggesting that women participate as fully as possible in the capitalist system so they could support themselves in style.

It makes sense that, given her political beliefs and individualist allegiance to the system, another of the key differences between Helen Gurley Brown and other feminists would be their takes on individual versus collective change. Gloria Steinem would admonish Brown that *Cosmopolitan* existed only on a personal level and failed to advocate for structural changes that would benefit all women. Brown recognized that she operated primarily on the individual level but refused to apologize for it. Dedicated as she was to each reader, Brown wanted to promote positive changes in individual readers' lives. She believed that change had to happen there first, with each woman feeling good about herself, her body, her sensuality, her power. Brown had no quarrel with advocacy on behalf of larger groups of women, and she publicly and professionally supported her twin causes of abortion rights and the ERA, but she felt her best contribution to women would be made on the personal level. Interestingly, Gloria Steinem and many other second-wave feminists would, in their later years, write books advocating working on the self as a necessary first component of social change. In Steinem's *Revolution from Within: A Book of Self-Esteem*, she writes, "I began to understand that self-esteem isn't everything, it's just that there's nothing without it."[11] Helen Gurley Brown supported that notion—and maintained that she and *Cosmopolitan* always acknowledged and furthered just the inner sensibility that women's liberation required.

In addition to her refusal to blame capitalism for women's woes, and in keeping with her sense that women sometimes stood in their own way, Brown refused to view men as enemies of women. In an April 1970 "Step into My Parlor" column, she explained, "We're for many of the tenets (equal-with-men pay for women, equal job opportunities, inexpensive child-care centers) while being against the hostile-to-men (surely, how we are can't be all their fault!) anti-sex aspects of the movement."[12] Men still tried to thwart women's potential on the job market, she acknowledged, but women could not simply hold men responsible for their lack of movement. Though men had been a "real pain in the neck in terms of job progress," women had to deal with them. Men existed on the job and elsewhere, and the pragmatic realist in Brown assured her audience that women had to and could make the most of that reality. "If you use your brains and guts and whatever modest talent you have," she advised, "you can get everywhere." Furthermore, men could prove women's allies on the job market, sexuality aside, and women needed all the allies they could get. Brown would maintain that, in an era in which such sentiments might well result in charges of naïveté, women's liberation was men's liberation, too. "It's equality and humanity for both men and women," she proposed in 1970 and then promoted as a key component of her feminism throughout the decades of her involvement in *Cosmopolitan*.[13]

If her contemporaries considered her viewpoint one of accommodation to male privilege, Brown considered it the only way for heterosexual women, sexual creatures that they were, to get what they wanted and needed. "I acknowledge that men keep women back," she argued, "but since sex is terrific and it comes from men, you can't rule men out of this world and say they're all terrible and rotten, because you're going to need them for your own purposes."[14] Brown understood that some among her contemporaries argued for various degrees of separation from men. Some advocated lesbianism as a political choice so that women could avoid the most harmful effects of heterosexuality, which demanded that women essentially put men first. Brown's more libertarian stance on sexuality found such a view confounding, as it ultimately attempted to limit rather than expand women's sexual experiences. She viewed feminists who chose separation from men, sexually, as manifestations of a growth process, as engaging in "emotional blackmail," not only of men but of themselves. If otherwise heterosexual women refused to have sex with men, she reasoned, they denied their bodies, their pleasures, and hence their selves.[15] In her mind, there were other, preferable means of simultaneously understanding the female body, achieving sexual pleasure, and communicating messages to men.

Helen Gurley Brown's understandings of feminism made some women in the movement uneasy to the point that they found it embarrassing to be in her company. Some even asked her not to espouse their cause because of her ideas about men and about female sexuality.[16] Nevertheless, Brown did join their ranks on occasion, even for overtly political demonstrations. In August of 1970 she joined thousands of other women for the Women Strike for Equality, a march down Fifth Avenue that featured as speakers such feminist luminaries as Gloria Steinem, Betty Friedan, Kate Millett, and Ti-Grace Atkinson. Not surprisingly, Brown was invited to participate but not to speak.

In the face of what Brown considered many feminists' negative understandings of female sexuality, she determined to put a positive spin on women's sexual realities and potential. For one thing she refused, from *Sex and the Single Girl* straight through to *Cosmopolitan,* to consider the sexual objectification of women as simply negative. "When feminists tell me that *Cosmo* is making sex objects out of women, I say bravo," she argued. "I think it's important to be valued as a sex object just as I think it's also important to be able to work, to have equal rights and abortion reform."[17] When Betty Friedan described *Cosmopolitan* under Brown's reign as a "quite obscure and quite horrible monthly embracing the idea that woman is nothing but a sex object," and demonstrating "nothing but contempt for women," Brown could not help but respond. "One thing I do quite well," she quipped, "is deal with reality."[18]

When *Cosmopolitan* covers became a lightning rod, and feminists juxtaposed "real" feminism with such blatantly sexualized images, Brown balked, refusing to parse feminism and sensuality. "Feminists didn't see past the sexy covers," she argued, when asked to compare her philosophy to feminism and recalling years of feminist complaints. "But no one can look like the *Cosmo* covers. There's nothing immoral about looking as good as you can." In the same breath, she concluded, seeing no disjuncture between the two statements, "How could any woman not be a feminist?"[19] What others might mockingly call "deep cleavage feminism," Brown took seriously.[20]

Helen Gurley Brown often found herself on the defensive, attempting simply to claim a presence in a larger movement that seemed repeatedly either to treat her as suspect or to cast her out altogether. At times she attempted to foster an argument rather than simply mount a defense, raising issues about her critics and placing their analyses in troubling relief. Perhaps the most significant place in which her process of defining and redefining feminism occurred was in relation to women's beauty practices. Whether or not they honed in on women's magazines specifically, many critics took issue with women's displays of, or, as they might have put it, subservience to beauty culture. Whether it was fashion or cosmetics, high heels or hair dyes, Brown's detractors complained that these things came between a woman and her true or authentic self.[21] However, the Cosmo Girl did not wear makeup because she had to but rather because she could. She was not a slave to fashion or to falsies but a thoughtful, fun-loving practitioner of pleasurable artifice. Brown's loyal reader, she stated, "is a feminist, but this feminist really enjoys wearing make-up, not so much for the effect it has on other people but because it makes her feel more alive and exciting and it's fun to put on—it's an art form."[22] She would make these same arguments about fashion, declaring it another art form that women, thankfully, had the freedom to experiment with.

Through the 1960s and 1970s, and on into the 1980s, the miniskirt would prove an intermittent target of fashion's critics. Helen Gurley Brown never lost her affection for this icon of female style, and she grew annoyed with feminists who tried to halt or even limit women's wearing of short skirts. She expressed her frustration in a *New York Times* opinion piece, complaining that feminists, "of whom I am proudly one, but not on this issue," had taken things too far in their "haranguing" about miniskirts. "You would think women today were about to be sold into a harem or that we already had been," she complained. Her studied defense of the miniskirt rested on three issues: the business of fashion, the pleasure of fashion, and the feminist necessity for more rather than fewer choices for women's lives.[23]

While some women complained that the fashion industry, with its constantly changing offerings, preyed upon women's bodies and wallets, Brown deemed it a wonderful business that supported women. "Why would you want a nice industry like that to go flat?" she asked with a simplicity that hides a fairly sophisticated understanding of the impact of one industry not just on New York City but on the country. "It supports a lot of people—more than 100,000 in New York City alone—and brings pleasure to a lot of us others." On top of her free enterprise- and pleasure-based endorsements of the fashion industry, Brown bristled at the very idea that some women deemed themselves worthy of making decisions for others. "We're really talking about choices here, and what we feminists must be careful about is not making decisions for all of us," she argued. "What we want and have always wanted are options—be they something as trivial as the mini or as profound as legal abortion."[24]

Brown developed a sophisticated understanding of her critics, pointing out the various inconsistencies or contradictions in their arguments. For one thing, she understood that no woman, regardless of her politics, existed outside of fashion dictates of one kind or another. No woman could operate, as some of her peers might have put it, "outside of the patriarchy." Whether a woman presented herself to the world as sexy, brainy, hip, conservative, corporate, or slutty, she dressed a part to fit the image she wanted to convey. And nowhere did what Brown considered the naive anti-fashion stance vex her more than in some women's demands that other women go "natural" by renouncing makeup, refusing to shave their legs, and dressing in androgynous, body-masking clothing in order to demonstrate their feminist credentials.[25] She aimed her most serious diatribe at the hippies. "Those back-to-goodness-and-nature hippies are certainly not natural," she argued. "They may not wear make-up, but some of them bleach their hair and their fringy, furry, funky costumes certainly didn't grow on their bodies (though they sometimes smell like it); the clothes are carefully, 'unnaturally,' collected from thrift shop and Army surplus stores."[26] On this she was determined to go on the offensive, if not regularly in the magazine then certainly in some of her hundreds of interviews with other journalists. So many feminist critics, Brown pointed out, never actually read *Cosmopolitan* to get a real sense of its contents, so she had to respond to at least some of their claims about *Cosmo*'s dangerous messages.

In fact, many of Brown's detractors likely did not read *Cosmopolitan*, which points to another of the distinctions—that of social class—that separated Helen Gurley Brown's readers from other feminists. As she claimed with conviction, only the most educated and privileged women could afford not to wear makeup or not to dress in ways deemed appropriate or necessary in many female occupations. Most women workers still found that, working as secretaries, receptionists, flight attendants, or nurses, or in any of the other myriad forms of female employment, they had to look and act a certain way to remain employed. These women had no choice but to wear pantyhose, eye makeup, and dresses. When Brown claimed, "My relevance is that I deal with reality," she meant that many women responded favorably to her version of reality. She also meant, however, that the "reality" of women's lives was that few women, even if they wanted to, lived outside of the demands of mainstream society.

At times Brown would call attention to other feminist slights against working-class women. Many women responded to Betty Friedan's *The Feminine Mystique* precisely because it encouraged their desires to engage in a world larger than the home. That engagement, tied in as it was with middle-class aspirations, often demanded that women pursue careers rather than simply work for a living, and women who worked in traditionally female occupations subsequently found their intelligence doubted, not just by men but by feminists. In a *New York Times* article, the feminist writer Deirdre English declared Gloria Steinem "America's first smart blonde." According to English, Steinem represented a shift from Helen Gurley Brown's single girl, "little more than a Playboy bunny with a clerical job," to a more admirable woman, "today's feisty feminist professional." Brown had to respond. "There is nothing wrong with being a Playboy bunny," she wrote in a letter to the *Times,* "but Cosmo's 11 million readers range from clerical workers and secretaries to television producers and psychiatrists. I don't know whether they are feisty... but they certainly are feminist and they certainly are professional."[27]

As for cosmetics, in a proposed newspaper column, "Doing What Comes Unnaturally," Brown explained that she had been waging "a personal war against naturalness" for several years. Admitting to coloring her hair, capping her teeth, having cosmetic surgery, and wearing the occasional wig, Brown asserted that what she did was "totally, unrelentingly, gloriously, brazenly unnatural!" She expressed frustration with what seemed a feminist mandate for things natural, singling out for criticism women who either go natural or use cosmetics but "go to pieces" when anyone can actually tell they are doing so. "Cosmetics were never meant to be natural, and men have always known it is fun to be fooled," she wrote.[28] Brown would approach the issue most often with complete seriousness, but sometimes what she saw as the absurdity of the situation would encourage her to make fun. "Have you ever seen me looking fresh and natural?" she asked a group of women. "Do you want to start dogs barking and children screaming for their mommies?"[29]

Furthermore, Brown found the feminist "rules" both unnecessary and dishonest. She was acutely aware of the ways in which many women, including not only the media's appointed darling, Gloria Steinem, but also others who were equally committed to the movement, dressed differently for different audiences and, often, dressed stylishly. Gloria Steinem, who did not wear lipstick, and cultivated a "natural" look, wore lip gloss and streaked her hair. Brown often replied by using Steinem as her proof that "you don't have wear turtlenecks and have greasy hair to be a feminist." When one interviewer asked Brown if her enterprise really constituted anything more than "selling out to the enemy," Brown attempted to complicate the discussion. "That presupposes that you only look glamorous for men," she argued, "and if it were left up to you, you would wear a pillowcase and go dusty and dirty, never use a deodorant, never comb your hair. There's no reason you can't be a strong feminist and look sensational." Her Cosmo Girl, she explained, used cosmetics not so much to gain the attention of others but instead because she enjoyed having fun and looking fabulous.[30]

Not surprisingly, in the wake of Betty Friedan's condemnation of traditional women's magazines and their promotion of female subservience in the home, feminists increasingly began to identify women's magazines of various sorts as the enemies of women's liberation. One of their first targets was the *Ladies' Home Journal*. In 1970, media-savvy feminist journalists, organized as Media Women, planned and carried out a sit-in at the editorial offices of the *Ladies' Home Journal*. The *Journal* at that time was run by John Mack Carter, a young, accomplished editor and publisher who belonged to Sigma Delta Chi, a fraternity of distinguished journalists that had, until the previous year, excluded women from its membership. When Media Women met to organize their action, one woman put together twenty pages of article ideas for stories noticeably absent from the *Ladies' Home Journal*, including pieces about the Vietnam War and the harmful environmental effects of household detergents. The group also suggested several new kinds of service articles, including pieces on how to get an abortion, how to obtain a divorce, and how to achieve an orgasm.

Joined by members of ten other groups, including New York Radical Women, NOW, OWL (Older Women's Liberation), and student representatives from Women's Liberation at Columbia University and Barnard College, and flanked by a large cadre of reporters from major media outlets,

Media Women occupied the *Ladies' Home Journal* offices. They presented John Mack Carter with an ultimatum, which concluded with the following demand: "The Women's Liberation Movement represents the feelings of a large and growing mass of women throughout the country. Therefore, we demand that as an act of faith toward women in this country, the *Ladies' Home Journal* turn over to the Women's Liberation Movement the editorial content of one issue of the magazine, to be named the *Women's Liberated Journal*. We further demand a monthly column." The room became fairly still as the women anticipated Carter's response. As the journalist Susan Brownmiller later recalled, "The man who had built his career by speaking for women had lost his own voice."[31]

This occupation, which at its height included as many as two hundred protesters, lasted eleven hours and nearly ended terribly when one well-known feminist, Shulamith Firestone, leaped from a desk in an attempt to attack John Mack Carter. As Brownmiller remembers it, Karla Jay, a member of the feminist group Redstockings, intervened, flipping Firestone across the room. What nearly ended in a melee instead ended as it had started, peacefully, and Carter, who acted throughout the ordeal with great dignity, said the experience had been the most interesting and transformative day of his career. In the end, the *Journal* granted the group eight pages of the magazine's August issue and agreed to explore on-site daycare for its employees' children. Circulation rose dramatically following the *Ladies' Home Journal*'s discussions of women's rights, and other mainstream women's magazines, anticipating profits from changing their focus to keep up with changing times, fell into line. *McCall's* magazine, for example, began to include feminist news under the heading "Right Now."[32] In 1972 the *Ladies' Home Journal* hired the feminist Letty Cottin Pogrebin, Helen Gurley Brown's former publicist at Bernard Geis Associates, to write a regular column on working women's issues.[33]

The *Ladies' Home Journal* incident was the most successful and most documented sit-in, but it was by no means the only time that feminists targeted media enterprises. Not surprisingly, they also honed in on Helen Gurley Brown and *Cosmopolitan*. Kate Millett, who would be both shocked and dismayed to discover herself declared the leader of the women's liberation movement by *Time* magazine, which put her portrait on the cover of the August 1970 issue, led the group that invaded Brown's office. In Millett's opinion, *Cosmopolitan* engaged in the same kinds of woman-hating practiced by the literary masters she debunked in her doctoral thesis and soon-to-be-published manifesto on feminism,

Sexual Politics. According to Millett, "The magazine's reactionary politics were too much to take."[34]

Helen Gurley Brown remembered the incident with an indignity tempered with humor. "I was backed up against the radiator," she related, "but it wasn't very hot."[35] By the time the feminists invaded *Cosmopolitan,* other media bosses, including John Mack Carter, had capitulated to their demands, but in Brown these women encountered something different and perhaps unexpected: a woman who considered herself one of them. When Kate Millett demanded that *Cosmo* undergo a transformation and begin to advocate for women, Brown came right back at her: "I said . . . we were already a feminist book."[36] When they asked for space in which to place their own articles, Brown made it clear that she was willing to add to the feminist content of *Cosmopolitan,* but she was in charge. "I told them I would be glad to have articles written about feminists by feminists, but they would have to do the writing, we the editing."[37]

A few but not many articles dribbled in, and Brown continued with her own formula, which included occasional direct references to the women's movement. In her May 1970 editor's column, she discussed what happened during and then in the aftermath of the takeover of *Cosmopolitan's* editorial offices. Kate Millett and the other "interlopers," as Brown described them, ended the occupation by inviting Brown and her staff to attend a consciousness-raising session. Both a theoretical and a recruiting tool of the second wave of feminism, the consciousness-raising session was formed when a small group of women gathered to talk about their personal lives and then relate their own personal issues with larger social forces, namely sexism and male supremacy. Helen Gurley Brown, by now approaching fifty, may have felt too old for such personal revelations, or politically disinclined to see this as the solution for women. Whatever her motivations, she recalled the incident in *Cosmopolitan* with a good degree of humor: "Twelve of us—I almost said girls, but they say I must stop that and refer to us as women—sat about and related our hangups. Frankly, I was only into my eighth hangup when I had to relinquish the floor to the next hangup-ee."

Brown continued in this half-joking, half-serious tone. She couldn't reveal what was said at the consciousness-raising session, she explained, since that had to remain secret, but it reminded her very much of the group therapy she had undergone years earlier, "the difference being that in that group we blamed life, parents, bosses, poor nerves, and arrested development for our problems, while Women's Lib feel many of their/our problems stem from society's attitude toward women." In her conclusion, turning serious, Brown asserted that although some women went too far with this, all of her readers should take advantage of consciousness-raising opportunities.[38] Several months later, Brown published an excerpt from Millett's *Sexual Politics*.[39] She often described her own incredulity at the vehement disdain with which other advocates for women viewed her magazine. She purported, simply, not to get it. "The girl I'm editing for is the one who wants to achieve," she reasoned. "She wants to be known for herself. If that's not a feminist message, I don't know what is."[40]

For the most part, Brown refused to impugn others in the women's movement in her speeches or public appearances. In fact, with a generosity of spirit, she repeatedly wrote or spoke about how the same women who disparaged her magazine had moved the mainstream in positive directions. "Those hard-core, militant and even violent feminist leaders," she explained in a 1979 speech in Japan, "have led her [the American woman] to re-evaluate and even question views she hasn't dared to question for many generations or ever before." Essentially, as she saw it, radical elements had moved the middle in meaningful and profound ways, and she was not about to let her pride get in the way of praising any and all efforts that improved women's lives. "These revolutionary cries have stirred a quiet re-examination by women of what is right and proper for us to achieve and what will not work for us," she asserted. From subtle issues like communication between men and women to legal issues like sexual harassment and marital rape, Brown explained, those with the loudest voices had forced change to happen.[41]

On other occasions, too, she touted the benefits that the organized women's movement had provided women. In one piece she argued that the militants had never worried her. "They made such a clang and clatter," she stated admiringly. They were noisy and "a bit unfeminine," she granted, but she gave them credit in that department as well. "If they had been Southern belles the whole thing would not have happened. I give them total credit."[42] Brown believed that any woman who identified as a mouseburger, as she had, could hardly afford not to give the women's movement its due. As she saw it, only women who resented other women for having it easier than they had it, or who did not actually want to pursue meaningful work, or who were "rich, spoiled and reactionary" could ignore something as profound as women's liberation. Conversely, however, anyone pursuing liberation could hardly afford to ignore the mouseburger philosophy of hard work and individual achievement. "Maybe you won't have to work as hard as I did to arrive—I hope not—but believe me, pussycat, mouseburger rules are valid now even with Lib."[43]

Brown engaged with the most visible, at least in the media, feminists of her day. She took many opportunities to praise Gloria Steinem and Betty Friedan, but she also maintained that when they agreed on issues it was because they, rather than she, had revised their view of womanhood.[44] "The feminist movement has come more to my viewpoint, I believe," she stated. "They have acknowledged that men are necessary. You can be a feminist and still like men. You don't have to like all men, but you need one for you."[45] For decades, she would receive letters from readers who appreciated and identified with this point of view. On the eve of her departure from *Cosmopolitan,* one reader remembered the impact that Brown had had on her in the 1970s. "You liberated us," she wrote, "taught us to use our brains and not just our looks, and in the seventies when women suppressed their femininity in order to fit into the male-dominated workplace and the feminist revolution... you went right on telling us it's OK to be women, to use our beauty and our brains and to be confident about who we were as individuals." That kind of sentiment meant a tremendous amount to Brown, who clearly moved the mainstream, even if in less visible ways than did some of her contemporaries.[46]

As much as Helen Gurley Brown would encourage her readers to strive for sexual and economic independence, she certainly remained guilty of at least one of the practices attributed to her. For decades, she held on to the argument that women vastly outnumbered men in the sexual and relationship marketplace. As a result, she and *Cosmopolitan* would tell readers, women had to act coy, manipulative, coquettish, or downright dishonest in order to get one—or more—of these male creatures in their lives. In an interview Gloria Steinem conducted with Brown in the mid-1980s, Brown admitted that *Cosmopolitan* counseled women not to be honest with men but rather to engage in manipulation. Steinem confessed how as a young woman she, too, had behaved that way, "giggling and chuckling and saying how clever of you to know what time it is." She had outgrown it, thankfully, and found *Cosmo's* approach quite disturbing. Brown readily admitted her guilt. Her reasoning, however, exemplifies both her reluctance to expect too much of men and her "realism" feminism at play: "It's hard enough, Gloria, to get a man into your life if you're over the age of 40 without saying to him, 'Look, I've slept with about 35 people before I met you, I want to tell you that the speech you made at the Kiwanis Club was so boring I couldn't sit through it or I don't think it was your best work.'" She continued: "There's enough trouble having a man in your life without saying to him, 'Look, I didn't have an orgasm last night, I haven't had an orgasm with you, and I may never, the way things are going.'"

Again, a difference in how feminists would define or employ "truth" was at play, with Steinem advocating honesty between partners and Brown preferring not dishonesty but rather artifice, performance, and playing well the games women and men alike played. When Steinem pressed that Brown wouldn't want that kind of man in her life anyhow, Brown continued, "I'm exaggerating, of course. There are ways of saying the truth, but my observations are that men do not want the truth." Steinem countered that Brown, rather than seeing women and men as fundamentally similar, as she claimed to do, advocated treating men as though they were a different species, needing to be lied to for the sake of relationships. "I think that [this practice of putting men first] in us—in you and me," she advised Brown, "comes from an economic dependence, feeling that we want a meal ticket." Steinem was right on this count. Helen Gurley Brown, for all her support of women's independence, held deep fears that women did need men for survival. It would remain difficult for her, given her own past, to accept that working-class women in particular could thrive without some degree of support by better-off men.[47]

Helen Gurley Brown's version of human relationships never included complete truth telling between women and men, and she considered honesty a particularly overrated theme. Her all-time favorite *Cosmopolitan* piece, "The Contraception Capers," offered a humorous 1970s look back on sexual practices during the 1950s, when diaphragms provided the best means of birth control but were available only by prescription and given for the most part only to married women. Men, eager to have sex but buying into the double standard about sexual readiness or preparedness, proved skeptical or even fearful of women who had secured their own diaphragms. The article explored how women would attempt to convince men that they had never used a diaphragm before and had obtained it specifically for this relationship. "Women's lib extremists call this manipulation," the article informs its readers. "I call it manipulation, too. I also call it tact, diplomacy, common sense and dire necessity. Women simply could not afford to be honest twenty years ago." For Brown, even years later, the sexual playing field remained inherently unequal. Given such conditions, complete truth was unnecessary; it was also, very likely, problematic if not dangerous.[48]

What would become known in the late 1970s and 1980s as politically correct manifestations of female sexuality, or the "sex wars," included demands for outlawing pornography and talking through each step of a sexual relationship to ensure equality of understanding between potential sexual partners. Such measures would terrify Helen Gurley Brown even more than would demands for honesty. A lifelong advocate for women's assertion of their own sexuality, she nevertheless feared that feminists demanding political correctness would clean sex up to the point of sterility. "I'd like somehow to get the mystery back into sex," she wrote in the late 1970s about the move to sanitize sexual behaviors. She feared that sex had become "about as mysterious as a bowl of granola." For Brown, squeaky clean sex would lead only to a return of repression of women's sexuality, not its further liberation: "I wouldn't want to have the hypocrisy and guilt also returned with the mystery," she maintained, "but it would be wonderful to resurrect that feeling of naughtiness and joy and discovery and enchantment which existed before sex was so clean and accessible."[49]

By the mid-1980s, Brown had become increasingly frustrated with and vocal about what she considered the anti-sex elements of feminist thinking and practice. When feminists attempted literally to legislate sexual behaviors among consenting adults, Brown had to join the fray. "It seems to me the most specious idea that there is some standard of sexual conduct...some prima facie correct way for everybody to behave that we can all be turned into so many slices of white bread," she argued in an Oxford debate on sexuality. "Sexual storm troopers" or "a Big Brother in every bedroom," as she put it, would set women back decades. Men, she advised knowingly, would escape the worst of the repression, as a double standard for male and female sexual behavior would be one residual if not immediate result of any regulation.[50] As the sex wars continued, other feminists would voice similar concerns. In a 1985 *New York Times* article titled "How to Get the Women's Movement Moving Again," Betty Friedan warned that the pornography question had split the movement and had given the impression on college campuses "that to be a feminist is to be against sex." Friedan certainly moved closer to Brown on this one. "Whoever said that feminism shouldn't be sexy!" she exclaimed.[51]

If other feminists could be faulted for holding too closely to mainstream media, or to capitalism, or to men as the source of women's problems, Helen Gurley Brown could be faulted for clinging too tightly to motherhood as the insurmountable obstacle to real liberation for women.[52] As early as 1966 Brown claimed, quite simply, that the thing that held women back was the "built-in mechanism in their bodies that allows them to have babies." Women were encouraged to want babies and then, once pregnant, "the babies give them a way of life presumably to the exclusion of their needing to do anything else."[53] In the hierarchy of feminist complaints, Brown ranked motherhood far above other issues. When Naomi Wolf published *The Beauty Myth,* in which she asserted that standards of beauty proved women's continued undoing, Brown sparred with Wolf on a television show hosted by Ronald Reagan Jr., the president's son. "There is a conspiracy against women, and I'd be the first to say so," asserted Brown in as close to a fighting voice as she could muster. "I am a practicing feminist.... But getting us to be beautiful ain't the problem! We are encouraged to be mothers, to be pregnant." She described the pro-life movement as one manufactured to keep women "encumbered with children."[54]

Given her anti-motherhood predilections, Helen Gurley Brown refused, until 1986, to produce a special issue on mothers for *Cosmopolitan.* She admitted that it was "ridiculous" to avoid writing on children simply because she did not "understand" them, yet that was the magazine's general practice. In all fairness, when she finally commissioned the special section, "Mothers Who Work," the twenty-four-page spread addressed many of the issues Brown had raised in one way or another over the years as she covered the economic and dating realities of single parents and divorced mothers. Nevertheless, *Cosmo* was behind the curve, and Brown was criticized for her late entry into the motherhood discussion. Gloria Steinem remarked that although *Cosmo* had introduced sex into women's magazines in the 1960s, in the case of motherhood, they were "the last." Steinem took her critique a step further. "Hopefully this means that the Cosmo girl is finally becoming the Cosmo woman." It didn't mean that at all. Overall, it meant that Brown would acknowledge what she knew well, that working women with children faced many obstacles in their personal and professional lives.

There was, however, no chance that the child would usurp the woman, or girl, as *Cosmo*'s premier audience or concern, and Brown refused to place a child alongside the woman on the magazine's cover. Steinem would describe this lack of children in the magazine as its myopia: "It's a fantasy world in which women all look beautiful and have enormous bosoms, and [yet] there's a remarkable absence of children."[55] What Steinem refused to see was the degree to which women desired that representation, a decided escape into a world in which they were not defined primarily through motherhood or their domestic affiliations. The remarkable absence of children would appeal not just to single women but also to mothers who relished the release not from womanhood but from the relentless images of women defined by pregnancy, childbirth, and childrearing.

As a childless woman, Brown would always advocate for women to maintain personal lives after they had children, but she was most concerned with single parents rather than with women in committed relationships who bore joint responsibility for their children's care. She knew little of these women's actual lives. If some feminists thought women's liberation would be achieved if they only dropped men from their lives, Brown could prove equally myopic in claiming that women's liberation would be achieved only after women dropped babies from their lives. "We have the babies," she told a group of women, as though it was the having them, rather than the imbalanced ways in which families raised them, that put women at risk.[56] When at times journalists called Brown on the lack of information about motherhood in the magazine, she admitted that it was her own reluctance that dictated magazine policy.[57]

The truth is, however, that single parents, the kinds of economically challenged women she could best relate to, had a presence in the magazine from the first days of Brown's *Femme* proposal, in which she described the magazine as one for women who had to cope with dating when they were single parents and in which she suggested an article titled "I'm Not Married to the Baby's Father and Never Was."[58] Women's abilities to survive with children and maintain their own lives and identities, rather than their relationships with their children, constituted Brown's concerns. She always found motherhood a challenging issue, and at one point in the early 1990s she acknowledged that David had offered her some sage advice on the subject: "My husband says I should shut up about children because it makes you so unpopular."[59]

Within the pages of *Cosmopolitan*, Helen Gurley Brown put forward her version of feminism, which was most often cultural rather than political. However, she felt strongly enough about two political issues in particular, abortion rights and the Equal Rights Amendment, to work them directly into her magazine. Even more profoundly, these issues would encourage Brown, uncharacteristically, to enter into agreements with other women's magazines about shared political content. In 1975 she met with a group of women's magazine editors representing *Glamour*, *Redbook*, *Ms.*, *Woman's Day*, and *McCall's* to discuss what women's magazines could or ought to be doing in relation to the ERA.[60] As national voices, the magazines had the potential to influence readers, who might in turn influence legislators in the four states that still needed to ratify the amendment. Some of the editors felt they should collectively endorse it, while others wanted to stop short of doing so. In the end, each agreed to run something and disseminate "actual" information, as opposed to much of what passed for information in a highly charged media environment that often lionized opposition to the amendment. The group of editors also agreed to include contact information to assist readers who might want to get involved in the cause. In short, each would indirectly promote the ERA and encourage their readers to support it more directly.[61]

Helen Gurley Brown followed up the meeting by writing to, among others, John Mack Carter, now editor of *Good Housekeeping*, inviting him to join the group.[62] In the end, during the country's bicentennial celebration in July 1976, thirty-five women's magazines produced special issues that dealt to one degree or another with the Equal Rights Amendment.[63] Even after the group effort, Brown would pen a Cosmo Girl ad for the *New York Times* in which the ERA featured prominently:

> Do I support the ERA? Of course I do. I find it incredible that anybody could seriously not support it. If our country can put a man on the moon—a totally astounding accomplishment—why can't we also guarantee that a woman will not be discriminated against just because she's female? My fav mag has always believed a woman should go where her talent and desire take her, whether it's mothering, modeling, plumbing or piloting a 747—the ERA will just make that freedom of choice a law (which it should have been already). That magazine says love and friends are very important to a woman, but so is her job. Well, we can have (if we try) the man we want, and the friends we cherish, but now it's time to guarantee the *life* we want—and deserve! I love that magazine. I guess you could say I'm That COSMOPOLITAN Girl.[64]

This overtly political action invited appreciation from a range of feminists, Betty Friedan among them. "If the Cosmo girl is for the ERA, then I'm for the Cosmo girl," she declared. "I don't mind the Cosmo girl being boldly sexy. Whoever said that feminism had to be against sex?" she inquired, erasing very real and divisive disputes within the movement but no doubt pleasing Brown at the same time.[65]

However much Helen Gurley Brown, or more likely Gloria Steinem, would see *Cosmopolitan* and *Ms.* as magazines with starkly different agendas, many readers during the second wave refused to view one as feminist and the other as not. Readers might prove more loyal to one magazine or the other but often viewed the magazines' dedication to women as an overriding, and shared, characteristic. One journalist discussed the ways in which women's lives had changed from 1962, when *Sex and the Single Girl* first hit the shelves, to 1977. In that fifteen years, as one young woman included in the interview explained, high school and college girls had been educated "by magazines like *Ms.* and *Cosmopolitan*" to consider options other than early marriage and homemaking.[66] Readers, apparently, could discover politics in culture, culture in politics, sexiness in feminism, and feminism in sexiness. Amid the "how to please a lover" pieces that *Cosmopolitan* surely featured, readers encountered, read, and responded positively to Brown's entreaties to treat themselves, first and foremost, well.

On behalf of her Cosmo Girl, Helen Gurley Brown would reach out to other magazine editors on just one other occasion, this time concerning reproductive rights. In August 1986 she sent out a host of invitations, courting editors for lunch with Kate Michelman, then the executive director of the National Abortion Rights Action League (NARAL). To her delight, editors from *Glamour, Self, New Woman, Woman's Day, Good Housekeeping, Redbook, Parents, Harper's, Elle, Savvy, Family Circle,* and the *Ladies' Home Journal* accepted. In addition, *Ms.* and *Mademoiselle* sent representatives. Brown spoke at the meeting, and the editors agreed to run pieces supporting the protection of abortion rights in their March 1987 issues. *Cosmopolitan* featured several items, including "Abortion: Your Right Under Attack," "Choice: Separating Myth from Fact," "My Illegal Abortion," and an article on why eight prominent women, including Katherine Hepburn, Gloria Steinem, and Julia Child, were pro-choice.[67] Brown felt herself most "actively" feminist in her work on behalf of abortion rights. "I don't know if strident is the right word," she reported, musing on the terminology most often applied to feminists, "but I'm as vocal as I can be. Rather than lose legal abortion, I think a lot of us have to speak out and make some noise."[68]

One of the most significant reasons Brown hesitated in giving much space in the magazine to overtly political elements of feminism was her resistance to feature or even acknowledge anything negative. She refused to include negative movie reviews, and she agonized for years over how to include articles on Phyllis Schlafly, whose anti-ERA stance she enjoyed mocking outside the pages of the magazine, or Anita Bryant, whose anti-gay stance angered Brown. As a former *Cosmo* writer put it, Brown had to figure out a way to make them look bad "by sticking little needles in them" rather than by criticizing them outright. Overtly feminist analyses, which by rights had many negative issues to raise and explore, did not fit into the overall zeitgeist of the magazine, which opted always for the benign rather than the belligerent approach, even when it tackled issues Brown herself felt most passionate about.[69] In a letter Brown wrote to the self-avowed feminist and longtime *Glamour* editor Ruth Whitney, she suggested that the movement had suffered from its negativity and had to find ways both to celebrate women's progress and to outline women's limitations. What feminism needed, she told Whitney, was more women who cared about how they looked and cared about moving ahead. "Somehow *Glamour* always delineated this idea," she wrote, "that gorgeous is good and so is achievement."[70]

Helen Gurley Brown's positive outlook extended to her support for other women's magazines. She claimed a niche with *Cosmopolitan* and readily defended her magazine against its competitors, but she also offered, often unsolicited—and one wonders how welcome—comments on other magazines and how they might improve themselves. She corresponded with Ruth Whitney at *Glamour* several times, and she once wrote to Gloria Steinem about *Ms.*, including a thousand-dollar check from her own account for the Ms. Foundation and letting Steinem know that she had some suggestions for improving the magazine. "Please don't think I'm being patronizing and please don't think I have any wish to have any other women's magazines prosper because of anything that I might know or pass along," she told Steinem, "but *Ms.* is different and I do know something. If this is a crummy idea (meeting to talk), don't worry that you'll hurt my feelings by not responding."[71] Later she attempted to assist Steinem in getting support from the Hearst Foundation for what had become, in one of *Ms.*'s many incarnations, an ailing publication. She explained her willingness to reach out from *Cosmo* to *Ms.* because of their complementary natures, labeling *Ms.* "a kind of early warning system on emerging issues that is helpful to other women's magazines."[72]

Brown felt that other magazines, including *Ms.*, increasingly copied *Cosmo* by featuring pieces on women's sexuality, but she never felt they threatened her magazine by doing so. "If you have one good women's magazine," she explained, "it does not mean that you cannot have three or four or nine."[73] Brown envisioned a sisterhood among the magazines, just as many feminists envisioned a sisterhood among women, even when the focus of one group or another differed. Importantly, Brown looked for similarities, not only with the likes of *Ms.*, but also with women's service magazines like the *Ladies' Home Journal*, not erasing their differences but instead looking for points of contact. And as she began to see herself as the wildly successful editor she had become, she reached out to other kinds of magazines. When she criticized *Reader's Digest*, a much-maligned but highly successful magazine that she enjoyed reading, the editors invited her to visit and she provided them with an enormous amount of advice. She did the same with advertising clients, including Foster Parents Plan, Saks Fifth Avenue, and Bloomingdale's, seeing her work as much allied with the advertising industry and the larger magazine industry as it was with the feminist movement.

Helen Gurley Brown had many admirers within the women's magazine ranks, partly because of her generosity in reaching out. Marcia Ann Gillespie, editor-in-chief of *Essence* in the 1960s and then editor of *Ms.* in the 1980s, viewed Brown as an important role model. "I frequently referred to you," she told Brown in the 1990s, "as in 'what would Helen Gurley Brown do with this subject?'" Gillespie explained that the admiration was professional but also extended to the ways in which Helen Gurley Brown, the person, emerged in her work. She called it the Helen Gurley Brown touch: "not just what you accomplished with the magazine but also your genuine caring and concern for others, the thoughtful notes and all the other ways you reached out to others."[74]

Whether or not her critics appreciated it, Helen Gurley Brown undoubtedly helped define the second wave of feminism, in part through her Cosmo Girl. Occasionally, Brown would be asked to name women in contemporary life who could be called Cosmo Girls. In 1990 she named Madonna, Ivana Trump, Joan Lunden, and Margaret Thatcher. She thought through her last nomination, though, and eventually took it back. "Her husband knew politics was more important to her than he was," she mused, admiring Thatcher's dedication to her professional life. "The only thing is that she's not a feminist. I don't know whether you could be a Cosmo woman and not be part of the feminist movement."[75] In the end, Brown would find a variety of ways to respond to the many critics who could not square women's liberation and *Cosmopolitan*. "Most so-called feminists like me when we're together," she explained at one point, "but they don't really get it with *Cosmo*. They don't realize that *Cosmo* is a feminist magazine." Brown maintained that women's liberation was entirely compatible with the *Cosmopolitan* philosophy: "Nobody should be held back because of race or sex or color. And that goes for men, too—we want them to be comfortable and happy. But we don't want to live totally through men and children; we don't want to get our identities from these other people; we want to do something on our own. We want to achieve. That is *Cosmo's* message."[76]

Sometimes journalists would reveal, in confessional tones, the private joys and the public shame of living as intellectuals or as feminists and reading *Cosmopolitan*. One reporter rationalized her early-1980s reading habits by explaining that *Cosmopolitan* was selling around six times more copies than *Ms.* was, contrary to feminist arguments about what women wanted. The reporter bought *Cosmo* on her birthday, whenever she wondered about a lover's compatibility, when she was feeling down, or when she just gave in to it all and coveted prize thighs. "But before you condemn me as terminally silly," she urged her readers, "let me tell you why Helen Gurley Brown has done every bit as much to liberate women as Gloria Steinem and Betty Friedan put together." She focused on the ways in which Brown began to erase the sexual double standard. The most important contribution Brown made, however, one visible in every issue of *Cosmo*, "is that men will not rescue you. Helen knows that life is cruel, painful and unfair and if you sit around like a wimp you will never achieve love, a good job or prize thighs."[77] One wonders just how many closet feminist *Cosmopolitan* readers there were, complaining about the system but working it to their best advantage, enjoying their sexuality and their smarts, and following, more or less, the dictates of Helen Gurley Brown.

Certainly Brown's philosophy lives on in the twenty-first century, as new groups of women, calling themselves the third wave, enjoy sexy and revealing clothing, reclaim the term "girl," explore a variety of sexual practices, acknowledge the pleasures capitalism affords and the problems it inflicts, and attempt to make feminism more fun if not more youthful. Like their predecessors in the first and second waves, who fought for suffrage and then for women's liberation, these more recent advocates consider themselves the vanguard of feminism, raising the issues that remain unspoken, or unrelenting, or even unthinkable in the aftermath of the second wave.[78] More than those earlier feminists, they argue, they accept living in mainstream worlds, acknowledge and understand the diversity of women's lives, and celebrate not only heterosexuality but also all other possible sexual identities. When they push for these freedoms in women's lives and refuse to be considered victims regardless of the obstacles they face, they draw, knowingly or not, on their most striking second-wave predecessor, Helen Gurley Brown.

11

aging, resisting, redefining

When Helen Gurley Brown first stepped into the editor's office at *Cosmopolitan* in 1965, she was forty-three years old. It was not unusual to encounter an editor a generation older than a magazine's audience, particularly when the target audience was that coveted eighteen-to-thirty-four age group. Experience and business acumen often compensated for the difference, and in Brown's case the degree of identification she accomplished with her particular audience more or less buried criticisms of her age—at least for a time. Inevitably, though, the topic of her age and the growing disparity between her age and that of her readers would become more and more of a story in itself. And through the years, as Helen Gurley Brown encountered her own aging process and that of family and friends, she attempted to resist and redefine what it meant to grow older. Not surprisingly, given her Cosmo Girl predilections and her dedication to individual achievement, Brown would claim repeatedly and in terms courageous, saucy, and at times outlandish, that all women, even old ones, can have it all.

During her years at *Cosmo*, Brown continued to look for additional opportunities to reach her loyal *Cosmopolitan* fans, speak to an even wider public, and make more money, and in this process she revealed an awareness of aging almost from the start. Helen Gurley Brown the editor insisted that the *Cosmo* reader, by rights, ruled the world, but at the same time Helen Gurley Brown the woman also sought a vehicle with which to claim that life remained exciting, sensuous, and fully engaging after age thirty-five. Helen and David began together to consider the cultural shifts in women's and men's lives that almost before their eyes might allow for the successful marketing of a magazine aimed at an older crowd. Perhaps they wondered just how long the already middle-aged Helen would be able to continue in her capacity as editor of a magazine for young women. Perhaps they wondered if Helen would grow tired of endlessly pleasing and appeasing this younger crowd. Perhaps they feared she would be driven out of *Cosmopolitan*, given the age consciousness and rapid turnover within the industry. Whatever their motivations, as early as 1967 Helen and David attempted to make concrete their wishes, and they submitted a proposal to Hearst for a magazine they tentatively titled *Lifeline*.

Aimed at an urban audience over thirty-five who had "decided to 'hang in there' and be part of the alive, sexy and functioning human race," *Lifeline* would deal principally with health, nutrition, and "good looks." In the proposal, the Browns envisaged their reader as someone who wanted to remain vigorous, attractive, and sexy, but who lacked information on and affirmation about how to live such a life. As the Browns saw it, their generation, not the baby boomers, would be the first to reject the unpleasant elements of aging. Half of the magazine would be devoted to health-related issues such as diet, nutrition, exercise, and emotional well-being; a quarter would offer profiles of individuals, famous and otherwise. The final quarter would consist of illustrations to accompany the other sections. The proposal might have worked well in the late twentieth century, with extensive market research pointing to the lucrative nature of recognizing not only the over-thirty-four market but also those who, decades older, exercised "gray power," but in attempting to target even a slightly older than the coveted eighteen-to-thirty-four-year-old group the Browns were once again ahead of their time.[1]

Predictably, perhaps, for the day, regardless of the convincing nature of the Browns' description of this emerging demographic, their own standing in the industry, and Helen's proven success at making money for her company, Hearst declined, stating simply that they were not interested in an "older" crowd. It would be another twenty years, in the late 1980s, before Frances Lear, the wife of the television producer Norman Lear, would launch *Lear's,* a magazine for women in their late thirties and older, whose slogan read "For the Woman Who Was Born Today." As for Helen Gurley Brown, she let go of the idea for a magazine for older women and would not raise it again until she readied herself for retirement from *Cosmopolitan.* But she would hardly be deterred from looking at other avenues, age-related and otherwise, to keep herself and her messages in public view.[2]

From her 1969 *Single Girls Cookbook,* to an updated *Sex and the Single Girl* in 1971, to four additional books in the next three decades, Brown promoted her sex-friendly message to women young and old while she sat at the helm of the thriving *Cosmopolitan.* She composed her books at night and on weekends, and she was almost never without a project.[3] Her day job, which provided her continuous contact with so many young women, along with her own positive attitude, kept her young. But as time went on, she read her age on the face she saw in the mirror and on the faces of her contemporaries, and she determined to discover the secrets of fighting age—and to share them. In addition to her mandatory daily exercise and strict diet, Brown began to undergo cosmetic surgery. Because the age disparity between Brown and her readers continued to grow, because she never lied about how old she was, and because she never relinquished an opportunity to extol the virtues of cosmetic surgery and diet to offset the ravages of aging, it soon became impossible to read anything about Helen Gurley Brown that did not mention her age. In article after article, interview after interview, journalists remarked not only on the dedication with which she continued to promote her messages but also on the ways in which she aged, counter to or in tandem with her chronological age. They counted the years, noting in particular her fiftieth, sixtieth, and seventieth birthdays and the degree to which she could measure up to existing beauty standards—or set new ones. For many observers, Brown's age increasingly became the story. But lest we fall into the same trap, let us move away for a time from the aging story to some other stories of Helen Gurley Brown's middle and later years: her home life and relationships with her mother and sister, her relationships with friends, and her professional successes in and outside of *Cosmopolitan.*

Inside the home and with her husband, Helen experienced the challenges of contemporary marriage and the support two people so dedicated to professional life and to each other could provide one another. In David Brown, Helen had found a mate who was her match in professional aspiration. They experienced the ups and downs of work life together, with each as the other's most loyal source of support. As David explained it, "Our marriage is such that you can't divide us. She couldn't make it without me, nor I without her." He claimed that their very compatibility explained their desire not to have children: "We're just too selfishly well-mated."[4] Their career lives, which for both included a fair amount of risk taking, provided many occasions on which they would rely almost exclusively on each other for support. For David, the first occasion occurred soon after their marriage, when, as he put it, his career at Twentieth Century Fox "went bust" just as *Sex and the Single Girl* "headed for immortality."

Although David had had measurable success at Twentieth Century Fox, even given the challenges that television posed to film, he was, much to his surprise and chagrin, fired in the ugly aftermath of the filming of the 1963 film *Cleopatra*. Budgeted at ten million dollars and eventually costing thirty million, *Cleopatra* demonstrated the vagaries of the Hollywood formula in a time of flux. David's friend and coworker Dick Zanuck was charged with the task of firing a thousand people, and David found himself ousted. It pained Zanuck to fire David, with whom he worked particularly closely and well, but he had no say in the matter. As he would put it later, "I was in charge of a firing squad."[5]

David recovered quite quickly, almost immediately securing a position as executive vice-president of New American Library's hardcover division in New York, but professional uncertainty loomed during the next few years, and David's emotional recovery from the experience was slow. He had suffered intermittent bouts of depression since childhood—with the sole exception of the period he spent in the Army, when he was "too busy staying alive" to notice troubling mood swings—and his occasional excessive drinking darkened his moods further. "I've come closest to wrecking my marriage and friendships while drinking, even moderately," he later recalled.[6] Things became particularly difficult at home when David was either out of work altogether or mired in work that left him dissatisfied professionally.

David Brown would never become an alcoholic, in part because Helen so carefully controlled his eating and his drinking. For the most part he welcomed the discipline she imposed, finding difficulty in imposing it on himself, but he occasionally joked publicly about his unrequited desires for food, liquor, and cigars. "I used to be fat," he quipped, "but you can't stay that way around Helen. She doesn't say it out loud, but you get the message." Helen insisted that David weigh himself daily, and her passion for cooking for him was in part a means to control his caloric intake. She had developed an interest in dieting, nutrition, and exercise in her thirties, and she would remain passionate, if not fanatical, about staying slim—and keeping David slim. In the end, David had to learn to live with Helen's controlling nature, particularly where food was concerned, and Helen had to learn to live with what sometimes amounted to a depressive pall permeating their home life.[7]

Once Helen had quit her job at Kenyon & Eckhardt in order to promote *Sex and the Single Girl,* and David had secured his position at New American Library, where he would, among other things, edit the James Bond novels, the couple relocated from Los Angeles to Park Avenue and 65th Street in Manhattan. Helen was then in a particularly convenient location when she took over at *Cosmopolitan,* which was housed in the Hearst building not too far across town, on West 57th Street. Within a year, however, David would face a job change again. Although he had offers in New York, including the editorship of the *Saturday Evening Post,* in 1964 he returned to Twentieth Century Fox and began to commute to Los Angeles. He later claimed that, had he not received an offer from Fox, he would likely have taken over as publisher of *Cosmopolitan* when Helen became editor. As much as they operated as a unit of one, this might well have proved too close a relationship. "I don't think it would have worked," he mused. "My job was clearly to launch Helen and not hang around."[8] David continued to commute; once Helen became established at *Cosmopolitan,* they would not leave New York City. David began to work again with Dick Zanuck, now on a series of hit films that included *Patton, Butch Cassidy and the Sundance Kid,* and *MASH.* Regardless of their success, however, which was considerable, conflicts between Dick Zanuck and his father, Darryl, the head of Fox, would emerge and reemerge, and in 1970 both Zanuck and Brown lost their jobs at Fox.

After a quick stint with Warner Brothers, David Brown and Dick Zanuck decided to form their own production company, the Zanuck/Brown Company. As agonizing as the Fox years had been, David later expressed gratitude for the difficult trajectory of those early days. "Had we not left Fox involuntarily," he stated generously but sincerely, "we would never have chosen to become entrepreneurs."[9] As supervising executives for Fox, Brown and Zanuck had overseen hundreds of films but had their names attached to none of them. They now had an

bad girls go everywhere

opportunity to make a name for themselves as producers, and beyond that, they relished the newfound freedom the disassociation provided. They worked alternately out of Dick's house and David's hotel room, making appointments from phone booths and delivering dictation to secretaries in car rides around Los Angeles. It would prove to be not only a liberating but also an enormously lucrative partnership. Their first big hit, *The Sting,* received ten Academy Award nominations and won seven Oscars, including Best Picture.

It befits Helen and David's relationship that his active support of *Sex and the Single Girl, Cosmopolitan,* and most of Helen's other professional endeavors would be complemented by her serendipitous contribution to one of the most significant decisions of his career. The Zanuck/Brown collaboration's blockbuster hit, *Jaws,* would initially arrive on David's desk via *Cosmopolitan* magazine. Helen's book editor at *Cosmo* regularly wrote brief synopses of the books she read and then passed her note cards on to Helen, who would select a few from among the stack for inclusion in the magazine. On one such card the editor noted, "This would make a good movie." Intrigued, Helen passed the card on to David who, equally intrigued, read the book, Peter Benchley's *Jaws.* David contacted Benchley, secured the film rights, and went on to produce the highest grossing box office hit to date. Directed by the young Steven Spielberg, *Jaws* initiated the summer blockbuster pattern, in which studios would attempt to make film releases events in themselves. From there Zanuck/Brown went on to continued success with hits that included *The Verdict* and *Cocoon.*

After David had acquired the film rights to *Driving Miss Daisy,* which itself eventually won four Oscars, he ended his more than thirty-year relationship with Dick Zanuck to go out on his own. He founded The Manhattan Project in 1988, producing a more eclectic line of work that included films, a classic short-story series for HBO, and highly success-ful live drama, including shows for the Broadway theater. In 1990 David Brown and Dick Zanuck would be awarded the Irving G. Thalberg Memo-rial Award by the Academy of Motion Pictures Arts and Sciences, an award presented to producers for their entire body of work.

David's career path, impressive as it has been, also included some diffi-cult times for the couple's relationship. He took his travails with Twentieth Century Fox personally, and the intermittent depressions he experienced over the years were in no small part related to work. As Helen well under-stood, David's one passion, aside from her, was work. "I have never seen a more company-oriented man than my husband," she explained. "He has no interest in sports...no intense interest in politics unless they affect his business life...no women or gambling (so far as I know!)...just BUSINESS."[10] Acutely aware that such a description fit her equally well, Helen defended this approach to life. "I don't mean to say he isn't widely read or curious about the world...but this is a man who simply cared more about 20th Century Fox, I believe, than Richard Milhous Nixon could care about his country." Some might dispute the logic implicit in Helen's comparison, but the sentiment rang true. For the Browns, work and identity, personal and professional, could never be disentangled.

David's success with *Jaws* was a professional coup, but it was also, importantly, quite rewarding financially, and he invested the money wisely and fairly conservatively in government bonds and then in real estate. Against Helen's wishes, David purchased a spectacular apartment on Manhattan's West Side. By now having absorbed much of elite New York's preference for the East Side, Helen found David's choice confounding. She blamed Dick Zanuck for the decision, as he had for years been telling David about the wonderful apartment that the film director and producer Mike Nichols owned on West 81st Street. When the apartment came on the market, David went after it. Helen moved across town reluctantly, but over the years she would come to believe, with good reason, that they must have some of the best views in Manhattan. The Browns' four-story penthouse apartment, whose twenty-third-story terrace on Central Park West overlooks the entirety of Central Park, is a one-of-a-kind dwelling in the Beresford, a building adjacent to the Museum of Natural History that houses celebrities from the worlds of Hollywood and of sports, legendary entrepreneurs, and less well known but no less wealthy New York citizens. Along with the Dakota and the San Remo, the Beresford is considered one of the three most prestigious addresses on Manhattan's Upper West Side.[11]

As Helen and David Brown eased in to New York celebrity life themselves, with their increasingly visible personalities and professional accomplishments, Helen relied for sustenance on her continued relationships with family and friends in Arkansas and Oklahoma. She talked twice a week by phone, briefly during the week and for an hour on Saturdays, with her mother and sister, and would continue to find her relationships with them both supportive and vexing. Mary, who would never recover from the damaging effects of her polio, became an alcoholic. Helen would make mention of Mary's drinking in letters, and one gets the sense that Helen felt that if she expressed sufficient belief in Mary's power, Mary, too, would take on that certainty as her reality. "I worry about your drinking too much," she wrote once, "but somehow that is none of my business and I have a deep core of conviction that whatever pertains to your self you can manage and keep under control." Helen recognized that Mary held far more of the responsibility for their mother than she did, even if Helen contributed financially on a regular basis, and she considered that responsibility alone enough to drive Mary to drink. "I think that whatever stubbornness and resentments you show are based on long years of bearing up under mother," she wrote. "This is certainly not to minimize her burdens and griefs. But while you and I are 'hard on her,' she is also 'hard on us.'"[12] Helen, too, would suffer a strained relationship with Cleo, and as always she would feel both grateful for and guilty about the distance between them.

Mary Gurley married George Alford, whom she met in a veterans' rehabilitation hospital in Okmulgee, Oklahoma, where they both spent some time seeking treatment. George had been in a grain-elevator accident that crushed his shoulder and left him facing chronic pain. His pain exacerbated an existing dependency on alcohol and led to a newfound dependency on drugs. Mary's long-hoped-for remedy to her own physical and financial dependency on her mother, through a successful marriage, would not materialize. As Helen explained, "It looked for one shining moment as though there might be somebody to take care of her and even ease the financial burden; that halcyon prospect didn't last long." It was certainly an odd coincidence, if not a cruel irony, that Mary lost her father to an elevator accident and then later married a man who had been seriously and permanently injured, also in an elevator accident. The couple moved to Shawnee, Oklahoma, where they would live for the rest of their lives. Cleo, who lived with her sister in Osage, Arkansas, for a number of years after Mary married, would eventually move in with her daughter and son-in-law, but by this time not any one of them could do much for the others. Helen attempted to remain supportive of her brother-in-law and her sister. "George belonged to my sister, was usually good and helpful with her, so he went with the territory for me," Helen would explain simply.[13]

In her adult life, Mary would hold an occasional job but found it difficult to maintain full-time employment. She kept the books for a company in Shawnee, but her passion in life was the organization that eventually saved her, Alcoholics Anonymous. She initially traveled thirty miles each way to Oklahoma City to attend AA meetings but eventually started and became the mainstay of a branch in Shawnee. When anyone looked up AA in the Shawnee telephone directory, they would find Mary's number.[14] Helen would occasionally accompany Mary to meetings and always remained proud of her sister's dedication to her community of active and recovering alcoholics. Mary was generous not only to her peers but also to Helen, never asking her, as so many others did, for money. In fact, every year Mary would invite Helen to choose a gift for herself from one of the many catalogs she kept at home.

Helen and David helped with George's health care, bringing him to New York so that he could seek specialized nerve surgery at New York University Hospital. But the surgery proved unsuccessful. They paid for his acupuncture and psychiatric treatments, neither of which proved palliative. His chronic pain would take its toll on the entire family. Mary would call Helen about George, oftentimes at work, which Helen found both difficult and instructive.[15] The experience helped her understand how personal issues sometimes invaded work life, and she vowed to remain understanding when her own employees found themselves such a position.

Helen solicited help for George from others as well. On one occasion she wrote to the Christian televangelist Oral Roberts, whom she had met on the *Merv Griffin Show,* asking him to have someone from his church see George about his chronic pain. This pain may or may not be real, she explained, "nevertheless, it's 'real' enough to practically have wrecked the life of my brother-in-law, my sister (the one I really care about), and, up to a point, my husband and myself." She praised Roberts, regardless of their monumental differences in worldview, noting his reputation for helping others. Roberts answered affirmatively, perhaps out of his Christian principles and perhaps from more self-serving motives. He had already called George and invited him to come in, he reported. He then asked Helen Gurley Brown to consider excerpting his wife's forthcoming book in *Cosmopolitan.* His wife, he reported in the letter, had balked at his audaciousness when he mentioned the idea to her. "Oral, *Cosmopolitan?*" she laughed. "Honey, they have the readers," he explained, "and besides I like Helen Gurley Brown!"[16] Roberts ended up sending a plane for George Alford, but the treatment he provided did not result in any significant healing. As thanks for the effort, Helen convinced the Hearst Foundation to make a ten-thousand-dollar contribution to Oral Roberts University.

In another instance, Helen again solicited the help of the Hearst Foundation, this time to purchase a van to pick Mary up at home and take her to church. By the early 1980s, George was confined to a nursing home, making occasional visits home, and Cleo's health had further deteriorated. Mary, always confined to a wheelchair and increasingly overweight as the years went by, found it hard to get around, and her already limited social life began to constrict further. Helen recognized that Mary needed to get out of the house, but she could not do so without assistance. With the support of her employer, Helen was able to donate to the church a van with a hydraulic lift. Helen also paid for live-in help for her mother and sister, but managing that help proved difficult, particularly from afar. She recognized that her family could be difficult, and she tried to treat the employees with care. At one time she used her celebrity to try to hold on to one such employee by securing her an autograph of the singer Larry Gatlin. This woman, "about as deranged as a human being can get over an entertainer," would be tremendously appeased by such a gift and might as a result stay on even though her working conditions in the Alford–Bryan household were admittedly far from perfect.[17]

In her later years, after George died, Mary was often bedridden, struck annually by pneumonia and generally weak for long periods afterward. During Helen's visits the sisters would watch the Westminster Kennel Club Dog Show, which Mary would tape and save for Helen, or "deep-dish soul visit," talking about their parents and their childhoods in Little Rock. Mary's sentimentality, at once understandable, would at times grate on Helen's nerves, but they generally got along well. "The girl was never jealous," Helen explained about Mary. "She cared deeply about whether I was happy, never hit me for money, cars, jewelry—except occasional costume. She was amazing!"[18]

Mary outlived both her husband and her mother, who, in 1980, at age eighty-seven, succumbed to arterial sclerosis. After Cleo's death, Helen lived with the regret many have when difficult relationships remained troubled through to the end. Their relationship had benefited from the distance and the only occasional visits, but they never fully reached a comfortable peace with each other. "Jesus, though, I wish I had lots more years to be nice to her," Helen would assert. "You know what we could have used— a referee!" If someone from the outside had been able to explain Cleo to Helen, the daughter might have been far more understanding and tolerant of her anxious and pessimistic mother. "When I heard it from her," Helen explained honestly about Cleo's continual complaints, "I just wanted to leave the room."[19] Cleo's death signified additional heartache for Helen, as it left Mary alone. One day Helen was in a meeting when a call came through from her sister. The most recent live-in employee, there just a few months, had walked out. Mary sat in her living room, completely alone, unable to take care of herself.[20] Helen again stepped in, but she recognized that Mary most often suffered in silence. Helen experienced some survivor's guilt that Mary had acquired polio and she had not, that she had been able to go on and live out her dreams and Mary had not, but their relationship was based, by and large, not on guilt but on mutual affection. Helen admitted after Mary's death that she didn't miss the "60 years of worry and anxiety" about her sister but that she did miss her.[21]

Helen Gurley Brown worked long days in the office and then much of every weekend at home, but when she had free time, she exchanged letters and phone calls with her childhood friends from Arkansas, Elizabeth Biltheimer and Betty Tab Hearst Murray. She and David occasionally went out to dinner with Charlotte Kelly, who, like Helen, had moved from a secretarial to a professional career, becoming a public relations executive and eventually head of public relations at Hearst. Brown's lifelong friends include Faith Stewart-Gordon, former owner of the Russian Tea Room, and gossip columnist Liz Smith, who would find in Brown first an indomitable employer and then a dear friend. "I find it difficult to recall a time," she would write in her autobiography, "when my life wasn't dominated in one way or another by the dynamic Helen Gurley Brown."[22] Another of Brown's most longstanding New York friendships, with Ann Siegel, ended in disagreement. According to Brown, Ann Siegel's husband, Mort, wanted Helen to endorse Hillary Clinton's opponent when Clinton ran for the Senate seat in New York State. When Helen indicated that she would support Clinton, Mort asked Ann to stop speaking to Helen.

But as important as any friendships might be, Helen's relationship with David always took precedence, and most evenings would find them at home, working or reading. They rarely entertained at home, and they accepted even the most coveted social invitations with some reluctance. The couple had an understanding when they went out. Helen would signify her readiness to leave by bending a spoon; David, if he wanted to avoid being embarrassed by leaving damaged cutlery in full view, would extricate himself from conversation and begin the process of leaving. David enjoyed the social events more than Helen did, as she never considered herself adept at small talk.

In the end, Helen Gurley Brown's strongest passions mirrored those of David: she wanted to work, and she wanted to be with her husband. She found—or perhaps made—little time for anything or anyone else. And as many times as she recalled for journalists the fact that her sister had polio and that her mother was a difficult parent, Helen nevertheless kept much of her family business, and David's, private. They grieved in private the death of David's son and Helen's stepson, Bruce, who, as described earlier, died after years of struggling with a drug addiction he could not conquer.[23] Over the years they had two cats, Samantha and Gregory, who provided both Helen and David with valued companionship. In the end they made only one other addition to their family, "adopting" a tree in Central Park, one they could see from their living room window and from their terrace; they named it Calliope and cherished watching it grow healthy and tall.

If Brown allowed herself one concern outside of work, her husband, and her few friendships, it was her body. She became notorious for her girly figure, which she achieved not naturally but through hard work and dieting. She exercised ninety minutes a day and took pride in claiming that she had foregone her exercise routine only twice in eight years, then in ten years, then in twenty. She fit her exercise routine in even on the day of her mother's funeral, perhaps in part because her obsession about her weight stemmed from the messages she got from Cleo about her unattractiveness. If she was not to be beautiful, she had to at least remain trim. "Helen's a fanatic," Liz Smith explained. "The perfection of her body is a form of religious fanaticism. She saw herself as very unattractive and felt she could rise above it. And she did."[24] It is true. As she became increasingly successful professionally, Brown remained unable to relinquish what she called that "feeling of great inadequacy." Instead, she shifted its focus to one area, her body.

Brown kept annual records of her measurements and justified her expenditures on haute couture in the interest of her never-changing weight. On Christmas Day 1978, in a particular fit of passion about her body, she gave up sugar, cold turkey; following that she also gave up coffee and alcohol for a number of years. She admitted to dieting to deprivation, tossing her champagne into houseplants at parties, and routinely downing protein tablets for dessert after an almost nonexistent lunch. She weighed herself daily and remained on a permanent diet. "I love food like a normal person," she stated, "but I love being skinny more."[25] The discipline she exercised in the workplace carried over to her personal life, particularly where diet and exercised were concerned. As one journalist remarked when Brown turned sixty, "It may be easy for a slip of a girl to be a *Cosmo* cover-girl clone, with tumbling hair and a dazzling smile, but to manage it when you reach pensionable age takes diamond-hard determination."[26]

Those who interviewed Brown would alternately marvel at, or meet with disdain, the sometimes extreme leanness of her frame. Brown would be referred to with descriptions that included "stringbean skinny" and "almost skeletal," and in a *New York Times* crossword puzzle she would be dubbed, jokingly, the "muscular magazine editor."[27] Others would prove less polite. One journalist described how Brown had "exercised, steamed and starved her 5-foot-4 body to a state of near concentration-camp leanness,"[28] and another would argue, about Brown among others, that an inverse relationship existed between a woman's dress size and the size of her New York apartment. Why is it, this writer wondered facetiously, that a size-two woman would have a fourteen-room apartment and a size-fourteen woman a two-room apartment?[29] Brown, too, acknowledged that her practices bordered on the problematic. "You can't be too thin unless you're anorexic," she stated in 1970. In 1980 she admitted, "I'm always hungry," and in 1987 stated, "I'm always feeling guilty or hungry—one or the other."[30]

Ironically, of course, the woman who equated sex with food would barely eat, and this spokesperson for women would exhibit little understanding of disordered eating, her own or that of others. She counted calories, restricting herself to fifteen hundred a day. When she splurged, which she defined as taking in more than eighteen hundred calories a day, she would follow up with a thirty-six-hour fast. At times in her adult life Brown took as many as sixty vitamins a day, hoping to maintain optimum health with minimal caloric intake. She cooked regularly for David but often abstained from eating herself.

When journalists asked Brown if she was anorexic rather than simply thin, she replied that her practices were in keeping with what other women did to maintain their ideal weight. "I think you may have to have a tiny touch of anorexia nervosa to maintain an ideal weight," she suggested at one point, and on another occasion she stated, "I am either starving or sinning (and suffering remorse) every day of my life, and lots of skinny ladies are just like I am."[31] She felt similarly toward feminist diatribes about dieting as she did about feminist diatribes about cosmetics. Feminists, too, dieted, she maintained, and when they did they reached for women's magazines rather than feminist activists to steer them in the directions they wanted to go. Brown rarely reacted negatively to people's observations about her weight, as she readily admitted to dieting, exercising, and medically altering her body in her quest for an eternally thin, youthful body. On only one occasion did she get angry: "They can say I'm too thin or that I look like I'm suffering from a slight case of anorexia nervosa," she pleaded. "They can even say I'm painfully thin. This thinness is perhaps neurotic, but that doesn't mean I like being called a plucked chicken."[32]

Helen Gurley Brown would never give up her prejudice against fat, in herself or others. The body is, she would write, "what you make love with," and she felt that women just had to keep it in as good a shape as possible to attract men. Her man-scarcity argument provided justification for this obsession. Fat women might attract men, she admitted, but they were less likely to attract the more desirable men, who had certain expectations of women. Ironically but perhaps predictably, Brown's own husband felt that her obsession far outranked his own expectations. Had he the power to determine such things in their household, they might both have grown fat happily. But for Brown, letting herself go implicitly also meant letting herself grow older, and the fitness regime was a welcome imposition, a necessary corrective to the many other unavoidable signs of the aging female body. A lean, exercised body, she would argue, "along with other attributes," could keep one "attractive to men indefinitely." She added, "It's simply up to you."[33]

While other women might find the "it's simply up to you" message off-putting if not impossible to implement, it worked for Brown until she was well into her seventies. Only then did she find that she lacked the drive to keep her fitness regimen strictly intact. She started to let up on her rules and began again to indulge in sweets and small amounts of alcohol. Alcohol dependency terrified her, given that she had several alcoholic aunts and uncles, so although she stopped refusing alcohol altogether, she would never have more than one drink. Because of some arthritis in her hip, Brown found exercising increasingly difficult, but she kept it up as best she could. As time went on, she put on weight. She regretted that she could no longer fit into some of her favorite Emilio Pucci dresses, but rather than preferring thinness to food, she realized she now preferred sweets to starvation.

A self-declared chocolate lover and "cookieholic," at age eighty-six Brown weighed 125 pounds, not her almost lifelong 100 pounds, and she tried only occasionally, and generally unsuccessfully, to diet her way back to her preferred weight. "I seem to be unwilling to do what it takes," she lamented simply.[34] And although she could have indulged her newfound or at least newly tolerated desires with fine, dark, French or Belgian chocolates, the ever-thrifty Brown kept a brown paper lunch bag filled with

Hershey's Kisses and mini Snickers bars at work, asking her secretary to dole out a few each afternoon but to keep the rest under wraps.

Even if she would eventually lose her determination to stay ultra-thin, Helen Gurley Brown would never relinquish her desire to stay young. And like many of her contemporaries, and then many women years and even decades younger, Brown would look to cosmetic surgery as her most significant ally in the fight against age.[35] The numbers of people, particularly women, indulging in surgeries of one kind or another grows exponentially every year in the United States. From facelifts and eyelid reconstruction to liposuction and nose surgery, women who can afford it increasingly consider cosmetic surgery an integral part of staving off old age. Every woman she knows, Brown guesses, has undergone some cosmetic surgery, and she ventures further to guess that every famous woman, even those who might be considered the most "technically beautiful," has indulged. She defends the practice vehemently.[36]

For Brown, altering the physical body in the pursuit or maintenance of beauty is neither new nor problematic, and in her mind surgery is simply an extension of other, less controversial practices some feminists might decry but many women, feminists among them, seriously consider in their lives. Hair coloring, as one example, is so commonplace that it provides job security for hair stylists across the United States, since women have come to equate gray hair with looking old. Diatribes against cosmetic surgery have again provided Brown the means to quarrel with "natural," that feminist stronghold. "Natural at our age is droops and folds," she writes about women over fifty. "Capped teeth, pacemakers, polio vaccine, hip-replacement surgery and blood transfusions are not natural either, but do we want to do without those things?"[37] And as Brown ages, technologies for addressing the aging body continue to be developed. Cosmetic surgery, now one more way for women to "do femininity," provides a means for women whose bodies no longer conform to the mandates of desirability to continue to look—and feel—younger.[38] Many feminists might acknowledge but lament this reality, finding in it evidence of just how little things have changed for women. Others will warn of the potentially harmful side effects of cosmetic surgeries gone wrong. The intrepid Brown, however, finds cosmetic surgery a perfectly acceptable means of making it as an old woman in a world that women have neither designed nor feel welcome in.

Helen Gurley Brown's only concern about cosmetic surgery is its expense and the ability of her "girls" to access it. "You might need to save money or take a second job," she argues, "but I absolutely recommend it."[39] She recognizes that good looks remain important through the lifespan and that, thanks in part to her, women find themselves playing the beauty game for years longer. They now stay in the workplace and the dating marketplace not only through middle age but through what many consider old age. As a result many women, feminists included, will make a variety of choices in their attempts to remain at home in their bodies. Like Brown herself, the practice of cosmetic surgery is likely to remain controversial. Without apology, Brown has had multiple surgeries, including dermabrasion, facelifts, silicone injections, and breast augmentation. The way she sees it, "You have to put yourself against age if you intend to be a vital, sexual woman all your life as I do."[40]

Even as she did what she could to forestall aging, Brown occasionally encountered reminders that she was growing older. One morning, when she was in her early sixties and riding the bus to work, a young woman offered to give Brown her seat. "It was a big shock," she admitted, "but I've recovered fairly well." For Brown, recovering meant engaging in further opposition to, rather than acceptance of, the process of aging, and she vowed to fight in every way she could. Cosmetic surgery was one way, but for Brown, work was another, equally important means of staying young. "There is just no way that I can believe I'm the real age that I am," she mused. "I think older age is just the pits, but you have to be some kind of nutcase to assume that you're escaping it. So I escape it as best I can, through my work."[41] In this regard Brown would be joined by countless women of her generation and later who would find identity through work and fight the invisibility of the aging woman, and the aging induced by inactivity, by remaining in the workplace as long as possible.

In 1993 Brown brought many of her ideas and experiences together in a book, *The Late Show: A Semiwild but Practical Plan for Women over 50*, an advice manual and memoir about growing older. As early as the 1980s, it had seemed inevitable that she would write more directly about aging. Although she protested that she remained "one of the girls," Brown was by then two generations older than many of her readers.[42] Other women her age had begun to publish books about aging, but Brown attempted, for some time, to postpone that discussion. As she told Gloria Steinem in the mid-1980s, "The next subject I'm trying to resist dealing with is age, because it's so cliché, because I would now start talking about how you can be older and you can be happy and your sexuality does not have to diminish." Having spent much of her life cheering up "single women and poor girls and girls who've started from behind and girls with their noses pressed to the glass," she was reluctant to move into the role of cheerleader for older women.[43] In 1982, after all, at age sixty, she had published *Having It All: Love, Success, Sex, Money, Even If You're Starting with Nothing*, and although this book acknowledged that she drew on her many years of experience to offer advice about living well, Brown did not include aging among the book's many thematic chapters.

Nevertheless, as Brown grew older she discovered that other people increasingly considered her age her story, and she eventually moved in the direction of addressing it. She attempted to write some fiction to shake things up and avoid the age question, but she found that her own voice was too dominant; she could not sufficiently get out of herself to create believable characters. She talked with several editors about potential projects and eventually heeded the advice of Charlotte Mayerson, an editor at Random House, who suggested Brown consider writing not for the *Cosmo* audience but for her own contemporaries. "In other words, your own audience may be slightly different," she prodded gently. "It is, I suspect, 5–10 years older, and we ought to be trying to figure out what that age group wants to hear from you."[44]

In *The Late Show*, Brown chronicles the process of aging in ways that would resonate for many women. She describes how she initially believed that no one, herself included, would be able to detect that she was growing older, particularly because she followed such a strict regime of diet and exercise, supplemented not only with vitamins but with cosmetic surgery. Little by little, though, she began to read the reactions to her aging self on the faces and through the body language of others; that, coupled with hard looks in the mirror, landed her in therapy. Her therapist told her, simply, "Older is what we get." The psychiatrist, herself seventy-three, benefited at that moment from her own advanced age. "If she'd been forty," Brown quipped, "I think I would have hit her."[45] As someone who had always prided herself on her ability to live in the real world, Brown found herself uncharacteristically unprepared to deal with this simple and inevitable reality. This fact, in and of itself, provided her impetus to write.

With *The Late Show*, Helen Gurley Brown would again tap into the approach she had relied on so successfully almost forty years earlier with *Sex and the Single Girl*: self-help. The self-help approach focused on personal issues and personal experiences. Unlike many feminist works outside of this genre, but in keeping with Brown's particular approach to women's lives, the therapeutic nature of self-help called most often for personal rather than social change. Brown's approach in *The Late Show* suggests that women, by recognizing the realities of aging in the United States, may be better able to change some facts and cope with others. Such a strategy certainly deemphasizes women's abilities to change those larger and perhaps damaging realities, including the notion that older women are unattractive and incapable of making significant contributions to the workplace. While other writers in this genre, including Gloria Steinem and Germaine Greer, would see old age in part as women's liberation from the demands of certain expectations, including the imperative to be beautiful, Brown maintained that those expectations never do, and never fully should, disappear. She would certainly agree with some elements of these other books, which emphasize acknowledging age, remaining active, and accessing role models of all ages who live—really live—in the present. Certainly, Steinem's response to how it felt to turn seventy would resonate with Brown: "It is different because it has a ring of mortality—so it has a big message of stop wasting time."[46]

Much of *The Late Show* provides practical advice for women who, having reached "that certain age," find themselves simultaneously being looked at differently by those around them and looking at themselves differently. They exist as they age in "a sort of sexual and social limbo in the eyes of a society still shackled by its old taboos."[47] Age is, Brown writes, "a careless jailer," receding in importance for weeks at a time for women. In contemporary life, however, it rears up again and again, and women are ill-prepared to deal with it. Brown recognizes that this may change, but she is more interested in living well in her lifetime than attempting to await the changes that will likely take generations. "Some lovely day perhaps we will all be judged strictly by what we are—not one scrap of attention paid to creamy thighs, goddess cheekbones, Mona Lisa lips, but that isn't the situation now and I'm not sure we, the getting-up-there group, are the ones to strike out and demand love and appreciation totally without artifice."[48] In chapters on health, exercise, work, clothes, money, beauty, and, of course, sex, Brown describes how to approach aging "with verve, clout and self-reliance—sans depression—even if there's not a man around."[49] She advises women to admit to their age but challenge its definition by remaining active at work and at play.

Sex features prominently in Brown's discussions. "How much sex should we have at our age?" she asks. "None, if you don't want it, I guess, and lots of women don't, but if you masturbate, that means your body feels desire, so whom are we kidding?" In blunt form, she advocates sex as important for her intended, heterosexual audience: "Welcoming a penis just seems more womanly to me than baking chocolate chip cookies or doling out money for a grandchild's college tuition."[50] Work, of course, also remains critical and as always, on par with sex: "For me," she writes, "work surely is the ultimate seduction."[51] Brown acknowledges that both sex and work become more difficult in later life, but her advice to her readers is that they accept themselves as older, not as old. She offers practical advice about pursuing sex as a means of enjoying sex and pursuing work as a means of enjoying work. Peppered among her own stories, Brown offers the experiences of women she knows who speak directly to their insecurities and their individual attempts to "beat the rap" of aging.[52]

Brown published *The Late Show* with William Morrow, and it reached Number 8 on the *New York Times* best-seller list. Reviews varied, as they did for all of Brown's books, with a lively group of fans staving off the complaints of those who found the book and its message of accommodation disturbing. Several devoted fans wrote that too many feminist messages left no room for women who continued to care about their looks. "In a perfect world people wouldn't care much about your looks or achievements, because by some magic they could see directly into your soul," one reasoned. "But alas, there's a word for such a place—heaven. Not earth." Others, however, found Brown's messages outdated but nevertheless realistic. "This book tickles the innate socio-sexual schizophrenia of post-menopausal women," wrote one reviewer. "Despite a seriousness about ourselves and our society, we can still be impressed back into old prisons in which we aim to remain sexual ornaments for men to admire eternally."[53] Judith Viorst, writing in the *New York Times*, was less harsh, claiming as her title suggested that "Age Cannot Wither a Girl Like Her."[54]

As much as Helen Gurley Brown would assert that her advice was practical as surely as it was "semiwild," the book stood out less for the practical and more for the outrageous elements of its message. Two pieces of advice received mention again and again in reviews. In the first, Brown advised post-menopausal women to keep vaginal lubricant on hand so they could make themselves ready for sex if an appealing invitation materialized. In the second, Brown advised women who wanted sex, but did not get it at home, to borrow someone else's husband to jumpstart her own sex life. In addition, the graphic language put some people off. Brown's message was, in essence, an updated version of her decades-long advice: sex, work, money, fashion, beauty—these things remained the purview of all women, old and young, and could be manipulated and enjoyed in such a way as to prevent anyone from becoming a "prim, stuffy, puffy, correct, respected, respectable, finished old person."[55]

Helen Gurley Brown followed her own advice and remained sexually and professionally active into her eighties. She survived breast cancer, lived with the chronic pain of arthritis, and assisted her husband as he dealt with kidney disease and other ailments of old age. She continued to focus on what she had to be grateful for and to recognize that her comfortable financial position facilitated her and David's everyday existence. She still identified with the mouseburger, however, and believed that every young woman, regardless of beauty, brains, money, or age, could, with hard work and a belief in the self, have it all.

12

an editor steps down, reluctantly

D uring the 1980s a few things happened that made Helen Gurley Brown's departure from *Cosmopolitan* seem increasingly imminent. Most importantly, perhaps, after reaching a peak in circulation, the magazine began a slow but steady decline. Brown herself would attribute the downturn—ironically, she would admit—to her profound success. *Cosmopolitan* under her reign had so influenced the women's magazine industry that copycat magazines regularly popped up; some of them even managed to take away some of *Cosmo*'s readership. On top of that, long-standing women's magazines such as *Glamour* and even *Seventeen* had begun to imitate *Cosmopolitan*'s more sex-friendly style. Finally, with more-sophisticated demographic data at its disposal, the magazine world proved eager to divide women into increasingly smaller categories and target magazines specifically toward women's beauty concerns, their health, their professional lives, or their fashion choices. Although *Cosmopolitan* continued to address the whole woman rather than target one discrete element of her life, and maintained a significant market share by doing so, it inevitably felt the competition.

Brown understood, as well as anyone could, that the market ruled. She realized that if the decline in circulation continued she would have to leave the magazine sooner than she wished, and that, in any case, she would eventually have to step down. As early as the mid-1980s, she vowed to start looking for a successor: "I hope not to be one of those people who has to hang on until she withers away," she said in 1983 of her own plan to retire at sixty-five. "I have a good husband and he has encouraged me to leave at the height of my power."[1] In another interview at the time, however, she revealed her hesitation about actually stepping aside: "There are 62-year-olds—and there are 62-year-olds. I am one of the latter."[2]

In the end, Helen Gurley Brown would prove an exceedingly difficult person to nudge from her coveted but comfortable position, and it took another decade for Hearst executives to force the issue. They would, in the aftermath of several controversies, the first of which concerned sexual harassment.[3] As early as 1979, Brown had publicly taken a stand against sexual harassment. Giving credit once again to "the feminists," she asserted in a speech that their "revolutionary cries" had caused women around the country to reexamine gender roles. "Sexual harassment in offices, for example, is no longer considered a joke," she argued, "but a serious offence against women's dignity." Brown linked sexual harassment with marital rape and claimed that the courts had finally begun to take women's charges against men seriously.[4] Nevertheless, because she generally avoided including negative issues in her magazine, over the next decade Brown failed to provide information about the increasingly public issue of sexual harassment. When she made several politically incorrect statements in the early 1990s, her previous silence in a magazine that targeted working women exacerbated the effect of her remarks.

During the Senate hearings on the nomination of Clarence Thomas to the U.S. Supreme Court, Anita Hill testified that Thomas had sexually harassed her for years while she worked for him at the Equal Employment Opportunity Commission. The media, responding to Thomas's claims that the hearings were little more than a lynching, sought out equally controversial statements, particularly by women. Helen Gurley Brown wrote an opinion piece on sexual harassment for the *Wall Street Journal* and admitted to having stated, in response to a question about whether or not sexual harassment existed at *Cosmopolitan*, "I certainly hope so. The problem is that we don't have enough men to go around for harassing." Brown defended her statement, claiming that she had simply been facetious— and that she supported Anita Hill vigorously and unequivocally. At the same time, she revealed a tortured stance on the issue. "I think we should come down hard on the creeps and bullies," she stated, "but not go stomping out sexual chemistry at work." Brown admitted to having neglected the issue of sexual harassment in *Cosmo* but defended her right to focus instead on the positive inroads women had made in the workplace: "I feel men and women are in the best shape we have ever been with each other and I don't want to stress negatives."[5]

Brown confessed that her perspective might be outdated. "I have this possibly benighted idea that when a man finds you sexually attractive, he is paying you a compliment," she explained. "When he doesn't, that's when you have to worry." She believed that women had the power to stave off most unwanted sexual advances and felt, furthermore, that the sexual harassment issue put women in the victim position, which she had always considered anathema. The *Wall Street Journal* article earned what one editor at the paper called an "explosive reaction," resulting in a great many letters to the editor, most of which took Brown to task for her substitution of understanding or advocacy for women with a flip disregard for their workplace realities.[6] She repeated the faux pas a few years later, defending Senator Robert Packwood, who had been accused by ten women, mainly former staff members and lobbyists, of making unwanted sexual advances. On television's *Dateline NBC*, Brown dubbed him "poor old Senator Packwood." When pushed on the issue, she excused his actions on the grounds of political expediency, which she saw practiced by so many others. "My darling," she told a journalist, "would you please remember that he was one of the congressmen who supported legal abortion. He was one of us, so we've got to forgive him for being a jerk."[7]

Other feminists disagreed. The National Organization for Women, after supporting Packwood for many years, turned against him, and the senator resigned before the Senate took the likely path of expelling him. Again Brown would fail to understand the degree to which women had not only entered multiple realms in the American workplace but also changed that workplace—and its rules—in the process. Regardless of her own enormous success, or that of the women she profiled in *Cosmopolitan*, Brown still viewed women, to a degree, as guests in many workplace settings. And since she viewed sex far more as a tool used by women than as a weapon used by men, she was reluctant to attempt to rid the workplace of sex altogether.[8]

The second issue that suggested that Helen Gurley Brown's disconnect from her readers had grown, and that again pointed to a generational divide she may have had difficulty overcoming, concerned her coverage of AIDS. In a January 1988 *Cosmo* piece, "Reassuring News about AIDS: A Doctor Tells Why You May Not Be at Risk," Dr. Robert Gould outlined— and minimized—the risk of HIV infection for the magazine's readers. In his assessment, if women's lovers were neither homosexual nor bisexual nor intravenous drug users, the women themselves faced little risk of contracting HIV. The piece generated significant controversy, and even the Surgeon General of the United States, C. Everett Koop, felt compelled to write a personal letter to Brown to correct the misinformation present in Gould's article. Brown's defensive response, which she maintained in print, in speeches at advertising lunches, and on television's *Nightline*, made her appear further entrenched in outmoded ideas.

As editor of *Cosmopolitan*, Helen Gurley Brown had no difficulty asking her authors to revise their contributions, sometimes in significant ways. In this case, following the controversy generated by the article on HIV transmission, one might expect that she would have published an update on the issue, sought additional medical research, or invited another opinion. Her refusal to do any of those things points not only to a generational divide but also to her longstanding and sometimes problematic refusal to present female sexuality as anything other than positive and self-fulfilling. It highlights her very real fear that women's sexual freedom would prove, without continued vigilance, little more than a fleeting reality. Brown interpreted the media blitz on the risks of HIV infection not as an attempt to assist women but rather in the context of a more general societal backlash against sex. She considered the attention to AIDS specifically as symptomatic of a renewed attack on women's sexual freedoms.

"We spent such a long time getting sexual equality for women," she lamented, "and just when we're beginning to enjoy ourselves, somebody's got to come along and say sex kills." She was also unhappy that the backlash extended not simply to heterosexual women but to homosexual men as well. "It seems to me," she continued, "that the most specious idea is that there is some standard of sexual conduct...some prima facie correct way for everybody to behave, that we can all be turned into so many slices of white bread, including the homosexual community." Brown's diatribe went on:

> Any healthy society thrives on variety of creative thought and activity. It is called freedom. Freedom always has its hazards... excesses. It carries with it responsibility...we can't live without

laws but people have to decide what is logical to regulate and I don't think sexual freedom, specifically for women, is one of those things. The price of having totally chaste teenage girls, chaste single women, monogamous marriage—for women only, of course...men would continue to enjoy sexual freedom as they always have—with motherhood as the only acceptable sexual goal for women would have to be a totalitarian state....Does anybody really want that?[9]

The insights Brown offered, which were considerable, became lost in her defense of indefensible information, and in the end her response, perhaps the result of feeling wounded in the battle, was to leave the AIDS story to others. During the remainder of her tenure at *Cosmo*, there would be no significant analysis of the AIDS crisis in the magazine. Not surprisingly, Brown's successor, Bonnie Fuller, overtly signaled changes in the magazine, and in its editorial direction, by running an article on heterosexual couples living with AIDS in her first issue and a piece on sexual harassment in her second.[10]

Given her longevity in the business and her relatively few forays into significant controversy, it was difficult for Hearst to decide, and for Helen Gurley Brown to agree, that it was time for her to step down. In the end, she would have to be pushed out of the magazine. She would remain unaware of the behind-the-scenes machinations, however, until nearly the end. Hearst executives publicly pledged their loyalty, but they began privately to consider when and how to move her out. As one journalist put it afterward, "The top brass began to fret that Mrs. Brown's high profile as aging—albeit gracefully—adventuress was an image younger readers couldn't identify with."[11] The company put a process in place, a process that in hindsight appears to have been clear to everyone except Helen Gurley Brown. For someone who studiously avoided the notion of leaving her job, the company's signals offered a variety of readings. First, Claeys Bahrenburg, the president of Hearst, ordered a redesign of the magazine without Brown's approval. Then he hired the *Harper's Bazaar* photographer Patrick Demarchelier to replace Brown's longtime cover photographer Francesco Scavullo. Brown's public response, which may well have reflected a reluctant but growing awareness of her own marginalization, was that she remained in charge and would gladly use both photographers.

On February 18, 1996, Hearst announced that Helen Gurley Brown would be stepping down as editor of *Cosmopolitan* and moving into a leadership position with *Cosmopolitan*'s international publications. She would be replaced by the thirty-nine-year-old Bonnie Fuller, who had successfully launched the U.S. edition of the French magazine *Marie Claire* for Hearst. Fuller would join as deputy editor in June 1996 and take over as editor in February 1997, at Brown's departure; Fuller would launch her first issue in March 1997. In the interim, the two women would work together. It was, as Brown admitted, an "unusual" arrangement, but, she added, "She's not a bitch and I'm not a bitch. We can work together."[12] As reality set in, Helen Gurley Brown found it difficult to name exactly what had happened. At times she would state that she had been fired; other times she would suggest that her new assignment at Hearst, one with considerably less responsibility, could be called a lateral move. "Despite all the ingratiating, the respect proffered, the work-obsessed, never-look-up-or-back hours, days, years you've put in, despite your being pussycat nice and decent, you can get fired—surprise!" she told a reporter for *Fortune* magazine. In the same breath, though, she moved away from the uncomfortable notion that she had been forced out. "My recent firing—well, it wasn't really a firing, I was moved—was done with all kinds of consolation prizes…money, contracts, perks, flowers and a new Mercedes Benz S500."[13]

In the end, Brown was indeed shifted from her position as editor of *Cosmopolitan* to the position of editor-in-chief of Cosmopolitan International, the branch of Hearst that oversaw the twenty-nine international editions of the magazine. With her assistance, the numbers would grow from twenty-nine to sixty editions. Although the magazines are not individually under her editorial control, she sends comments on their aesthetic appeal, content, and layout to editors around the world. She works full-time in her New York office, travels to launch new editions of *Cosmopolitan*, invites international editors to New York for meetings, and collects a wildly high salary. Hearst benefits, certainly, from having an icon like Helen Gurley Brown walk through its office doors every day. Brown benefits not simply or even primarily because of her two-million-dollar salary, but because she remains employed. Her identity as a working woman, a significant component of her identity as a person, remains intact. If in the end she does, as one Hearst executive joked, leave the building feet first, her own needs will have been met.[14]

When Helen Gurley Brown left the helm of *Cosmopolitan* magazine, after thirty-two years, she was one of the most highly paid editors in the business. Rarely had a magazine been so identified with its editor, and people in and outside of the magazine both welcomed and worried over her departure. A new editor might well tap more directly into the needs and desires of that coveted younger demographic. At the same time, the magazine's philosophy had been Brown's philosophy, and it had worked enormously well for more than three decades. As a privately owned business, Hearst keeps its financial results confidential, but *Cosmo* was widely believed to be its most lucrative magazine. Brown herself claims that the top brass admitted to her that *Cosmopolitan*'s success paid for the sleek and elegant new Hearst building in Manhattan.[15] Certainly top levels of management had legitimate concerns as they contemplated Brown's departure: Would a new editor feel the need to make her own mark on the magazine and in the process change it enough to take away its unique— and uniquely successful—look and approach? Could a magazine so identified with Helen Gurley Brown survive without her?

Regardless of anyone's desires for or fears about *Cosmopolitan*, the magazine changed little following Brown's departure. Because of her experience with *Marie Claire*, Bonnie Fuller brought more fashion and more fashion advertising to the magazine. She declared *Cosmo* the home of the "fun, fearless female," but when focus groups with readers revealed that they liked the magazine the way it was, she made few substantial changes. Fuller stuck to the basic Helen Gurley Brown formula, which included four pillars: relationship issues, emotional issues, career issues, and sexual issues. After a year and a half on the job, Fuller left *Cosmopolitan* to take over as editor of *Glamour*, where she replaced Brown's friend and colleague Ruth Whitney—who, like Brown, had been pushed out in part at least because of her age.

Hearst replaced Bonnie Fuller with forty-six-year-old Kate White, who had worked as editor of the women's magazines *Working Woman*, *McCall's*, and *Redbook*. As Brown had a generation earlier, White first became acquainted with magazines by winning a *Glamour* magazine contest. Helen Gurley Brown had won Ten Girls with Taste; Kate White had won the Top Ten College Women contest, for which she secured a spot on the cover of the magazine. Also like Brown, White had written a sexy book for career women, titled *Why Good Girls Don't Get Ahead...But Gutsy Girls Do: Nine Secrets Every Working Woman Must Know*.[16] Regardless of the things they shared, people expected a clean sweep after White took over at *Cosmo*. In the end, she, too, has done little to change the magazine. In fact, her additions, which include "Cosmo Gyno," a health column, and "Ecstasy," a sex column, remain true to concerns Helen Gurley Brown had brought to *Cosmopolitan* thirty-five years earlier.

The truth is that Helen Gurley Brown has proven an exceedingly difficult act to follow. At the time of her retirement, *Cosmopolitan* was selling 2.8 million copies a month, had long maintained its top sales spot in college bookstores, and sold the vast majority of issues it published in any given month.[17] As one journalist remarked admiringly, it would be difficult for anyone to come close to replicating the impact she had on *Cosmo,* "which she took from the remainder racks of the Hearst magazine group and transformed into the Bible of a certain sort of feminist—the Cosmo Girl."[18]

Brown's move to Cosmopolitan International occasioned a good deal of attention to the global reach of the magazine. Charlotte Bunch, the editor of *Sisterhood Is Global* and a champion of a global feminist politics, mused about the positive and the negative implications of this particular version of global sisterhood: "It definitely shows that women around the world have more access to money to buy magazines, more interest in various questions about how they're going to live and more space to explore those questions, even if some of the articles seem regressive."[19] The new editor in chief's own analysis of that sisterhood was far more direct, concise, and Helen-Gurley-Brown-like: "We all have a vagina, a heart, a brain, and we're all subject to the seven deadly sins."[20]

While many feminists grappled, importantly, with global differences among women and the difficulty of writing to or on behalf of women in various locations, Brown now put her faith in the international market, believing that if local editors and writers could tap in to the psyches of women in those settings, the magazines would sell. If they could not, the magazines would flounder. Her philosophy on sex, men, and femininity would be viewed as problematic by many, but once again, the numbers sided with Brown. In both the international and the national arenas, *Cosmopolitan*'s fairly libertarian stance on sexuality for contemporary women drew readers in.

The Russian edition of *Cosmopolitan,* which began publication in 1995, provides an interesting case in point. For decades, Soviet, and then Russian, women had access to just two women's magazines, *Rabonitsa (Factory Worker Lady)* and *Krestyanka (Peasant Woman).* But with the significant capitalist inroads made in the 1990s, it seemed possible that there existed a sufficient audience, particularly in Moscow and St. Petersburg, to sustain a radically different, radically capitalist, magazine. The publisher Derk Sauer, who successfully launched the Russian *Good Housekeeping, Harper's Bazaar,* and *Playboy,* felt that Russia, with its size, had the potential to become a significant magazine market. More and more products aimed at women were being produced there, but there were few vehicles to enhance sales; magazines, of course, selectively and productively provide that service. Sauer's business partner, Annemarie van Gaal, described how she chased the Hearst Magazines International president George Green all over the world to make her case for a *Cosmo* launch. "I knew *Cosmo* could work here," she explained. "You looked at Russian women and you saw how they dressed, how they looked to the West, how they wanted to improve themselves. I knew that if there was one magazine that shows how your life can be, a shop window you can look in, this educational element that says you can do it this way or that way, and that empowers you to do it, it was *Cosmo*."[21]

Van Gaal got her wish, and with the seventy-two-year-old Helen Gurley Brown, then still editor of *Cosmopolitan,* on hand, the Russian version hit the newsstands in 1994. It took little time either for the initial Hearst investment to see returns or for the magazine to overtake even the U.S. edition in sales figures. As a *Washington Post* reporter put it, the Russian edition of *Cosmo* caught on "faster than you can say 'extramarital affair.'"[22] The inaugural edition, a run of 60,000 copies whose cover featured Cindy Crawford, sold out almost immediately in Moscow and St. Petersburg. Some of the articles were translated directly from the English versions published in the United States, but like every other foreign edition, the Russian magazine hired local staff writers who tailored their particular efforts to the concerns of "Russian Cosmo Girls."[23] As Brown describes the Russian edition now, it is as heavy as the New York phone book.[24] *Cosmopolitan* has continued its international reach, marking its territory on every continent, and recently becoming one of the first Western magazines to receive permission to publish in mainland China. Even the government of Singapore, which initially banned *Cosmopolitan* as an unhealthy influence on its citizens, has since relented.

The sixty editions, published in thirty-six languages and distributed in more than one hundred countries, now reach more than 100 million women around the world. They are a long arm for Helen Gurley Brown's continuing philosophy. Brown continues to share the generalities and the specifics of her approach with the international editors in meetings at home and abroad. These editors, described by one journalist as "lifestyle evangelists," follow their mentor closely, for like "all good evangelists," their work will not be completed "until the Cosmo Girl confidently struts the boardrooms and the bedrooms of the whole civilized world."[25] As Brown herself perceives it, her goal, more simply, is to help those editors "put out the right magazine."[26]

Brown has also continued to pursue outside projects, including three books. In 1999 she published *The Writer's Rules: The Power of Positive Prose, How to Create It and Get It Published,* a writing guide that drew on and finessed the advice she gave *Cosmopolitan* writers as mimeographed handouts over the course of several decades.[27] Brown's advice proved most useful for those who aspired to magazine writing, which demands concise information rather than longer narrative development. Her own writing habits, which include the overly generous use of italics, ellipses, and capital letters, hardly seem in keeping with a guide for writers. The book received lukewarm reviews, and Brown herself admitted that the chapter on letter writing was the only strong piece. A lifelong letter writer herself, she instructed would-be letter writers about how to connect with celebrities, largely through flattery. She also offered tips on writing résumés, thank-you notes, and even love letters. It seemed logical to follow this up with a collection of her own letters, and in 2004 she published *Dear Pussycat: Mash Notes and Missives from the Desk of Cosmopolitan's Legendary Editor,* a sampling of the many letters she wrote to fans, celebrities, employers, employees, and friends.[28]

In 2000 Brown published her memoir, *I'm Wild Again,* which before publication included the subtitle "Snippets from My Life and a Few Brazen Thoughts."[29] Dedicated to Frank A. Bennick Jr., Helen Gurley Brown's longtime boss at Hearst, and David Brown, "the world's greatest husband," the book covers a great deal of ground Brown had previously covered in her earlier writings and in interviews, but it pulls her story together in one place, if not in one narrative. Broken up into dozens of subheadings, including "How Big Is He?"—which includes a highly nonscientific means of estimating the size of a man's penis before he takes his clothes off—the book also offers a very personal look at Brown's experience with breast cancer, which included radiation treatment. Brown alternates between heartfelt personal advice and some rather playful observations about contemporary life and relationships. Interestingly, although this book was published years after *The Late Show,* Brown does not target, to any considerable degree, the "older" woman reader. Instead, she again attempts to connect, regardless of age, with those women who, like the Cosmo Girl, forever like money, work, life in the female body, and, of course, sex.

Brown concludes *I'm Wild Again* with a chapter called "Letter to My Daughter," in which she outlines the advice she would give "Anna Marie," if there were such a young woman. Brown asserts again that she had no regrets about not having had a child. "Why should I start lying now?" she ponders. Much of the advice for Anna Marie mirrors Brown's philosophy for herself and for Cosmo Girls over the years. Believe in yourself, she exhorts. Like yourself, but then feel utterly guiltless for working to look your best. Fashion is silly, but enjoy taking it seriously. Accept that bad things happen; do not be afraid to ask for help from professionals when you need it. Sex is good, even when it is not great. Money matters; so does being smart and acting smart. Good health is critical; exercise facilitates it. Exercise empathy; do not put up with foolishness. Someday Mr. Right will come along. "He will be a good man, delicious in bed but also kind, gentle, smart, mad about you." With her customary wit, Brown inserts herself carefully but firmly into her hypothetical daughter's future: "Grab him," she instructs about the right man when he comes along. "You'll need to read Mommy's books to find out how to do that."[30]

Although Helen Gurley Brown never did have children, many of her readers would eagerly have put themselves in the place of the fictional Anna Marie. Countless women wrote to Brown over the years suggesting that they considered her a close friend if not a family member. Not just *Cosmopolitan,* but also every book she published, from *Sex and the Single Girl* to *I'm Wild Again,* provided the occasion for fans, mostly but not exclusively women, to write to her about the impact her work and example had had on their lives. Brown's fan mail includes correspondence from working-class and wealthy women; white teenagers and middle-aged black women; feminists and anti-feminists. The letter Brown identified as "the best Cosmo fan letter I ever received" came from a woman from Alexandria, Virginia. "This letter is about ten years overdue but better late than never!" wrote Patricia Myles, who first encountered *Cosmopolitan* while a disgruntled teenager in Buffalo, New York. The magazine encouraged her to strike out on her own, so she moved to Washington, D.C., where she read all of Brown's books, made the bold decision to become a police officer, and stayed single until age forty-six. "You were my cheerleader," she said, claiming that with Brown's encouragement she married only when she was sufficiently independent to make the best choices for her life.[31]

Many other fans have written about how Brown inspired them to make professional choices that seemed daunting at best and dangerous at worst. Often these were working-class women who, with Brown's help, found the courage to start their own businesses, seek additional training, resign from unrewarding positions, move to new cities, or end dissatisfying professional relationships. "Over the years, while trying to create a comfortable place for myself, I would ask myself over and over—'What would Mrs. Brown do in this situation?'" one woman wrote. "I read and reread your books until they actually did fall apart, searching for the clues I knew were there that would allow me to accomplish something, anything." That woman eventually became a Canadian Woman of the Year and president of a United Steel Workers of America local.[32]

Others, too, have expressed the support they felt in pursuing nontraditional careers. One started as a secretary in an auto repair business but eventually become the resident expert on big rigs. Another revealed that she had, with what she felt was Brown's permission, become an entrepreneur and started her own nail polish business. Another, an "ex-sacrificial wife," was building her own house. Finally, one woman revealed that she was on welfare when she first encountered Brown, but she was now "mouseburgering" her way to "bigger and better things."[33] Mainstream women, including those marginalized not only by "the system" but also by a middle-class feminist movement, found an ally in Brown. Occasionally, though, a letter would reveal how even some of the most privileged women found Brown's diatribes about work inspirational. Mitzi Purdue explained how, with Brown's encouragement, she skipped the Social Register life offered to her as the daughter of the founder of the Sheraton Hotels and "instead became the first woman in [her] family ever to work." Through her career she met the chicken baron Frank Perdue, a man she said "never would have looked" at her if she had been "nothing more than an idle heiress."[34]

One of the writers claimed that Brown spoke on behalf of "gals from 15 to 100," and indeed the fans range tremendously in age.[35] Many of the older women asked Brown to start a new magazine for older women; some asked for other services, like mouseburger clinics.[36] There's the fifteen-year-old African American girl who claimed Brown speaks to and for her, regardless of race or age; the twenty-something who found in Brown her own "terrific coach"; the fifty-eight-year-old who had finally become her own person; and the eighty-two-year-old writing from a nursing home in the Bronx and wondering what she missed more, high heels or sex. On the topic of sex, women of varied ages wrote about how Brown inspired them to seek it out and enjoy it. One woman in her fifties spoke about how intimidating it was to enter the dating scene but said that she felt Brown supporting her in her ventures. Many women found Brown enormously helpful as they worked through what they initially perceived as their lack of sensuousness after their husbands left them for younger women. Even men wrote about the ways in which they identified with Brown. An Ethiopian man told of the difficulty of speaking about sex in his culture and the solidarity he felt when he read a piece Brown had published in *Newsweek*. Midway through the letter, the writer had to change pens. "Sorry for the change of ink," he stated. "The first pen could not go on. I think it was shy to talk about sex, like every Ethiopian."[37]

Many of the letters Brown received were confessional in tone and content: writers revealed the mouseburger secrets they had long harbored, sometimes in detail, and explained how Helen Gurley Brown had helped them live fuller lives. "All women probably tell you 'I could have written that myself,'" one writer suggested aptly.[38] Many stated that their degree of identification with Brown was so complete that they actually felt related to her. "You are more than a friend, more than a mother, more than a sister, more than an advisor to me," explained one woman. "I don't know what word adequately expresses how I feel about you; you have had the single most powerful influence on my life to date."[39] Another stated, explaining her salutation, "The reason I didn't write 'Mrs. Brown' was because I feel like you are my best friend." At times they acknowledged that their identification was acute regardless of the differences between them. "I'm about as sexy as a box of cornflakes," claimed one, while another argued that she connected with Brown even though she was "forty-one, of Afro-American heritage and . . . divorced . . . certainly not your typical mouseburger."[40] Characteristic is this quote: "Mrs. Brown, my God, it's me in your book!"[41]

At times the writers revealed that they had been in dire need of a friend when Brown's work came along. Two women wrote about being "on the brink," and others talked about entering therapy, finding in Brown's work both permission and encouragement. "At 35 years of age, you have really clarified things for me. I am not too crazy, dumb, or over-sexed. I am Me. There must be millions of women out there you have pulled back from the brink of insanity."[42] One woman, whose husband of twenty-seven years left her for another woman, felt Brown had given her permission to feel and act. "Being a product of the 50s left so many of us with suppressed desire and feelings," she wrote. "Would you believe a woman who only began using Tampax a year ago, gave up Carter's cotton underpants only recently and began to feel proud of her body and self—Well, I know you understand."[43] Some simply identified Helen Gurley Brown as a friend. One woman invited her to visit her at her home in Magnolia, Arkansas.

"I've met lots of charming men, none of whom I'd like to spend the rest of my life with," she stated simply, but as a black, Southern woman she wanted to be sure to extend her full hospitality to Helen Gurley Brown.[44]

Several of the writers indicated that writing letters to anyone, never mind someone of Helen Gurley Brown's stature, was new to them. "I'm one of those people who never have written to a celebrity and probably won't do so again," explained someone typical of this group.[45] One fan confessed that she was "better at hairdressing than English grammar and spelling," but felt compelled to write, while another demonstrated the same when she wrote, and misspelled, "You are my idle."[46] Yet another explained, "Helen, I am not much of a writer but it seemed to me working as hard as you do to communicate I wanted you to know it's damn well appreciated."[47]

Many of the letter writers explained that their relationships with Brown were longstanding. A woman from Britain wrote that she had read *Sex and the Single Girl* when she was in her thirties; at that point the book encouraged her to get a better job, learn to drive, and buy a car. Now, twenty years later, following a divorce and depressed from the demands of caring for her mother, who was suffering from dementia, she had rediscovered Helen Gurley Brown. "You have done it again!" she exclaimed, celebrating Brown's latest work.[48] A fan from Alberta, Canada, wrote, "You have been my constant ally in 'femaleness,'" revealing that she had relied on Brown's companionship, month after month, for thirty years.[49] The most poignant of these long-term relationship letters came from a woman who recalled reading *Sex and the Single Girl* twenty years earlier, when she was nineteen, pregnant, and living in a small town in Illinois. Helen Gurley Brown, she said, gave her permission to give the baby up for adoption rather than view that moment as the end of her life. She went on to travel, learn new languages, and earn two master's degrees at Columbia University. "I'll never forget the hope you gave a 19-year-old who felt as if the world were caving in," she stated.[50]

These fan letters represent only a fraction of the letters Brown received because, unfortunately, none of the letters written in the aftermath of *Sex and the Single Girl*, when Helen Gurley Brown first had such an impact on women's lives, remain. But regardless of when or in what context they encountered Brown, her fans paid her, in some form or fashion, what surely she would consider the highest compliment: "You made a believer out of me."[51]

That's Helen Gurley Brown, and that is the legacy of her particular form of feminism.

acknowledgments

I am exceedingly grateful to the organizations and institutions that supplied generous financial assistance for this work. In addition to providing a sabbatical to facilitate my writing, Bowdoin College supported my travel and research through a Fletcher Family Research Grant and a Faculty Leave Supplement. The American Philosophical Society, through a Franklin Research Grant, provided me the opportunity to do the initial research and confirm the viability of the project. The Sophia Smith Collection at Smith College, through a Travel-to-Collections Grant and then a Margaret Storrs Grierson Scholar-in-Residence fellowship, provided intellectual validation and financial support. I am indebted to the Sophia Smith Collection curator, Amy Hague, and to the helpful and professional staff members who welcomed me to the collection, took an interest in my work, provided their own insights about Helen Gurley Brown, and offered intellectual camaraderie during my stays there. Susan Sanborn Barker, the collection's administrative assistant, was particularly generous in her response to my many queries and requests for help.

The staffs at the New York Public Library, the Schlesinger Library on the History of Women in America, and the Bowdoin College Library assisted me as I searched for documents relevant to the project. On research trips I benefited from the hospitality of Daniel Horowitz and Helen Lefkowitz Horowitz in Northampton, Massachusetts; Larry Scanlon and Mary Grace Gannon, and Anthony Arthur and Dahlia Galan, in New York City; and Laura and Peter Cavicchi and Julie Boss and Donna Klein in Boston. Helen Gurley Brown and David Brown both took time from their busy schedules and full lives to meet with me and fill in some of the gaps. They then left me free to write this book. Their generosity has been extraordinary. Susan Gordon, the executive assistant to Helen Gurley Brown, graciously helped gather photographs for the book.

At each stage of the project, a variety of people read parts or all of the manuscript and offered helpful suggestions. From the very first stages of the book proposal, I received support and guidance from Sarah Elbert, Daniel Horowitz, Susan Ware, and Dana Heller. My earliest readers, Charlotte Daniels, Michael Arthur, and Kristen Ghodsee, also read the final manuscript, and their support and insights helped throughout. I am enormously grateful to spend my workdays with Kristen and with Anne Clifford, who contributed to the manuscript in many invisible but invaluable ways. Through the challenges and the fortunes of the past few years, including this project, Marilyn Reizbaum and Rachel Connelly have also been wonderful and supportive colleagues and friends. I am indebted as well to many other of my colleagues at Bowdoin, too numerous to mention by name, who enrich my personal and intellectual life.

Julie Gallagher and Daniel Horowitz provided invaluable historical insights on the workings of the second wave of feminism and the ways in which Helen Gurley Brown fits in with their own readings of the era. Dan's published work on Betty Friedan has helped encourage many scholars to complicate our understandings of and approaches to the second wave, and his critique of my reading of Betty Friedan influenced the final manuscript in important ways. Oxford University Press's readers also helped shape the project, and I trust that they see their mark in these pages. Readers for *Feminist Media Studies,* which published a version of one chapter of the book, contributed to my thinking about that piece and about the project as a whole. I am also indebted to my editor at Oxford, Nancy Toff, whose thoughtful editing and good humor made our many interactions both enjoyable and productive.

This book, like much of my work, owes a special debt to my students, past and present. On several research trips I had the good fortune to share coffee or a meal with former students from Bowdoin College and from Plattsburgh State University. Their enthusiasm extended literally to a sense of shared ownership for the project across the years and the miles and through our intellectual kinship. My current students enliven my thinking with their curiosity and engagement. I offer special thanks to Alana Wooley and Courtney Eustace, for their research support, and to my Feminist Theory students, whose contribution to my thinking in the last stages of the project was surely more significant than they realized.

When Hillary Clinton publicized the African proverb, "It takes a village," she did not have Brunswick, Maine, in mind, but she might well have. In conversations on the playground in the afternoons, at sporting events on the weekends, or over glasses of wine at night, and through their generous support in taking care of my children during vacations, snow days, research trips, and times I needed to care for my parents, my community has been there both to inquire about and offer encouragement for my work and to provide concrete support. Fynn and Maeve surely benefit from the many adults in their lives who open their homes to them, offer them a variety of perspectives on daily life and on family, and validate, contrary to my own predilections, their enthusiasm for New England sports teams.

I am indebted to my family for its generous support of this project and all that I do. My sabbatical leave coincided with the last year of my father's life, and allowing me in to everything he experienced that year was just one of the many gifts he gave me. My mother, born four days before Helen Gurley Brown, provides me with ways of thinking about women's lives, and with inspiration, every day. My siblings, my Bajan in-laws, and my extended family of nieces, nephews, and cousins keep me connected. My family life includes Julie Boss and Donna Klein, who did not need to be stranded with us in the middle of a lake, on the top of a mountain, in a lightning storm, to get it, but nevertheless, that did happen and they do get it.

Michael Arthur, my partner, is the only person I have ever met whose passion is balanced in equal parts by his equanimity. He, along with our children, Fynn Ajani and Maeve Emia, have been supportive of this project in the most significant, everyday, and heartfelt ways. They inspire me always not only to work hard at this work that I love but also to walk away from it at the end of the day to enjoy, in full, the gifts of family. This book is dedicated to them.

notes

PREFACE

The Sophia Smith Collection at Smith College, Northampton, Massachusetts, houses the Helen Gurley Brown Papers. The papers are referred to, in this manuscript, as HGB-SSCSC, followed by the archival box number within parentheses.

1. Each year the New York Landmarks Conservancy names as Living Landmarks people who have made outstanding contributions to New York City. Helen Gurley Brown was so named in 2003. Among her many other awards, Brown received an award for editorial leadership from the American Newspaper Women's Club in Washington, D.C.; a Distinguished Achievement Award in Journalism from Stanford University; a New York Women in Communications Matrix Award; and the Henry John Fisher Award, the magazine industry's highest honor. The Helen Gurley Brown Research Professorship was established in her name at Northwestern University's Medill School of Journalism, and she also was inducted into the Publisher's Hall of Fame.

2. Helen Gurley Brown, "Step into My Office," *Cosmopolitan*, February 1997, 20.

3. Helen Gurley Brown quoted in Carol Krucoff, "Wanting It All!" *Washington Post*, November 10, 1982, 20. On the multiple meanings of feminism, see Nancy F. Cott, *The Grounding of Modern Feminism* (New Haven, CT: Yale University Press, 1987); Michael S. Kimmel, ed., *Against the Tide: Pro-Feminist Men in the U.S., 1776–1990: A Documentary History* (Boston: Beacon, 1992); Rebecca

Walker and Tom Digby, ed., *Men Doing Feminism* (New York: Routledge, 1993); Judith Butler, "Feminism by Any Other Name," *differences: A Journal of Feminist Cultural Studies* 6, no. 2–3 (Summer–Fall 1994), 27–61; Katha Pollitt, *Reasonable Creatures: Essays on Women and Feminism* (New York: Vintage, 1995); Rebecca Walker, *To Be Real: Telling the Truth and Changing the Face of Feminism* (New York: Anchor Books, 1995); Rosalyn Baxandall, "Re-visioning the Women's Liberation Movement Narrative: Early Second Wave African American Feminists," *Feminist Studies* 27, no. 1 (2001), 225–45; Ruth Rosen, *The World Split Open: How the Modern Women's Movement Changed America* (New York: Viking, 2000); Estelle Freedman, *No Turning Back: The History of Women and the Future of Feminism* (New York: Ballantine, 2002); and Sara M. Evans, *Tidal Wave: How Women Changed America at Century's End* (New York: Free Press, 2003).

4. The first wave of feminism refers to the activists who worked in the late nineteenth and early twentieth centuries to gain suffrage for women, which they did with the passage of the Susan B. Anthony Amendment in 1920. The second wave of feminism refers to the activists who emerged from a variety of locations, in the 1960s and 1970s, to advocate for a wide spectrum of legal, economic, and social changes. The third wave refers to those activists coming of age in the early 1990s and since, advocating for a new feminism distinguished from the second wave by, among other things, its emphasis on female empowerment rather than women's victimization.

5. The "long decade" of the postwar period ran from 1947 until the early 1960s. See Stephanie Coontz, *Marriage, A History: From Obedience to Intimacy, or How Love Conquered Marriage* (New York: Viking, 2005), 226.

6. Betty Friedan, *The Feminine Mystique* (New York: W. W. Norton, 1963).

7. Few histories of the second wave of feminism include any consideration of Helen Gurley Brown. Among the exceptions are Barbara Ehrenreich, Elizabeth Hess, and Gloria Jacobs, *Re-Making Love: The Feminization of Sex* (Garden City, NY: Anchor Books/Doubleday, 1987); Susan Ware, *Modern American Women: A Documentary History* (Belmont, CA: Wadsworth, 1989); Susan Douglas, *Where the Girls Are: Growing Up Female with the Mass Media* (New York: Times Books, 1994); Joanne Meyerowitz, ed., *Not June Cleaver: Women and Gender in Postwar America, 1945–1960* (Philadelphia: Temple University Press, 1994); Rosen, *World Split Open*; David Allyn, *Make Love, Not War: The Sexual Revolution, an Unfettered History* (New York: Routledge, 2001), and Patricia Bradley, *Mass Media and the Shaping of American Feminism, 1963–1975* (Jackson: University Press of Mississippi, 2003). Some historians might argue that to be considered part of the feminist movement, Helen Gurley Brown would have to have had an organizational base and be part of a movement. I would argue that *Sex and the Single Girl* and then *Cosmopolitan* served as Brown's organizational bases, much as *Ms.* magazine could be said to represent an organizational base for another form of second-wave feminism.

8. Gloria Steinem, "In Step with Helen Gurley Brown" (Palm Springs, CA: TAE Productions, 1985), HGB-SSCSC (16).

9. Helen Gurley Brown, *Sex and the Single Girl* (New York: Bernard A. Geis, 1962), 70.

10. Helen Gurley Brown quoted in Daniel Meacham, *The Magic of Self-Confidence* (New York: Simon & Schuster, 1985), HGB-SSCSC (36).

11. On Helen Gurley Brown's relationship to *Playboy* magazine, see Carrie Pitzulo, "The Battle in Every Man's Bed: Playboy and the Fiery Feminists," *Journal of the History of Sexuality* 17, no. 2 (May 2008); Beth Bailey, "Sexual Revolution(s)," in *The Sixties: From Memory to History*, ed. David Farber (Chapel Hill: University of North Carolina Press, 1994), 248–49. Over the years Brown has been deemed the female equivalent of *Playboy*'s Hugh Hefner. In one of the most recent examples of that, Maureen Dowd calls Helen Gurley Brown "the perfect twin to Hugh Hefner" in her *Are Men Necessary? When Sexes Collide* (New York: Berkeley Books, 2005), 170.

12. Brown, *Sex and the Single Girl*, 4, 8.

13. Helen Gurley Brown, "HGB Remembers the *Cosmo* Years," *Cosmopolitan*, February 1997, 345, HGB-SSCSC (44). This remark formed part of Helen Gurley Brown's farewell address to her readers when she stepped down as editor of *Cosmopolitan* and assumed the position of editor in chief at Cosmopolitan International in 1997.

14. On Helen Gurley Brown's work in relation to the history of self-help, see Micki McGee, *Self-Help, Inc.: Makeover Culture in American Life* (New York: Oxford University Press, 2005).

15. For *Cosmopolitan* statistics, see Helen Gurley Brown, "HGB Remembers the *Cosmo* Years," 345.

16. Over the years journalists have made repeated mention of Helen Gurley Brown's obsessive dieting and exercise regimens. Most recently Eve Ensler highlights Helen Gurley Brown as a sad example of what women need to fight against, in "Helen Gurley Brown: Author and Pioneering Editor of *Cosmopolitan* Magazine," in *The Good Body* (New York: Villard, 2004), 11–14.

17. Helen Gurley Brown quoted in "Helen Gurley Brown," Contemporary Authors Online (Belmont, CA: Gale Group, 2006), http://galenet.galegroup.com/servlet/GLD/hits?r=d&origSearch=true&o=DataType&n=10&l=d&c=1&locID=main e&secondary=false&u=CA&u=CLC&u=DLB&t=KW&s=1&NA=brown%2C+helen+gurley (accessed September 29, 2008).

18. Brown, *Sex and the Single Girl*, 259.

CHAPTER 1

1. Helen Gurley's sister, four years her elder, was christened Eloine but was always known as Mary.

2. For the history of Oklahoma in general and the Ozarks in particular, see Brooks Blevins, *Hill Folks: A History of Arkansas Ozarkers and Their Image* (Fayetteville: University of Arkansas Press, 1986); and C. Fred Williams et al., eds., *A Documentary History of Arkansas* (Fayetteville: University of Arkansas Press, 2005). For the history of the Gurley and Sisco families, see letter from Helen Gurley Brown to Carl Stamps, August 13, 1981, HGB-SSCSC (13); letter from Claude Cisco to Cleo Sisco Gurley, February 21, 1929, HGB-SSCSC (13); and Will of

Charles Sneed, December 2, 1865, HGB-SSCSC (13); and Helen Gurley Brown, unpublished autobiography, 1962–1963, HGB-SSCSC (35).

3. On the history of Hot Springs National Park, see Ray Hanley and Steven Hanley, *Hot Springs, Arkansas* (Mt. Pleasant, SC: Arcadia, 2000).

4. See Anita Loos, *Gentlemen Prefer Blondes—and—But Gentlemen Marry Brunettes: The Illuminating Diary of a Professional Lady* (New York: Penguin, 1998). Quote from p. vii of Regina Barreca's introduction. All background information about *Gentleman Prefer Blondes* is from Barreca's insightful and informative introduction.

5. "Big Sister," *Time*, vol. 91, no. 6 (February 9, 1965), 60. Anita Loos wrote an article for the May 1974 issue of *Cosmopolitan*. Brown wrote to thank her, stating, "We all consider you the Cosmopolitan girl…you were being sexy and having a fantastic career at the same time before anybody!" Loos wrote back, claiming about Brown's letter, "I shall treasure it among the best things that have happened to me in a very long career!" Letters between Helen Gurley Brown and Anita Loos, February 26, 1974, and March 4, 1974, HGB-SSCSC (8).

6. Helen Gurley Brown, Canadian syndicated radio show, August 17, 1963, HGB-SSCSC (17).

7. The University of Arkansas holds the Orval Faubus papers, a series of ten oral histories, and two boxes of FBI records pertaining to the desegregation of Central High School in Little Rock. Little Rock Desegregation Records, Special Collections Library, University of Arkansas. See also John A. Kirk, *Redefining the Color Line: Black Activism in Little Rock, Arkansas, 1940–1970* (Gainesville: University Press of Florida, 2002).

8. Helen Gurley Brown, *I'm Wild Again* (New York: Warner Books, 2000), 7, 23, 286.

9. During Helen Gurley's childhood, former slaves still resided in Arkansas, and their life stories, recorded by the Federal Writers Project during the Great Depression, would attest to the continuingly difficult living conditions of blacks in the region, who faced the presence of the Ku Klux Klan and other forms of intimidation. These stories would also reveal the extreme efforts required by black communities to keep people alive when so few opportunities were available to them. The Federal Writers Project interviewed 233 African Americans in Arkansas as part of the Works Progress Administration's Folk History of Slavery. Transcripts of these interviews, *Born in Slavery: Slave Narratives from the Federal Writers Project, 1936–1938, Arkansas Narratives,* are available online through the Library of Congress, http://memory.loc.gov/ammem/snhtml/.

10. On the flood, see John M. Barry, *Rising Tide: The Great Mississippi Flood of 1927 and How It Changed America* (New York: Simon & Schuster, 1998). On the Works Progress Administration, see Federal Writers Project, *The WPA Guide to 1930s Arkansas* (Lawrence: University Press of Kansas, 1987).

11. Helen Gurley Brown, unpublished autobiography, 1962–1963, HGB-SSCSC (35).

12. Letter from Elizabeth Jessup Bilheimer to Helen Gurley Brown, December 1989, HGB-SSCSC (6). Brown and Bilheimer would remain lifelong friends.

13. On protective labor legislation, see Stephanie Coontz, *Marriage, A History: From Obedience to Intimacy, or How Love Conquered Marriage* (New York: Viking, 2005); Susan Lehrer, *Origins of Protective Labor Legislation for Women,*

1905–1925 (Albany, NY: SUNY Press, 1985); Ulla Wikander, Alice Kessler-Harris, and Jane Lewis, eds., *Protecting Women: Labor Legislation in Europe, the United States, and Australia, 1880–1920* (Champaign: University of Illinois Press, 1995); and Alice Kessler-Harris, *In Pursuit of Equity: Women, Men, and the Quest for Economic Citizenship in 20th-Century America* (New York: Oxford University Press, 2003).

14. Helen Gurley Brown, unpublished autobiography, 1962–1963, HGB-SSCSC (35).

15. See letter from Helen Gurley Brown to Dorothy London, May 25, 1989, HGB-SSCSC. On the history of Chicago, see Robert G. Spinney, *City of Big Shoulders: A History of Chicago* (DeKalb: Northern Illinois University Press, 2000); Donald L. Miller, *City of the Century: The Epic of Chicago and the Making of America* (New York: Simon & Schuster, 1997).

16. Helen Gurley Brown, unpublished autobiography, 1962–1963, HGB-SSCSC (35).

17. Helen Gurley Brown, "Things I Wish I'd Known at 18," *Sunday Express Magazine,* April 9, 1983, HGB-SSCSC (2).

18. Helen Gurley Brown, "Rich Girls," unpublished manuscript, n.d., HGB-SSCSC (36).

19. "My sister Mary says there's going to be a riot if I don't stop calling our family hillbillies," Brown stated in a lecture at Stanford University. "She says we are not hillbillies. We are mountain people." Helen Gurley Brown, author's luncheon, May 17, 1993, HGB-SSCSC (37). Brown's use of the term "hillbilly" arguably said as much about her desire to have overcome an identity as it said about the identity itself. On the history of hillbillies, see Anthony Harkins, *Hillbilly: A Cultural History of an American Icon* (New York: Oxford University Press, 2005).

20. Brown, "Things I Wish I'd Known at 18."

21. Richard Wright, "Inner Landscape," *New Republic* 103 (August 1940), 195; Helen Gurley Brown, notes for the *Late Show,* HGB-SSCSC (29).

22. Brown, notes for the *Late Show.*

23. Letter from Helen Gurley Brown to Carl Stamps, August 13, 1981, HGB-SSCSC (13).

24. Helen Gurley Brown, "History," unpublished manuscript, no date, HGB-SSCSC (35).

25. Helen Gurley Brown, in *Teachers Make a Difference,* Harris County Department of Education, 1987, 13, HGB-SSCSC (35). Well into her eighties, she remembered her teachers, particularly Charlotte McGee and Ethel Davis in Los Angeles, as important influences. From Helen Gurley Brown, interview by Jennifer Scanlon, June 11, 2007.

26. Caroline Clark, "Helen Gurley Brown—She Can't Recall a Dull Moment," *Arkansas Gazette,* November 19, 1967, 4E, HGB-SSCSC (2).

27. On the history of polio, see David M. Oshinsky, *Polio: An American Story* (New York: Oxford University Press, 2006), and Jeffrey Kluger, *Splendid Solution: Jonas Salk and the Conquest of Polio* (New York: Putnam, 2005). When the daughter of the book and film critic Gene Shalit was paralyzed in an accident, Helen Gurley Brown wrote him a letter in which she revealed more of the history of her sister's polio. The best way to help people in these circumstances, she wrote, is to care for them, lavishly, and "also to lead your own life because you can't join them in

the wheelchair; it doesn't help if you go down the drain with grief and caring and actually you can both live good lives with lots of trying." Helen Gurley Brown, letter to Gene Shalit, June 1, 1989, HGB-SSCSC (9).

28. Helen Gurley Brown, *I'm Wild Again* (New York: Warner Books, 2000), 6–7, 10–13. On the history of disability, see Peter K. Longmore and Lauri Umansky, eds., *The New Disability History: American Perspectives* (New York: New York University Press, 2001).

29. Brown, *I'm Wild Again*, 10.

30. Helen Gurley Brown, unpublished autobiography, 1962–1963, HGB-SSCSC (35).

31. Letters from classmates to Helen Gurley Brown, June 1939, HGB-SSCSC.

32. See *Yearbook* and accompanying articles from June 1939, HGB-SSCSC.

33. Deirdre Donahue, "Brown Lives Magazine's Message," *USA Today*, April 13, 1980, 1D-E, HGB-SSCSC (2); Gloria Steinem, "In Conversation with Helen Gurley Brown," (Palm Springs, CA: TAE Productions, 1985), HGB-SSCSC (16).

34. Florence Stanley, letter to Helen Gurley Brown, March 29, 1939, HGB-SSCSC (1).

35. Anne Eaton, "The Girl with Her Nose Pressed to the Window," *Suburbia Today*, September 26, 1982, 9, HGB-SSCSC (28).

36. On cultural ideas of beauty during Helen Gurley's day, see Lois Banner, *American Beauty: A Social History Through Two Centuries of the American Idea, Ideal, and Image of the Beautiful Woman* (Los Angeles: Figueroa Press, 2006).

37. Virginia Garrison, "Helen Gurley Brown: Mama Hen to Swinging Chicks," *Arkansas Democrat*, July 6, 1969, 3C, HGB-SSCSC (2).

38. Texas State College for Women became Texas Women's University in 1957 and a coeducational institution in 1994. Woodbury College, founded in 1884, became Woodbury University in 1974.

39. On the history of women's access to higher education, see Barbara Miller Solomon, *In the Company of Women: A History of Women in Higher Education in America* (New Haven, CT: Yale University Press, 1986); John Mack Faragher and Florence Howe, eds., *Women and Higher Education in American History* (New York: W. W. Norton, 1988); Lynn D. Gordon, *Gender and Higher Education in the Progressive Era* (New Haven, CT: Yale University Press, 1992).

40. Helen Gurley, unpublished manuscript, n.d., HGB-SSCSC.

41. Helen Gurley Brown, unpublished autobiography, 1962–1963, HGB-SSCSC (35).

42. James Kaplan, "The Mouseburger That Roared," *Vanity Fair* 53, no. 6 (June 1990), 153, HGB-SSCSC (2); see also Brown, *I'm Wild Again*, 11.

43. Helen Gurley, unpublished manuscript, n.d., HGB-SSCSC.

44. Brown, *I'm Wild Again*, 11.

45. Helen Gurley Brown, unpublished autobiographical piece, HGB-SSCSC (36).

46. File not used for *The Late Show*, HGB-SSCSC (29).

47. Helen Gurley Brown, manuscript notes for *The Late Show*, HGB-SSCSC (29).

48. On the cachet of the Wilshire Boulevard address, see Kevin Roderick, *Wilshire Boulevard: Grand Concourse of Los Angeles* (Santa Monica, CA: Angel City, 2005).

49. Helen Gurley Brown, letter to Paul Ziffren, July 20, 1988, HGB-SSCSC (10).

50. Helen Gurley Brown, manuscript notes for *The Late Show*, HGB-SSCSC (29).

51. Helen Gurley Brown, letter to Steve Rubell, November 6, 1980, HGB-SSCSC (9). Brown wrote this in-depth letter, perhaps a means of working through her

mother's recent death, to a prison inmate. She acknowledges in the letter that they are not close and wonders why she has shared these details with him.

CHAPTER 2

1. Jesse Kornbluth, "The Queen of the Mouseburgers," *New York,* September 27, 1982, 38, HGB-SSCSC (28).
2. Leo Robin, "Little Girl from Little Rock," lyrics composed for Broadway musical production of *Gentlemen Prefer Blondes,* 1949.
3. On the history of Jews in Hollywood, see Neal Gabler, *An Empire of Their Own: How the Jews Invented Hollywood* (New York: Anchor Books, 1989); Paul Buhle, *From the Lower East Side to Hollywood: Jews in American Popular Culture* (New York: Verso, 2004); J. Hoberman and Jeffrey Shandler, *Entertaining America: Jews, Movies, and Broadcasting* (Princeton, NJ: Princeton University Press, 2003).
4. Helen Gurley Brown, "The Year of Being Kept (But Not Very Well)," in *I'm Wild Again* (New York: Warner Books, 2000), 17. On the history of Hollywood, see Gregory Paul Williams, *The Story of Hollywood: An Illustrated History* (Los Angeles: BL Press, 2006); Allen J. Scott, *On Hollywood: The Place, The Industry* (Princeton, NJ: Princeton University Press, 2005).
5. Brown, "Year of Being Kept (But Not Very Well)," 17.
6. Helen Gurley, unpublished manuscript, no date, HGB-SSCSC (26).
7. As mentioned in chapter 1, the similarities between Helen Gurley Brown and the fictional Lorelei Lee, "just two little girls from Little Rock," are fascinating and worthy of further study. See Anita Loos, *Gentlemen Prefer Blondes: The Illuminating Diary of a Professional Lady* (London: The Folio Society, 1985 [1925]); see also the film version, featuring Marilyn Monroe: *Gentlemen Prefer Blondes* (Twentieth Century Fox, 1953).
8. See Brown, *I'm Wild Again,* 15–28.
9. "Whatever Happened to Don Belding?" *Sales Management,* January 7, 1966, HGB-SSCSC (21).
10. Gloria Steinem, "In Conversation with Helen Gurley Brown" (Palm Springs, CA: TAE Productions, 1985), HGB-SSCSC (16).
11. Steinem, "In Conversation with Helen Gurley Brown."
12. Helen Gurley Brown, draft of *Sex and the Office,* chapter 3, HGB-SSCSC (22).
13. Steinem, "In Conversation with Helen Gurley Brown."
14. See Norman Brokaw and Norm Meyer, *The Mailroom: Hollywood History from the Bottom Up* (New York: Ballantine Books, 2003).
15. On the history of women's work in the United States, see Alice Kessler-Harris, *Out to Work: A History of Wage-Earning Women in America* (New York: Oxford University Press, 2003); Teresa Amott and Julie Matthaei, *Race, Gender, and Work: A Multi-Cultural Economic History of Women in the United States* (Boston: South End Press, 1999). On secretarial work, see Marjorie W. Davies, *Woman's Place Is at the Typewriter; Office Work and Office Workers, 1900–1930* (Urbana: University of Illinois Press, 1992), and Angel Kwolek-Folland, *Engendering*

Business: Men and Women in the Corporate Office, 1870–1930 (Baltimore: Johns Hopkins University Press, 1998).

16. Steinem, "In Conversation with Helen Gurley Brown."

17. The follow-up in *Glamour* in November 1953, p. 131, included three photos of Helen Gurley in Hawaii, HGB-SSCSC (1).

18. Stephanie Coontz, *Marriage, A History: From Obedience to Intimacy, or How Love Conquered Marriage* (New York: Viking, 2005), 227. See also Beth Bailey, *From Front Porch to Back Seat: Courtship in Twentieth-Century America* (Baltimore: Johns Hopkins University Press, 1988); Betsy Israel, *Bachelor Girl: The Secret History of Single Women in the Twentieth Century* (New York: William Morrow, 2002); and Wini Breines, *Young, White and Miserable: Growing Up Female in the Fifties* (Boston: Beacon Press, 1992).

19. On *Playboy*, see Barbara Ehrenreich, *The Hearts of Men* (Garden City, NY: Anchor, 1983); Carrie Pitzulo, "The Battle in Every Man's Bed: *Playboy* and the Fiery Feminists," *Journal of the History of Sexuality*, 17, no. 2 (May 2008); Beth Bailey, "Sexual Revolution(s)," in *The Sixties: From Memory to History*, ed. David Farber (Chapel Hill: University of North Carolina Press, 1994).

20. Helen Gurley, unpublished manuscript, no date, HGB-SSCSC (35).

21. Elaine Tyler May, *Barren in the Promised Land: Childless Americans and the Pursuit of Happiness* (Cambridge, MA: Harvard University Press, 1997), 12, 39, 152. See also William H. Chafe, *The Paradox of Change: American Women in the Twentieth Century* (New York: Oxford University Press, 1992); Joanne Meyerowitz, ed., *Not June Cleaver: Women and Gender in Postwar America, 1945–1960* (Philadelphia: Temple University Press, 1994); and Juliet Mitchell, "Procreative Mothers (Sexual Difference) and Child-Free Sisters (Gender)," *European Journal of Women's Studies*, vol. 11, no. 4 (November 2004), 415–26.

22. Helen Gurley Brown, unpublished manuscript, HGB-SSCSC (35).

23. Helen Gurley Brown, speech to USO, May 10, 1991, HGB-SSCSC (15). On the history of women and the USO, see Meghan K. Winchell, *Good Girls, Good Food, Good Fun: The Story of USO Hostesses During World War II* (Chapel Hill: University of North Carolina Press, 2008).

24. Helen Gurley Brown, *Sex and the Single Girl* (New York: Bernard A. Geis, 1962), 4.

25. Helen Gurley, journal entry, March 19, 1953, HGB-SSCSC (35).

26. On Helen Gurley's relationship with W.G., see unpublished autobiographical pieces, n.d., HGB-SSCSC (36), and draft notes for *The Late Show* HGB-SSCSC (29).

27. Shirley Low, "Sex and the 61-Year-Old Ms.," *Boston Globe*, November 14, 1982, HGB-SSCSC (2).

28. On Helen Gurley's relationship with Jack Dempsey, see Helen Gurley Brown, letter to Noreen Nash Siegel, August 4, 1989, HGB-SSCSC (40).

29. On women in the advertising profession, particularly in copywriting, see Jennifer Scanlon, *Inarticulate Longings: The "Ladies' Home Journal," Gender, and the Promises of Consumer Culture* (New York: Routledge, 1995). Although many of the early women in the field had college degrees, if not graduate degrees, advertising remained a profession with career ladders for less educated but ambitious individuals, primarily men, of course.

30. Runner Associates, "Miss Helen Marie Gurley," February 1957, HGB-SSCSC (4).
31. Helen Gurley Brown's files contain ad copy she wrote, HGB-SSCSC (35).
32. Helen Gurley Brown muses about her reasons for not marrying in her unpublished autobiography, 1962–1963, HGB-SSCSC (35). On the history of psychotherapy, which Brown would recommend repeatedly to her growing audiences of women, see Philip Cushman, *Constructing the Self: A Cultural History of Psychotherapy* (Cambridge, MA: Da Capo Press, 1996); and Ellen Herman, *The Romance of American Psychology: Political Culture in the Age of Experts* (Berkeley: University of California Press, 1999).
33. Helen Gurley Brown, speech to Parents without Partners, early to mid-1960s, HGB-SSCSC (15).
34. The following references, all journal entries dated 1953, can be found in HGB-SSCSC (35).
35. Helen Gurley, unpublished material, 1956, HGB-SSCSC, (36).
36. Ibid.
37. Ibid.
38. Ibid.
39. Brown, unpublished manuscript, n.d., HGB-SSCSC (35).
40. Rock, "Little Girl from Little Rock," 1949.
41. Brown, *I'm Wild Again*, 33.
42. On Helen Gurley Brown's time at Kenyon & Eckhardt, see Helen Gurley Brown, unpublished autobiography, 1962–1963, HGB-SSCSC (35).
43. Helen Gurley Brown, "What the Women's Movement Means to Me," *Ms.*, July 1985, 118.
44. Steinem, "In Conversation with Helen Gurley Brown."
45. Helen Gurley Brown, *The Late Show* (New York: William Morrow, 1993), 52.

CHAPTER 3

1. Helen Gurley Brown, *The Late Show* (New York: William Morrow, 1993), 52.
2. Ibid.
3. Ibid.
4. Carl Henneman, "Best-Sell Author Pens 'Better One,'" *St. Paul Dispatch*, May 20, 1964, 58, HGB-SSCSC (24).
5. David Brown, "Long Island and the Single Boy," *On the Sound* 2, no. 8 (August 1972), 52, HGB-SSCSC (36). On the history of Long Island, see Bernie Bookbinder, *Long Island* (New York: Harry N. Abrams, 1998); and Marilyn Weigold, *The Long Island Sound: A History of Its Peoples, Places, and Environments* (New York: New York University Press, 2004). For a short history of Prohibition, see Thomas R. Pegram, *Battling Demon Rum: The Struggle for a Dry America, 1800–1933* (New York: Ivan R. Dee, 1998).
6. David Brown, "Long Island and the Single Boy," 50.
7. Ibid.," 54.
8. David Brown, *Let Me Entertain You* (New York: William Morrow, 1990), 60. This book, rich with insights about Hollywood insiders is, as the inside cover

states, "a self-portrait, in selective memory, of a man who has lived many lives, all of them full of risk, accomplishment, and above all, humanity."

9. Ibid., 60–61.

10. Ibid., 61.

11. Ibid., 63. On David Brown's college career, see Chit L. Lijauco, "Cosmo Couple," *Savvy*, June 2, 1997, 16, HGB-SSCSC (1). Brown himself notes that in 1933, when he attended Stanford, tuition was $115 a quarter and the trip from New York to California took three weeks by ship. He continues: "Martinis were twenty-five cents. At Stanford, meals and lodging at a dormitory cost nine dollars a week. Sex at a San Jose bordello was two dollars... AIDS was nonexistent but condoms were de rigueur. The greatest sexual fears were unwanted pregnancy (abortion was illegal and dangerous) and venereal disease (incurable then). Brown, *Let Me Entertain You*, 182.

12. Thomas Quinn Curtiss, "David Brown," *International Herald Tribune*, November 29, 1884, n.p, HGB-SSCSC (1); James Brady, "In Step With: David Brown, *Parade*, September 13, 1987, 30, HGB-SSCSC (1).

13. Brown, *Let Me Entertain You*, 19–24.

14. On the history of these magazines, see Theodore Peterson, *Magazines in the Twentieth Century* (Urbana: University of Illinois Press, 1956); and John Tebbel and Mary Ellen Zuckerman, *The Magazine in America, 1741–1990* (New York: Oxford University Press, 1991).

15. Brown, *Let Me Entertain You*, 28. On the history of television in this period, see Gary Edgerton, *The Columbia History of American Television* (New York: Columbia University Press, 2007). See also chapter 8 of this volume.

16. Brown, *Let Me Entertain You*, 35, 250–51.

17. Herb Stein, "Hollywood," *Morning Telegraph*, February 9, 1961, HGB-SSCSC (1). On the cultural history of Hollywood before and during David Brown's era, see Robert Sklar, *Movie-Made America: A Cultural History of the American Movies* (New York: Vintage, 1994).

18. Brown, *Let Me Entertain You*, 38.

19. Helen Gurley Brown, unpublished autobiography, 1962–1963, HGB-SSCSC (35).

20. Cindy Adams, "He Made Her a Married Woman," *Pageant*, December 1963, 68, HGB-SSCSC (1).

21. Ibid., 69.

22. Brown, unpublished autobiography, 1962–1963.

23. Ibid.

24. Ibid.

25. Ibid.

26. Ibid.

27. Helen Gurley Brown, "So He Won't Marry You," *Women and Beauty*, April 1964, 24, HGB-SSCSC (36).

28. Brown, unpublished autobiography, 1962–1963.

29. Ibid.

30. Jean Walker, "Marriage? Three Modern Misses Discuss an Up-to-Date Dilemma," *Los Angeles Mirror News*, May 5, 1959, HGB-SSCSC (2).

31. Brown, unpublished autobiography, 1962–1963.

32. Ibid.

33. Ibid.
34. Helen Gurley Brown, interview by Jennifer Scanlon, June 18, 2007; David Brown, interview by Jennifer Scanlon, March 27, 2008.
35. Brown, unpublished autobiography, 1962–1963.
36. Helen Gurley Brown, unpublished manuscript, n.d., HGB-SSCSC (35).
37. On the history of marriage—and gendered changes in the nature of marriage—over the course of the twentieth century, see Stephanie Coontz, *Marriage—A History: From Obedience to Intimacy, or How Love Conquered Marriage* (New York: Viking, 2005); to get a sense of how much the institution has and has not changed during Helen Gurley Brown's lifetime, see Anne Kingston, *The Meaning of Wife: A Provocative Look at Women and Marriage in the Twenty-First Century* (New York: Picador, 2006).
38. Helen explained that David didn't like that she worked Saturdays. See Jack Curry, "Two on an Island," *New York Daily News* (September 10, 1980), 8, HGB-SSCSC (36).
39. Adams, "He Made Her a Married Woman," 71.
40. Joyce Gabriel, "Efficient, Feminine—That's Helen Gurley Brown," *Escort,* January 24, 1971, 9, HGB-SSCSC (2).
41. Adams, "He Made Her a Married Woman," 68.
42. Curry, "Two on an Island," 8.
43. Helen Gurley Brown, unpublished manuscript, 1995, HGB-SSCSC (35).
44. Henneman, "Best-Sell Author Pens 'Better One,'" 58.
45. Brown, *Let Me Entertain You,* 70.
46. Curry, "Two on an Island," 8.
47. Judy Bachrach, "Couples," *People,* November 1, 1982, 55–56, HGB-SSCSC (1).

CHAPTER 4

1. April Levy, "The Blond Who's Had More Fun," *New York,* http://nymag.com/personals/articles/02/02/singles/bushnell1.htm (accessed October 8, 2008).
2. "Review: *Sex and the City,*" BBC News, February 24, 2004, http://news.bbc.co.uk/1/hi/entertainment/tv_and_radio/3512669.stm (accessed October 8, 2008).
3. Quotation from book jacket, Helen Gurley Brown, *Sex and the Single Girl* (New York: Bernard A. Geis, 1962).
4. Laurie Ouellette, "Inventing the Cosmo Girl: Class Identity and Girl-Style American Dreams," *Media Culture & Society* 21 (1999), 361.
5. For statistics on *Sex and the Single Girl,* see scrapbook, HGB-SSCSC (47).
6. Helen Gurley Brown, "Brief Resume of What's Happened with the Book So Far," July 1962, HGB-SSCSC (31).
7. Helen Gurley Brown, account of origins of *Sex and the Single Girl,* in David Brown manuscript, November 17, 1989, HGB-SSCSC (35).
8. Ibid.
9. Ibid.
10. Helen Gurley Brown, letter to Judith Krantz, April 5, 1978, HGB-SSCSC (8).

11. On the ways in which pregnancy outside of marriage was viewed, see Rickie Solinger, *Wake Up Little Susie: Single Pregnancy and Race Before Roe v. Wade* (New York: Routledge, 1992).

12. All of the quotes in this section are found in letters between Helen Gurley and Bill Peters, May 1949 to January 1951, HGB-SSCSC (9).

13. Helen Gurley Brown, *The Writer's Rules* (New York: William Morrow, 1998), xix.

14. Brown, *Sex and the Single Girl,* back cover.

15. Brown, *Sex and the Single Girl,* 5–6.

16. Brown, *Sex and the Single Girl,* 4; on expectations of women during the postwar period, and the multiple ways in which women responded to those expectations, see Elaine Tyler May, *Homeward Bound: American Families in the Cold War Era* (New York: Basic Books, 1988); Stephanie Coontz, *The Way We Never Were: American Families and the Nostalgia Trap* (New York: Basic Books, 1992); Susan Douglas, *Where the Girls Are: Growing Up Female with the Mass Media* (New York: Times Books, 1994); Joanne Meyerowitz, ed., *Not June Cleaver: Women and Gender in Postwar America, 1945–1960* (Philadelphia: Temple University Press, 1994); Beth Bailey, *Sex in the Heartland* (Cambridge, MA: Harvard University Press, 1999); and Jessica Weiss, *To Have and To Hold: Marriage, the Baby Boom, and Social Change* (Chicago: University of Chicago Press, 2000).

17. Jennifer Jarratt, "Marriage Hasn't Changed the Single Girls' Champion," *Free Press,* March 19, 1966, HGB-SSCSC (1).

18. Helen Gurley Brown, town hall speech, October 8, 1964, HGB-SSCSC (15).

19. Joseph Adelson, "Is Women's Liberation a Passing Fad?" *New York Times Magazine,* March 19, 1972, 94.

20. "Boy Meets Girl in Wartime," Pamphlet A496, 1943, quoted in May, *Homeward Bound,* 68–69.

21. Richard Hoffman, "I Met the Wrong Man," in *Why Are You Single,* quoted in Betsy Israel, *Bachelor Girl: The Secret History of Single Women in the Twentieth Century* (New York: William Morrow, 2002), 233.

22. Israel, *Bachelor Girl,* 6.

23. Ibid., 6.

24. Coontz, *Marriage, A History,* 227.

25. Helen Gurley Brown, speech to Parents without Partners, early to mid-1960s, HGB-SSCSC (15).

26. Coontz, *Way We Never Were,* 186.

27. Brown, *Sex and the Single Girl,* 7, 8.

28. Ibid., 7.

29. Ibid., 257.

30. *Kinsey in the News,* PBS American Experience, http://www.pbs.org/wgbh/amex/kinsey/sfeature/sf_response_female.html (accessed October 8, 2008).

31. *Late Scene,* BBC interview with Helen Gurley Brown, October 20, 1964, HGB-SSCSC (21).

32. Israel, *Bachelor Girl,* 208.

33. Ibid., 210.

34. Barbara Ehrenreich, Elizabeth Hess, and Gloria Jacobs, *Re-making Love: The Feminization of Sex* (Garden City, NY: Doubleday, 1987), 60.

35. Willard Waller quoted in May, *Homeward Bound*, 69; Reuben Hill and Howard Bakers, eds., *Marriage and the Family* (Boston: D. C. Heath, 1940), 587–88, quoted in May, 69.
36. May, *Homeward Bound*, 99.
37. Ibid., 101.
38. Ibid., 123.
39. Brown, *Sex and the Single Girl*, 22.
40. Ibid., 23–24.
41. Ibid., 24.
42. Ibid., 237.
43. Ibid., 24.
44. Ibid., 25.
45. Judy Bachrach, "When It Comes to *Having It All*, HGB Wrote the Book—With a Little Inspiration from Her Dear David," *People*, November 1, 1982, 54–61, HGB-SSCSC (28).
46. Brown, *Sex and the Single Girl*, 167, 174, 179–80, 185.
47. Ibid., 104–5.
48. Ibid., 105.
49. Ibid., 196.
50. Ibid., 111, 112, 115.
51. Ibid., 239.
52. Ibid., 105.
53. On the contested nature of sexual and financial relationships between women and men, see Kathy Peiss, *Cheap Amusements: Working Women and Leisure in Turn-of-the-Century New York* (Philadelphia: Temple University Press, 1986), Beth Bailey, *From Front Porch to Back Seat: Courtship in Twentieth-Century America* (Baltimore: Johns Hopkins University Press, 1988); and Joanne Meyerowitz, *Women Adrift: Independent Wage Earners in Chicago, 1880–1930* (Chicago: University of Chicago Press, 1988).
54. Brown, *Sex and the Single Girl*, 89.
55. Ibid., 90.
56. Ruth Rosen, *The World Split Open: How the Modern Women's Movement Changed America* (New York: Viking, 2000), xi.
57. "Special Report on Women," *Life*, 1956, quoted in Israel, *Bachelor Girl*, 181.
58. Brown, *Sex and the Single Girl*, 103.
59. Ibid., 98.
60. Ibid., 99.

CHAPTER 5

A version of chapter 5 was published as "Sensationalist Literature or Expert Advice? Helen Gurley Brown's *Sex and the Single Girl* in its Publishing Context," *Feminist Media Studies* 9, no. 1 (Spring 2009).
1. David Brown," Sex and the Single Girl As Seen by David Brown," *Cavalier*, April 1964, HGB-SSCSC (1).

2. Letter from David Brown to Bernard Geis, July 24, 1962, HGB-SSCSC (19).

3. Kenneth C. Davis, *Two-Bit Culture: The Paperbacking of America* (Boston: Houghton Mifflin, 1984), 101, 103. On the history of the paperback industry, see also Clarence Peterson, *The Bantam Story: Thirty Years of Paperback Publishing* (New York: Bantam Books, 1975); Allen B. Crider, *Mass Market Publishing in America* (Boston: G. K. Hall, 1982); and Lee Server, *Over My Dead Body: The Sensational Age of the American Paperback, 1945–1955* (San Francisco: Chronicle Books, 1994).

4. Barbara Seaman, *Lovely Me: The Life of Jacqueline Susann* (New York: William Morrow, 1987), 270. According to Geis's son, Stephen, Geis used to give out Bernard Geis Associates pens, which featured a miniskirt-clad woman sliding down a pole in a liquid-filled chamber, to anyone who dared the descent on the pole. Letter from Stephen Geis to Jennifer Scanlon, March 4, 2008.

5. Joan Didion, "Bosses Make Lousy Lovers," *Saturday Evening Post,* January 30, 1965, 36, HGB-SSCSC (21); letter from Stephen Geis to Jennifer Scanlon, March 4, 2008.

6. Seaman, *Lovely Me,* 270.

7. Davis, *Two-Bit Culture,* xii, 41.

8. Ibid., 305, 361.

9. See Ann Barr Snitow, "The Front Line: Notes on Sex in Novels by Women, 1969–1979," in *Women: Sex and Sexuality,* ed. Catharine R. Stimpson and Ethel Spector Person (Chicago: University of Chicago Press, 1980); Madonna M. Miner, *Insatiable Appetites: Twentieth Century American Women's Bestsellers* (Westport, CT: Greenwood, 1984); and Ruth Pirsig Wood, *Lolita in Peyton Place: Highbrow, Lowbrow, and Middlebrow Novels of the 1950s* (New York: Garland, 1995). Interestingly, *Peyton Place* was published by Kitty Messner, president of one of only two female-run publishing companies of the day. Like Bernard Geis did with Helen Gurley Brown, Messner felt an affinity for her author and the book's racy contents. See Emily Toth, *Inside Peyton Place: The Life of Grace Metalious* (Jackson: University Press of Mississippi, 2000). It is worth noting that Truman Capote's *Breakfast at Tiffany's,* published in 1958 as a novella and then produced in 1961 as a film, also featured a young, sexually active single woman.

10. David Halberstam, *The Fifties* (New York: Villard Books, 1993), 579.

11. Davis, *Two-Bit Culture,* 258; Ardis Cameron, "Open Secrets: Rereading Peyton Place," introduction to *Peyton Place,* by Grace Metalious (Boston: Northeastern University Press, 1999), xv; Toth, *Inside Peyton Place,* 143; Halberstam, *Fifties,* 580.

12. Quoted in Mitchell Owens, "Rona Jaffe, Author of Popular Novels, Is Dead at 74," *New York Times,* December 31, 2005 [online], available at http://www.nytimes.com/2005/12/31/arts/31jaffe.html (accessed February 27, 2008).

13. Betsy Israel, *Bachelor Girl: The Secret History of Single Women in the Twentieth Century* (New York: William Morrow, 2002), 206.

14. Helen Gurley Brown, *Sex and the Single Girl* (New York: Bernard A. Geis, 1962), 249.

15. In an interview with *Playboy,* Brown explained that she had attempted to include abortion in *Sex and the Single Girl.* See "Playboy Interview: Helen Gurley Brown," *Playboy,* April 1963, 53–54.

16. Halberstam, *Fifties,* 580.

17. Davis, *Two-Bit Culture*, 259.

18. In her biography of Grace Metalious, Emily Toth describes the many clandestine readers of *Peyton Place*, who knew, as Toth puts it, "they weren't supposed to be reading *Peyton Place*. They also knew they had to read it." Emily Toth, *Inside Peyton Place*, 138.

19. Elaine Tyler May, *Homeward Bound: American Families in the Cold War Era* (New York: Basic Books, 1988), 187.

20. Brown, *Sex and the Single Girl*, 3.

21. Ibid., 5.

22. Barbara Ehrenreich, Elizabeth Hess, and Gloria Jacobs, *Remaking Love: The Feminization of Sex* (Garden City, NY: Anchor Books, 1987), 25.

23. David Brown, unpublished manuscript, October 17, 1989, HGB-SSCSC (35).

24. See Laurie Ouellette, "Inventing the Cosmo Girl: Class Identity and Girl-Style American Dreams," *Media, Culture & Society* 21 (1999), 369–83.

25. Terry Galanoy, "You and Your Love Life," *Rogue*, September 1962, 37, HGB-SSCSC (21).

26. Bernard Geis, letter to Saul David, June 19, 1962, HGB-SSCSC (19).

27. Letter from Bernard Geis to Helen Gurley Brown, June 26, 1962, HGB-SSCSC (19).

28. Letter from Stephen Geis to Jennifer Scanlon, March 4, 2008.

29. Letter from Helen Gurley Brown to Letty Cottin, June 26, 1962, HGB-SSCSC (19); letter from Helen Gurley Brown to Letty Cottin, March 19, 1962, HGB-SSCSC (19); letter from Helen Gurley Brown to Letty Cottin, March 26, 1962, HGB-SSCSC (19); letter from Helen Gurley Brown to Letty Cottin, April 10, 1962, HGB-SSCSC (19).

30. Letter from Helen Gurley Brown to Bernard Geis, January 11, 1963, HGB-SSCSC (19).

31. "Foreign Affairs Need Research," *New York World Telegram*, July 18, 1962 (21); Item, *New Yorker*, February 29, 1964, 24 (21).

32. John D'Emilio and Estelle B. Freedman, *Intimate Matters: A History of Sex in America* (Chicago: University of Chicago Press, 1997), 159.

33. On the history of the censorship of paperbacks, see Davis, *Two-Bit Culture*, 216–47.

34. Letter from Letty Cottin to Helen Gurley Brown, March 14, 1962, HGB-SSCSC (19); letter from Helen Gurley Brown to Letty Cottin, March 19, 1962, HGB-SSCSC (19); letter from Bernard Geis to Helen Gurley Brown, August 29, 1962, HGB-SSCSC (19).

35. Robert Kirsch, "Sex and the Single Girl Falls Short of Its Promising Title," *Los Angeles Times*, July 6, 1962, 2; Norman Vincent Peale, "Where Do You Draw the Line?" *Miami Herald*, February 3, 1966, 2C; letter to the editor, *San Francisco Chronicle*, July 12, 1962; Cleo Brown, letter to Helen Gurley Brown, May 3, 1962, all from HGB-SSCSC (6).

36. Kirsch, "Sex and the Single Girl Falls Short," 2; Virginia Tackett, "Arkansas Writer Has a Good One for the Distaff Side," *Arkansas Gazette*, June 3, 1962.

37. Anne Eaton, "The Girl with Her Nose Pressed to the Window," *Suburbia Today*, September 26, 1982, 10 HGB-SSCSC (28).

38. Didion, "Bosses Make Lousy Lovers," 36.

CHAPTER 6

1. Linda Kerber, "'I Was Appalled': The Invisible Antecedents of Second-Wave Feminism," *Journal of Women's History* 14, no. 2 (Summer 2002), 94.

2. Janaan Sherman, introduction to *Interviews with Betty Friedan,* ed. Janaan Sherman (Jackson: University Press of Mississippi, 2002), ix.

3. Alice Steinbach, "The Cosmo Girl at 60 Fights Back the Jungle," *Sun,* November 21, 1982, 6, HGB-SSCSC (28). Daniel Horowitz's groundbreaking work, *Betty Friedan and the Making of the Feminist Mystique: The American Left, the Cold War, and Modern Feminism* (Amherst: University of Massachusetts Press, 1998), demonstrates that Friedan wrote her book within a larger context of critical social commentary. See also Eva Moskowitz, "'It's Good to Blow Your Top': Women's Magazines and a Discourse of Discontent," *Journal of Women's History* 8, no. 3 (Fall 1996), 66–98; and Joanne Meyerowitz, "Beyond the Feminine Mystique: A Reassessment of Postwar Mass Culture," in *Not June Cleaver: Women and Gender in Postwar America* (Philadelphia: Temple University Press, 1994). The first work to compare Friedan and Brown, and argue that Brown's analysis was "in some ways the more radical," was Barbara Ehrenreich, Elizabeth Hess, and Gloria Jacobs, *Remaking Love: The Feminization of Sex* (Garden City, NY: Anchor Books, 1987), 56–57. Ruth Rosen makes a similar argument in *The World Split Open: How the Modern Women's Movement Changed America* (New York: Penguin, 2000), 51. At times Brown claimed a position as second-wave pioneer. "I was there before Betty Friedan and *The Feminine Mystique,*" she told one reporter. "I was there saying 'You're your own person, go out there and be somebody... You don't have to get your identity from being somebody's appendage.'" Quoted in Imelda Whelehan, *The Feminist Bestseller: From "Sex and the Single Girl" to "Sex and the City"* (New York: Palgrave Macmillan, 2005), 30.

4. See Horowitz, *Betty Friedan and the Making of the Feminist Mystique,* 87.

5. Michelle Kort, "Portrait of a Feminist as an Old Woman," in Sherman, *Interviews with Betty Friedan,* 126; on writing, see Lyn Tornabene, "The Liberation of Betty Friedan," originally printed in *McCall's* magazine in May 1971 and reprinted in Sherman, *Interviews with Betty Friedan,* 30.

6. On cultural expectations around motherhood and domesticity, see Juliet Mitchell, "Procreative Mothers (Sexual Difference) and Child-Free Sisters (Gender)," *European Journal of Women's Studies* 11, no. 4 (November 2004), 415–26.

7. Betty Friedan quoted in Mary Walton, "Once More to the Ramparts," in Sherman, *Interviews with Betty Friedan,* 45; Tornabene, "Liberation of Betty Friedan," 30.

8. Lesley Johnson, "Revolutions Are Not Made by Downtrodden Housewives: Feminism and the Housewife," *Australian Feminist Studies* 15, no. 32 (2000), 243; Betty Friedan, *The Feminine Mystique* (New York: W. W. Norton, 1963), 334. In chapter 14, "The Forfeited Self," Friedan cites the work of Rollo May, Erich Fromm, David Riesman, and Abraham H. Maslow. Micki McGee identifies Brown and Friedan as the originators of the notion that self-actualization, particularly through work, belonged to both women and men. See her discussions of Brown, Friedan, and Maslow in *Self-Help, Inc.: Makeover Culture in American Life* (New York: Oxford University Press, 2005), 39–43.

9. Self-help books of the sort written by Helen Gurley Brown and Betty Friedan arguably assist, as Lesley Johnson argues about conduct books, "not only in shaping a reflexive self but [also] incite the desire to have such a sense of self." See Johnson, "Revolutions Are Not Made by Downtrodden Housewives," 243; Friedan, *Feminine Mystique*, 79.

10. Friedan, *Feminine Mystique*, 177, 180.

11. Rosemary Hennessee, *Betty Friedan: Her Life* (New York: Random House, 1999).

12. Whelehan, *Feminist Bestseller*, 27.

13. Jennifer Jarratt, "Marriage Hasn't Changed the Single Girls' Champion," *Free Press*, March 19, 1966, HGB-SSCSC (1).

14. "The Browns," 1963, HGB-SSCSC (1).

15. Helen Gurley Brown, speech, early 1960s, HGB-SSCSC (15).

16. Ibid.

17. For histories of the second wave of feminism, see Ruth Rosen, *The World Split Open: How the Modern Women's Movement Changed America* (New York: Viking, 2000); Estelle Freedman, *No Turning Back: The History of Women and the Future of Feminism* (New York: Ballantine, 2002); and Sara M. Evans, *Tidal Wave: How Women Changed America at Century's End* (New York: Free Press, 2003).

18. Friedan, *Feminine Mystique*, 206–32, 333, 334, 344.

19. Joanne Hollows provides an enormously helpful discussion in "The Feminist and the Cook: Julia Child, Betty Friedan and Domestic Femininity," in *Gender and Consumption*, ed. Emma Casey and Lydia Martens (Aldershot, UK: Ashgate, 2006), 59–84.

20. See Philip Wylie, *Generation of Vipers* (New York: Farrar & Rinehart, 1942); William H. Whyte Jr., *The Organization Man* (New York: Simon & Schuster, 1956); David Reisman, et al., *The Lonely Crowd: A Study of the Changing American Character* (New Haven, CT: Yale University Press, 1969).

21. On the connections between Friedan's Old Left past and the popular feminism she espoused in *The Feminine Mystique*, see Horowitz, *Betty Friedan and the Making of the Feminine Mystique*.

22. Jane Howard, "Bettty Friedan's Pet Pique: *The Feminine Mystique*," in *Interviews with Betty Friedan*, 3.

23. Hollows, "Feminist and the Cook," 71–72.

24. Helen Gurley Brown, *Sex and the Single Girl* (New York: Bernard A. Geis, 1962), 120.

25. Friedan, *Feminine Mystique*, 232; Brown, *Sex and the Single Girl*, 124, 138, 139, 140.

26. Brown, *Sex and the Single Girl*, 134, 135.

27. Ibid., 246.

28. "Bad Girl," *Psychology Today* (March/April 1963), 71, HGB-SSCSC (2).

29. Friedan, *Feminine Mystique*, 43.

30. Ibid., 336. On Friedan's use of the Holocaust analogy, see Kirsten Fermaglich, *American Dreams and Nazi Nightmares: Early Holocaust Consciousness and Liberal America, 1957–1965* (Hanover, NH: University Press of New England, 2006); Alyson M. Cole, " 'There Are No Victims in This Class': On Female Suffering and Anti-Victim Feminism," *NWSA Journal* 11, no. 1 (Spring 1999), 72–96.

31. See Susan Estabrook Kennedy, *If All We Did Was to Weep at Home: A History of White Working-Class Women in America* (Bloomington: Indiana University Press, 1979); bell hooks, *Ain't I a Woman? Black Women and Feminism* (Boston: South End, 1981).

32. Chris Mazza and Jeffrey DeShell, eds., *Chick-Lit: Postfeminist Fiction* (Normal, IL: FC2, 1995).

33. Much as Helen Gurley Brown's writings on sexuality became less radical as they reached publication because of editorial interventions, Betty Friedan's writings became less radical where they concerned race and class as *The Feminine Mystique* reached publication. See Daniel Horowitz, *Betty Friedan and the Making of the Feminist Mystique*, 228.

34. Helen Gurley Brown, transcript for radio program, n.d., HGB-SSCSC (17).

35. Helen Gurley Brown, "Sex in Marriage," *Neue Illustrierte* (1963–64), HGB-SSCSC (36).

36. Friedan, *Feminine Mystique*, 261.

37. Brown, *Sex and the Single Girl*, 257.

38. Meredith Miller, "*The Feminine Mystique*: Sexual Excess and the Pre-Political Housewife," *Women: A Cultural Review* 16, no. 1 (2005), 7.

39. Miller, "Feminine Mystique," 12.

40. Anne Eaton, "The Girl with Her Nose Pressed to the Window," *Suburbia Today* (September 26, 1982), 7, HGB-SSCSC (28).

41. "Bad Girl," 70.

42. Betty Friedan, *Feminine Mystique*, 276, 277.

43. Jeannine Locke, "The Pippy-Poo World of Helen Gurley Brown," Johannesburg *Star Weekly*, January 1, 1966, HGB-SSCSC (21).

44. Helen Gurley Brown, speech, early 1960s, HGB-SSCSC (15).

45. Letter from Helen Gurley Brown to Betty Friedan, June 6, 1963; letter from Betty Friedan to Helen Gurley Brown, July 14, 1963; letter from Helen Gurley Brown to Betty Freidan, July 16, 1963. All letters quoted above from the Schlesinger Library, Radcliffe Institute for Advanced Study, Harvard University, Betty Friedan Papers, Folder 1790.

CHAPTER 7

1. Helen Gurley Brown, draft outline of *Sex and the Office*, n.d., HGB-SSCSC (22); Paul Rosenfeld, "'Deja Forward' With Helen and David Brown," *Los Angeles Times*, May 11, 1979, 21.

2. Eloise Duncan, "Sex Has Snowballed," *News-Call Bulletin*, December 14, 1962, HGB-SSCSC (21).

3. Letter from David Brown to James J. Shea, December 17, 1963, HGB-SSCSC (20). Albert Ellis, *Sex and the Single Man* (New York: Lyle Stuart, 1963). "Sex and the…" titles today include *Sex and the Single Person* (1995); *Sex and the Single Sister* (2002); *Sex and the Single Christian* (2005); *Sex and the Single Zillionaire* (2006); and *Sex and the Single Savior* (2006).

4. David Brown lays out the details of the contract in letter to Bernard Geis, July 24, 1962, HGB-SSCSC (19); the most comprehensive discussion of the book's metamorphosis into a film appears in Joe Hyams, "Sex and the Single Girl," *Cosmopolitan*, April 1964, 16–19, HGB-SSCSC (21). See also Shana Alexander, "Singular Girl's Success," *Life*, March 1, 1963, 64–67, HGB-SSCSC (2).

5. Helen Gurley Brown, *Lessons in Love*, GNP-Crescendo Records, 1962. Helen Gurley Brown's papers include the contract and royalty statements, HGB-SSCSC (33).

6. See letter from Bernard Geis to Helen Gurley Brown, March 14, 1962, HGB-SSCSC (19).

7. Letter from David Brown to Gene Norman, February 4, 1964, HGB-SSCSC (33).

8. Letter from Helen Gurley Brown to Elizabeth Weston, January 15, 1963, HGB-SSCSC (36).

9. Letter from Helen Gurley Brown to Jeanette Sarkisian, September 6, 1962, HGB-SSCSC (19).

10. See letter from law offices of Mitchell, Silberberg & Knupp to Helen Gurley Brown, January 3, 1963, HGB-SSCSC (31); Helen Gurley Brown, "The Fourth Dimension" *Woman Alone*, June 18–19, 1964, HGB-SSCSC (31). All *Woman Alone* columns referenced here may be found in the Helen Gurley Brown Papers.

11. Helen Gurley Brown, "Calling All Widows, Divorcees, Bachelor Girls," *Woman Alone*, April 1963; Helen Gurley Brown, "New Glamour Girl of Our Time," *Woman Alone*, April 1963.

12. On these themes see these *Woman Alone* columns: "Why Isn't a Nice Girl Like You Married?" April 1963; "We Save Rent, She's More Like My Age, But…," May 2–3, 1962; "Lift That Mop!" May 28–29, 1963; "Show Them Your Brain," June 6–7, 1963; "The Florence Nightingale in You," June 16–17, 1963; "I'd Rather Wake Up by Myself," February 11–12, 1964; "What Is Heaven Doing for the Really Poor Working Girl?" July 11–12, 1963; "The Friendly Forties," May 17–18, 1964; "How to Live on Your Income," October 13–14, 1964; "Fun and Games with the Kids," September 19–20, 1963; "Escape into Alcoholism," December 27–28, 1964; "Scared Stiff? That's Good!" February 20–21, 1964; "Hey, Mom, They're Separating the Girls from the Boys Again!" November 19–20, 1963; "See Europe and Live," May 24–25, 1964; "Make Your Job Bring More Happiness Units," November 17–18, 1964.

13. Helen Gurley Brown, "Is Mother Crazy?" *Woman Alone*, May 21–22, 1963; Helen Gurley Brown, "In Love with a Younger Man," *Woman Alone*, June 11–12, 1963.

14. Helen Gurley Brown, "How to Live on Your Income," *Woman Alone*, October 13–14, 1963; Helen Gurley Brown, "Mommy's Dating Again," *Woman Alone*, October 17–18, 1963.

15. Helen Gurley Brown, "A Shade of Difference," *Woman Alone*, November 24–25, 1963; Helen Gurley Brown, "Parting Is No Fun at All," *Woman Alone*, April 24–25, 1964.

16. Helen Gurley Brown, *Outrageous Opinions* (New York: Bernard Geis Associates, 1964). On Jacqueline Susann, see Barbara Seaman, *Lovely Me: The Life of Jacqueline Susann* (New York: Morrow, 1987).

17. Helen Gurley Brown, "Make Your Job Bring More Happiness Units," *Woman Alone,* November 17–18, 1964; Helen Gurley Brown, "The Proper Attitude about Money," *Woman Alone,* March 14–15, 1965.

18. Susan Hartmann, "Women's Employment and the Domestic Ideal in the Early Cold War Years," in *Not June Cleaver: Women and Gender in Postwar America, 1945–1960,* ed. Joanne Meyerowitz (Philadelphia: Temple University Press, 1994), 86; Ellen DuBois, "Women's and Gender History in Global Perspective: North America after 1865," in *Women's History in Global Perspective,* ed. Bonnie Smith (Chicago: University of Illinois Press, 2005), 245. See also Julie Matthaei, *An Economic History of Women in America* (New York, Schocken Books, 1982).

19. Letter from Bernard Geis to Helen Gurley Brown, June 7, 1962, HGB-SSCSC (19).

20. Helen Gurley Brown, speech, early 1960s, HGB-SSCSC (15).

21. Ibid.

22. Sara Evans, *Born For Liberty: A History of Women in America* (New York: The Free Press, 1989), 183. See also Rosabeth Moss Kanter, *Men and Women of the Corporation* (New York: Basic Books, 1977); Margery W. Davies, *Woman's Place Is at the Typewriter: Office Work and Office Workers, 1870–1930* (Philadelphia: Temple University Press, 1982); Sharon Hartman Strom, *Beyond the Typewriter: Gender, Class, and the Origins of Modern American Office Work, 1900–1930* (Urbana: University of Illinois Press, 1992); and Angel Kwolek-Folland, *Engendering Business: Men and Women in the Corporate Office, 1870–1930* (Baltimore: Johns Hopkins University Press, 1998).

23. Julie Berebitsky's discussion of *Sex and the Office* provides the most comprehensive and astute analysis of this publication and its publishing context. See Julie Berebitsky, "The Joy of Work: Helen Gurley Brown, Gender, and Sexuality in the White-Collar Office," *Journal of the History of Sexuality* 15, no. 1 (January 2006), 89–127. Sharon Hartmann Strom argues that even if a woman was not expected to provide sexual services for her boss, she was "to give him the services of her gender: domesticity, passivity, charm, and endless patience," 372–73.

24. See Berebitsky, "Joy of Work"; and Laurie Ouellette, "Inventing the Cosmo Girl: Class Identity and Girl-Style American Dreams," *Media, Culture & Society* 21 (1999), 359–83.

25. Helen Gurley Brown, *Sex and the Single Girl* (New York: Bernard A. Geis, 1962), 30.

26. Brown, draft of *Sex and the Office,* 7, HGB-SSCSC (22).

27. Brown, draft of *Sex and the Office,* n.d..

28. Letter from Bernard Geis to Helen Gurley Brown, February 4, 1964, HGB-SSCSC (19).

29. Ibid.

30. Helen Gurley Brown, *Sex and the Office* (New York: Bernard Geis Associates, 1964), 22.

31. Letter from Helen Gurley Brown to Bernard Geis, November 8, 1962, HGB-SSCSC (19); letter from Bernard Geis to Helen Gurley Brown, February 10, 1964, HGB-SSCSC (19).

32. Helen Gurley Brown, "The Seduction…with a Difference," in *Three Little Bedtime Stories,* n.d., HGB-SSCSC (22).

33. Helen Gurley Brown, draft of *Sex and the Office,* n.d., HGB-SSCSC (22).

34. Letter from Bernard Geis to Helen Gurley Brown, February 10, 1964, HGB-SSCSC, (19); letter from Bernard Geis to Helen Gurley Brown, February 19, 1964, HGB-SSCSC (19).

35. Letter from Helen Gurley Brown to Bernard Geis, February 8, 1964, HGB-SSCSC, (19).

36. Letter from Bernard Geis to Helen Gurley Brown, February 28, 1962, HGB-SSCSC, (19); letter from Helen Gurley Brown to Bernard Geis, February 8, 1962, HGB-SSCSC (19).

37. Helen Gurley Brown, "Rape—More or Less," in *Three Little Bedtime Stories*, n.d., HGB-SSCSC (22).

38. Letter from Bernard Geis to Helen Gurley Brown, February 19, 1964, HGB-SSCSC (19).

39. On the issue of contraception and *Sex and the Office*, see letter from Letty Cottin to Helen Gurley Brown, August 23, 1962, HGB-SSCSC (19), in which Cottin explains that Geis's decision to cut out material on contraception was justified.

40. On lesbians in the postwar period, see Donna Penn, "The Sexualized Woman: The Lesbian, the Prostitute, and the Containment of Female Sexuality in Postwar America," in Meyerowitz, *Not June Cleaver*, 359. In a letter to Geis dated February 8, 1964, Brown writes that although he perhaps wisely excised references to abortion from *Sex and the Single Girl*, lesbian sexuality is "not all that taboo," HGB-SSCSC (19).

41. Linda Klein, "Sex in Office Handbook," *Wilmington DE News*, September 7, 1964, HGB-SSCSC (47); "Sex and the Office," no source identified, HGB-SSCSC (47); "Sex and the Office," *Psychiatric Quarterly*, n.d., HGB-SSCSC (24); Gloria Steinem, review, *New York Herald-Tribune*, October 18, 1964, HGB-SSCSC (47); "Secretary's Guide to Sex at High Noon," *Life*, August 28, 1964, HGB-SSCSC (47); miscellaneous reviews, HGB-SSCSC (47).

42. Discussions of and newspaper clippings about the West German lawsuit can be found in the Helen Gurley Brown Papers. See letter from Judy Ezer to David Brown, June 21, 1965, HGB-SSCSC (19).

43. Phyllis Battelle, "Who Needs Her?" *Cleveland Plain Dealer*, November 22, 1964, HGB-SSCSC (47).

CHAPTER 8

1. Sonny Curtis, composer, "Love Is All Around," theme song for *The Mary Tyler Moore Show*, CBS, 1970.

2. On the history of television and its gendered implications in the postwar period, see Ella Taylor, *Prime-Time Families: Television Culture in Postwar America* (Berkeley: University of California Press, 1989); and Lynn Spigel, *Make Room for TV: Television and the Family Ideal in Postwar America* (Chicago: University of Chicago Press, 1992). Statistics from Taylor, 20; Spigel, 1.

3. Taylor, *Prime-Time Families*, 27.

4. See Mary Beth Haralovich, "Sitcoms and Suburbs: Positioning the 1950s Homemaker," *Quarterly Review of Film and Video* 11 (1989), 61–83. On women

in television outside of the situation comedy genre, see also Moya Luckett, "Sensuous Women and Single Girls: Reclaiming the Female Body on 1960s Television," in *Swinging Single: Representing Sexuality in the 1960s*, ed. Hilary Radner and Moya Luckett (Minneapolis: University of Minnesota Press, 1999), 277–98.

5. Taylor, *Prime-Time Families*, 28. As Taylor puts it, "The widowed state became a popular device in 1960s comedy and drama for opening up the lives of characters to romance and increased contact with the outside world without risking the stigma of divorce," 28.

6. Ibid., 31–32.

7. Ibid., 85.

8. Ibid., 85.

9. Letter from Helen Gurley Brown to Lucy Kroll, December 8, 1962, HGB-SSCSC (19).

10. Letter from ABC Television to Helen Gurley Brown and David Brown, November 23, 1962, HGB-SSCSC (35).

11. All descriptions and quotes from *The Single Girl Sandra* are found in various manuscript copies, notes, and proposals in Helen Gurley Brown's papers (19; 35).

12. Letter from Helen Gurley Brown to Lucy Kroll, August 30, 1962, HGB-SSCSC (19).

13. Taylor, *Prime-Time Families*, 115–18.

14. Letter from Helen Gurley Brown to Lucy Kroll, August 30, 1962.

15. Ibid.

16. Helen Gurley Brown, proposal, *Single Girl—Sandra*.

17. Ibid.

18. On the ways in which family was defined on *The Mary Tyler Moore Show*, see Taylor, *Prime-Time Families*, 99–100; quotes from "Memorable Quotes for *Mary Tyler Moore*," http://www.imdb.com/title/tt0065314/quotes (accessed June 10, 2008).

19. Helen Gurley Brown, proposals for *That Tully Girl* and *Normal Like Me*, HGB-SSCSC. The setting of the therapist's office would work well for CBS when it introduced the Emmy Award–winning comedy, *The Bob Newhart Show*, in 1972; and of course, HBO's *The Sopranos* would make good use of this setting decades later.

20. Helen Gurley Brown, proposals for *Personal and Confidential* and *What Is Your Problem?* HGB-SSCSC (35).

21. Helen Gurley Brown, proposals for *Making Marriage Work, Behind the Scenes*, and *Frankly Female*, HGB-SSCSC (35). Sherri Finkbine, a children's television actress, sought an abortion after being prescribed thalidomide, a drug linked to serious birth defects, during her pregnancy. The 1962 case drew a tremendous amount of attention and helped raise awareness about the need for legalized abortion.

22. Helen Gurley Brown, proposals for *Sex: Female and Cook's on the Fire*, HGB-SSCSC (35).

23. Jeremy Campbell, "Joe Pyne: TV's Biggest Bully?" *Rocky Mountain News*, March 5, 1967, 10, HGB-SSCSC (18).

24. *Good Morning America* discontinued Helen Gurley Brown's contract in 1978. David Brown protested the decision and its delivery, but the chairman of the board of CBS wrote David back, arguing that the decision was "backed up by

some extensive research studies." This did not mean they did not want her at all; rather, they hoped to draw on her from time to time. See letter from Leonard Goldstein to David Brown, May 16, 1978, HGB-SSCSC (6).

25. Information about *Outrageous Opinions*, HGB-SSCSC (43); Moya Luckett, "A Moral Crisis in Prime Time: *Peyton Place* and the Rise of the Single Girl," in *Television, History, and American Culture: Feminist Critical Essays*, ed. Mary Beth Haralovich and Lauren Rabinowitz (Durham, NC: Duke University Press, 1999), 81.

26. Judy Klemesrud, "Mrs. Brown, Your Subject Is Showing," *New York Times*, December 31, 1967, n.p., HGB-SSCSC (21).

27. Helen Gurley Brown, *I'm Wild Again* (New York: Warner Books, 2000), 46–49.

28. Letter from David Brown to Bernard Geis, August 17, 1964, HGB-SSCSC (37).

CHAPTER 9

1. Helen Gurley Brown, "How the 'New *Cosmopolitan*' Got to Be," circa 1990s, HGB-SSCSC (41); David Brown, *Let Me Entertain You* (New York: William Morrow, 1990), 111.

2. On the history of each of these other women's magazines, see Kathleen L. Endres and Therese L. Lueck, eds., *Women's Periodicals in the United States: Consumer Magazines* (Westport, CT: Greenwood, 1995); Brown, *Let Me Entertain You*, 111.

3. Helen Gurley Brown, *Femme* proposal, HGB-SSCSC (37).

4. Ibid.

5. Ibid.

6. Ibid.

7. David Brown, letter to Bernard Geis, October 14, 1964, HGB-SSCSC (37).

8. Bernard Geis, *Femme* proposal, 1964, HGB-SSCSC (37); letter from David Brown to Bernard Geis, October 14, 1964, HGB-SSCSC (37).

9. Gloria Steinem, "In Conversation with Helen Gurley Brown" (Palm Springs, CA: TAE Productions, 1985), HGB-SSCSC (16).

10. Helen Gurley Brown, "A Proposal for *Cosmopolitan* Magazine from Helen Gurley Brown," HGB-SSCSC (37).

11. Helen Gurley Brown, "How the New Cosmo Got Started," notes for *Let Me Entertain You*, HGB-SSCSC (4).

12. Brown, *Femme* proposal; Steinem, "In Conversation with Helen Gurley Brown"; Brown, "How the 'New *Cosmopolitan*' Got to Be."

13. On the history of *Cosmopolitan*, see Jon Bekken and Lisa Beinhoff, "Cosmopolitan," in *Women's Periodicals in the United States: Consumer Magazines*, ed. Kathleen L. Endres and Therese L. Lueck (Westport, CT: Greenwood, 1995), 49–57. According to Helen Gurley Brown, Ulysses S. Grant Jr. "was as big a loser as a magazine publisher as his father was as president"; see Helen Gurley Brown, speech made to *Cosmopolitan* sales force, San Juan, Puerto Rico, March 1978, HGB-SSCSC (37).

14. On Brown's attitude toward existing *Cosmopolitan* readers, see "Interview with Helen Gurley Brown," n.d., HGB-SSCSC (28); Helen Gurley Brown, "Step into My Parlor," *Cosmopolitan*, July 1965, HGB-SSCSC (43).

15. Rodger Streitmatter, *Sex Sells: The Media's Journey from Repression to Obsession* (Cambridge, MA: Westview, 2004), 6. On the history of the birth control pill, see Elizabeth Siegel Watkins, *On the Pill: A Social History of Oral Contraceptives, 1950–1970* (Baltimore: Johns Hopkins University Press, 1998).

16. Robert Kline, "In Conversation with Helen Gurley Brown," 1985, HGB-SSCSC (2); Julia Hinds, "Sex and the Singular Gurley," *Detroit News,* May 9, 1990, HGB-SSCSC (2); "Interview with Helen Gurley Brown," n.d., HGB-SSCSC (28).

17. Chris Welles, "Soaring Success of the Iron Butterfly," *Life,* November 19, 1965, 65; Richard Berlin, letter to Helen Gurley Brown, June 25, 1969, HGB-SSCSC (39).

18. A. R. Roalman, "The New *Cosmopolitan*," *Writers' Digest,* August 1966, 51, HGB-SSCSC (38).

19. Joan Sutton, "That Cosmo Girl a Few Years Later," *Toronto Sun,* December 14, 1978, 99, HGB-SSCSC (2).

20. Richard Berlin, letter to Helen Gurley Brown, June 25, 1969, HGB-SSCSC (39).

21. Helen Gurley Brown, notes, n.d., HGB-SSCSC (42).

22. Bonnie Hearn, "Connecting with Your Readers: Helen Gurley Brown Tells You How," *Editor & Writer* 1, no. 2 (April 1997), 15, HGB-SSCSC (36); UPI Financial Wire, April 9, 1990, HGB-SSCSC (47).

23. Stephanie Harrington, "The Two Faces of the Same Eve: *Ms.* vs. *Cosmo*," *New York Times Magazine,* August 11, 1974, 10, HGB-SSCSC (38).

24. Ron Rosenbaum, "Grill Talk: Liz Smith and Helen Gurley Brown at the Four Seasons," *Manhattan, Inc.,* December 1984, 44–49, HGB-SSCSC (2); Helen Gurley Brown quoted in David Brown manuscript proof pages, 1989, HGB-SSCSC (35); Helen Gurley Brown, "Letter to Editor," *MORE,* September 30, 1977, HGB-SSCSC (36).

25. James Kaplan, "The Mouseburger That Roared," *Vanity Fair,* 53, no. 6 (June 1990), 152; Rona Jaffe, letter to Helen Gurley Brown, May 4, 1967, HGB-SSCSC (8).

26. Kaplan, "Mouseburger That Roared," 186; Helen Gurley Brown, interview by Jennifer Scanlon, June 11, 2007.

27. Helen Gurley Brown, interview by Jennifer Scanlon, June 11, 2007.

28. David Friedman, "She Loves Being a Girl!" *Newsday,* April 26, 1980, 9 (2); Kaplan, "Mouseburger That Roared," 186.

29. Laura Green, "A Mouseburger Roars," *Sunday Sun-Times,* October 3, 1982, 9, HGB-SSCSC (28); Judy Bachrach, "When It Comes to Having It All, Helen Gurley Brown Wrote the Book—With a Little Inspiration from Her Dear David," *People,* November 1, 1982, 56, HGB-SSCSC (28); Roberta Ashley, letter to Helen Gurley Brown, 1972, HGB-SSCSC (11).

30. Helen Gurley Brown, "How to Be a Good Executive," August 1996, HGB-SSCSC (36), published in part as "Management Wisdom from the Ultimate Cosmo Girl," *Fortune,* October 28, 1996, 103–5.

31. Helen Gurley Brown, "The Cosmo Format and Ground Rules," November 30, 1996, HGB-SSCSC (41).

32. Helen Gurley Brown, art format memo, 1972, HGB-SSCSC (41); Helen Gurley Brown, notes for media directors and presidents lunch, December 1995, HGB-SSCSC (37).

33. Helen Gurley Brown explained about the Cosmo Girl that "a guy reading *Playboy* can say, 'Hey, that's me.' I want my girl to be able to say the same thing," Brown quoted in *Providence Journal,* 1965, HGB-SSCSC (8).

34. Profile of *Cosmopolitan* reader, Simmons Research, 1980, Helen Gurley Brown Papers (47). The profile did not include race or ethnicity.

35. "Interview with Helen Gurley Brown," n.d., HGB-SSCSC (28).

36. Friedman, "She Loves Being a Girl!" 9; Philippa Toomey, "Love, Work, and Helen Gurley Brown," London *Times,* February 24, 1982, HGB-SSCSC (38); Helen Gurley Brown, advertising presentation, September 1980, HGB-SSCSC (37); Helen Gurley Brown, "The Cosmo Format and Ground Rules," November 30, 1996 (41).

37. Steinem, "In Conversation with Helen Gurley Brown"; Helen Gurley Brown, letter to Gilbert C. Maurer, November 13, 1989, HGB-SSCSC (42). On the issue of racial representation in *Cosmo,* the cover photographer, Francesco Scavullo, stated that before the 1980s, the cover beauties were "blonde, blue-eyed women with perpetual suntans" but that by the 1980s the trend had turned toward "universal and international beauty." Nevertheless, as in most mainstream magazines, women of color remained underrepresented in *Cosmopolitan* throughout Scavullo's and Brown's tenure. Quotes from Cara Appelbaum, "Beyond the Blonde Bombshell," *Adweek's Marketing Week,* June 3, 1981, 18, HGB-SSCSC (38).

38. Helen Gurley Brown, advertising luncheon notes, 1991, HGB-SSCSC (38).

39. Ibid.

40. Helen Gurley Brown, Los Angeles speech, 1986, HGB-SSCSC (37); "Mothers Who Work," special issue of *Cosmopolitan,* November 1986.

41. Helen Gurley Brown, *Cosmo* ads, 1978–1984, HGB-SCSSC (46).

42. Ivor Williams, "The Pious Pornographers: Sex and Sanctimony in the Ladies' Home Jungle," *Playboy,* October 1957, 25; Helen Gurley Brown, notes for speech at Edgewater Hotel, July 19, 1963, HGB-SSCSC (15).

43. Earl F. Holbrook, "Mrs. Brown's Elixir," *Media Agencies Clients,* July 2, 1962; Nora Ephron quoted in Kaplan, "Mouseburger That Roared," 152.

44. Steinem, "In Conversation with Helen Gurley Brown"; Helen Gurley Brown, letter to J. M. Jack, HGB-SSCSC (40); Helen Gurley Brown, memo, March 25, 1975, HGB-SSCSC (42).

45. Steinem, "In Conversation with Helen Gurley Brown."

46. "Bad Girl," *Psychology Today,* March/April 1963, 22, HGB-SSCSC (2).

CHAPTER 10

1. Tess Lawrence, "That Cosmopolitan Lady, Helen Gurley Brown," *Herald,* October 2, 1982, 18, HGB-SSCSC (28); Helen Gurley Brown, interview by Jennifer Scanlon, June 11, 2007; "Proust Questionnaire: Helen Gurley Brown," *Vanity Fair,* August 2007, 185.

2. For a discussion of what she calls "radical-libertarian" and "radical-cultural" feminist ideas about differences between women and men, and additional

readings on this influential focus of feminist thinking during the second wave, see Rosemary Tong, *Feminist Thought: A More Comprehensive Introduction* (Boulder, CO: Westview Press, 2009), 48–95.

3. Daniel Meacham, "The Magic of Self-Confidence," n.d., HGB-SSCSC (35).
4. Helen Gurley Brown, notes from *Cosmo* lunch, Fall 1981, HGB-SSCSC (37).
5. Nikki Finke, "Birthday Girl," *Los Angeles Times,* May 1990, clipping, HGB-SSCSC (47).
6. Helen Gurley Brown, unpublished article ideas, HGB-SSCSC (42).
7. "Helen Gurley Brown," *Playboy,* April 1963, 60. According to Dale Spender, as early as the eighteenth century, feminist Mary Wollstonecraft made the connection between marriage and prostitution. See Dale Spender, *Women of Ideas and What Men Have Done to Them* (London: Routledge, 1982), 151.
8. Feminist artists also struggled with these issues. On the history of pin-ups, another sometimes feminist practice of marketing women's bodies, see Maria Elena Buszek, *Pin-Up Girls: Feminism, Sexuality, Popular Culture* (Durham, NC: Duke University Press, 2006).
9. See bell hooks, *Feminist Theory: From Margin to Center* (Boston: South End, 1984), 150; Buszek, *Pin-Up Girls,* 7–13. For an early discussion of the ways in which different groups of feminists viewed sexuality, see Ann Ferguson, "Sex War: The Debate between Radical and Liberation Feminists," *Signs: Journal of Women in Culture and Society,* 10, no. 1 (Autumn 1984); for a recent overview of the debates, see Rosemary Tong, *Feminist Thought,* 65–73.
10. Helen Gurley Brown, edits on pieces for *Cosmopolitan,* HGB-SSCSC (42).
11. Gloria Steinem, *Revolution from Within: A Book of Self-Esteem* (Boston: Little, Brown, 1993), 26.
12. Helen Gurley Brown, "Step into My Parlor," *Cosmopolitan,* April 1970, HGB-SSCSC (43).
13. Diana Lurie, "Living with Liberation," *New York,* August 31, 1970, 22–23.
14. "Bad Girl," *Psychology Today,* March/April 1963, 71.
15. Lurie, "Living with Liberation," 22–23. On feminist arguments on separation, see Marilyn Frye, "Some Reflections on Separatism and Power," in *The Politics of Reality: Essays in Feminist Theory* (Freedom, CA: Crossing Press, 1983) 95–109, and Lee Schwing, "On Separatism," *Women: A Journal of Liberation,* April 1973, reprinted in *Dear Sisters: Dispatches from the Women's Liberation Movement,* ed. Rosalyn Baxandall and Linda Gordon (New York: Basic Books, 2000).
16. Joyce Gabriel, "Efficient, Feminine—That's Helen Gurley Brown," *Escort,* January 14, 1971, HGB-SSCSC (1). For a description of the organizing of the Woman Strike for Equality, see Marcia Cohen, *The Sisterhood: The True Story of the Women Who Changed the World* (New York: Simon & Schuster, 1998), 266–87.
17. Joan Sutton, "That Cosmo Girl a Few Years Later," *Toronto Sun,* December 14, 1976, 99, HGB-SSCSC (2).
18. Judy Bachrach, "Couples," *People,* November 1, 1982, 56, HGB-SSCSC (1); Friedan quoted in Anne Eaton, "The Girl with Her Nose Pressed to the Window," *Suburbia Today,* September 26, 1982, 7, HGB-SSCSC (28).
19. Daniel Kahn, "At 20, The Cosmo Girl is a Career Woman," *Newsday,* September 23, 1985, HGB-SSCSC (38).

20. Maggie Alderson, "Cosmo's Stars Make a World of Difference," *Sydney Morning Herald,* May 5, 1998, HGB-SSCSC (38).
21. In an influential discussion, Alison M. Jaggar described the alienation women felt from their own bodies. See her *Feminist Politics and Human Nature* (Totowa, NJ: Rowman & Allanheld, 1983).
22. Helen Gurley Brown, speech, 1986, HGB-SSCSC (37).
23. Helen Gurley Brown, "Better a Miniskirt Than a Minnie Mouse Gray," *New York Times,* April 16, 1988, HGB-SSCSC (36/5).
24. Helen Gurley Brown, speech, 1986, HGB-SSCSC (37).
25. Feminists more radical than Brown did not present a unified voice on androgyny. See Alice Echols, "The New Feminism of Yin and Yang," in *Powers of Desire: The Politics of Sexuality,* ed. Ann Snitow, Christine Stansell, and Sharon Thompson (New York: Monthly Review Press, 1983), 439–59.
26. Helen Gurley Brown, rewrites for *Sex and the Single Girl,* HGB-SSCSC (25).
27. Helen Gurley Brown, letter to the editor, *New York Times,* n.d., HGB-SSCSC (36).
28. Helen Gurley Brown, "Doing What Comes Unnaturally," n.d., HGB-SSCSC (31).
29. Helen Gurley Brown, speech, 1997, HGB-SSCSC (15).
30. Ned Zeman, "Sex and the Senior Girl," *Newsweek,* March 22, 1993, 71, HGB-SSCSC (30).
31. Susan Brownmiller recounts the organization and the takeover in her memoir, *In Our Time: Memoir of a Revolution* (New York: Dial, 1999).
32. Ruth Rosen, *The World Split Open: How the Modern Women's Movement Changed America* (New York: Viking, 2000), 301.
33. Ibid., 309.
34. David Friedman, "She Loves Being a Girl!" *Newsday,* April 26, 1980, HGB-SSCSC (2). The sit-in at *Cosmopolitan* represents on some levels the increasing split in the second wave about women's relationships with men. Radical feminists often portrayed heterosexuality as the condition women needed to escape in order to live healthy lives. *Cosmopolitan*'s stance would have proven particularly troubling in this regard. See Ti-Grace Atkinson, "Radical Feminism and Love," in *Amazon Odyssey* (New York: Links Books, 1974); Kate Millet, *Sexual Politics* (Garden City, NY: Doubleday, 1970); and Shulamith Firestone, *The Dialectic of Sex: The Case for Feminist Revolution* (New York: Farrar, Straus, and Giroux, 1970).
35. David Brown, unpublished manuscript, 1989, HGB-SSCSC (35).
36. Joy Hakanson Colby, "The Cosmo Girl's a Foxy, Frisky 20," *Detroit News,* November 5, 1985, 2B, HGB-SSCSC (38).
37. Maureen Spagnolo, "Two Decades of That Cosmo Girl," *Washington Times Magazine,* October 29, 1985, 5M, HGB-SSCSC (38).
38. Helen Gurley Brown, "Step into My Parlor," *Cosmopolitan,* May 1970, HGB-SSCSC (43); see also Helen Gurley Brown, "Step into My Parlor," *Cosmopolitan,* November 1985, HGB-SSCSC (43). Regardless of her mocking of consciousness-raising, one can argue that *Cosmopolitan,* like much of the popular fiction aimed at heterosexual women during this period, performed a kind of consciousness-raising itself. See Lisa Maria Hogeland, *Feminism*

and Its Fictions: The Consciousness-Raising Novel and the Women's Liberation Movement (Philadelphia: University of Pennsylvania Press, 1998). For another perspective on feminism and consciousness raising, from one of Brown's contemporaries and friends, see Liz Smith, *Natural Blonde: A Memoir* (New York, Hyperion, 2000), 222–25.

39. Kate Millett, excerpt from *Sexual Politics, Cosmopolitan,* November 1970, HGB-SSCSC (38).

40. Sarah Pattee, "The First Cosmo Girl," *San Antonio Light,* March 3, 1985, HGB-SSCSC (38).

41. Helen Gurley Brown, MORE speech, 1979, HGB-SSCSC (15).

42. "10 Questions We Finally Got the Nerve to Ask Helen Gurley Brown," *Madison Avenue,* September 1985, 108–110, HGB-SSCSC (2).

43. Helen Gurley Brown, "The Women's Movement Is Your Ally but You've Still Got to Get There Yourself," draft copy of *Having It All,* HGB-SSCSC (27).

44. Spagnolo, "Two Decades of That Cosmo Girl," 4M-5M.

45. "Bad Girl," 22–24, 70–71.

46. Cindy Sperling, letter to Helen Gurley Brown, January 25, 1996, March/April 1963, HGB-SSCSC (41).

47. Gloria Steinem, "In Step with Helen Gurley Brown" (Palm Springs, CA: TAE Productions, 1985), HGB-SSCSC (16).

48. Florence King, "The Contraception Capers," *Cosmopolitan,* October 1974, 124, HGB-SSCSC (44).

49. Helen Gurley Brown, letter to George Sullivan, July 11, 1979, HGB-SSCSC (35).

50. Helen Gurley Brown, Oxford debate, October 13, 1986, HGB-SSCSC (15).

51. Betty Friedan, "How to Get the Women's Movement Moving Again," *New York Times Magazine,* November 3, 1985.

52. The radical feminist Shulamith Firestone would deem heterosexuality women's primary enemy; Helen Gurley Brown would claim the same of motherhood. See Firestone, *Dialectic of Sex.*

53. Helen Gurley Brown, "... What Makes Women Women," *Printer's Ink,* April 22, 1966, 40, HGB-SSCSC (36).

54. Text of television show, July 24, 1991, HGB-SSCSC (15).

55. "Mothers Who Work," *Cosmopolitan,* November 1986, HGB-SSCSC (38); Michele Ingrassia, "Now, the Cosmo Baby," *Newsday,* August 20, 1986, 4, HGB-SSCSC (38).

56. Helen Gurley Brown, speech to Houston Forum, January 14, 1988, HGB-SSCSC (37).

57. Helen Gurley Brown, unpublished piece, HGB-SSCSC (28).

58. Helen Gurley Brown, *Femme* proposal, HGB-SSCSC (37).

59. Valerie Grove, "Sexy and Sassy at Seventy," *Times,* October 12, 1992, 2, HGB-SSCSC (38).

60. Flora Davis writes that after the Senate passed the Equal Rights Amendment in 1972, its proponents felt that ratification on the part of the states would be "quick and easy." Due in large part to the efforts of the anti-ERA advocate Phyllis Schlafly, the amendment was never fully ratified. See Flora Davis, *Moving the Mountain: The Women's Movement in America since 1960* (New York: Simon &

Schuster, 1991), 386; and Donald T. Crichlow, *Phyllis Schlafly and Grassroots Conservativism: A Woman's Crusade* (Princeton, NJ: Princeton University Press, 2005).

61. Helen Gurley Brown reported on her pro-ERA efforts, reflecting her fear that the anti-ERA leadership of Phyllis Schlafly was formidable. "All the magazines together may not be as effective as Phyllis Schlafly with her rabble-rousing TV appearances," she explained. "But we hope reason will prevail." See Helen Gurley Brown, "All for ERA," *Time,* October 29, 1979, 99.

62. Helen Gurley Brown, letter to Elizabeth Whelan, January 30, 1980, HGB-SSCSC (39); Helen Gurley Brown, memo to John Mack Carter, December 30, 1975, HGB-SSCSC (39).

63. Beth Bailey, "She Can 'Bring Home the Bacon': Negotiating Gender in the 1970s," in *America in the Seventies,* ed. Beth Bailey and David Farber (Lawrence: University Press of Kansas, 2004), 113.

64. Helen Gurley Brown, *Cosmopolitan* advertisement, *New York Times,* April 27, 1978, D22, HGB-SSCSC (46).

65. Karen Heller, "Sexcess!" *USA Weekend,* October 15–27, 1985, 5, HGB-SSCSC (38).

66. Carole Ashkinaze, "Sex and the Single Girl," 1977, HGB-SSCSC (21).

67. Helen Gurley Brown, unpublished notes, HGB-SSCSC (45).

68. "10 Questions," 110.

69. Laura Green, "A Mouseburger Roars," *Sunday Sun-Times,* October 3, 1982, 9, HGB-SSCSC (28).

70. Helen Gurley Brown, letter to Ruth Whitney, July 26, 1977, HGB-SSCSC (10).

71. Helen Gurley Brown, letter to Gloria Steinem, December 19, 1978, HGB-SSCSC (10).

72. Letter from Helen Gurley Brown to Gloria Steinem, August 8, 1989, HGB-SSCSC (10).

73. "Visitors in Town," *Japan Times,* October 28, 1978, 2, HGB-SSCSC (2).

74. Marcia Ann Gillespie, letter to Helen Gurley Brown, May 6, 1996, HGB-SSCSC (7).

75. "Helen Gurley Brown's Picks for Cosmo Girls of the 1990s," *Detroit News,* May 9, 1990, 11c, HGB-SSCSC (2).

76. Bob Frost, "Helen Gurley Brown," *San Jose Mercury News,* October 31, 1993, HGB-SSCSC (2).

77. Margaret Wente, "Ah Men! Darling Creatures from Another Planet," *Toronto Star,* November 12, 1983, HGB-SSCSC (38).

78. Astrid Henry provides the most comprehensive history of the development of the third wave. As she puts it, the wave metaphor "allows one both to identify and disidentify with the past." See Astrid Henry, *Not My Mother's Sister: Generational Conflict and Third-Wave Feminism* (Bloomington: Indiana University Press, 2004), 25. Many third-wave feminists identify with the Third Wave Foundation, founded by Rebecca Walker, herself the daughter of the second-wave feminist writer Alice Walker. The foundation describes itself on its Web site as a "feminist, activist foundation that works nationally to support young women and transgender youth ages 15 to 30." http://www.thirdwavefoundation.org/about (accessed October 8, 2008).

CHAPTER 11

1. See proposal for *Lifeline*, HGB-SSCSC (36).
2. In a letter to a fan written during her last month at the magazine, Brown responded to the fan's lament about the magazine world's loss of Helen Gurley Brown. Perhaps she would start a magazine for older women, she wrote, revealing that in the past Hearst had rejected that idea, not imagining it to be "commercially feasible." But she suggested she might "try them again." Helen Gurley Brown to Ann Reynolds, February 12, 1997, HGB-SSCSC (41).
3. Helen Gurley Brown's *Single Girls' Cookbook* was published in May 1969. A reviewer called the book "trash," but the book sold more than 147,000 copies and was published in ten more countries. Ironically, of course, the woman who published a cookbook and who equated food with sex actually ate very little food herself for most of her adult life. See Robert Glasgow, "Helen Gurley Brown: The Fanny Farmer of the Boudoir," *Los Angeles*, February 1963, 36–39, HGB-SSCSC (2).
4. Cindy Adams, "He Made Her a Married Woman," *Pageant*, December 1963, 70, HGB-SSCSC (1).
5. Joyce Haber, "Zanuck/Brown: An Odd Couple of Executives," *Los Angeles Times*, July 22, 1973, 15, HGB-SSCSC (1).
6. David Brown, *The Rest of Your Life Is the Best of Your Life: David Brown's Guide to Growing Gray Disgracefully* (Fort Lee, NJ: Barricade Books, 1991), 83.
7. Brown, *Rest of Your Life*, 44; Chloe Rolfes, "The Cosmo Girl," *Fair Lady*, November 5, 1980, 80, HGB-SSCSC (1).
8. David Brown, *Let Me Entertain You* (New York: William Morrow, 1990), 111.
9. Steven Flax, "A Boffo, Socko Portfolio," *Forbes*, April 13, 1981, 163.
10. Helen Gurley Brown, letter to Harold Berkowitz, December 5, 1971, HGB-SSCSC (5).
11. Andrew Alpern, *Luxury Apartment Buildings in Manhattan: An Illustrated History* (Mineola, NY: Dover, 1992).
12. Helen Gurley Brown, letter to Mary Gurley, n.d., HGB-SSCSC (6).
13. Helen Gurley Brown, *I'm Wild Again* (New York: Warner Books, 2000), 13.
14. Ibid., 13.
15. Brown, *I'm Wild Again*, 87–88.
16. Helen Gurley Brown, letter to Oral Roberts, May 28, 1976, HGB-SSCSC (9); Oral Roberts, letter to Helen Gurley Brown, July 15, 1976, HGB-SSCSC (9).
17. Helen Gurley Brown, letter to Fred Laurence, June 16, 1981, HGB-SSCSC (13).
18. Helen Gurley Brown, draft of *The Late Show*, HGB-SSCSC (29).
19. Helen Gurley Brown, letter to Berna Linden, n.d., HGB-SSCSC (8).
20. Brown, *I'm Wild Again*, 88.
21. Ibid., 15.
22. Liz Smith, *Natural Blonde: A Memoir* (New York: Hyperion, 2001), 213. Smith provides a vivid account of Brown's first days as editor of *Cosmopolitan*.
23. Helen Gurley Brown, interview by Jennifer Scanlon, October 20, 2007.
24. Judy Bachrach, "Couples," *People*, November 1, 1982, 54, HGB-SSCSC (1).
25. Carol Sarler, "Cosmo's Climax Control," *Sunday Times Magazine*, February 28, 1993, HGB-SSCSC (38).

26. Valerie Grove, "Helen Gurley Brown: On Staying Sexy at 60," *New York Post*, March 8, 1982, HGB-SSCSC (2).

27. Deidre Donahue, "Brown Lives Magazine's Message," *USA Today*, April 13, 1980, 1D, 1E, HGB-SSCSC (2); *New York Times*, August 26, 1980.

28. Kathy Hacker, "A Guru Finds Some Women Are Ingrates," *Philadelphia Inquirer*, November 11, 1982, 4D, HGB-SSCSC (28).

29. Nell Scovell, "Too Rich and Too Thin," *Spy*, March 1987, 42–44, HGB-SSCSC (2).

30. Peter Castro, "Chatter," *People*, 1970, n.d., HGB-SSCSC (2); Rolfes, "Cosmo Girl"; Scovell, "Too Rich and Too Thin," 42.

31. Susan Toepfer, "That Cosmo Girl at 60!" *Sunday News Magazine*, October 31, 1982, 22, HGB-SSCSC (28); Helen Gurley Brown, letter to Paul Solomon, February 16, 1979, HGB-SSCSC (10).

32. Margarita Fichtner, "She's Mother Mouseburger, Not a Plucked Chicken," *Miami Herald*, January 16, 1983, HGB-SSCSC (28).

33. Helen Gurley Brown, notes for *Sex and the New Single Girl*, HGB-SSCSC (25).

34. Helen Gurley Brown, interview by Jennifer Scanlon, October 20, 2007. In this interview Brown spoke about alcoholism among her mother's siblings.

35. Kathy Davis, *Reshaping the Female Body: The Dilemma of Cosmetic Surgery* (New York: Routledge, 1995).

36. Helen Gurley Brown, interview by Jennifer Scanlon, October 20, 2007.

37. Helen Gurley Brown, *The Late Show: A Semiwild but Practical Survival Plan for Women over 50* (New York: William Morrow, 1993), 110.

38. Davis, *Reshaping the Female Body*, 163.

39. Helen Gurley Brown, interview by Jennifer Scanlon, October 20, 2007.

40. Rolfes, "Cosmo Girl," 79.

41. "Bad Girl," *Psychology Today*, March/April 1963, 22, HGB-SSCSC (2).

42. Helen Gurley Brown, unpublished notes, 1993, HGB-SSCSC (36).

43. Gloria Steinem, "In Conversation with Helen Gurley Brown" (Palm Springs, CA: TAE Productions, 1985), HGB-SSCSC (16).

44. Charlotte Mayerson, letter to Helen Gurley Brown, December 5, 1984, HGB-SSCSC (31).

45. Brown, *Late Show*, 13.

46. Gloria Steinem, *Doing Sixty and Seventy* (San Francisco: Elders Academy Press, 2006), inside jacket.

47. Isabelle de Courtivron, "Nothing to Fear but Fear Itself?" *Women's Review of Books* 12, no. 2 (November 1994), 15.

48. Brown, *Late Show*, 125.

49. Ibid., book jacket.

50. Ibid., 61.

51. Ibid., 284.

52. Ibid., 373.

53. Barbara Raskin, review of *The Late Show*, n.d., HGB-SSCSC (30).

54. Judith Viorst, "Age Cannot Wither a Girl Like Her," *New York Times*, March 14, 1994, 8.

55. Brown, *Late Show*, 57.

CHAPTER 12

1. Charlene Canape, "The New Money Makers at Hearst," *New York Times,* March 6, 1983, 1, 8, HGB-SSCSC (38).
2. Philip Dougherty, "Taking a Hard Look at TV," *New York Times,* October 25, 1984, n.p., HGB-SSCSC (38).
3. The term "sexual harassment" was coined in a 1975 lawsuit. The *New York Times* featured a piece on sexual harassment in 1975, and *Redbook* in a survey in 1976. Both pieces elicited many responses from women who had themselves been harassed. On the history of the depiction of sexual harassment in the media, see Carrie N. Baker, " 'He Said, She Said': Popular Representations of Sexual Harassment and Second-Wave Feminism," in *Disco Divas: Women and Popular Culture in the 1970s,* ed. Sherrie Inness (Philadelphia: University of Pennsylvania Press, 2003), 39–53. See also Carrie N. Baker's *The Women's Movement against Sexual Harassment* (New York: Cambridge University Press, 2007). Susan Brownmiller also recounts the history of feminist naming of and responses to sexual harassment in "Its Name Is Sexual Harassment," in her *In Our Time: Memoir of a Revolution* (New York: Dial Press, 1990), 279–94.
4. Helen Gurley Brown, MORE speech, 1979, HGB-SSCSC (15).
5. Helen Gurley Brown, "At Work, Sexual Electricity Sparks Creativity," *Wall Street Journal,* October 29, 1991, HGB-SSCSC (36).
6. Brown, "At Work, Sexual Electricity Sparks Creativity"; Melanie Fitzpatrick, letter to Helen Gurley Brown, November 4, 1991, HGB-SSCSC (36).
7. Nancy Lloyd, "Helen Gurley Brown: Still the Same Ol' Tease," *Modern Maturity,* May/June 1997, 56.
8. A year after the term "sexual harassment" was coined, *Quest,* a feminist journal, published an article criticizing *Cosmopolitan* for contributing to the problem by advocating that women use sex for their own advantage. See Deirdre Silverman, "Sexual Harassment: Working Women's Dilemma," *Quest* 3 (Winter 1976/77), 20. On the history of sexual harassment legislation, see Laura Stein, *Sexual Harassment in America: A Documentary History* (Westport, CT: Greenwood, 1999).
9. Helen Gurley Brown, untitled article, HGB-SSCSC (36). Brown sent this piece to the *New York Times,* but they did not publish it.
10. Melanie Warner, "The Mouseburger That Roared," *InsideMedia,* July 12, 1995, 25, HGB-SSCSC (38).
11. Patrick Reilly, "Helen Gurley Brown Finds That 'Nice Girls' Sometimes Finish Last," *Wall Street Journal,* February 1, 1996, A1 (38).
12. Ibid.
13. Helen Gurley Brown, "How to Be a Good Executive," August 1996, unpublished and longer version of "Management Wisdom from the Ultimate Cosmo Girl," *Fortune,* October 28, 1996, 103–5, HGB-SSCSC (36).
14. Helen Gurley Brown revealed her salary to the author in an interview, New York City, June 11, 2007; Reilly, "Helen Gurley Brown Finds That 'Nice Girls' Sometimes Finish Last," A1.
15. Helen Gurley Brown, interview by Jennifer Scanlon, October 20, 2007.

16. Kate White, *Why Good Girls Don't Get Ahead . . . but Gutsy Girls Do: Nine Secrets Every Working Woman Must Know* (New York: Grand Central, 1996).
17. Helen Gurley Brown, interview by Jennifer Scanlon, October 20, 2007.
18. Charles Laurence, "Why Cosmo's Cobra Is Still Baring Her Fangs," *Daily Telegraph*, n.d., HGB-SSCSC (2).
19. Susan H. Greenberg, "Your Very Own Cosmo," *Newsweek*, May 18, 1998, 25 (38).
20. Ibid.
21. Lee Hockstader, "The Culture Czar," *Washington Post*, February 22, 1995, D4, HGB-SSCSC (38).
22. Ibid., D1.
23. Margaret Shapiro, "Post-Communist Cosmo Girl," *Washington Post*, April 29, 1994, C1, HGB-SSCSC (38).
24. Helen Gurley Brown, interview by Jennifer Scanlon, October 20, 2007.
25. "The World According to Cosmo," *Sunday Times'* March 3, 1990, n.p., HGB-SSCSC (38).
26. Helen Gurley Brown, interview by Jennifer Scanlon, October 20, 2007.
27. Helen Gurley Brown, *The Writer's Rules: The Power of Positive Prose, How to Create It and Get It Published* (New York: William Morrow, 1998). Much of the book is based on William Strunk Jr. and E. B. White, *The Elements of Style* (New York: Allyn & Bacon, 1999).
28. Helen Gurley Brown, *Dear Pussycat: Mash Notes and Missives from the Desk of Cosmopolitan's Legendary Editor* (New York: St. Martin's, 2004).
29. Helen Gurley Brown, *I'm Wild Again* (New York: Warner Books, 2001).
30. Ibid., 347, 356.
31. Patricia Myles, letter to Helen Gurley Brown, September 25, 2000, HGB-SSCSC (13).
32. Frances Soboda, letter to Helen Gurley Brown, January 30, 1983, HGB-SSCSC (12).
33. Ouida Ray, letter to Helen Gurley Brown, January 26, 1983, HGB-SSCSC (12); Kingi Carpenter, letter to Helen Gurley Brown, n.d., HGB-SSCSC (13); Dorothy Smalley, letter to Helen Gurley Brown, January 18, 1964, HGB-SSCSC (12); Simone Marie Baxandall, letter to Helen Gurley Brown, March 9, 1986, HGB-SSCSC (12).
34. Mitzi Purdue, letter to Helen Gurley Brown, June 25, 1989, HGB-SSCSC (9).
35. Barbara Schumacher, letter to Helen Gurley Brown, April 21, 1983, HGB-SSCSC (12).
36. Helen Gurley Brown, letter to Ann Reynolds, February 12, 1997, HGB-SSCSC (13); Jean Daniel, letter to Helen Gurley Brown, November 21, 1982, HGB-SSCSC (12).
37. Gloria Rose, letter to Helen Gurley Brown, January 11, 1983, HGB-SSCSC (12); Laura Richards, letter to Helen Gurley Brown, n.d., HGB-SSCSC (12); Isabel Loofbourow, letter to Helen Gurley Brown, February 1983, HGB-SSCSC (12); Sadie Friedlander, letter to Helen Gurley Brown, January 31, 1987, HGB-SSCSC (12); Milly Broughs, letter to Helen Gurley Brown, May 30, 1984, HGB-SSCSC (12); Shirley Erwin, letter to Helen Gurley Brown, October 18, 1983, HGB-SSCSC (12); June Canepa, letter to Helen Gurley Brown, May 10, 1984, HGB-SSCSC (12); Teodros Ghebremichael, letter to Helen Gurley Brown, September 23, 2000, HGB-SSCSC (13).

38. Jean Leich, letter to Helen Gurley Brown, January 13, 1983, HGB-SSCSC (12).
39. Frances Soboda, letter to Helen Gurley Brown, January 30, 1983, HGB-SSCSC (12).
40. Eleanor Andrews, letter to Helen Gurley Brown, August 19, 2000, HGB-SSCSC (13); Patricia Jennings, letter to Helen Gurley Brown, n.d., HGB-SSCSC (25).
41. Susan Baker, letter to Helen Gurley Brown, October 12, 1983, HGB-SSCSC (12).
42. Ibid.
43. Jane Paquin, letter to Helen Gurley Brown, January 17, 1985, HGB-SSCSC (12).
44. Ruby Pickens, letter to Helen Gurley Brown, April 29, 1983, HGB-SSCSC (12).
45. Shelley Vitale, letter to Helen Gurley Brown, August 2, 1983, HGB-SSCSC (12).
46. Letter to Helen Gurley Brown, HGB-SSCSC (21); Debbie Lloyd, letter to Helen Gurley Brown, September 21, 1983, HGB-SSCSC (12).
47. Sally Cook, letter to Helen Gurley Brown, June 7, 1983, HGB-SSCSC (12).
48. D. Walmsley, letter to Helen Gurley Brown, September 17, 1983, HGB-SSCSC (12).
49. Mrs. S. Stevens, letter to Helen Gurley Brown, September 3, 1996, HGB-SSCSC (13).
50. Norma Elliott, letter to Helen Gurley Brown, April 11, 1993, HGB-SSCSC (13).
51. Mary Harms, letter to Helen Gurley Brown, June 3, 1983, HGB-SSCSC (12).

index

ABC (TV network), 135, 138
abortion
    Brown and, xii, 61, 145, 146, 169,
        186–89
    Sex and the Office and, 126
    television and, 139
Abzug, Bella, 140
adultery
    American culture and, 28–30, 71–72
    Brown and, xv, 23–25, 28–30, 34,
        36–37, 69–70, 72–73
advertising
    Brown and, 32–33, 38–39, 159–60,
        163–64, 190
    sex and, 165–66
    television and, 135–36
advice
    Brown and, 86–87
    Friedan and, 98
    television and, 138–39
African Americans
    in Arkansas, 5–6
    Brown and, 121, 223–24, 253n37

    as fans, 224–25
age
    American culture and, 193
    Brown and, 120, 192–211
agency, Brown and, 106–7
AIDS, 215–16
Alcoholics Anonymous, Mary and,
    199–200
Alford, George, 199–200
Allen, Kelcey, 43–44
Allen, Woody, 140–41
ambition
    Brown and, 27–28
    Cosmopolitan and, 155
    Sex and the Office and, 126–27
American culture
    and age, 193
    and birth control, 70–71
    Brown and, 86–87
    and experts, 85–86, 98
    and feminism, 94–111
    and lesbians, 130
    and marriage, 28–29, 67–68 ∎

American culture (*continued*)
  and men, 29–30
  and motherhood, 29
  and publishing industry, 81–85
  and sex, 71–72, 153
  and *Sex and the Single Girl*, 66
  and television, 44–45, 133
  and working women, 123
anorexia nervosa, 204
appearance
  Brown and, 15–17, 20, 177–78, 203–9
  feminism and, 175–77
Appleton, Myra, 155
Arkansas, 1–3, 6, 9–10, 12
Arnaz, Desi, 133
Ashley, Roberta, 157

Bahrenburg, Claeys, 216
Ball, Lucille, 133–34
Bantam Books, 80
Barr, Candy, 51
beauty culture, ix, x, xiii–xiv, 174–75,
  177–78, 194, 206, 209
Behind the Scenes, 139
Belding, Alice, 26–27, 32
Belding, Don, 26–27, 32, 50, 89
Benchley, Peter, 197
Bennick, Frank A., Jr., 221
Beresford, 198
Berlin, Richard E., 45, 152–53
Bernard Geis Associates, 81
Best of Everything, The (Jaffe), 83–85
Biltheimer, Elizabeth, 202
birth control
  American culture and, 70–71
  Brown and, 183
  Cosmopolitan and, 150–51
  Sex and the Office and, 130
Bosko, Nathalie, 42
Bradshaw, Carrie, 78
Brodgon, Jim, 30–31
Brown, Bruce, 45, 47–49, 51–52, 203
Brown, David, 40–56, 73
  and age, 193, 196, 211
  background of, 41–43
  and career, 43–46, 195–98
  and *Cosmopolitan*, 44–45, 145

and depression, 55, 195
and fan mail, 143
and memoir, 221
and motherhood, 186
and promotion, 79–80, 91–92,
  112–13, 116, 118
and *Sex and the Single Girl*, 60–62, 65
and support, 54–55, 153, 194–95, 221
and television, 133, 138
Brown, Edward Fischer, 41–43, 79
Brown, Helen Gurley
  and aging, 192–211
  awards, 229n1
  background of, 1–22
  and beauty, 15–16, 20, 96–97, 99
  at *Cosmopolitan*, 143–67
  and David Brown, 40–56, 73
  and feminism, 94–111, 168–91
  legacy of, 225
  and promotion, 79–93
  and relationships, 21–22
  retirement from *Cosmopolitan*, 212–25
  and *Sex and the Single Girl*, 57–78
  and television, 132–42
  and *Woman Alone*, 118–22
Brown, Lillian, 41
Brown, Tibbi, 45, 47
Brown, Tina, 167
Brown, Wayne, 43, 45, 53
Brown v. Board of Education, 5
Brownmiller, Susan, 179
Bryan, Cleo. *See* Gurley, Cleo
Bryan, Leigh, 2, 7–8, 19–20
Bryant, Anita, 189
Bunch, Charlotte, 219
Bushnell, Candace, 57

Campbell, Mary, 32
Can This Marriage Be Saved? 139, 165
capitalism, Brown and, 101, 168–70, 172
Carnegie, Dale, 82
cars, Brown and, 37–38, 217
Carter, John Mack, 178–79, 187
Celebrity Chefs, 140
censorship
  and *Sex and the Office*, 128–29
  and *Sex and the Single Girl*, 89–90

Child, Julia, 103, 188
childcare
    feminism and, 179
    Lessons in Love and, 116
children. *See* motherhood
China, *Cosmopolitan* and, 220
CinemaScope, 46
class
    Brown and, 9, 20, 222–23
    feminism and, 176–77
    Friedan and, 97
    See also working class
Cleopatra, 195
Clinton, Bill, 169
Clinton, Hillary, 202
Comstock laws, 89
conduct books, 98
consciousness-raising sessions, 180–81,
    255–56n38
Cook's on the Fire, 139–40
copywriting, Brown and, 27–28, 32–33
cosmetic surgery, Brown and, 194, 206–8
Cosmo Girl, x, 158–64, 175, 187, 190, 220
Cosmopolitan
    Brown's editorship of, 141, 143–67
    Brown's retirement from, 212–25
    circulation of, 166–67, 212, 219
    cover blurbs, 150, 153, 158
    cover images, 150–51, 154, 158–59,
        174–75
    David Brown and, 44–45
    feminism and, 179–91
    Friedan and, 109
    and *Jaws*, 197
    Russian edition of, 219–20
Cosmopolitan International, 217,
    219–20
Cottin, Letty, 88, 90, 116, 179
Crawford, Cindy, 220
Crawford, Joan, 89
Crossfire, 140
culture. *See* American culture
Curtis, Sonny, 132
Curtis, Tony, 113

David, Saul, 113
David Brown Associates, 44

Dear Pussycat (Brown), 221
Deems, Dick, 152
Demarchelier, Patrick, 216
Democratic Party, Brown and, 169
Dempsey, Jack, 32, 34
Dick Van Dyke Show, 134
Didion, Joan, 81, 93
diet
    Brown and, 74, 195–96, 203–6
    feminism and, 204
discrimination, in working world, 77
divorce
    Brown and, 120
    television and, 134
Driving Miss Daisy, 197
Dupuy, Frank, Jr., 151
Dystel, Oscar, 79

eating disorders, 204
economic-sexual exchanges
    Brown and, xii, 23–25, 30–31, 34–35
    feminism and, 104–5, 170–71
    Lessons in Love and, 115
    Loos and, 5, 23–24
    Sex and the Single Girl and,
        72–73, 76
education, Brown and, 11, 14, 17–18
Eisenhower, Dwight D., 5, 89
Elder, Glen, 68–69
Ellis, Albert, 113, 145
empowerment, Brown and, 110
English, Deirdre, 177
Ephron, Nora, 165
Equal Rights Amendment, Brown and,
    xii, 186–87, 257n61
Esquire, 150
Ettinger, Maggie, 45
exercise, Brown and, 74, 196, 203
experts
    American culture and, 85–86
    Brown and, 86–87

fan mail, for Brown, 88, 143, 222–25
fashion, Brown and, 161, 175–76
Faubus, Orval E., 5
Feminine Mystique, The (Friedan), x, 94,
    96–111, 177

feminism
  Brown and, ix–xv, 95, 168–91
  Cleo and, 11
  and cosmetic surgery, 206
  and diet, 204
  Friedan and, 99
  and globalization, 219
  and *Sex and the Single Girl,* 78
  See also second-wave feminism;
    third-wave feminism
Femme, 144–47
Firestone, Shulamith, 179
Fonda, Henry, 113
Foote, Cone & Belding, 32–33
Fortune, 157–58
Fox, William, 42
Frankly Female, 139
freedom, Brown and, 215–16
Freundlich, Isador, 41
Friedan, Betty, x, 94–111, 174, 177, 182,
  184, 187, 191
Fuller, Bonnie, 216–18

Gatlin, Larry, 201
Geis, Bernard
  and magazine, 146
  and *Sex and the Office,* 126
  and *Sex and the Single Girl,* 80–81,
    88–89, 112, 121
gender, Brown and, 169
Gentlemen Prefer Blondes (Loos), 4–5,
  10, 23–24, 38, 76
Geraldo, 140
Getty, Ron, 50
Gillespie, Marcia Ann, 190
girl
  term, 191
  See also Cosmo Girl
Glamour, 27–28, 32, 189, 218
globalization, Brown and, 219–21
Goldstein, Betty. *See* Friedan, Betty
Goldstein, Miriam, 95–96
Good Morning America, 140
Gordimer, Nadine, 150
Gould, Robert, 215
Grant, Ulysses S., Jr., 149
Great Depression, 6, 13, 41–42, 68–69

Grosset & Dunlap, 80
Gurley, Cleo Fred Sisco (mother), 2–3,
  16–17, 22, 25, 97
  and beauty, 16, 96
  in later life, 198–99, 201
  and marriage, 6–7, 19–20, 50
  and *Sex and the Single Girl,* 79, 91
  and work, 7–8, 10–11
Gurley, Helen. *See* Brown, Helen Gurley
Gurley, Ira Marvin (father), 2–3, 6–7, 10
Gurley, Mary (sister), 2, 7, 9, 12–13, 22
  in later life, 198–202

Hainsworth, Marilyn, 121
Having It All (Brown), 208
Healy, Robert, 45
Hearst, William Randolph, 149
Hearst Corporation, 193–94
  and Brown's retirement, 213, 216–17
  and *Cosmopolitan,* 147, 151–52, 161,
    166
  David Brown and, 45
Hearst Foundation, 189, 200–201
Hedley, Pamela, 51
Heffner, Richard, 141
Helen Gurley Brown at Town Hall, 116
Heller, Joseph, 113
Hepburn, Katherine, 188
Hill, Anita, 213–14
Hite, Shere, 140
HIV/AIDS, 215–16
Hoffman, Joseph, 113
Hollywood, CA, 24, 26, 45–46
home life
  Brown and, 48–49, 103–5, 198
  Friedan and, 102–4
  television and, 136
homosexuality
  Brown and, 108, 127–29, 145, 215–16
  Cosmopolitan and, 166
  television and, 137
  See also lesbians
honesty, Brown and, 36, 183
Howells, William Dean, 149

identity
  Friedan and, 108–9

Sex and the Single Girl and, 76–77
I'm Wild Again (Brown), 221–22
individualism
    Brown and, 17, 121
    feminism and, 172–73
    Friedan and, 97–98

Jaffe, Rona, 83–85, 124, 150, 155
Jaffee agency, 26
Jaws, 197–98
Jay, Karla, 179
Jessup, Elizabeth, 7, 12
Joan Rivers Show, 140
Jong, Erica, 140

Kelly, Charlotte, 30–31, 144, 202
Kenyon & Eckhardt, 38–39, 59, 80, 114
Khrushchev, Nikita, 68
Kinsey, Alfred, 70–71, 87
Kitchen Debate, 68
Koop, C. Everett, 215
Krantz, Judith, 155
Kroll, Lucy, 135

Ladies' Home Journal, 139, 165, 178–79
Larry King Live, 140
Late Show, The (Brown), 207–11
Lear's, 194
Lee, Gypsy Rose, 89
Lehman, Ernest, 44
lesbians
    American culture and, 130
    Brown and, xiii, 108, 127–29
    feminism and, 173–74
    See also homosexuality
Lessons in Love (Brown), 114–16
Levin, Martin, 84
Liberty, 44
Lifeline, 193–94
Lindbergh, Charles, 42
Linkletter, Art, 80
lipstick feminism, x
Little Rock, AR, 3–6, 9–10, 28
Loos, Anita, 4–5, 10, 23–24, 38, 76,
    235n7
Lucy Show, The, 134
Lunden, Joan, 190

Mademoiselle, 165
Madonna, 4, 190
Mailer, Norman, 140
mailroom system, 27
Making Marriage Work, 139
management, Brown and, 153–58
Manhattan Project, the, 197
manipulation
    Brown and, 30–31, 89–91
    feminism and, 172, 182–83
marriage
    age and, 194–96
    American culture and, 28–29, 67–68
    Brown and, 18, 30, 33–34, 37, 48–56,
        73, 105–6, 119
    Cosmopolitan and, 162
    feminism and, 171
    Lessons in Love and, 114–16
    Sex and the Single Girl and, 58–59,
        66–67
    television and, 137–38
Mary Tyler Moore Show, The, 132–33,
    138
Maslow, Abraham H., 97
mass-market paperbacks, 82
materialism, Brown on, 5
Mayerson, Charlotte, 208
Mayes, Herbert R., 44–45
McCall's, 117, 179
McCullers, Carson, 10
Meade, Walter, 152
Media Women, 178–79
men
    American culture and, 29–30
    Brown and, 21, 224
    Cosmopolitan and, 162
    feminism and, 173–74, 182–83
    Lessons in Love and, 115–16
    Sex and the Single Girl and, 76, 104–5
Mencken, H. L., 4
Merv Griffin Show, 140
Metalious, Grace, 83
Michelman, Kate, 188
Mike Wallace Show, 140
Millett, Kate, 179–81
Milton Bradley, 113
miniskirts, 175

money
  Brown and, ix, 16–17, 20, 24, 35–38,
    122, 161
  Cosmopolitan and, 155
  David Brown and, 47–48, 52–54,
    91–92, 198
  feminism and, 170
  Lessons in Love and, 115
  and marriage, 52–53
  Sex and the Single Girl and, 65, 74–75
  See also economic-sexual exchanges
Monroe, Marilyn, 46
Moore, Mary Tyler, 131, 132–34
motherhood
  Brown and, 29, 96–97, 120, 184–85,
    221–22
  Cosmopolitan and, 162, 185–86
  Friedan and, 96–97
  Lessons in Love and, 116
mouseburger
  and feminism, 181–82
  term, 14–15
Mr. Right Is Dead (Jaffe), 150
Ms. magazine, 188–89, 191, 230n7
muckraking, term, 149
Murray, Betty Tab Hearst, 202
Music Corporation of America, 26
Myles, Patricia, 222

NARAL (National Abortion Rights
    Action League), 188
National Organization for Women, 214
Neale, housekeeper, 48–49, 51
New American Library, 195
New York Times, 163–64, 175
New Yorker, 152
newspaper column, Brown and, 117–21
Nichols, Mike, 198
Nightline, 140
Nixon, Richard, 68
Normal Like Me, 138
Norman, Gene, 114

objectification
  Brown and, 109, 174
  feminism and, 171–72
  Friedan and, 108–9

O'Connor, John, 80
Oprah, 140
optimism, Brown and, 149, 156–57,
    188–89, 215
Oral Roberts University, 200
Our Miss Brooks, 134
Outrageous Opinions (Brown), 121–22,
    140–41

Packwood, Robert, 214
paperback industry, 82–83
Park La Brea, 47
Peale, Norman Vincent, 86, 91
Pearson, Drew, 44
performance, Brown and, 99, 175, 183
Personal and Confidential, 138–39
Peters, Bill, correspondence with, 61–65
Peyton Place (Metalious), 83, 85
Phil Donahue Show, 140
Phillips, David Graham, 149
philosophy, Brown's, 16, 34, 78, 221–22
  and *Cosmopolitan*, 147–49, 218
  and feminism, 169, 190–91
Playboy, xii, 28, 36, 110, 124, 146–47,
    164, 253n33
Pocket Books, 82
Pogrebin, Letty. *See* Cottin, Letty
polio, 12–13
political correctness, Brown and, 184
politics, Brown and, 169, 186–89
pornography, feminism and, 184
Preminger, Otto, 141
promotion
  of Brown, 112–31
  of *Sex and the Single Girl*, 79–93
prostitution
  feminism and, 171
  Sex and the Office and, 130
  See also economic-sexual exchanges
publishing industry, American culture
    and, 81–85
pulp fiction, 81–82
Purdue, Mitzi, 223
Pyne Show, 140

rape, Brown and, 129
Reader's Digest, 190

Reagan, Ronald, 169
Reagan, Ronald, Jr., 185
realism, Brown and, 72–73, 78
Red Lion, 53
Redstockings, 179
Roberts, Oral, 200
Roosevelt, Franklin D., 13
Roosevelt, Theodore, 149
Rose, Charlie, 141
Russian edition of *Cosmopolitan,* 219–20

Saturday Evening Post, 117
Sauer, Derk, 219
Scavullo, Francesco, 154–55, 216
Schlafly, Phyllis, 188–89
Schwartz, David, 113
Screen Gems, 135
second-wave feminism, x–xiv, 168–91
    definition of, x, 230n4
    early years of, 94–111
secretarial work, 87, 126, 160
    Brown and, 21, 26
Segma Delta Chi, 178
self, focus on
    early experiences and, 11–12
    feminism and, 173
self-improvement
    Brown and, 99–100, 127, 208–9
    Friedan and, 98
Selznick, David O., 144
sex
    advertising and, 165–66
    age and, 209–10
    American culture and, xii, 71–72, 153
    Brown and, 36–37, 65, 141, 209–10
    Cosmopolitan and, 150, 154–55, 166
    desire and, 107–8
    feminism and, 171–72, 184
    Friedan and, 107–10
    Loos and, 4
    television and, 136–37, 140–41
    third-wave feminism and, 191
    women's magazines and, 164–65
    and work, 21, 23, 123–24
    See also economic-sexual exchanges
Sex: Female, 139
Sex and the City, x, 57–58, 131

Sex and the Office (Brown), 123–31, 136
    reviews of, 130–31
Sex and the Single Girl (Brown), 57–78
    film of, 113–14
    promotion of, 79–93
    reviews of, 91–92
    update to, 194
sexual harassment, Brown and, 19,
    213–14
sexual objectification, 109
sexual violence, Brown and, 129, 146
Shandorf, Ruth, 40–41, 46, 51
Siegel, Ann and Mort, 202
Singapore, *Cosmopolitan* and, 220
Single Girl Sandra, The, 132–42
Single Girls Cookbook (Brown), 194, 258n3
single women
    American culture and, 27–29, 67–69
    Brown and, 65
    Cosmopolitan and, 144, 162
    demographics of, 70–71
    newspaper column and, 118–20
    television and, 132–34
    See also Sex and the Single Girl
Sisco, Cleo. *See* Gurley, Cleo
60 Minutes, 140
Smith, Liz, 156, 202–3, 256n38
social life, Brown and, 29–30, 202
sociology. *See* American culture
Spielberg, Steven, 197
Spock, Benjamin, 86
Stanley, Florence, 15
Steinem, Gloria, xi, 15, 94, 172–73,
    177–78, 182–83, 188, 191
    on *Cosmopolitan,* 166, 185–86
    on *Sex and the Office,* 130–31
    on women's magazines, 151
Stewart-Gordon, Faith, 202
Sting, The, 197
Susann, Jacqueline, 81, 92, 121–22
Susskind, David, 140
syndicated newspaper column, Brown
    and, 117–21

television
    American culture and, 44–45, 133
    Brown and, 132–42

television (*continued*)
    and promotion of *Sex and the Single Girl*, 88
Texas State College for Women, 17
Thatcher, Margaret, 190
That Girl, 132, 134
That Tully Girl, 138
therapy
    Brown and, 34, 48, 96, 154–55, 208
    David Brown and, 47
    fans and, 224
    Sex and the Single Girl and, 88
    television and, 138
third-wave feminism
    Brown and, 103, 191
    definition of, x, 230n4
    and victimhood, 107
Thomas, Clarence, 213
Thomas, Marlo, 132
Times-Mirror Corporation, 118
Tonight Show, 140
Trump, Ivana, 190
Twentieth Century Fox, 45–46, 195–96
20/20, 140

van Gaal, Annemarie, 220
Veal, Charlotte. *See* Kelly, Charlotte
victimhood
    Brown and, 106–7, 121
    Friedan and, 106–7
    third-wave feminism and, 107, 191
Viorst, Judith, 210
Vreeland, Diana, 151

Wall Street Journal, 213–14
Waller, Wilkard, 71
Walsh, George, 152
Walters, Barbara, 140
Warner Brothers, 113, 138, 196
Warwick & Legler, 31
W.G., 31–32
Wharton, Edith, 4
What Is Your Problem? 139
White, Kate, 218
Whitney, Ruth, 189, 218
Wilkinson, Bill, 30–31
William Morris Agency, 26–27

Wolf, George, 42
Wolf, Naomi, 185
Woman Alone, 118–22
Women Strike for Equality, 174
women's magazines, 144, 151, 164–65
    competition among, 189–90, 212
    feminism and, 178–79
    and politics, 186–88
Women's Wear Daily, 43–44
Wood, Natalie, 113
Woodbury Business College, 18
work
    age and, 207, 210, 217
    American culture and, 77
    Brown and, 18–19, 21, 23–39, 100–101
    Cosmopolitan and, 160–61
    David Brown and, 43–44, 195–98
    Friedan and, 95–96, 101–2, 110
    newspaper column and, 120
    sex and, 21, 23, 123–24
    Sex and the Office and, 123–31
    Sex and the Single Girl and, 74–78
    television and, 134–35
working class
    Brown and, x, 100–101, 222–23
    Cosmopolitan and, 152, 176–77
    Geis and, 81
    Sex and the Single Girl and, 74–75
working women
    American culture and, 123
    Brown and, 27, 35–36
    Cleo and, 7–8
    Cosmopolitan and, 160–61
    mouseburger and, 14–15
    Sex and the Single Girl and, 74–75
    television and, 134
Works Progress Administration, 6
Wright, Richard, 10
Writer's Rules, The (Brown), 156, 221
writing
    Brown and, 36, 59–61, 65
    David Brown and, 44

Zanuck, Darryl, 45–46, 73, 196, 198
Zanuck, Dick, 195–96, 198
Zanuck/Brown Company, 196–97
Ziffren, Paul, 21